Quality and Research in Higher Education

Quality and Research in Higher Education

Edited by
Dr. Gedam Kamalakar

KALPAZ

First Published, 2020

Published by

Kalpaz Publications
C-30, Satyawati Nagar,
Delhi – 110052
Ph.: 011-47034999, 9811692060
www.kalpazpublications.com
E-mail: kalpaz@hotmail.com

Printed at: G. Print Process, Delhi

Cataloging in Publication Data—DK
Courtesy: D.K. Agencies (P) Ltd. <docinfo@dkagencies.com>

Quality and research in higher education / edited by Dr. Gedam Kamalakar.
pages cm
Includes index.
ISBN 9789353242305

1. Education, Higher—India. 2. Education, Higher—Standards—India. 3. Education, Higher—Research—India. 4. Higher education and state—India. I. Kamalakar, G. (Gedam), 1980- editor.

LCC LA1153.Q35 2019 | DDC 378.54 23

Contents

Foreword 9
Preface 13
Acknowledgements 15

1. Data Protection: In the Era of Globalisation 17
Dr. S. Sudhakar
2. Quality Education and its Imperativeness in Modern India- A Review 23
Dr. V. Vijay Durga Prasad
3. Challenges & Opportunities in Higher Education: A Case Study on Indian Perspective 33
Dr. Debarun Chakraborty, Wendrila Biswas
4. Quality and Excellence of Higher Education in India: Issues and challenges 43
Dr. D R S Reddy
5. Qualitative Dimensions in Higher Education 49
C. Jyothi
6. Need for a New Education Policy Higher Education in India- Challenges, Issues and Opportunities 59
Dr. Challoju Jyothsna
7. Academic Leadership A Need For Quality Higher Education 69
Mrs. K. Malathi Devi, Dr.R.Komala
8. Higher Education in India Issues and Challenges 73
Dr. P. Prameela Margaret
9. Role of Research in Higher Education 79
Dr. K. Rajesh kumar
10. Privatization in Higher Education in India: A Reflection of Issues 87
Dr. Sampath kumar, Dr. P. Prameela Margaret
11. Higher Education in India: Current Challenges, Issues and Remedies 93
G. Shekar
12. Reforms in Higher Education in Telangana State 99
B. Shirisha, Dr. Raja reddy

13. Reforms of Higher Education in India 109
Dr.G.Sreenivasulu, B.Ravi Kumar

14. Genesis of an Ecosystem for Innovation in Research and Development 117
Dr. Sumit Ghosh

15. Role of Research in Higher Education in India 123
Ujjwal Ashutosh, Sushree Sunanda Sahu

16. Higher Education Quality-Need of Reforms 131
Dr. Thanneeru Sujatha

17. Quality Concerns in Indian Higher Education: Challenges and Opportunities 139
Ms. Shivani Seth

18. Higher Education Policy in India 149
Dr. Kamala

19. Higher Education in India: Issues, Concerns and New Directions 161
Dr. S. Venkatesh

20. Quality of Research in Higher Education in India 167
Dr. Akthar Parveen

21. Higher Education in India – Issues and Challenges 175
Dr. D. CH. Apparao

22. Need To Encourage Intellectual Property Research in Higher Education 185
Dr. K. Srinivasa Raju, Dr. D. Ashok Kumar

23. esearch Ethics in Social Science 193
Dr. Jagdish Buwade

24. Higher Education in India-issues, challenges and suggestions 197
T. Kalpana

25. Accessibility of Higher Education through ICT 205
Dr. M. RAVI BABU

26. Reforms in Quality of Higher Education 211
Reddeppa Tagadi

27. Research Ecosystem and Plagarisum 221
Sathyanarayana G

28. Current Status and Problems of Higher Education Among Tribals in Telangana State 231
D. Shiva

29. Implications for Higher Education in India 241
Dr. J.Ratna Prabhakar

30. Reforms of Higher Education 249
Baby Kumari

31. Reforms in Higher Education in India: Prospects and Challenges 257
Dr. S. Chandra Shekar

32. A Qualitative Study to Improve the Quality of Higher Education by Promoting Research and Innovation 263
Naghma Shahida, Asma

33. Information and Communication Technologies (ICTS): Means to Quality Higher Education in Kashmir 273
Ferooz Akram, Ravees Ahmad

34. Quality, Content and Context in Higher Education 281
Joginapallyramesh

35. Issues and Challenges – Higher Education in India 289
Ravi Kaka

36. Improving Quality and Research in Higher Education-A Case Study Analysis 297
Dr.P.Srinivasa sastry, Ananth Narayan Tripurari

37. Student Based Financial Support System in Higher Education: Challenges in Implementation of Centrally Sponsored Schemes 305
Dr. Vetukuri P. S. Raju

38. Rusa in Higher Education in West Bengal- A Study 323
Arnab Chowdhury, Jayanta Mete Professor

39. Financing Higher Education 341
S. C. Bhandari, CEO

40. Professional Ethics: Predicament in Higher Education 349
Dr. P. Venu Gopal

41. Contemporary Issues in Higher Education- Liberalization Privatization, Globalisation 357
Priyanka Mokale

42. Education System: Role of Stakeholders, Impact on Nations Growth– A Case Study on South Korean Higher Education System .. 361
K. Prabhu Sahai, L. N. Gupta

43. Mentoring system in Higher Education: A Case Study of ICFAI Law School, Hyderabad 371
S. Kannan

44. Finances in Higher Education in India- An Introspection 385
Bibhudendu Das

45. Role of Higher Education and Employability in India - Challenges and Solutions 391
Cyril T

46. Role of Private Sector in Higher Education 397
Dr. N. Gopal

47. A Study on Reformsin Education System in India 403
Ch.V. S Varma, Y. Srinivasa Rao

48. Higher Education in India: An empirical study of Jammu and Kashmir 407
Tariq Ahmad Malik, Haamid Amin Mir, Ajaz Ahmad Dass

49. Significance of Institutional Infrastructure in Development of Higher Education 417
M. V. Rama Mohan Rao

50. Impact of Globalisation on Higher Education in India – Challenges and Opportunities – An Insight 427
T. Y. Nirmala Devi

51. The Commercialisation of Higher Education: A Paradigm Shift from Educating All to the Facilitating Few 437
Maruthi. O, Dr. J. Rani Ratna Prabha

52. Women in Higher Education: Issues and Challenges 449
Manjula A

53. Higher Education in India: Opportunities, Issues, Challenges and Suggestions 455
B. Venkateshwarlu

54. Privatization of Higher Education in India 465
Md. Amzad

55. History of Higher Education in India 471
Dr. C. Kista Reddy

56. Indian Higher Education System in India - Challenges and Suggestions 481
Dr. K. Peddi Raju

57. A Critical Analysis of Ranking System and Parameters and How They Result in Poor Ranking of Indian Universities and Institutions at Global Level 487
Dr. K. Raja Ram

58. Expansion in Indian Higher Education in Recent years: Impact of Technological Innovations for excellence 493
Dr. Santhosh Mathew

Index 501

Foreword

Over the last seven decades many far-reaching changes have taken place in the development of higher education in India. Today we have the second largest system of higher education system in the world, having diverse effects, some highly momentous, on the nation's socioeconomic progress, political development and technological advancement at the national and global level as well.

However, higher education today is facing umpteen challenges. While the student numbers and also the number of institutions are rapidly increasing, the quality of higher education is becoming a major concern, with poor quality of graduates resulting in rising graduate unemployment – open and hidden, and poor quality and quantum of research output. Not even one among the existing one thousand Indian universities figures in the top one hundred universities in the global rankings. There are several reasons for the dismal state of affairs. The entire system of higher education – from under graduate colleges to central universities, including institutions like the Indian Institutes of Technology, suffers from a severe shortage of quality teachers. Not only in quality, but also in terms of number of teachers, almost all institutions are facing a high degree of shortage. Second, a large number of institutions of higher education have very poor quality infrastructure – classrooms, lecture halls, libraries, laboratories, playgrounds, and facilities for accommodation of students and teachers, and all are working in impoverished conditions. High technology based laboratories, smart classrooms etc are severely limited in number. Third, we do have a small number of high quality institutions like the Indian Institutes of Technology, Indian Institutes of Management, Indian Institutes of Information

Technology, central universities, central laboratories, etc., but all, working in isolation, have very little effect on the vast system, having no horizontal or vertical linkages. Fourth, the curriculum and the pedagogic methods that are currently in practice are found to be no more relevant for the country's transformation into a vibrant knowledge society of the 21st century associated with a new industrial revolution (industry 4.0), artificial intelligence, and an altogether new knowledge society. Fifth, the inefficient structures and mechanisms of governance that we have have their own adverse effects on the overall environment, which result in demotivated teaching faculty, dissuaded student community and lacklustre research output. The severe shortfall of funds that almost every institution faces is perhaps one of the most important reasons for the crisis in higher education.

While the small number of central institutions tend to focus on quality and standards, the large number of state level institutions of higher education aim at expansion of higher education, rather massification. The state level institutions, in their task, heavily depend upon private sector. As a result, today we have one of the largest private systems of higher education in the world, which depends exclusively on student fees. In fact, growth in private universities, private colleges and other institutions of private higher education which are based on pecuniary motives, has been alarming, unregulated and somewhat chaotic, producing devastating effects on the quality of and equitable access to higher education and on the values that education imparts among the youth..

While the union government and some states have taken important policy initiatives in the recent past towards reforming higher education, they are found to be not sufficient. Quality enhancement programmes are being launched on a large scale. The absence of a long term policy for the development of higher education is being addressed with the most recent efforts to make a new National Policy on Education. The *Policy* promises development of 'a new architecture for higher education, with large, well-resourced, vibrant multidisciplinary institutions of higher education.' Aiming at excellence in higher education as the most important goal, the *Policy* promises integration of higher education of all levels and types – under graduate, post graduate and research; professional, technical, and general; and liberal, classical and modern, in such a way that an organically closely linked higher education system is evolved that will contribute to the national transformation in diverse ways in the years to come.

It is in this overall background, this book edited by Dr Gedam Kamalakar, consisting of more than 50 articles contributed by a galaxy of young and experienced scholars, deserves a mention. These papers were intensively discussed in a seminar organised by the New Government Degree College, Serilingamaplay, and Hyderabad. Addressing a wide variety of issues relating to higher education in India, I am sure, it will attract the wide attention of all those who are engaged in higher education development in the country.

25 December 2019

Jandhyala B G Tilak

Former Vice Chancellor, NUEPA

Currently ICSSR National Fellow & Distinguished Professor

Council for Social Development, New Delhi

Preface

In Modern times education has come to play an important role in the life of individuals and in determining power and prestige of nations at the global level. Individual's value, position in society, economic status and personality are determined by education one attains. A nation's competency, place in the comity of nations, wealth and prosperity, growth rate, and comparative advantage in the production process are also linked to education. Individuals' choice and access to higher learning are closely associated with quality of education available in an institution or in a country. There are multiple factors which also play a role in determining quality of higher education. In the era of Globalisation, people have become mobile in pursuit of higher education with the tag of quality. In a sense wherever quality is available irrespective of form, people are ready to move to that place or institution to get the best and agree to pay for it, if not all, at least the middle class. The measurement of quality is undergoing change from time to time depending upon demand a course is having in market place and skills imparted and how long the skills have demand in market. As knowledge and skills are not static so is the quality of higher education. Thus one finds many assessment agencies across national boundaries assessing the quality of institutions and courses as per certain parameters to sustain quality whether they are in the public jurisdiction or private jurisdiction.

In India, higher education is under state control. There are many regulatory bodies at state and central levels to set standards and supervise quality. Institutions are assessed from time to time and new institutions are established upon the prior approval of these bodies. As a result there is a huge expansion of higher education sector in the last several decades. Only with the introduction of economic reforms higher education sector is opened for private participation to meet the increasing demand. With the opening of gates of higher education sector for private participation there arose issues like access, quality and equity. From time to time these issues are raised and assessed by scholars and educational commissions. At present, more or less, everybody is agreeing that quality in higher education has declined in the last few years. The reasons given are that per capita expenditure either remained constant or declined and quantity has over taken the quality. Regulatory bodies failed to arrest the trend and they are not in a position to assess the institutions properly due to push-pull pressures, due to withdrawal of state from its responsibility in the form of enhancing finances to support institutions, indifference to recruitment, putting aside quality, emphasis on expansion, mismanagement of institutions, over control of policy initiatives by bureaucracy and political class. When universalization of higher education is taking place and recognized as the need of the hour, trivial issues are gaining upper hand resulting in policy paralysis and indifference to new initiatives. Thinking out of box, major restructuring of higher education and freeing it from vested interesting is the need of the hour to take to the doorsteps of the needy which requires political will on the part of the policy makers of the present times to make India a competitive nation in shaping the future world.

Present volume is an effort made by scholars who raise a few questions related to quality and research in higher education in India. Issues discussed may not provide final answers but it is an attempt to understand the issues and processes. The effort has to be appreciated to take the questions forward. Many more such efforts are to be taken up to analyse and to understand higher education sector in India. I wish the endeavor reaches its fruition in the form of greater debate and action.

Prof. J. Lakshmi Narsimha Rao
Former Professor of Political Science
Osmania University Hyderabad

Acknowledgements

I express my special thanks to my research supervisor Prof.J.Lakshmi Narsimha Rao who has been a constant source of inspiration. I feel highly honoured and greatly indebted to him for sparing time to guide this work and motivating me for completion of the seminar proceedings in the form of book.

I would like to express my gratitude to Prof Ram Reddy, academic colleagues and students who took part in the seminar and shared their valuable views and experiences of quality evaluation in the higher education sector. I would like to express my thanks to the New Government Degree College serilingmapally for conducting such National seminar. Sincere thanks to ICSSR, TSCHE and RUSA for their staunch support and special thanks to Dr.Kamala, Asst. Professor of Political Science, Convener of National Seminar who has helped proofread this book. This book is dedicated to my family and thanks for their love and support.

Dr. G. Kamalakar

Chapter-1

Data Protection: In the Era of Globalisation

Dr. S. Sudhakar

Abstract

The growing importance of technology and its rapid spread in all areas of our social and economic fabric means that increasingly data and data privacy are becoming important aspects of our life. The higher education system is not immune from these changes in the larger society and economy.

Higher Education and Data privacy

Globalisation and increased emphasis on an interconnected world only forcefully draw our attention to these needs. As technology becomes important there is an increased need to protect the information technology backbone of the higher education institutions since they are increasingly becoming data driven as well as due to the unique intellectual property that various universities are investing in now-a-days. The recent news that about 750 million email accounts where comprised should be a sufficient cause for concern and should serve as a wakeup call. More importantly, most of our institutions now store the records, including sensitive private/personal information of their students, their economic and social profiles in their information technology systems. Hence, it would be a mistake to think that only large companies have vital data to protect. The higher education system, in its totality, has extremely sensitive and important information that needs to be protected. Hence, it is necessary for universities invest in the right solutions to protect student data from prying unauthorised networks.

In the year 2018 on 25th May, a new phase in global consumer data protection was inaugurated. On that particular day European Union's (EU) new and stringent General Data Protection Regulations (GDPR) came into force. These data protection rules come at a critical time when the world is in the midst of a major technology induced change. There is little doubt that India, like other parts of the world, is adopting technology rapidly. The result of this adaption is that millions of Indians are using various tools for an increasing number of activities in their everyday life. While cyber security has been a topic of much discussion one aspect that has largely been ignored is that related to **data protection**. If there is one aspect India definitely lacks, it is a complete lack of awareness and urgency to protect consumer-user data. In the age of information technology 'data is considered the new oil'; and, it is increasingly becoming critical to lubricate the economy. Most of the technology tools that we use today were either non-existent or were at best at nascent stages of development at the turn of the century. To understand the importance of technology and its impact on our everyday life we need to look at no further than statistics related to technology usage in the past few years: there were an estimated 1.6 crore (or 0.4 percent of world's population) internet users in 1995; by the end of 2017 it was an estimated 415 crore (or 54.4 percent of world's population)[1]. Nearly 1 billion people (or 100 crores) use Whatsapp every day; they share nearly 450 (4.5 billion) crores photos every day, 100 crore videos and, send nearly 5500 crore (55 billion) messages every day[2]. Nearly 40,000 people search for information on Google every second – that translates into 3500 crore searches every day. Facebook has nearly 200 crore active monthly users. The World's nine most popular mobile messaging apps have a cumulative 580 crore (5.8 billion) active users[3]. Apart from these, in different countries people use thousands, if not lakhs of other technology tools and apps like games, etc. Every online activity of a person generates data since technology leaves a digital footprint. So now, companies and governments not only know what we read but also which web pages we visit, their frequency, the time spent on each web page, what we buy, our chats, our online behaviour, etc. People think that their activities are anonymous, discreet and all the information is available free of cost. The only reason something is given free on the Internet is because there is a hidden, underlying commercial value to our use of that resource. Thus, we have to wake up to the reality that all our online activities are closely being tracked. Using our online behaviour companies generate an excellent profile of the user which they then sell to various others including among others advertisers.

Technology, Data and National Laws

As a generalisation, Data includes various kinds of data including those related to our banking and other financial transactions, sites we visit, the timings, the time we spend in them, our online purchases, bill payments, etc – all of which are increasingly becoming an important aspect of our everyday life. Increasingly, its protection is important for national security aspects too since paralysing data transfer and other IT networks will mean a large part of our economy will come to a standstill. Imagine what will happen if the bank servers, government departmental servers, electricity grid and our telephones stop working – all in the same day.

The important aspect of this technological change is that thanks to the internet, national boundaries are becoming increasingly more fluid. Almost all the largest technology companies of the world are based in one location but provide services to one and all across national boundaries. Till now, there were few laws in countries to regulate all these large companies. And, these laws can be implemented only if a country is very large and powerful. Little wonder that till date very few countries have been able to control the internet. So far, only China has been able to control the internet but that is because it is not a democracy. It is because of the increased importance of data for the wellbeing of the country that EU is introducing new conditions. Slowly there is a realisation in India that banking data is vital for our security concerns. It is for this reason that recently, the RBI passed guidelines that require all payments companies to physically store Indian Citizen's payment transaction history and data in the country. This is expected to give greater control to RBI and the government in implementing laws of the country. It has given companies six months to comply. This is important because increasingly private companies are allowed into the financial and payments sector. Payments are increasingly important for the national economy with lakhs of crores of payments being transferred electronically.

EU's Revolutionary Data Protection Rules

It is in the above context of the increased importance of technology and data that the importance of EU regulations can be understood. The European Union has taken up a major overhaul of regulation to protect data of consumers or personal data. This personal data is important because it can identify a person and their behaviour. EU provides for stringent conditions for sharing "any personal information including those related to name, identification number, location of data or any online identifier reflecting changes in the technology and the way organisations collect information about people". Thus, any information that can be used to directly or indirectly identify a person comes under the purview of this law. Any company, individual or website that uses technology to collect such information should seek the consent of the user for any use that the data is being put to. Users can object to any kind of data being collected, shared or any type of profiling – something which is simply not possible at present. The most important aspect of the rules is that for the first time it gives various rights including those related to access, any corrections, erasure, restrict processing of data, portability of data in easy readable format and not machine language. If the user so wishes the right to be forgotten they have to delete their data. The collector of the data has to inform the users about the data that is in their possession, what use it is being put to, whom this information is being shared, how long the data is being stored, how much information is shared and the and what information is being shared with others, what data protection policies and principles are in place. In case the data is being processed then, disclosures are required for the lawful basis for the processing this data. Users can complain to the regulatory agency if they have a problem with the way their data is being handled. Hence, it will not be possible for companies to survive on collecting data and analysing data discreetly without the permission of the user – something that is dominant today where companies collect data about user behaviour and sell it to advertisers. In case of children below the age of 16, parental consent/permission is required for online services. An important aspect of this is that the consent has to be in easy to understand and easy to access forms rather than that which uses complex legal terminology. All public authorities and organisations that engage in large scale processing of sensitive personal data of any kind are required to appoint Data Protection Officers (DPO) to look after compliance related issues. This effectively means that all government, public institutions, educational institutions, technology, financial, retail and other companies including banks who have any kind of personal information need to appoint such officers. A very important aspect of these changes is that these changes are applicable not just for companies based in Europe but for all companies which may be based anywhere in the world but provide services to citizens or residents of European Union. Thus, unlike most other laws these laws are applicable irrespective of the territory that a service provider may be based in as long as they have access to the personal data of the user.

Implications & Significance

These rules have immense implications for a country like India. The first and foremost is that the transition to these new guidelines is bound to be difficult for Indian companies. A recent report pointed out that while only 50 percent of the French companies are prepared; it is 33 percent in USA, around 35 percent in South Africa and a low 13 percent in India. Any non compliance and breach of GDPR will draw a maximum fine of up to

4 percent of annual global turnover or 20 million Euros (or about ₹120 crores) whichever is greater. Hence, non compliance will mean heavy penalties which most of the Indian companies cannot afford. Since the EU GDPR has expanded the definition it will mean that most of the companies that offer goods and services to EU citizens will be affected. The problem for these companies that do business in EU will be aggravated as there is a shortage of professional who have knowledge of the compliance system. It has been estimated that about 75,000 data protection officers are required around the world while India alone need about 1200 DPOs.

Second, it is high time that India learnt from the positive and proactive effort of data protection. In India we have had governments and private sector blatantly collecting data and violating the rules that exist. The lack of these rules is made worse by the fact that user grievance redressal mechanism is rare or when it exists is often slow to react. In some cases, the few laws that are meant to protect consumers completely violate the constitution. The case of grievance redressal in the case of Aadhaar is illustrative of this: Section 47 of the Aadhaar Act says that in case of grievance about Aadhaar misuse, citizens cannot directly approach a court of law. Instead they will have to complain to UIDAI and only the UIDAI can represent the matter to a court of law. This is completely against the spirit of natural justice. It becomes a bigger problem because UIDAI rarely takes action against those who misuse consumer data. The only time that it takes any action is when it faces an issue with their providers. No wonder they do not take any action when thousands or lakhs of Aadhaar numbers are stored or disclosed publicly – and, in contravention of Aadhaar Act. Another example are the frequent marketing calls from banks and insurance companies to people – even to those who are registered in "Do Not Call Registry" of those companies and Telecom Regulatory Authority of India (TRAI).

Notes

1. https://www.internetworldstats.com/emarketing.htm.
2. https://www.zdnet.com/article/whatsapp-now-one-billion-people-send-55-billion-messages-per-day/.
3. https://www.statista.com/statistics/258749/most-popular-global-mobile-messenger-apps/.

Chapter-2

Quality Education and its Imperativeness in Modern India-A Review

Dr. V. Vijay Durga Prasad,

Abstract

Education has been given high priority by India's central and state governments and continues to grow fast. School access has been expanded by investment in school infrastructure and recruitment of teachers. In higher education too, the number of providers continues to rise rapidly. A new law enshrining the rights of all children to free and compulsory education will further lift enrolment, bringing closer the government's goal of universal elementary education, which comprises eight years of schooling. Nevertheless, high drop-out rates and low attendance continues to be a challenge at lower levels and enrolment at higher levels remains modest by international standards. Private sector involvement is on the rise. While it helps expand education infrastructure, particularly in higher education, access has not always been assured and the availability of student loans for higher education needs to improve. Poor learning outcomes amongst school students and mediocre higher education provision call for more effective government regulation and funding arrangements. Expanding resources will help but they need to be deployed more effectively, while incentives and professional development systems for teachers need to be strengthened. In higher education the government has proposed reforms which have the potential to bring about much-needed improvements in regulatory effectiveness. Efforts should focus on reducing micro-regulation and improving institutional autonomy, in order to stimulate innovation and diversity. Increasing the number of institutions subjected to quality assessments will be important for lifting standards across the higher education system, while reform of recruitment and promotion mechanisms could help attract and retain talent in academia. The paper exemplifies the importance of success through quality education as well as the impediments and challenges to education faced by certain communities in industrial and emergent countries. No doubt, enhancement in education ensures success because it is the only discipline that develops awareness and builds excellent ethical personality. We could deem education as a token or a golden coin that brings not only immensity in knowledge but also superlative standard in life. The paper presents thirteen core barriers to quality education such as high fee structure, lack of awareness, and conversion of this field into business. The feeling of educationist to work for humanity by spreading education is now been sidetracked only to make money. Reasons for which these impediment come to pass are enlightened as well as the suggestions to lessen the affect of these barriers are also been discussed in the paper. Holding up with conclusion, it is education that provides distinction between good and bad, right and erroneous, so every one of us must need to comprehend the magnitude of education and strengthen its root as it manipulate our lives.

Keywords: *Human capital, literacy, vocational education, India, secondary education, primary education, universities, tertiary education, schools, education spending, education policy, quality education, success, awareness, growth of economy.*

Introduction

Post independence, it was believed that the education system in India requires an overall improvement in terms of the present day needs and fast changing technology. As previously there was no connection found between the education being imparted in our classrooms and employment opportunities present outside, the experts have set a keen eye on the syllabus and the framework of the Indian education system so much so that these can be adapted to the changing needs of the contemporary times. This would result in gaining better job prospects and we as a nation would then be able to keep a check on the problem of 'brain-drain'' and ensure that both the personal interest of the student and the national students can go hand in hand. There is no connection between the education being imparted to our students and the employment opportunities available in the outside world. As a result of which, the students find themselves unable to cope with the situation and get dejected. However, in recent times both the central as well as the state governments have begun paying attention to this serious challenge and are trying to bridge the gap between the two. Progress in the field of education has been really dismal. Our government only spends 3.85 percent of the GDP on education and millions of students still do not get the opportunity to enroll themselves in school even though the mark of improvement in the gross enrollment ratio. We should understand that the fate of our nation depends on our youth and if they are empowered no one can stop our nation from growing and accomplishing new heights on a global platform. If the resources are utilize correctly and properly than the success becomes certain. It is true that if the state is provided with financial resources as well as human resources than the step towards success is created but how can we correctly utilize these resources. For that education plays a vital role and brings awareness and enhances skills to utilize these resources properly. In modern world quality education is considered to be the basic reason that can only make a developing state a developed state. If the government of any country enable to provide good quality education to every person of her society than that state never depends upon loans and funds. To make the root level of economy strong there need to be such educational policies made by educational professionals that prove their loyalty with the nation and the people. The basic factor that needs to be included in these policies should be provision of quality education free of cost. As the paper is prepared on genuine thoughts and authentic perception there are certain core hurdles been discussed that influence education. There are many challenges that are faced by education like cultural, social, political, technological, and economical. To triumph over these challenges advanced educational technology should be introduced in every educational institute by developing advanced frameworks. New course of action should also be formulated to purify education quality. The basic theme of this paper is to identify the impediments and challenges faced by specific communities regarding education and to find solutions to those barriers. This paper also revels towards strengthening of success through education. As it is very clear that without enhancing access to education there exist no possibility to achieve success so every one of us must understand the enormity and value of education and make it in reach of every person.

Literature reviews

Today's world is the world of information, technology, internationalization and competition. Only those are successful who contribute their best potential into work and have a great charm of continuous learning. People put their efforts and polish their skills to get success but they are unaware of the correct medium to be used to achieve it. In meaningful words we can say that there are impediments and challenges to achieve success and people are unable to find solutions to lessen them. There are various researches that were conducted to find out the obstacles that create glass ceiling between education and success. The research conducted by Yuksel Goktas etal, Soner Yildirim etal and Zahide Yildirim etal, (2009) examine the foundation of barriers that appears when information and communication technologies (ICT) are integrated in teacher educational courses. Quantitative as well as qualitative methods were used by the researchers. Some of the main barriers that appear while conducting quantitative approach were lack of in-service training, shortage of appropriate software/materials, and lack of fundamental knowledge/skills for ICT. In addition to the aforesaid barriers they also talked about the barriers appeared while conducting qualitative method such as jam-packed classrooms, insufficient number of ICT-related courses, lack of computers, unavailability of presentation equipment in classrooms, lack of computer laboratories for use in free time, and lack of technology plans etc. The paper also discusses that if the positive strategies are adopted than it will put a great impact on decreasing the hub barriers and for that institutes must have technology plans and allocating budget. On the other hand a brief literature study by A. Abrizah etal and Ruslina Ahmad etal (2010) reveals towards Special Education Needs (SEN). The paper is about those students who are having disabilities and face great level of difficulties in learning and are traditionally excluded from school libraries. The paper also discusses that without excellent mentoring and provision of special educators children with disabilities can't move forward in life. Libraries are considered to be the best source to enhance knowledge but disable children are unable to access to libraries. Six core obstacles were discussed by the researchers that influence disable children to get access to libraries. Some suggestion are also been given to overcome these barriers.

Importance of Education in Modern World

We can perceive education as a human asset that enhances knowledge, skills, talent, abilities and capabilities to make person's life much more valuable. When we talk about quality education it is the excellence of knowledge and information that spreads from educational professionals and platforms to make bright future. It is desire of every individual to spend a comfortable life by following ethics of life, and education is considered to be the only key that can fulfil this statement. As technology is changing new modes to spread education are orienting. Previously education was just used to spread by teaching styles and limited to institutes but technology brings it to advancement. Today we can use internet to educate our self, E-education is also been introduced and we can also find online educational courses and recorded lectures on CDs but question arises here, is education free? Or does every individual can get free access to education in this world of competition? We always hear that, it is right of every individual to get education or the only way to help a child is to educate him but we may not find any statement that "it is right of every individual to get quality education free of cost". No person can deny, to get education is a right but unfortunately when it comes to money than law also modifies it. Today almost everyone has become self-centred and concern to himself. Only those are successful who have money and can let their children to get good quality education in world famous institutes. The feeling to work for humanity is now been altered to make money by any means. Nations are divided into different sects and admissions in schools, colleges and universities are offered on quota system. Only those people suffer who belongs to deprived families and not able to pay high fees for their underprivileged children. These people are always been degraded in high societies just because they don't have access to education. In high level communities there exists a very untrue concept that money is everything. "Money supports a person to be a better person but it doesn't make a better person, which is only education that identifies what you are" (Ali Muslim). This statement shows that it is only quality education that leads a person to achieve success not money. To make education common it is not only the responsibility of government but it is also the responsibility of all of us to provide better solutions to our state leaders so that they can provide justice and make education accessible to everyone. If we talk about access it can only be enhanced towards education if the government would be having enough financial resources that it can spend on education as well as human resources that can provide quality of education. Word education is a broader term and having many sections or subsections such as education could be on health, safety, discipline or quality and must be of quality. No doubt when access is enhanced towards education it ensures success but there are many impediments and challenges to education which are faced by certain communities in industrial and emergent countries. Developed countries are much more successful in providing quality education than developing countries and able to find hurdles that influence education.

Following are the main obstacles that prevent an individual to get access to education:

First core barrier to education is improper allocation of budget by the government on educational sector. As we know government role has always been considered as a backbone to develop economic growth but unfortunately it is neglecting the educational sector that generates and stabilizes economy.

Second obstacle that influences education is incorrect implementation of educational policies. If the process of policy making is correct and implementation is not done properly vice versa than how could that state proves she to be the best in the world.

Third hurdle is the language. Countries that have strong economic growth they have their course books in their mother language but unfortunately it is lack of awareness that government is unable to implement such educational policy that includes such section.

Fourth impediment to education is conversion of this sadqa-e-jaria (work for ALLAH by helping his creation) into business. Work for humanity has now been substituted by earning money.

Fifth core obstacle that manipulates education is lack of educational platforms that make education accessible to every individual free of cost. We can see many tuition centres in our society that only provide education and their basic purpose is to earn money not to polish educational skills of students.

Sixth obstacle to education is, countries which have quality education their fee structure is very high and unaffordable for low salary earners. This happens when the involvement of state leaders becomes zero in education sector and education policies are made out of way by immature people. By this people open private institutes and charge as much fee as they want.

Seventh barrier and biggest challenge to education are those students who go abroad for higher studies and don't wish to come back to home countries. Government institutes usually offer scholarships for brilliant students and provide them a golden chance to travel abroad for higher studies but these students usually start to do jobs rather than studying. These students are considered to be the asset of that country but unfortunately due to the neglect ion of their parents, relatives and state leaders, state is losing this golden asset.

Eighth obstacle is lack of awareness. People who belong to deprived families are not aware of the value of education because poverty inherited them and they just desire to earn for hand to mouth. These people never wish to make their lives standard able. Second reason is that they don't have enough money to spend on their children to educate them so they are not aware of importance of education. They do labour work and also encourage their children to never think about getting education and work as they do.

Ninth obstacle is construction of educational institutes on long distances. Students having travelling problem can't make so long to travel each and every day to learn. We can take an example of students who are living in villages and can't afford to live in hostels situated in rural areas so how can they pay each day for transportation.

Tenth hurdle to education is insufficient availability of teachers. They teach many subjects as they are master in one subject. We could say without hesitating that one teacher who is master in one subject teaches many subjects throughout the day and get exhausted at the end than how could he get prepared for the next day lecture. As quantity increases quality decreases, so when more subjects are allotted to one teacher then quality of teaching suffers.

Eleventh sturdy barrier to education is insufficient availability of educational institutes for disable children. Disability is not a fault of a child or his parents, it's by nature. In our societies disable children are always underestimated because they need special attention and special schools. If nature fetches any ability it provides any other skill that a normal person don't have. We can see many disable children in our society having much more intelligence and good brain power. These special students are also not been provided with special teachers to mentor them, they are just restricted to their homes and feel like burden on their parents for the rest of their lives.

Twelfth impediment to education is existence of funeral system. This happens mostly in urban or tribal areas where the head of a village do not allow his area people to get education with the fear that if they become educated than they will ask for their rights and no more be slaves.

Thirteenth barrier to education is deployment of such person as a Minister of education who does not belong to educational background. We could also say he is not aware of educational policies and procedures. There exists many responsibilities as a Minister of education and unfortunately this barrier influences education the most. When there is no standard of merit is set for higher jobs and people hire people by references than that state never ever proves to be successful. That state than always rely on other countries to provide funds and loans and work like slaves and her identity is lost.

The major problems of the Education Planning in India as far as analysts opinion are as under:

- high drop-out rates
- low levels of learning achievement
- low participation of girl students
- inadequate school infrastructure
- teacher absenteeism rate high
- large-scale teacher vacancies
- inadequate teaching/learning material
- lack of public involvement in provisioning of educational services

- variation in the literacy rates for the Special Groups of citizens
- variation in inter-state literacy rates

Challenges to implement integrated education

- The challenge of poverty associated with disability
- The challenge of modifying deeply held attitudes
- Dissemination and public education
- The challenge of providing adequate levels of training to key stakeholders
- Inadequate resources

Conclusion

India has joined the few countries that have legislation to promote integrated education. This is a landmark step as India has now overcome a major legislative hurdle. A number of unique challenges still needs to be overcome in order to implement the key objectives enshrined in the legislation. Attitudinal barriers engrained as part of India's historical response to disability must be changed through education programs for both teachers and the general populace. The basic purpose of education is to make a man a real gentleman, so every person must craft himself to become aware of significance to enhance access to education that leads to success. We mostly observe people from business families prioritize money on education. They recognize money much more imperative than of getting education, so along with themselves they also don't bother to let their children to be educated. This concept should be eliminated by developing awareness. Furthermore by deploying teachers separately for secondary and intermediate level will help in reducing the core impediment to education and will make success certain. Without the involvement of state leaders it is impossible to promote education and make economy stabilize therefore it is the responsibility of government to make root level of education strong, promote its importance and make it free of cost. As it is very obvious that growth of economy of any state totally hinges upon education, hence it is also the duty of the government to endow with such educational platforms that make education accessible to every person of the country. We know it is education that provides distinction between good and bad, right and erroneous, so every one of us must need to understand the meaning of education, encourage others to get education and strengthen the heart of education as it manipulate our living standards.

References

1. Altekar A.S., *Education in Ancient India*, Benaras, 1948
2. Azad, Y. A. (1996). *Integration of disabled in common schools: A survey-study of IEDC in the country.* New Delhi: National Council of Educational Research and Training.
3. Baquer, A., & Sharma, A. (1997). *Disability: Challenges vs. responses*. New Delhi: Concerned Action Now.
4. Canadian International Development Agency (CIDA). (2003). *India Country Program Framework (2002-2007)*. Retrieved 10th June, 2003.
5. Chatterjee, G. (2003, April). *The global movement for inclusive education*. Retrieved 10th July, 2003.
6. Das, A. K., & Pillay, A. N. (1999, December). *Inclusive education for disabled students: Challenges for teacher education.* Paper presented at the 5th UNESCO-ACEID Conference, Bangkok, Thailand.
7. Dutt, Sukumar, *Buddhist Monks and Monasteries of India* (Their History and Their Contribution to Indian Culture.) London, 1962.
8. Halappa, G.S. (Ed.), *Studies in Education and Culture* (Dr. D. C. Pavate Felicitation Volume), Dharwad, 1960.
9. Jangira, N. K. (1995). Rethinking teacher education. *Prospects, 25*(2), 261-272.
10. Kamat, Jyotsna K., *Social Life in Medieval Karnataka(SLMK)*, New Delhi, 1980.
11. Leela, Shanta Kumari, S, *The Agrahâras in Karnataka*, 400-1300, Madras, 1986.
12. Sampatgiri Rao. K.(Ed.), *Karnataka through the Ages*, Bangalore, 1968
13. Upadhya, A. N., *Pravachanasârâ of Kundâjundâchârya* (Trans.) Bombay, 1945.
14. Yazdani, G., *The Early history of the Deccan*, parts I and II. London, 1960.

Chapter-3

Challenges & Opportunities in Higher Education: A Case Study on Indian Perspective

Dr. Debarun Chakraborty,
Wendrila Biswas,

Abstract

The world has understood that the monetary accomplishment of the states is specifically dictated by their instruction frameworks. Training is a Nation's Strength. A created country is unavoidably an informed country. Indian advanced education framework is the third biggest on the planet, by the United States and China. Since freedom, India as a creating country is antagonistically advancing in the training field. In spite of the fact that there have been parcel of difficulties to advanced education arrangement of India however similarly have parcel of chances to beat these difficulties and to improve advanced education framework much. It needs more prominent straightforwardness and responsibility, the job of schools furthermore, colleges in the new thousand years, and rising logical research on how individuals learn is of most extreme imperative. India require all around gifted and exceedingly taught individuals who can drive our economy forward. India gives exceedingly gifted individuals to different nations in this way; it is simple for India to exchange our nation from a creating country to a created country. The present examination means to feature the difficulties and to bring up the openings in advanced education framework in India.

Keywords: *Indian Higher Education, UGC, Challenges, Opportunities, GER*

Introduction

India's advanced education framework is the world's third biggest regarding understudies, beside China and the United States. In future, India will be one of the biggest training center points. India's Higher Education part has seen a colossal increment in the quantity of Universities/University level Institutions and Colleges since freedom. The 'Right to Education Act' which stipulates mandatory and free training to all kids inside the age gatherings of 6-14 years, has achieved an unrest in the instruction arrangement of the nation with measurements uncovering a stunning enrolment in schools throughout the most recent four years. The contribution of private segment in higher training has seen radical changes in the field. Today over 60 percent of advanced education foundations in India are advanced by the private part. This has quickened foundation of establishments which have begun over the a decade ago making India home to the biggest number of Higher Education foundations on the planet, with understudy enrolments at the second most astounding (Shaguri, 2013).The number of Universities has expanded multiple times in last few years. Notwithstanding these numbers, universal instruction rating offices have not set a significant number of these foundations inside the best of the world positioning. Likewise, India has neglected to create world class colleges.

Today, Knowledge is control. The more information one has, the more engaged one is. In any case, India keeps on confronting stern difficulties. Regardless of developing interest in instruction, 25 percent of its populace is still uneducated; just 15 percent of Indian understudies achieve secondary school, and only 7 percent graduate (Masani, 2008). The nature of training in India whether at essential or advanced education is altogether poor when contrasted with real creating countries of the world. Starting at 2008, India's post-auxiliary establishments offer sufficiently just seats for 7 percent of India's school age populace, 25 percent of showing positions across the nation are empty, and 57 percent of school teachers need either an ace's or PhD degree (Newsweek, 2011). Starting at 2011, there are 1522 certificate conceding building schools in India with a yearly understudy admission of 582,000 (Science and Innovation Education, 2009) in addition to 1,244 polytechnics with a yearly admission of 265,000. Be that as it may, these foundations confront deficiency of staff and concerns have been raised over the nature of training (Mitra, 2008).

Regardless of these difficulties advanced education arrangement of India similarly have parcel of chances to survive these difficulties and have the capacity to make its personality at worldwide dimension. In any case, it needs more prominent straightforwardness and responsibility, the job of colleges and universities in the new thousand years, and developing logical research on how individuals learn is of most extreme essential. India gives exceptionally gifted individuals to other nations in this manner; it is simple for India to exchange our nation from a creating country to a created country.

Objectives

- To find out the current status of Indian higher education.
- To find out the challenges in Indian higher education.
- To find out the opportunities Indian higher education.
- To find out the suggestions to improve Indian higher education.

Research Methodology

The optional information has been assembled at first. Therefore, extraordinary magazines and journals have been used as it is a determined paper. Henceforth, the fixation is to get some answers concerning the thought, its application and the impact on economy. Thusly abstract data have been used. As the examination paper is of determined and review nature, the pro has associated exploratory research arrangement by using changed auxiliary information benefitted from the discretionary data sources. In perspective of the assistant data and review, the researcher has expounded on various rising examples and issues and troubles in cutting edge India. Research report, journal and day by day paper articles from popular writers have been kept an eye on.

Current Status of Indian Higher Education

Indian training comprises of "islands of greatness gliding in an ocean of average quality". This open decision, voiced in 2014 by the nation's at that point clergyman of state for human asset improvement Shashi Tharoor, is especially valid in the circle of advanced education. Since freedom, the difficulties of building a mass advanced education framework in a setting of deficient government subsidizing has implied low quality, expanding privatization, and politicization.

In 2013, the Indian government propelled a noteworthy change activity. Known as RUSA, it expects to give extra key financing to state advanced education establishments in an offer to drive up quality and limit in the framework. B. Venkatesh Kumar and Ashok Thakur from the Indian Institute of Technology Bombay take note of that this financing expanded India's entrance rate to advanced education from 19.4 percent of the qualified populace to 25.2 percent somewhere in the range of 2013 and 2017, and diminished staff opportunities from 60 percent to 19.4 percent in government-subsidized post-optional establishments. In any case, understudy consummation rates stay risky and staff opening is still altogether higher at "unaided" establishments that get no immediate open financing. Additionally, while later research demonstrates that the entrance rate additionally expanded to 25.8 percent in 2018, the quantity of instructors in advanced education has been declining amid the previous couple of years, and the student to-educator proportion in colleges and schools stays just 1 to 30.

Open venture additionally keeps on being disseminated incredibly unequally. Late information partook in the Indian national parliament by Satyapal Singh, pastor of human asset advancement in charge of advanced education, uncover that amid the previous three years, more than 50 percent of the central government's financing for advanced education has just profited the 3 percent of the nation's understudies selected at midway supported establishments, for example, the Indian Institutes of Technology (IITs), Indian Institutes of Management (IIMs) and National Institutes of Technology (NITs). These foundations are among the islands of brilliance that Tharoor was insinuating. Different precedents incorporate the midway supported Indian Institute of Science, Tata Institute for Fundamental Research and Jawaharlal Nehru University, and private organizations, for example, the Manipal Academy of Higher Education, and the Birla Institute of Technology and Science, Pilani (BITS Pilani) – all exceptionally respected research and instructing foundations. There are a couple of others, as well. In any case, in a framework that currently enlists 35 million understudies – more than some other nation with the exception of China – these are for sure minor drops in the sea of average quality.

Periodic talk from authorities keeps on making a joke of Indian advanced education and science. An ongoing model is remarks that Singh made not long ago scrutinizing the legitimacy of Darwin's hypothesis of advancement. With such little confidence in science, India's expectation to dispatch a kept an eye on space mission by 2022, reported by leader Narendra Modi a couple of months after the fact, amid his Independence Day address on 15 August, appears to be probably not going to work out as expected.

Another stressing late advancement is the administration's expectation to supplant the University Grants Commission (UGC) – the focal organization in charge of both giving assets and supervising quality models – with another body, the Higher Education Commission of India (HECI), which would be centered only on enhancing scholastic measures and quality. The UGC's give granting job would go to the Ministry of Human Resource Development, conceivably enabling legislators to utilize their money related clout to abrogate institutional independence. In any case, southern states, for example, Kerala and Tamil Nadu have effectively contradicted the move (both the administrative and state governments have the ability to order advanced education enactment, yet on the off chance that there is a contention, the government's enactment wins). What's more, at present, the possibilities of the enactment being passed by the national parliament look thin.

Regardless of whether this bit of enactment is defective, it shows that in any event the focal government shows up at long last to have perceived the key job for advanced education in India's improvement and worldwide commitment. Also, following 50 years of scholarly laziness, different activities it has as of late presented are charmingly astounding and possibly amusement evolving.

Challenges in Indian Higher Education:

Since 1947 we became independent as a country but still our instruction framework has not been created completely. We are not ready to list a solitary college in best 100 colleges of the world. Different governments changed amid these six decades. They endeavored to help the instruction framework and actualized different training strategies however they were not adequate to put a case for the universe. UGC is consistently working and concentrating on quality instruction in higher instruction part. Still we are confronting parcel of issues and difficulties in our training framework. A portion of the essential challenges in advanced education framework in India are talked about beneath:

The Gross Enrolment Ratio of India in advanced education is just 15 percent which is very low when contrasted with the created and also, other creating nations. With the expansion of enrolments at school level, the supply of advanced education organizations is inadequate to meet the developing request in the nation.

There is no value in GER among various orders of the general public. As indicated by past examinations the GER in advanced education in India among male and female shifts to a more noteworthy degree. There are provincial varieties took a few states have high GER while as some is very behind the national GER which mirror a critical irregular characteristics inside the advanced education framework.

Quality in advanced education is a multi-dimensional, staggered, and a dynamic idea. Guaranteeing quality in advanced education is among the premier difficulties being looked in India today. Nonetheless, Government is ceaselessly concentrating on the quality training. Still Large number of universities furthermore, colleges in India can't meet the base prerequisites set somewhere around the UGC and our colleges are not in a situation to check its place among the best colleges of the world.

Poor foundation is another test to the advanced education arrangement of India especially the establishments kept running by general society area experience the ill effects of poor physical offices and framework. There are extensive numbers of universities which are working on second or third floor of the expanding on ground or first floor there exists readymade hosieries or photocopy shops.

Most of the instructive Institutions are claimed by the political pioneers, who are assuming key job in administering assemblages of the Universities. They are utilizing the guiltless understudies for their narrow minded methods. Understudies compose battles, overlook their very own goals and start to build up their professions in legislative issues.

Faculty deficiencies and the powerlessness of the state instructive framework to draw in and hold well qualified educators have been presenting difficulties to quality instruction for a long time. Substantial quantities of NET/PhD hopefuls are jobless even there are parcel of opportunities in advanced education, these meriting hopefuls are then applying in different offices which is a greatest hit to the higher training framework.

There are extremely ostensible researchers in our nation whose composing is referred to by popular western creators. There is deficient spotlight on research in advanced education organizations. There are inadequate assets and offices, and additionally, constrained quantities of value staff to exhortation understudies.

The greater part of the exploration researchers are without partnerships or not getting their cooperation's on time which straightforwardly or in a roundabout way influences their exploration. Besides, Indian Higher training establishments are ineffectively associated with research focuses. In this way, this is another zone of test to the advanced education in India.

Management of the Indian training faces difficulties of over centralization, bureaucratic structures and absence of responsibility, straightforwardness, and demonstrable skill. As a consequence of increment in number of partnered universities and understudies, the weight of authoritative elements of colleges has fundamentally expanded and the center spotlight on scholastics and research is weakened (Kumar, 2015).

Opportunities in Indian Higher Education

India is an expansive nation, with an expected populace of youngsters matured between 18 to 23 years to be near 150 millions. The sheer size of the market offers colossal open doors for advancement of the advanced education area in India. India presently gloats of having in excess of 33,000 schools and 659 colleges, which has been very a striking development amid the most recent six decades. The year 2018 saw more than 30 million enlistments, which makes India the third biggest instructive framework on the planet. Lamentably, the instructive framework of India is insufficient to deal with such immense volumes. In hate all the administration spending in the instructive division, it is simply too lacking to even consider meeting the developing prerequisites. Along these lines, advanced education division has now been recognized as one of the promising regions for private and remote ventures. It offers huge speculation openings in both non-managed and controlled portions (Nexus Novus, 26 July, 2013).

Indian advanced education framework is becoming quick regardless of different difficulties however there is no reason that these Challenges can't be survived. With the assistance of new-age learning devices, it is simple for nation like India to conquer these issues and bring a change in outlook in the nation's advanced education part. With such a dynamic nation with enormous populace legitimately taught, the potential outcomes are inestimable. On the off chance that information is granted utilizing progressed advanced educating and learning apparatuses, and society is made mindful of where we are right now lingering behind, our nation can without much of a stretch rise as a standout amongst the most created countries on the planet.

There are open doors for key commitment and limit working in advanced education authority also, the board at the state level. There are open doors for India to coordinated effort at national and global level on territories of foundational change, including quality confirmation, worldwide credit acknowledgment, and bound together national capabilities system. Uniformity of instructive open door in advanced education is considered basic in light of the fact that advanced education is an amazing asset for diminishing or killing salary and riches differences.

Equalizing instructive open doors additionally lies in the way that the capacity to benefit by advanced education is spread among all classes of individuals. There are incredible stores of undiscovered capacity in the general public; whenever offered the chance they can ascend to the best (Balachander, 1986).

The need to upgrade the employability of alumni is displaying section focuses for coordinated effort in undertaking instruction and business, joins with industry, inquire about abilities and the wide scope of transferable abilities, including English. The developing enthusiasm for Indian advanced education foundations in the professional abilities advertise gives territories to potential commitment with universal accomplices. There is a need to construct more grounded connections and increment shared comprehension in advanced education by expanding backing and interest in stages (meetings, workshops, courses) which empower discussion and discourse with different nations of the world (British Council, 2014).

Suggestions to Improve

There is a need to execute creative and transformational approach shape essential to higher training level to make Indian instructive framework all inclusive increasingly significant and aggressive. Higher instructive establishments need to enhance quality and notoriety. There ought to be a decent framework of schools and colleges which may draw in the understudies. Government must advance joint effort between Indian advanced education foundations and best International establishments and furthermore produces linkage between national research labs and research focuses of best organizations for better quality and community oriented research.

There is a need to concentrate on the alumni understudies by giving them such courses in which they can accomplish perfection, increase further information of subject with the goal that they will land positions after enlistment in the organizations which would diminish superfluous hurry to the advanced education. Universities and schools in both open private must be far from the political affiliations, Favoritism, cash making procedure ought to be out of training framework and so forth. There ought to be a multidisciplinary approach in advanced education so understudies information may not be limited just up to his very own subjects.

Conclusion

Instruction is a procedure by which an individual's body, psyche and character are framed and fortified. It is bringing of head, heart and mind together and accordingly empowering an individual to build up an inside and out identity distinguishing the best in that person. Advanced education in India has extended quickly over the most recent six decades after autonomy yet it isn't similarly open to all. India is today one of the quickest creating nations of the world with the yearly development rate going above 9 percent. Still a huge segment of the populace stays uneducated and a huge number of kids' don't get even essential instruction. This isn't just barred a vast area of the populace from adding to the improvement of the nation completely yet it has likewise kept them from using the advantages of whatever improvement have occurred to support the general population.

Presumably India is confronting different difficulties in advanced education yet to handle these difficulties and to support advanced education is most extreme vital. India is a nation of immense human asset potential, to use this potential legitimately is the issue which expected to examine. Openings are accessible however how to get profits by these chances and the most effective method to make them available to others is the matter of concern. So as to support that rate of development, there is need to build the quantity of establishments and furthermore the nature of advanced education in India. To reach and accomplish the future prerequisites there is a pressing need to relook at the Financial Resources, Access and Equity, Quality Models, Relevance, foundation and toward the end the Responsiveness.

References

1. Shaguri, Obadya Ray, Higher Education in India Access, Equity, Quality, EAN World Congress Scholar, Global Access to Postsecondary education, 2013.
2. Masani, Zareer, India still Asia's reluctant tiger, BBC Radio 4, 27 February 2008.
3. Newsweek, Special Report: The Education Race, August 18–25, 2011.
4. Science and Technology Education". Press Information Bureau, Retrieved 2009 08-08
5. Mitra, Sramana, How To Save The World's Back Office of Forbes, 03.14.2008
6. Henard, Fabrice, Report, Learning our Lesson: Review of Quality teaching in Higher Education, 2008.
7. Higher Education in India: Twelfth Five Year Plan (2012-17) and beyond FICCI Higher Education Summit 2012.
8. Kumar, Anuj & Ambrish, Higher Education: Growth, Challenges And Opportunities, International Journal of Arts, Humanities and Management Studies, Volume 01, No.2, Feb 2015.
9. Sharma, Sahil, Sharma, Purnendu, Indian Higher Education System: Challenges And Suggestions, Electronic Journal for Inclusive Education, Vol. 3, No. 4, 2015, pp.3-4.
10. Nexus Novus, Higher Education Opportunities in India, http://nexusnovus.com/higher-educationopportunities-india, Jul 26, 2013 accessed on 14/12/2018.
11. Balachander, K.K. "Higher education in India: Quest for Equality and Equity", Mainstream, 1986.
12. British Council, Understanding India- The Future of Higher Education and Opportunities for International Cooperation, 2014.

Chapter-4

Quality and Excellence of Higher Education in India: Issues and challenges

Dr. D R S Reddy,

Abstract

Across the Nation, there is a great concern about Quality in Education system. It has become a key concept in the world today. As globalization has sought world class technocrats, wealth managers, researchers and skilled labour for furtherance of their national objectives. Though it is very difficult to definite term quality However simply says that "Fit for use or purpose. Quality education ensures to achieve their goals and there by helps national development. Good educational institutions are built wit sustain and continues efforts of some committed personalities. These institutions have to play critical role in strengthening human resources and there by facilitating a smooth transition of the society.

Introduction

India has been a hub of education since time immemorial with the scholars drawn from different parts of the world. However, Ancient India consider education as an important aspect and taught in Gurkulas Agraharas and Madaras as throughout the country. The great world class universities such as Takshashila, Nalanda Ujjaini are flourished in India. During the colonial regime,westren thought and learning system introduced. However the first modern educational institutes such has Calcutta, Bombay and Madras universities sprang up in the year 1857.

Since Independence India made concerted efforts to improve access to higher education and the system grew rapidly. At the time of Independence there were just about twenty universities and around five hundred odd colleges. However, as of February 2017, there are 789 universities, 37204 colleges and 11443 standalone institutions functioning in the country. During the financial year 2016-17 the central government proposed to established twenty world class universities under public and private management. All these indicate higher education has registered an impressive growth in the last 80 years in the country. Also there has been steady growth in the student enrolment for collegiate education. Higher education in India is likely to surpass the US and china in another decade time. By 2030, India will be amongst youngest nation in the world with nearly 140miiloin people in the college going age groups.

This paper is trying to identify issues and challenges that facing in the field of higher education in India.

Issues and challenges in quality education

The current issues and challenges are pushing the educators teachers, students and the general public in to exploring new ideas, discussing new possibilities and pressing for new and quick solution. Some of the major ones are:

Selection of Faculty members

It is a serious issue and posing a great challenge to the section board. However to attract excellent teachers to the profession is the cry of today. Teachers are the pivot on which the society turned. They have the onerous responsibility of promoting good citizens also. Apart from academic achievements, the applicants vision of quality education to be examine. Also required to qualify in the national level tests in the concerned area.Definitly these measures will contribute produce the inspired and ignited minds of graduates and post graduates and scholars of eminence to fuel unprecedented growth and development. These in turn reduce poverty, hunger, debases, unemployment etc. Further the quality education will advance the frontiers of knowledge, shrink the boundaries of ignorance in the society.

Enhancement of salary and tenured faculty

To attract best brains in to academic institutions, salary should be negotiable. further you should also cover health,transport, liberary and lab expenses. For higher level post like professors principals, deans there should be tenural system to be implemented. There by eminent academicians may get opportunity to serve the institution the some of the western universities alredy practices in method. Also there must be periodical assessment of the faculty in practice.

Free mobility of researchers and faculty

The free Mobility among researchers and faculty between university to university, college to college are to eminent institutes like IITS, IIMs,

IISCs must be encourage. Hope that the relevance of our research and innovation and accelerated growth of start ups in the compasses to meet the future challenges and thus India become a world leader in education . We can remember the words of world renowned scholar and former precedence of India Prof S. Radhakrishnan that "The end-product of education should be a free creative man, who can battle against historical circumstances and adversities of nature. For this the universities should attract the best minds for its teaching faculty".

However the above words are more relevant today and universities and colleges have great responsibility to make India a vibrant nation. Further it indicate s that universities and institutions are lifeline to local industries and catalysts of change both at nation and global levels. It requires active participation of the industry and thus rice to the growth of new enterprises. As it calls for a major departure that universities as centers of learning and scholarship to universities as global knowledge enterprises. These changes accelerate the socio-economic development of the society.

Inter -Disciplinary approach

Different discipline teachers like scince, commerece arts to teach undergraduates students. Unless students are exposed to inter disciplinary and cross cultural studies, they will not be coped to face the ongoing changes in their career. For instance a student of commerce of science desiring to pursue political-economic or public policy paper can take up that course. Also creative writing, Philosophy, Psychology etc., should be available for interested student. Faculties should design combination of such electives to enable students get adequate knowledge of discipline.

Examination reforms

This area is one of great challenge for teachers to assess the students knowledge in the particular domain. Therefore gradual shifting from the traditional method to regular and continuous assessment of students performance to be implemented. Also a group of faculty members jointly examine the students to ensure a fair just assesment. Adoption of anti-plagiarisms software for assessing thesis and dissertations may promote original research in the campuses. Other changes like online practical examination and CC TV surveillance facility in examination centres may bring qualitative change in the campuses.

Establishment of e-class rooms and library

Even today most of the higher educational institutions are not equipped with ultra modern class room facilities to impart latest information. A library or class rooms must be conducive for serious study. Hence hi-tech ambience to be promoted.

Value based Education

As C S Lewis Says "Education without values as useful as it is Seems rather to make man a more clever Devil".

Hence true and quality education must promote and encourage noble motives, objective thinking, nation -building, service mindedness. Further the higher education beyond the preparation of intellectuals and knowledge contribution has to promote value-addition like deepening democracy in society and in turn stake holders become incubators of more empowered citizens.

Other Issues

There are several other issues posing a challenge to bring quality education in the country. They are Curriculum updating, R&D, E-Governance, healthcare,gender disparity, Funding institutions, international cooperation, action plan, student teacher ratio, personality development, linkages with industry, academic autonomy infrastructure, student scholarships and internships. Hence there is an urgent need to address these issues in order to accomplish quality education in the society.

Conclusion

It has been observe that higher education in India has been witness various changes,influencess and practies.The heightened pace of globalization mandates faster coping and adaptive capabilites, capacites in our higher educational institutions in the country to respond to changing economic order of the world. The emerging world view suggests that in the days to come, the role of knowledge capital in the process of development will predominate the physical capital and these clearly indicate that the importance and relevance of higher education. By way of cultivating academic culture and research and foster creativity and innovations and thus make India a world leader in quality education and reserch. The new approaches like participative and student-centric activates contributes significantly to the quality education. The competitiveness of nations-as the only way to achieve progress-should be balanced with inclusive social development and sustainability of the entire global population.

References

1. University Grants Commission report on "higher education in India at a glance"
2. All India survey on higher education (2015), MHRD
3. higher education in India and Yashpal Committee Recommendations
4. University News A weekly journal of higher educatinal,2017
5. Mishra, L (2013) globalization of higher education, new Delhi
6. Planning commission (2012), "higher Education in India" twelfth five year plan
7. Chaudhary, V S (2009), higher education : Today and tomorrow, new Delhi
8. The world university ranking 2018, times higher education

Chapter-5

Qualitative Dimensions in Higher Education

C. Jyothi,

Abstract

Higher Education appears as an important element in providing knowledge and growing qualified human power that a country requires. Higher education improves an individual's quality of life. Learning and creativity are reducing to a system of evaluation that places its focus on memory rather than understanding. Inadequate infrastructure, curriculum which has almost remained ;unchanged for decades have not kept pace with time, boundaries between disciplines have become dividing walls rather than constitute barriers to entitling for new disciplines. Studies show that compared to high school graduates college graduates have, access to health care, better dietary and health practices, greater economic stability and security, more prestigious employment and greater job satisfaction less dependency of government assistance, greater knowledge of government, greater community service and leadership and more self-confidence. Students, parents, teachers, governments and enterprise are the stakeholders in higher education. There are many dimensions for quality in higher education which include reliability, responsibility, competence, access, courtesy, communication, creativity and security. The emerging issues in higher education include deteriorating levels of teaching, financing of higher education, traditional methods of teaching privatization inadequate facilities and infrastructure. The challenges include heterogeneous education system, interference of political factors, economic difficulties, deteriorating moral values. Student centric education, examination reforms', international cooperation i.e., advancement and transmission of knowledge through traditional functions such as research to increase the quality of universities and high technology libraries. Education is the key to success as well as a very powerful tool for change and as such Higher education must be qualitatively strong so that it can guarantee higher employability and reputed positions. Improvement in quality of higher education will eventually draws more and more students and problem of low enrolment will get solved.

Keywords: *Quality, Infrastructure, security, economic, teaching, employability*

Introduction

Education beyond high school, specifically that provided by colleges and graduate schools and professional schools is known as higher education. Also known as post secondary education, tertiary education or third level education is an optional final stage of formal education that is accomplished by learning at a college or university.

Higher education appears as an important element in producing knowledge and growing qualified human power that a country requires. Higher education is also available through a certain college level institutions including vocational colleges and other career colleges that award degree or professional certifications.

The World Bank and UNESCO report (2000) rightly present a powerful message that higher education is no longer a luxury and is essential for survival. So we are interested in higher education because we are interested in our survival.

In the last two decades India has made rapid progress in the expansion of higher education facilities and institutions and at present, India in higher education system has expanded at a fast pace by adding nearly 20000 colleges and more than 8 million students in a decade from 2000 – 01 to 2010 – 11. As of 2011 India has 42 central universities 275 state universities 130 deemed universities 90 private universities 15 institutions of established and functioning under the State Act and 33 institutes of national importance. Other institutions include 33000 colleges as GDC's and PDCs including 1800 exclusive women's colleges functioning under these universities and institutions as reported by UGC 2012.

Need for quality in Higher Education

1. Curriculum which have almost remained unchanged for decades have not kept pace with the time.
2. Learning and creativity are reducing in a system of evaluation that places its focus in memory rather than understanding.
3. The atmosphere is not favorable to anything beyond the classroom for it is caught in 9:30 to 1:30 syndromes.
4. Infrastructure is not only inadequate but also in the threshold of collapse.
5. Academic calendar being untouchable.
6. The importance attached to research has ended gradually.

7. The boundaries between disciplines have become dividing walls that contribute barriers entry for new disciplines.
8. There is little accountability because there are no rewards for performances and penalties for non - performances.
9. Structures of governance are not responsible to changing times.

Importance of Higher Education

Higher education offers graduates more jobs to choose from than are open to those who don't pursue education beyond high schools and graduates typically earn more than non - graduates.

Higher education improves an individual's quality of life. Studies show that compared to high school graduates, college graduates have better access to health care, better dietary and health practices greater economic stability and security, prestigious employment and greater job satisfaction, less dependency of government assistance, greater knowledge of government, greater community services and leadership, more volunteers work once self confidence. In addition college graduates have greater access of internet, greater attendance at live performances, greater participation in commercial activities and high voting rates. Higher education also helps to expand knowledge and skills express their thoughts clearly in speech, group abstract concepts and theories and increase their understanding of the world and their community.

Quality in Higher Education

- Higher education is a service.
- Institutions of higher education are not the purpose for themselves.
- Higher education has been developed in varying degrees and at different times in different countries.
- The quality of education is not necessarily associated with the process of learning self.
- Education includes input process output vision goals.

Dimensions of quality in Higher Education

Detailed consideration of quality: Higher education at the beginning requires identifying the primary issues of services in higher education. namely the education process involves many stakeholders, students, parents, teachers, government enterprise.

Students are the most numerous stakeholders and are involved in different roles; they are the product of the process internal customers for company's facilities, laborers of learning process and the internal outcomes of the delivery of the course material. However students are primary customers not other prospective customers are such as alumni, parents, employees, government, industry and society may be considered secondary customer.

Consequently it becomes necessary to identify the determinants of service quality from the stand point of students being the primary customers. Developing a service quality model to measure the student's perception of quality is a key complex and tedious because the service quality dimensions cover may arise and therefore it is not possible to cover all.

Naturally defining the dimensions of quality in higher education is the dimensions of service quality in other areas. Exploring quality in different areas authorize state different dimensions i.e., they explore different aspects of satisfaction with some services. Different dimensions of services quality are used for different industries but there are some similarities between them (layrocan ET 2004). Also researchers agree that there is no single dimension which can be applicable for all the services sectors (Carner 1990 Bromet ET at 1993) and in the stated the most frequently mentioned authorities and the dimensions as for higher education as in other sectors are.

Parasurama et at (1991) initially developed ten dimensions in his research in 1985 reliability, responsiveness, competence, access, courtesy, communication, credibility, security, understanding the customer trouble and later reduced into 5 dimensions (research in 1988, tangible, reliability, responsiveness, assurance, empathy).

In paper in 1988 Gronroor lad identified 6 criteria of good perceived service quality professionalism and skill attitude and behavior, access and flexibility, reliability and trust worthiness, recovery, reputation and credibility and in his paper in 1990 he stated that the quality dimensions can be classified into 3 groups technical quality, functional quality and corporate image.

Athiyaman (1997) used 8 characteristics to examined university education services, teaching students were availability of staff for student consultation, library services, computing facilities, recreations facilities, class sizes, level and difficulty of subject content and student work load.

Carney (1994) variables of college image are student qualification (academic) student qualities (personal) faculty student interaction quality instruction (faculty) variety of courses, academic reputation class size, career preparation, athletic program, student activities (social life) community services, facilities and equipment, location physical appearance (campus) on campus residence, friendly atmosphere, religious atmosphere, safe campus (cost financial aid). Sargeeb ET (2004) noted five factors contribute competence, attitude, content, delivery, reliability.

Analyzing the listed dimensions authorities have came to the following conclusion:

1. There are significant similarities and also differences are the dimensions of services quality developed and used by various researchers.
2. Each of the developed dimensions is unique, therefore that supports the hypothesis that there are no single set of dimensions of service quality such as applicable and suitable for all types of service quality research.
3. Service quality dimension varies according to customers. Research objectives, institution, situation environment and time.
4. All the chosen dimensions for each of the studies are tailor made to meet different customer's perception and expectation.
5. Hence used to explain each dimensions varies according to research and customer group.
6. All dimensions used are acceptable and correct with qualitative and quantitative justification.
7. None of the dimensions are applicable for all types of service quality research without necessary modification.
8. The best way to identify the dimensions of service quality is by asking the customers. It is not possible to study the dimensions of service quality under the survey.

Emerging issues in qualitative dimensions of higher education

The role of higher education in the emerging scenarios of knowledge economy is very crucial and multi faceted for any country in general and India in particular. There are many basic problems faced by higher education system in India.

1. **Lower level of teaching quality**: our education system is formed by issues of quality in many of its institution and universities. Many of the issues like of lack of facility, poor quality teaching. Traditional teaching methods outdated curricula and pedagogy, lack of accountability and quality assurance and separation of

research and teaching are raising questions on Indian Education System.

2. **Financing of Higher Education**: One of the most important issues that have to be addressed is the use of financial constraints, regarding higher education before the government. Expenditure in education in common and in higher education in particular by the government is one of the parameters to judge the quality in education for allocation. The state government has already been spending 20-30 percent of its revenue budget in education. It cannot spend more. In India higher education has received less attention in terms of public spending than other levels. It's not feasible for India to make massive state investments in research and development that precede research led industries.
3. **Traditional methods of teaching**: Professor still sticks on to their old methods of teaching like board markers. They don't like to use audio; visual aids. Also they are not up to date with information available and what global industry demands.
4. **Privatization:** In the present scenario privatization of higher education is apparently a finding out welcome and is essential to maintain creativity, adaptability and quality. In India both public and private institutions operate simultaneously. Approximately 50 percent of higher education in India is imparted through private institutions mainly unaided involving high cost. Privatization works in the interest of maximizing profits, have every incentive to minimize costs by comparing the quality of education provided in this institution. Last but not the least quality of teaching staff is one of the considerable issues for higher education sector to sustain in the future. Earlier there were committed to their students to the subjects and to their profession. Today high salaries are available but the commitment is less. There is a need of the hour to free the higher education system from unnecessary constraints and political interference.
5. **Inadequate facilities and infrastructure**: In India many of the universities don't have adequate infrastructure or facilities to; teach students. Even many private universities are running courses without classrooms; internet and Wi-Fi facility is still out of reach of many students.
6. **Quota System**: Bringing the reservation and quota system for different categories in education but in quality. Even deserving candidates of general categories are ignored and on quota we have

to select other person from reserved category even though he is not suitable.

Emerging challenges in the qualitative dimensions of higher education.

The system of Indian higher education is the second largest in the world which fulfills the educational requirement of millions of millions who came from different sectors of the society since it is the student community that can help to generate healthy and academic atmosphere in institution of higher learning. No doubt India faces today a number of problems.

1. **Our heterogeneous education system**: Based on geographical rural labor, rich, poor set up have posed a great challenge for the educational institutions. Varieties of colleges, universities, and technical institutions have produced and different types and quality of education. Some of them are really imparting qualitative education although a few others are doing the worst job. We should be thankful of UGC for publishing to list of such a fake universities and institutions indulging in educational malpractices.
2. **Interference of political factors**: Most of the institutions imparting education are owned by dominant political leaders playing key role in governing bodies of the universities. They have established them, own youth and encourage student's organization on political basis. They exploit the student's energy for the political purpose. The students forget their own objectives and begin to develop their career in politics.
3. **Economic difficulties**: economic difficulties are one of the trouble some changes that the present higher education system has imposed on the communities. The numbers of students are coming from the ordinary classes many of them are unable to provide the minimum necessities of life for themselves. Economic miseries have grown due to the increased prizes habits of wasting money on luxuries increasing population, scarcity of food supply, corruption etc. students hold part time job in order to pay to their educational expenditure and should divide them between job and college. About 75 percent of the total students commonly have been facing the financial problem. Earn while learn scheme cannot adequately support student to face economic challenges.
4. **Lack of moral values**: Rapid growth of science and technology and subsequent industrialization has caused a great danger to our

old morals and values. The younger generations; dissatisfaction and revolt is the outcome of a decaying system of values.

Suggestions for improving the quality of Higher Education

1. **Student's centric education and dynamic methods**: methods of higher education also have to be appropriate to cater the needs of learning to learning, learning to do, and learning to become. Student centric education and employment of dynamic methods of education will require from teachers new attitude and new skills. Methods of distance education will have to be employed on a vast scale.
2. **Examination reforms**: examination reform gradually shifting from the terminal, annual and semester examination to regular and continuous assessment of student's performance in learning must be implemented.
3. **International cooperation**: universities in India have been a primary conduct for the advancement and transmission of knowledge through traditional functions such as research, innovation, teaching, and HRD and continuing education international cooperation gaining importance as yet another function. With the increased development of transport and communication the global village is witnessing a growing emphasis on international cooperation and action to find satisfactory solution to problems that have global dimensions and higher education is one of them.
4. **More Universitie**s To increase quantity of universities: we need more universities because we are more in number and universities are too less. On 13th June 2005 government of India contributed a high level advisory body known as national knowledge commission to advise the PM about the state of education in India and measures needed to reform the sectors. NKC has submitted its report in November 2007 and recommended setting up of 1500 universities by 2015 so that gross enrolment ratio increases to 15 percent. It has also called for establishing an independent regulations authority for higher education to monitor the quality of overall higher education in India.
5. **Gross cultural programmes** : After education tours to every places in India and world as far as possible with the cooperation of government is necessary so that one can understand about people, cultural, art, literature, religions, technological developments and progress of human society in the world.

6. **Action plan for improving quality**: academic and administrative audit must be conducted ones in 3 yrs in college 4 external experts for ensuring in all aspects of academic activities. The self finance colleges must come forward for accreditation and fulfill the requirements of accreditation. Universities and colleges should realize the need for education and come forward with action plan for improving quality in higher education institutions.

   World class education: Indian government should give priority to the development of standards in education India must aspire for the international standards of education for education. Many national universities like in the USA, UK, Australia, etc allow studies in higher education for foreign students in their countries and through correspondence courses at well. In the same way Indian universities of world class education can also offer courses of studies to the foreign students taking advantages of the globalization process. To achieve that goal it must adopt uniform international syllabus in it educational, institutions.

7. **Personality development**: Finally education must be in the flowering of personality but not for the suppression of creativity or natural skill. In the globalised world opportunity for the educated people are naturally expanded in scope. As a result business processing outsourcing activities have increased competition in the world trade leading towards the production quality goods and easy their way availability everywhere in the world market. That is the way the world can be developed for peace, prosperity and progress by able and skillful men.

8. **High tech libraries**: Our university libraries have a very good collection of books but they all in mess. Library must be conducive for serious study. Indian universities should concentrate more on providing quality education which is comparable to that of international standards.

Conclusions

Over the period of time growth have been taken place in higher education in terms of institutions, enrollment, etc but it is not sufficient. Indian economy a facing various challenge regarding higher education which needs to overcome through appropriate policy formation and their effective implementation.The policies have to be implemented and the changes have to be made keeping pace the social phenomena and economic policies which suit the development of higher education. Higher education in India is an extraordinary important part in modern Indian society and it is inter twinned in the political and social systems of the society. It is in need of change development and growth. In order to effectively plan for reform, it is necessary to have in realistic perception of what is possible and what is not.As higher education is the peak time of education accountability from the teacher's point of view information access to the students and parents play a very important role in achieving quality in higher education. Regular support from the management government, teachers and students as well as the readiness to change as per changing needs is very important for achieving quality in higher education.Improvement in quality of higher education will eventually draw more and more students and problem of low enrollment will get solved.

References

1. Mishra sharda (2006) UGC and higher education in India book enclave Jaipur 302006.
2. Padhi SK (2011) issues, Challenges and reforms in Higher Education for a knowledgeable society.
3. Ramesh G Indian higher education and the challenge of sustainability. An analytical study journalist of social science and inter disciplinary research 2013. 2 (9).
4. British council report. Understanding India. The future of higher education and opportunities for international cooperation.
5. Choudary S (2011) Problems and prospects of Indian higher education in the age of globalization. University news volume 49 (23 Delhi).
6. Dube SC (1988) higher education and social change in A Singh and GD Sharma(ED)(HE) in India. The social context Konark publisher's new deli.
7. Prem ji azim (2004) Importance of quality education in the development of the nation, legal news and views.

Chapter-6

Need for a New Education Policy Higher Education in India-Challenges, Issues and Opportunities

Dr. Challoju Jyothsna,

Abstract

The National Policy on Education was framed in 1986 and modified in 1992. Since then several changes have taken place that calls for a revision of the Policy. In 2016 the government constituted TSR Subramanyam committee to review and propose new education policy for the 21st century. But the government was unhappy with its recommendations appointed Kasturi Rangan Committee for further research in to the issue in 2017 July. But the committee recommendations are not yet publicised. In the wake of these issues, it is pertinent to identify certain challenges to the higher education in the contemporary Indian society. Higher education system is not meeting the needs of the market. There is no adequate attention to the Research and Development. Universities are politicised. Caste politics plaguing the management of the university education. PhD holders applying for the constable posts. In all our higher education system is producing only the well disciplined employees but not the innovators. It is producing followers but not leaders.

Introduction

Hence there is a need for concentrating on these issues which will have long term socio, economic and political implications. Budget allocated to the education is inadequate. But mere enhancement of the budget allocation will not solve the crisis. A political and policy commitment is needed to improve higher education that can impart knowledge, and has capacity to produce the leaders and initiators.

K. Kasturi Rangan Committee report on higher education is ready and the Central Government would declare National Education Policy very soon.

The National Institutional Ranking Framework (NIRF) would also be applicable for smaller universities. The government is trying to upscale and give new directions to the education system. Quality, Research and Innovation are the three pillars on which government is focusing. Outcome based education' seems to be the priority of government.

In this context it is pertinent to throw a bird's eye view on the higher education system in India, its issues, challenges and needed reforms.

Education Policy

The National Policy on Education was framed in 1986 and modified in 1992. Since then several changes have taken place that calls for a revision of the Policy. The Government of India would like to bring out a National Education Policy to meet the changing dynamics of the population's requirement with regards to quality education, innovation and research, aiming to make India a knowledge superpower by equipping its students with the necessary skills and knowledge and to eliminate the shortage of manpower in science, technology, academics and industry.

Let us review the issues in the existing education policy before analyzing the proposals for the new policy proposals.

Issues in the present university education

The major issue has been unemployability of the well educated people. The gross enrolment ratio in the country has risen sharply in the last decade but industry complains that most students are unemployable. Talented and skilled people are migrating abroad.

There is not even one truly outstanding institution among 700 universities and over 36,000 colleges. Universities are merely producing the degree holders.

A "casual" approach to higher education is adopted by the policy makers. There has been a too much government interference in top appointments in institutions. Political interference in top appointments is a crucial factor in the decline of institutions of higher learning. Particularly it is visible in the appointments of VCs, Directors and Principals. As a result, the academicians and management in the universities are politically active but academically weak. This has led to a leadership crisis in the universities.

There has been an Un necessary focus on managing an institution rather than fostering creativity, or encouraging a questioning spirit. Ideas from the Western universities are being mechanically borrowed for implementation in India. This clear and present in the case of the adoption the methods like - Choice based credit system (CBCS) and massive open online courses (MOOCS) and idea of Meta University (Meta university implies – having university departments in the same building, inter disciplinary approach which requires lot of synergy).

Academic leaders often make their institutions playgrounds for caste, regional, political and community politics. More over, there is also a feudal culture prevailing in most institutions of higher learning. It is marginalizing the excellence. As a result there is no innovation and no invention.

Wrong learning systems are adopted that focus more on learning by rote that kills inquisitiveness. Even in the IITs and IIMs – there is no scope for questioning because of the heavy dose of curriculum. Most teachers also learnt by rote and they reproduce that in the classroom. Exams test the capacity to mechanically reproduce what is mugged up. Exams and degrees have become a passport to a job.

In the present system of education, the students need not attend the classes need not be attended. As result, corruption has seeped into exams as found in the VYAPAM scam.

The shortage of faculty aggravates this crisis. Consequently, overworked, part-time and ad hoc teachers, lacking in skills, carry the burden and teaching suffers. Research guidance deteriorated.

Prescribing the standard qualifications like MPhil, PhD, NET, Refresher course completion, Academic Performance Index (API) for recruitment, promotions and better increments etc., are not achieving the standards in the education. Teaching is not viewed as a qualitative element but as a matter of time and motion studies.

Many academicians play the game cynically to earn points for promotion as a part of API score. Contact with students has been devalued since that gets few points. Poor quality dissertations, journals and conferences enable academics to collect points. Those playing the numbers game are accumulating points mechanically while genuine academics fail to do so for their promotion; mediocrity gets privileged over talent.

RUSA related failures

There has been a failure of RUSA in the strengthening the universities and colleges. States have failed to establish the project directorates of the RUSA.

Where they are established, the directors have no awareness of the RUSA.

There has been a failure on part of the states in utilizing the RUSA funds. Where they are with drawn, there is a misuse of funds.

There is also a problem of inaccessibility of the funds released under the RUSA. For instance in AP out of the 19 universities only 3 have got 100 percent funds.

The problem of job relevance

The relevance of the higher education and technical education to the job market is least in India when compared to other countries. The policy of the government is also paralytic. The report of the Ministry of labor says that, unemployment among the people in the age group of 18-29 is 13.3 percent.

A study by an organization called "Aspiring Minds" – Annually 1 million Engineers are produced by various engineering colleges in the country. Out of them , only less than 20 percent are qualified to be suitable to software jobs.

Factors responsible for this condition are multiple –

There is a lack of qualified teachers at the higher education level. There is dearth of synchronization between the professional colleges and the industry. Colleges are sanctioned permissions without minimum standards.

There is no policy to properly utilize the human resources in the country (there are 55 crores of young people who are below the age of 24 years). More over, Curriculum is not reflecting the requirements of the market. Even the lack of encouragement to research and development in the educational institutions as it is done in the western countries.

Most of the educational policies are still continue to be colonial hangover. The curriculum is not designed to create interest among the students. Lack of proper budget allocation to the higher education.

Consequences of improper development of higher education

The graduates are forced to take coaching after their academic education. There will be underemployment. Wide spread unemployment (not due to lack of jobs but due to lack of professionally qualified and eligible candidates) (unemployment rate by 2030 is estimated as 25 cr.). Unemployment results in convulsions.

The candidates are not having adequate skills like arithmetic, English language skills etc. As a result, the market requirements are not properly met. The young generations will not have security of their livelihoods. India emerge as largest youth country by 2020, but they will not have capacity to work.

Industrial growth will come down because of failure to utilize the human resources. There will be scarcity of skilled human resources in all the sectors ranging from industrial to infrastructure sector.

Recommendations of the TSR Subramanyam Committee

The T.S.R. Subramanian committee, entrusted with preparing a new education policy for India submitted the report to the government in May 2016 suggesting measures that the country must take to improve the sector that caters to over 300 million students in the country. Important among the 95 recommendations are —

(1) A new AIS for education:

An Indian Education Service (IES) should be established as an all India service with officers being on permanent settlement to the state governments but with the cadre controlling authority vesting with the Human Resource Development (HRD) ministry.

(2) Enhanced GDP:

The outlay on education should be raised to at least 6 percent of GDP without further loss of time.

(3) Minimum eligibility:

There should be minimum eligibility condition with 50 percent marks at graduate level for entry to existing B.Ed courses. Teacher Entrance Tests (TET) should be made compulsory for recruitment of all teachers. The Centre and states should jointly lay down norms and standards for TET.

(4) Teaching license:

Compulsory licensing or certification for teachers in government and private schools should be made mandatory, with provision for renewal every 10 years based on independent external testing.

(5) Pre school education right:

Pre-school education for children in the age group of 4 to 5 years should be declared as a right and a program for it implemented immediately.

(6) No Detention Policy:

The no detention policy must be continued for young children until completion of class V when the child will be 11 years old. At the upper primary stage, the system of detention shall be restored subject to the provision of remedial coaching and at least two extra chances being offered to prove his capability to move to a higher class.

(7) On demand Board exams:

On-demand board exams should be introduced to offer flexibility and reduce year end stress of students and parents. A National Level Test open to every student who has completed class XII from any School Board should be designed.

(8) Mid day meal:

The mid-day meal (MDM) program should now be extended to cover students of secondary schools. This is necessary as levels of malnutrition and anemia continue to be high among adolescents.

(9) UGC reforms:

UGC Act must be allowed to lapse once a separate law is created for the management of higher education. The University Grants Commission (UGC) needs to be made leaner and thinner and given the role of disbursal of scholarships and fellowships.

(10) Regional university campuses:

Top 200 foreign universities should be allowed to open campuses in India and give the same degree which is acceptable in the home country of the said university.

Kasturi Rangan Committee on New Education Policy

The recommendations of the T.S.R. Subramanian committee were not received well due to differences between some members the committee and the then HRD minister Smriti Irani. In view of this, the Union government in July 2017 formed another committee, headed by space scientist K. Kasturirangan, to come up with the blueprint / final draft for a new education policy. It takes at least six to seven months to submit the report.

The committee has been mandated to make Indian education contemporary, improve its quality, and internationalize it. It could also provide a roadmap for the entry of foreign universities into India.

The new committee would take into account the ground work done over last 30 months and inputs received from the Subramanian committee.

The recommendations of this committee will supersede the Subramanian committee.

What is needed to be done for a better Education Policy

1. **Consider the Ground Realities :** It requires a historical view essentially because the problems have not appeared overnight. Reports like the Ambani–Birla Report (1999) or the Knowledge Commission Report (2007) lacked a historical understanding of the evolution of the Indian system of higher education and did not address the ground realities of the system. They implicitly assumed that the system is flawed because of its public sector character and suggested its betterment and expansion through privatization. The pressure from the World Trade Organization (WTO) is also in the same direction and concerned people worry about the commitments there.
2. **Make the education autonomous:** As far as possible, education system should be left autonomous. It should be neither controlled by the market nor regulated by the state.
3. **Common syllabus need not be imposed:** A common syllabus result in standardization that will kill the creativity and teaching becomes mechanical
4. **Rationality in the privatization policy:** It leads to an increase in resource availability but often also to a demand to cut public funding for education. It should be recognized that the private sector is best suited to deal with the short-term issues and that reinforces narrowness of conception, which is counterproductive.
5. **Role of Central Government:** The seats in the government educational institutions should be increased. The government has to show its initiative as it shown in the implementation of the GST.

In brief, if talent is to be nurtured, the NEP must overhaul higher education based on the ground realities and a holistic perspective. For this, diverse academic voices need to be heard rather than only of those at the top and who have been the problem and whose agenda may not be real reform.

6. **Technology and education:** Digital India program is an attempt to use technology for the benefit of people in order to over come some of the challenges facing the country particularly in the field of education and health care, technology may be leveraged in the promotion of online courses in various fields of higher education.

Proposal to create HECI: The government has proposed to establish Higher Education Commission of India (HECI) to replace the UGC. It will have a chairperson, vice-chairperson and 12 members of whom which the first two shall be whole-time salaried individuals. The chairperson will be of the rank of Secretary to the Government of India. The secretary of the HECI will be an officer of the rank of joint secretary and above or a reputed academic and will serve as its member-secretary. Will she have voting rights as a member, as she will be appointed by the HECI? Besides, the secretary, higher education is envisaged to don many hats, serving as a member of the search-cum-selection committee of the chairperson and vice-chairperson, then processing their appointment as a key functionary of the government, and finally acting as a member of the HECI. Such multiplicity of roles may create difficulties and conflict of interest. Also, the power of the government to remove the chairperson and members is rather overwhelming and should be constrained.

It is intended to "provide for more autonomy and facilitate holistic growth" of the higher education sector and offer "greater opportunities to Indian students at more affordable cost". The new commission will cover all fields of education except medical and, presumably, agriculture, and institutions set up under the Central and State Acts, excluding those of national importance.

However, it is going to give whole sale regulation to the government over the higher education system. This is mainly because of a separation between academic functions and grant-giving ones, the former to be discharged by the HECI and the latter by the Ministry of Human Resource Development (MHRD) directly.

Conclusion

The government should play the role of a guide and philosopher and disseminator. It should only play a fiduciary role. Market system should not be allowed to penetrate in to the system. Education at the higher level should not be the domain of a handful of a few affluent sections. Universities should continue to remain autonomous, self financed, government budgeted, and market sponsored. Encouragement to the true research and developing indigenous systems to fulfil the dreams of make in India by the Indians.

References

1. The Hindu editorials
2. Various Articles from Economic and Political Weekly

3. Draft of the 12th Five Year Plan.
4. Draft National Policy on Education 2016, Ministry of Human Resource Development (Report of the Committee for Evolution of the New Education Policy).

Chapter-7

Academic Leadership A Need For Quality Higher Education

Mrs. K. Malathi Devi,
Dr.R.Komala,

Introduction

HEIs have got a vital role to play in generating the man power in required number for sustaining the socio economic growth of a nation. The quality in HEI is maintained by academicians. As the teachers are the nation builders, so the quality should be there in the very teaching of the nation builder. A good teacher need to foster innovations in teaching which are need based and promotes the quality of education. Educational Institutions cannot expect faculty with outdated knowledge and skills to help students meet today's changing expectations. It is essential that faculty continuously develop their intellectual capital, which includes technological literacy and knowledge of the current and evolving worlds, both within their disciplines and in related disciplines. Teachers need to be equipped with competencies and skills of self learning which would help them in keeping pace with the rapidly changing times to acquire new knowledge, techniques and instructional methodologies. Skill improvement programs like teacher seminars, conferences, workshops, should be properly implemented from time to time. Such programs should be given proper follow up so as to ensure effective roles in teaching, research and administration by the academicians in the higher educational institutions. Teachers are lifelong learners having commitment to the objectives of education, involving in planning and execution of activities, building strong team work and motivating young minds. Academic leaders need to have greater abilities and skills to fulfill mission and vision of the institution as they are actually a backbone of HEIs. They play a critical role in chalking out strategies and facilitating their execution which creates a glittering image of the organization in public. A good academic leader identifies the opportunities for the growth of the institution, identifies the potential of staff members, builds a strong team and utilizes resources available in the institution to the maximum to bring in a boom in quality teaching learning and research.

Enriching Teaching Skills

Education in its general sense is a form of learning in which the knowledge, skills and values are transferred from one generation to the next. The knowledge can be transformed through teaching, discussion and training especially to develop the reasoning, judgment and skill required in adult life and professional occupations. Higher education is an educational level that follows a completion of a school providing a secondary education. Under graduate and post graduate levels come under Higher education which includes teaching, research activity and social service activities of college or university .

Institutions must organize programs which promote the personal/social, educational, and career development of all students. *Higher education is perceived as extremely important, and for most students college education has become the necessary admission ticket to good jobs.* Higher educational institutes cannot survive without the efforts of dedicated and committed teacher. Academicians of HEI's play a significant role in moulding young citizens with high human values. The essential characters expected from an academician are commitment to profession, intellectual aspects, sound knowledge in a specialized area and correlate subject to the requirements of students. The commitment of the academicians will accelerate the educational process so that the student will succeed in developing potentialities to the maximum possible extent. Academicians should make sincere efforts for the wholesome development of the students in every respect under their caring nature. Academicians are expected to follow recent developments in their field of study, specialization/s, expertise and knowledge; so that the knowledge base remains up to date. The teaching skills and efficiency of the teacher can be increased by adopting various strategies such as organizing teacher improvement programs. As the years roll on the polishing of skills should be there. It is said that dust begins to settle upon if something is not dusted properly. Professional development for new teachers should be built on a framework of research-based instructional strategies. These skills help new teacher's bridge theory and practice and create high-quality learning environments in their classrooms. The strategies fall into three categories: organizing, instructing, and assessing.

Teaching resources like modern teaching methodologies – Multimedia, Webinar, Video Conference, usage of Internet for effective teaching and learning.

Opportunities must be provided to teachers to participate and present their technical papers in reputed national level seminars / conferences and workshops to enhance teaching abilities.

The academicians should be content experts, with better understanding of the syllabus and updated knowledge in their areas of concern and specialization. Staff development programs must be regularly arranged for quality improvement in the areas of teaching, research and administration. Such programs must boost up confidence in their teaching skills and develop their teaching ability. These programs are not just the concern of teachers who are new to the profession, but also of experienced teachers when they meet new challenges which seem to threaten their long-standing values and beliefs about learning and teaching, especially if these may imply changes to their teaching practices. The teacher with more teaching ability, will be more confident in teaching. In the same way, the more confident you become in your teaching skills. Teacher development is not just to do with language or even teaching: it's also about language development, counseling skills, assertiveness training, confidence-building , etc., Programs whose faculties do not keep current will find that demand for their services will diminish and that their students will move to corporate competitors.

Teachers must involve in research & undertake projects in their area/ s of concern/specialization which will facilitate them to present & publish high quality articles/papers in the leading, reputed journal/s of national and international levels. Faculty must attract external funds from research agencies, funding agencies, universities, State & Central Govt. for research activities while exploring new technology, training and executing the same in teaching and research areas. Faculty must attend research meetings, supervise juniors and should be able to generate exciting new ideas. Their external activities are increasingly important, such as acquiring funding, maintaining collaboration networks and disseminating knowledge to society at large. The balance of time spent on teaching, research and administration can vary widely according to the time in the academic year, experience and administrative responsibility that is assigned to a particular faculty. Two key factors are identified that positively influence the performance of research groups in higher education institutions. The first is academic leadership: the way researchers are guided and stimulated by the vision and inspiration of the group leader. The other key factor is network management: the way academic leaders position their groups in scientific and societal environments and how they respond to environmental opportunities and constraints.

Individuals who take on leadership positions in higher educational institutions help facilitate the mission of those institutions. However, they are often chosen on the basis of success in the core activities in research, teaching experience , leadership and management skills. A good academic leader must have command over vision, managerial style, knowledge, people skills, organizational orientation and personal development.

Conclusion

The academic leaders play a key role in developing cooperative culture which builds strong interpersonal skills and efficient team work. They are responsible for the results of the students, good placements, value added training, involving in admission, examination, administration processes and in achieving institutional goals. These varied subjects and activities have made the position of academic leader more demanding and need to have greater abilities and skills to manage the tasks effectively. They should be more creative and innovative in chalking out strategies that tend to emphasize improved communications, collaboration, mutual respect and teamwork. The role of a good academic leader is to lead a team successfully while mobilizing, allocating and controlling resources and giving research guidance to colleagues.

Teachers should aim at improving their ability to put all this knowledge into practice and become more skillful at teaching, research and administration. Institutions must offer Opportunities for leadership growth and development. Colleges must organize seminars, workshops and Club activities where the faculty hones their leadership skills.

References

1. http://en.wikipedia.org/wiki/Higher education.
2. http://www.rathenau.nl/en/publications/publication/dynamics-of-academic-leadership-in-research-groups.html.
3. Harish Kumar and Mohammad Rishad Faridi, University News, Dec, 2014 : 'Ensuring Quality in Higher Education Institutions through Improved Leadership'.
4. Amit Kauts and Vijay Kumar Chechi, University News, Dec, 2014 : 'Teacher Commitment: A requisite for Quality Assurance in Education.
5. http://www.ascd.org/publications/educational-leadership/mar02/vol59/num06/Essential-Skills-for-New-Teachers.aspx.
6. http://www.ncbi.nlm.nih.gov/pmc/articles/PMC3024119.

Chapter-8

Higher Education in India Issues and Challenges

Dr. P. Prameela Margaret,'

Abstract

Education is very important and essential to every human being, without education; it is very difficult to know the values of human society. With education only one can attain knowledge without education it is not possible to know the development of the society. Education is helps to develop our knowledge, values, culture, obedience, discipline and how to respect to others and how to behave in the society. Education helps to improve our personality in the different fields, Example political, economical, social fields. Education is social process. Particularly higher education as the instrument of the individuals with that we can understand the society, and to transform economic conditions of any nation in India the second half of the 20th century Education is social process. Education and particularly higher education as the instrument of the individual, societal and economic transformation in India became well recognized in the second half of the century. The transformation education from the ancient gurukula system in India to today's virtual learning system is reflection of the social context. Education is highly imperative for everybody in the society without any exception. Basic education happens to be a unique experiment in the field of education. It is the most important and the lasting gift of Mahatma Gandhi, the father of the nation, who formulated it in Indian context. It is outcome of his long experience. His educational philosophy is reflected in the scheme of Basic Education which is propounded by him. It is popularly called a silent revolution in the field of Indian education. Lord Curzon was the ablest viceroy that ever came to India. Education formed an important aspect in his scheme of administrative reforms.

***Keywords:** Higher education Importance, quality women role, and inequality in gender difference*

Introduction

The higher education system has experienced different phases of expansion in the first half of the 20th century. In higher education system, in most parts of the world, there existed a public system in 1960s and 1970s. The global expansion of education is also measured by the quality maintained. External quality assurance mechanisms and accreditation agencies are put in place across the world for maintaining the quality in higher education. In most countries, internal quality assurance cells are established in most of the institutions. One of the favorable climates for investing in higher education was a change in the perception regarding education and its potential contribution especially the economic value of higher education with the emerging expansion of knowledge, the capacity to produce and absorb knowledge production elsewhere became an influential factor in promoting growth and the pace of growth of knowledge economies (World Bank 2009). Education in India was governed by the Board of Directors of the East India Company under section 43 of the Chapter 1813. Lord Macaulay came to India in 1834 and was made the Chief of the Public instruction by the then Governor General Lord William Bentinck, a great reformer and visionary. The knowledge economy has increased the market demand for good quality higher education, enhanced the salaries for the educated and contributed to increased returns to investments in higher education.

Higher Education in India

The higher education in India too had similarities to many of the developments experienced on the international scene. The expansionary trends and efforts led to the establishment of internal quality assurance cells which led to the promotion of privatization of public institutions. India has a rich and glorious tradition of higher education from ancient times, Nalanda, Vikramashila, Thakhsila, and Vallabi were some of the important and well-known universities of ancient India and they occupy a special place in the history of higher education in India. The British Indian educational policy was clearly subservient to Imperial economic policy. After independence, India realized the fact that University education was essential for a cultural resurgence as well as for meeting the scientific, technical and other manpower requirements of the newly independent nation. As a result, the country started university education from the scratch. The significant step that was taken by the Government of India in the field of education was the appointment of the University Education Commission in 1948 under the chairmanship of Sarvepalli. Radhakrishnan (Ministry of education, 1950). The mandate of the commission was to report on university education and suggest improvements and extensions that may be desirable for the present and also for the future.

Role of higher education

Higher education plays an important role in the developing nations to a great extent. It helps the members of the society to improve their lives and also helps in the strengthening of the nation. It helps to reform conduct and behavior and the integrity of the personality of the individuals of the nation. Higher education reforms our society from different points of view. The class cultured people come out from the institutions of higher education colleges which happen to be the principal centers' for higher education. But universities are ultimate controller of them and are more responsible for it.

Education has to be a socially integrated institution that forms the part of human civilization. Real education is primarily the process of training of hand, heart and head. Thus, the purpose of education may be summed up into three fold viz.

- Attuning the capability to get a suitable profession
- Acquisition of a certain amount of knowledge
- Requisition of a knowledge

Women's role in higher education in India

In a democratic system, the place of women, like men is of great importance. These days' women are also conscious about the rights and obligations. In India, the percentage of women education is on the increase. It is about 39.19 percent in the eighth plan. The national government has launched a major scheme for development and improvement of women's education in the country. This will help to create proper awareness regarding education among women. This is highly necessary for the success of democracy in our country.

Mother is the first educator of the child from birth to school age. The home environment and the association of other members of the family play a vital role in developing proper attitude among the children but the most important is the influence of mother on the child. She is responsible for his or her upbringing and career. Therefore, it is highly necessary that mother is imbued with good qualities and acts as a role model for the child. She should be efficient and conscious of her responsibilities. Thus, education of women is of great importance in our nation and social life and we have to be very careful in this respect. It is the duty of the society and the government to provide adequate facilities for the education of women because by educating the girl we educate the whole family.

The University Education Commission noted the importance of women education and stated that there cannot be educated women If general education had to be limited to men. Women should be given opportunity to educate themselves and only then it would most surely be passed on to the next generation. In the modern world the role of women goes much beyond the home and bringing up of children. The Educational Commission (1964-66) fully endorsed the recommendations of the two committees which examined the role of the problem of women education in recent years. Women's studies programs would have dimensions namely, reaching training and extension. Women issues would be incorporated in courses under various disciplines.

Inequity in Gender Difference

A very serious problem in the domain of higher education system is the presence of a very high degree of inequity between different social groups, between men and women, between rural and urban areas and between the rich and the poor. Gender differences have narrowed down over the years to a substantial extent. Currently about 40 percent of the enrolments are women, though there is a concentration of them in some areas of study like primary education, healthcare etc. But this is changing, albeit slowly. Higher education is not a matter of right, leave alone a fundamental right. No person of any caste and community has a right to become a doctor, engineer or other kind of highly educated person. Everyone has the right to aspire to such status on a fair and equal consideration in the admissions process, according to specified norms of fairness and equality.

But no one has apriority right to actual admission. The aspect of gender difference does not confine to the walls of households. This is evident from the very foundation of even the old and reputed Universities of India. The recent incident of Eve teasing is one of the higher-level educational universities in India exemplifies the prevalent feeling of gender difference even at the higher level of education setups. The women students in education institutions encounter this discouraging the phenomenon which causes them to remain at the backstage in higher education.

Quality in Higher Education

Quality we mean the excellence in education in terms of its values, functionality and marketability. When National Assessment and Accreditation Council (NAAC) assess the university/college it emphasizes the following criteria to determine whether the institution is maintaining quality in education. The criteria are 1. Curricular activities, 2. Teaching-learning evolution, 3. Research consultancy and extension, 4. Infrastructure and learning and evolution, 5. Student support in progress in, 6. Organizational management and 7. Healthy practices. The quality of education is being decided on the basis of the infrastructure available. The type of curriculum and evolution of processes followed the teachers and the qualifications, their ability to teach using different techniques, availability of instructional materials and the facilities available for the personality development. Ancient Indian education system also insisted on vocational education, discipline and physical exercise and yoga for good physique and sound mind. Later, Indian leaders like she Aurobindo Ghosh, Rabindra Tagore and Mahatma Gandhi also tried to provide education that is suited to India and to Indian culture. Thus, the basic education in the Independent India emerged as the national system of education with some changes and modifications recommended by Dr. Zakeer Hussein.

Conclusion

The Indian women appear to have come a long way from an obscurantist past and complete subordination to the position where theoretically they are the equals of men and there is a vast array of laws, policies and programs trying to content with the cumulative disadvantage of women arising out of the predominant patriarchal family and kinship structures, customs, traditions and beliefs. Women are making a mark in all fields among the middle classes and the elite. Yet at the level of reality, the promise of equality and dignity remains an unfinished agenda.

In the last 60 years, the women's status has received a lot of attention from time to time resulting in policy changes and setting up of institutional structures that reflected the national policies, plans, programmes and schemes that are resulting in advancement of women in all fields. Besides, special committees and commissions on women have been appointed for implementing programs and schemes.

Reference

1. Higher Education in India: B.Deka
2. Women Education in India:S.P. Agraval & J.C. Agrrval
3. Women Education: R.C. Mishra
4, Education and Development: G.Pankajam
5. History of Indian Educational System: Y.K.Singh

Chapter-9

Role of Research in Higher Education

Dr. K. Rajesh kumar,

Introduction

Our education system faces a number of constraints and challenges—quality research is one of them. Barring few prestigious institutes, most display a dismal picture in terms of quality and quantity research. Not many institutes have mandatory research goals for individual faculty, and most do not have adequate systems or infrastructure for quality research. The lack of an encouraging academic environment, ill-equipped libraries, labs and equipment, inadequate infrastructure, lack of funds, faculty crunch, etc, are some of the factors contributing to the dismal picture of research in Indian academic institutions.

Need of the Study

This is a time of renewed enthusiasm for higher education and research as the way forward to world development, Human and social development through higher education and research capabilities are appropriate themes in a report dedicated to the future role of higher education in an era of globalization.

Objecticves

1. To know the importance of research in higher education.
2. To enquire about the usage of reaearch developments in the education system
3. To analyse the awareness among the students in research technologies.
4. To promote the research ethics for higher value education
5. To inculcate the research innovation and ideas in higher education.

Methodology

In a globalised world, the role of research in an academic institution is significant for its sustainability and development, and it is imperative to have knowledge-driven growth based on innovation. The quest for knowledge is the basic principle behind research. The quality of research work directly translates to the quality of teaching and learning in the classroom, thereby benefiting the students, the society and the country. The promotion of research in a huge and diverse country like India will help the nation evolve as a knowledge reservoir in the international arena.

Our education system faces a number of constraints and challenges—quality research is one of them. Barring few prestigious institutes, most display a dismal picture in terms of quality and quantity research. Not many institutes have mandatory research goals for individual faculty, and most do not have adequate systems or infrastructure for quality research. The lack of an encouraging academic environment, ill-equipped libraries, labs and equipment, inadequate infrastructure, lack of funds, faculty crunch, etc, are some of the factors contributing to the dismal picture of research in Indian academic institutions.

It is well-accepted that academic research has contributed enormously to find solutions to many problems faced by our society and industries. There have been multiple instances when industries have turned to academics for finding solutions to vital issues. The need for sharing knowledge between research institutions and industry has become increasingly evident. The emerging importance of interdisciplinary fields has given rise to institutional collaborations that allow knowledge to be pooled together. Often, it is industry which is the ultimate beneficiary. Research provides basic inputs that can be used for planning and policy decision-making. Needless to say, academic research is an integral part of global development.

Technology is dramatically changing educational research processes, at a time of high demand for 'evidence-based' policy and practice. It will interpret and evaluate research in technologyrich environments. Everybody is engaged in the critical study of original empirical research to learn about cutting edge methods of data collection and analysis. Philosophical assumptions underlying educational enquiry are to be examined.

To conduct research, one need to study and look for references, sources and market research and carefully analyze the topic you are researching, including evidence and theories. The need of performing educational Research will start from effective programs and teaching methods which will help students to learn what they really want to discover relationships between variables in educational settings to plan interventions. It will help them to understand cultural contexts of schools to create schools that embody justice and reduce prejudice and inequality. From the individual researcher's perspective we investigate topics about which we are curious or passionate; as well, we do research because it is an integral part of the academic role and a central factor in academic promotion. Individually and collectively, educational research is a part of a quest for meaning. Conceptions of knowledge, like linguistic and conceptual meaning, are both personal and contextually based. In recent years some educational researchers have focused on epistemological meaning.

Types of Education Research

1. Historical research generates descriptions, and sometimes attempted explanations, of conditions, situations, and events that have occurred in the past. For example, a study that documents the evolution of teacher training programs since the turn of the century, with the aim of explaining the historical origins of the content and processes of current programs.
2. Descriptive research provides information about conditions, situations, and events that occur in the present. For example, a survey of the physical condition of school buildings in order to establish a descriptive profile of the facilities that exist in a typical school.
3. Co relational research involves the search for relationships between variables through the use of various measures of statistical association. For example, an investigation of the relationship between teachers' satisfaction with their job and various factors describing the provision and quality of teacher housing, salaries, leave entitlements, and the availability of classroom supplies. Causal research aims to suggest causal linkages between variables by observing existing phenomena and then searching back through available data in order to try to identify plausible causal relationships. For example, a study of factors related to student 'drop out' from secondary school using data obtained from school records over the past decade.
4. Experimental research is used in settings where variables defining one or more 'causes' can be manipulated in a systematic fashion in order to discern 'effects' on other variables. For example, an investigation of the effectiveness of two new textbooks using

random assignment of teachers and students to three groups – two groups for each of the new textbooks, and one group as a 'control' group to use the existing textbook.

5. Case study research generally refers to two distinct research approaches. The first consists of an in-depth study of a particular student, classroom, or school with the aim of producing a nuanced description of the pervading cultural setting that affects education, and an account of the interactions.

Benefits of Research in Eduction

1. Research will help to understand any subject and its principals in much better and easier way which will encounter new questions and search for answers of those questions will lead you to learn new theories of any subject. Research means trying something out of the box. When it is done such things it will separate one from other students which will surely attract attention of your tutors as well which in turn benefit extreme need of help from someone who is more knowledgeable than the other.
2. Research is not always a concept that practitioners, managers and policy makers respect. Too often it is seen as an academic activity conducted by others – to the profession, not with the profession.
3. Research education professionals are always learning, finding out things, analyzing information, adapting their behavior according to information received, looking to improve and adapting to modern demands. Practitioners have to comply with policy. Teachers can adapt it to fit the individual needs of their own pupils. As teachers are accountable, the public must have faith in the profession – and attitudes to education vary across many social groups – so the performance of teachers can be demonstrated through the publication of research findings. Teachers project their own personality upon learning experiences. Sometimes this is intuitive and these decisions can either be successful or fail.
4. Research methodologies give teachers the tools to analyze and make informed decisions about their practice. Research helps teachers to share with colleagues. Too often research looks backwards and there are lessons to learn. However, it would be better to prefer a research in education as invention and innovation so that it should be future oriented and designed to benefit learners rather than the researchers themselves.

The research awareness in educational field can be implemented in the following forms which can lead into the improvement of in terms of progress can be observed. The various forms of research should suit policy makers, planners and implementers of policy. Large scale studies into pupil performance can help to identify trends and enable educational outcomes to be related to social and economic needs. Policy makers want to see the big picture. On the other hand, practitioners want to know why some techniques work and others don't. All professionals need to be able to trust the source of information – and strict research ethics provide that assurance. The profession as a whole needs access to a range of data/evidence types. Teaching does involve creative thinking and experimentation. Individuals and professional groups need to know what works and why. Whether a teacher's action lead to improved pupil performance, increased motivation, commitment, better behavior or not, but it will surely reflect that research is more formal. However, these all need to be connected, and too often research is conducted in isolation of others.

Recommendations of University Grants Commission

1. There should be regular monitoring and evaluation of teaching and research in the Universities and other Institutions of higher learning . A Monitoring & Evaluation (M & E) Unit should be set-up at State level preferably attached to Chancellor's Office; and for its effective functioning, a Statistical Cell should be set-up in each University in the State, under the over all supervision of the M & E Unit.
2. Many institutions of higher education in the country are excellent in the sense that their infrastructure, resources, faculty, programmes of teaching and research are almost as good as the best in the advanced countries. But, the same cannot be said of the average institutions of higher education in the country. They do not come anywhere near the level of average institutions of higher education in the advanced countries. This vast gap in standards and facilities has been a cause of constant anxiety and concern to the policy planners of higher education in India.
3. The issue of accessibility to quality higher education needs to be addressed in the light of the vast economic and social disparities, cultural and linguistic diversities, and extremely uneven opportunities of learning at the school level together with the aspirations and capacities of the potential students. Therefore, the question of access to higher education needs to be addressed at the

local, regional, national and international levels from transdisciplinary, inter-disciplinary and discipline-specific perspectives. The issue of accessibility of quality higher education arises in the context of the transition in the country from elitist to mass education in the post-independence period. The issue has significant implications in the sense that it demands a redefinition of the aims of higher education. This and related issues were discussed at this Seminar, resulting in the following major recommendations.

4. Quality of higher education can also be improved by inducting quality oriented objectivity in merit promotions of teaching faculty. Specification of weightages for teaching, research publications/ supervision would help in making this transparent and credible.
5. Policies of higher education should be designed to strengthen indigenous research agenda.
6. Outline of the strategies, the imperative scope of expansion, dimensions of diversification, potentials for both short and long-term planning and modalities of placid administrative processes warranted in the contemporary ambience, but in the changed context, have been discussed by experts and researchers.

Conclusion

The Importance of research in higher education say that knowledge is enough to make productive career but nowadays competition is so tough that higher education is must to make a mark at higher level. It doesn't really matter that whether we are interested in history or science, computer or management, higher education will provide you that extra bit of ease to pick up much required speed at corporate level in beginning. But main question is how to make your higher education more productive. It does not depend on university or college to be selected or it's a course selection that makes all the difference. The fact is all of those students who are cautious about their study are well enough to make good selection over course and college. Actually that makes difference is research in technical and higher education which holds the level holds its own importance.

References

1. www.financialexpress.com.
2. Pramodini D V, K. Anu sophia , Evaluation of research importance in education, IRJC International Journal of Social Science & Interdisciplinary Research Vol.1 Issue 9, September 2012.

3. https://www.researchgate. net.
4. Hiebert, J., Gallimore, R. & Stigler, J. (1992). A knowledge base for the teaching profession: What would it look like and how can we get one? Educational Researcher, 31(5), 3 – 15.
5. Kliebard, H. (1993). What is a knowledge base, and who would use it if we had one? Review of Educational Research 63, 295 – 303.
6. Higher education in India: Issues, concerns in new education, University grants commission New Delhi, December 2003.

Chapter-10

Privatization in Higher Education in India: A Reflection of Issues

Dr. Sampath kumar,
Dr. P. Prameela Margaret,

Abstract

The Indian higher education system has been witnessing a myriad of changes and challenges through the years. The phenomenal increase in enrollment of students in millions has been possible with the growth in the number of institutions of higher learning both in the public as well as private sector. The National Policy on Education (NPE) of 1986 emphasized the need of faculty enhancement and development. It also pointed out the lacuna in the system of evaluation and its need for further reinforcement. It states that "higher education has to become dynamic as never before and to this effect outlines a series of steps including encouraging autonomy, specializa-tion, vocationa-lization, emphasis on research and development."

Higher education has witnessed higher degree privatization in subjects like engineering, pharmacy, education, medicine, law, business management, allied science, biotechnology, biochemistry, and information technology. A majority of the institutions have been established by the private sector to meet the demands of the young generation with adequate scope for employment opportunities. Government-aided institutions are yet to strive toward the new challenges thrown up by the private sector. Private colleges and universities are surviving on the fees collected from the students and additional fees, which governments pay to the students as scholarships for candidates from disadvantaged communities. There is a wide variation in terms of students' admission policy, fee structure, students support facilities, research assistance, extension activity, and their participation. Most students from the lower middle class are unable to pay the fee prescribed by these institutions. It is the social responsibility of the governments to provide education to all. Central and respective state governments have tried to provide primary and secondary education free for all students up to the age of 14 years. Higher education has been kept under the state as well as the central government for effective governance and monitoring. The private

sector has used the new challenges as an opportunity and has created a number of higher education institutions (HEIs) throughout India.
Keywords: *Accreditation, Assessment, Higher education, Privatization of higher education*

Introduction

The higher education system has experienced different phases of expansion in the first half of the 20th century. In higher education system, in most parts of the world, there existed a public system in 1960s and 1970s. The global expansion of education is also measured by the quality maintained. External quality assurance mechanisms and accreditation agencies are put in place across the world for maintaining the quality in higher education. In most countries, internal quality assurance cells are established in most of the institutions. One of the favorable climates for investing in higher education was a change in the perception regarding education and its potential contribution especially the economic value of higher education with the emerging expansion of knowledge, the capacity to produce and absorb knowledge production elsewhere became an influential factor in promoting growth and the pace of growth of knowledge economies (World Bank 2009). Education in India was governed by the Board of Directors of the East India Company under section 43 of the Chapter 1813. Lord Macaulay came to India in 1834 and was made the Chief of the Public instruction by the then Governor General Lord William Bentinck, a great reformer and visionary. The knowledge economy has increased the market demand for good quality higher education, enhanced the salaries for the educated and contributed to increased returns to investments in higher education.

Higher Education in India

The higher education in India too had similarities to many of the developments experienced on the international scene. The expansionary trends and efforts led to the establishment of internal quality assurance cells which led to the promotion of privatization of public institutions. India has a rich and glorious tradition of higher education from ancient times, Nalanda, Vikramashila, Thakhsila, and Vallabi were some of the important and well-known universities of ancient India and they occupy a special place in the history of higher education in India. The British Indian educational policy was clearly subservient to Imperial economic policy. After independence, India realized the fact that University education was essential for a cultural resurgence as well as for meeting the scientific, technical and other manpower requirements of the newly independent nation. As a result, the country started university education from the scratch. The significant step that was taken by the Government of India in the field of education was the appointment of the University Education Commission in 1948 under the chairmanship of Sarvepalli. Radhakrishnan (Ministry of education, 1950). The mandate of the commission was to report on university education and suggest improvements and extensions that may be desirable for the present and also for the future.

Role of higher education

Higher education plays an important role in the developing nations to a great extent. It helps the members of the society to improve their lives and also helps in the strengthening of the nation. It helps to reform conduct and behavior and the integrity of the personality of the individuals of the nation. Higher education reforms our society from different points of view. The class cultured people come out from the institutions of higher education colleges which happen to be the principal centers' for higher education. But universities are ultimate controller of them and are more responsible for it.

Education has to be a socially integrated institution that forms the part of human civilization. Real education is primarily the process of training of hand, heart and head. Thus, the purpose of education may be summed up into three fold viz.

- Attuning the capability to get a suitable profession
- Acquisition of a certain amount of knowledge
- Requisition of a knowledge

Women's role in higher education in India

In a democratic system, the place of women, like men is of great importance. These days' women are also conscious about the rights and obligations. In India, the percentage of women education is on the increase. It is about 39.19 percent in the eighth plan. The national government has launched a major scheme for development and improvement of women's education in the country. This will help to create proper awareness regarding education among women. This is highly necessary for the success of democracy in our country.

Mother is the first educator of the child from birth to school age. The home environment and the association of other members of the family play a vital role in developing proper attitude among the children but the most important is the influence of mother on the child. She is responsible for his or her upbringing and career. Therefore, it is highly necessary that mother is imbued with good qualities and acts as a role model for the child. She should be efficient and conscious of her responsibilities. Thus, education of women is of great importance in our nation and social life and we have to be very careful in this respect. It is the duty of the society and the government to provide adequate facilities for the education of women because by educating the girl we educate the whole family.

The University Education Commission noted the importance of women education and stated that there cannot be educated women If general education had to be limited to men. Women should be given opportunity to educate themselves and only then it would most surely be passed on to the next generation. In the modern world the role of women goes much beyond the home and bringing up of children. The Educational Commission (1964-66) fully endorsed the recommendations of the two committees which examined the role of the problem of women education in recent years. Women's studies programs would have dimensions namely, reaching training and extension. Women issues would be incorporated in courses under various disciplines.

Inequity in Gender Difference

A very serious problem in the domain of higher education system is the presence of a very high degree of inequity between different social groups, between men and women, between rural and urban areas and between the rich and the poor. Gender differences have narrowed down over the years to a substantial extent. Currently about 40 percent of the enrolments are women, though there is a concentration of them in some areas of study like primary education, healthcare etc. But this is changing, albeit slowly. Higher education is not a matter of right, leave alone a fundamental right. No person of any caste and community has a right to become a doctor, engineer or other kind of highly educated person. Everyone has the right to aspire to such status on a fair and equal consideration in the admissions process, according to specified norms of fairness and equality.

But no one has apriority right to actual admission. The aspect of gender difference does not confine to the walls of households. This is evident from the very foundation of even the old and reputed Universities of India. The recent incident of Eve teasing is one of the higher-level educational universities in India exemplifies the prevalent feeling of gender difference even at the higher level of education setups. The women students in education institutions encounter this discouraging the phenomenon which causes them to remain at the backstage in higher education.

Quality in Higher Education

Quality we mean the excellence in education in terms of its values, functionality and marketability. When National Assessment and Accreditation Council (NAAC) assess the university/college it emphasizes the following criteria to determine whether the institution is maintaining quality in education. The criteria are 1. Curricular activities, 2. Teaching-learning evolution, 3. Research consultancy and extension, 4. Infrastructure and learning and evolution, 5. Student support in progress in, 6. Organizational management and 7. Healthy practices. The quality of education is being decided on the basis of the infrastructure available. The type of curriculum and evolution of processes followed the teachers and the qualifications, their ability to teach using different techniques, availability of instructional materials and the facilities available for the personality development. Ancient Indian education system also insisted on vocational education, discipline and physical exercise and yoga for good physique and sound mind. Later, Indian leaders like she Aurobindo Ghosh, Rabindra Tagore and Mahatma Gandhi also tried to provide education that is suited to India and to Indian culture. Thus, the basic education in the Independent India emerged as the national system of education with some changes and modifications recommended by Dr. Zakeer Hussein.

Conclusion

The Indian women appear to have come a long way from an obscurantist past and complete subordination to the position where theoretically they are the equals of men and there is a vast array of laws, policies and programs trying to content with the cumulative disadvantage of women arising out of the predominant patriarchal family and kinship structures, customs, traditions and beliefs. Women are making a mark in all fields among the middle classes and the elite. Yet at the level of reality, the promise of equality and dignity remains an unfinished agenda.

In the last 60 years, the women's status has received a lot of attention from time to time resulting in policy changes and setting up of institutional structures that reflected the national policies, plans, programmes and schemes that are resulting in advancement of women in all fields. Besides, special committees and commissions on women have been appointed for implementing programs and schemes.

References

1. Higher Education in India: B.Deka.

2. Women Education in India:S.P. Agraval & J.C. Agrrval.
3. Women Education: R.C. Mishra.
4. Education and Development: G.Pankajam.
5. History of Indian Educational System: Y.K.Singh.

Chapter-11

Higher Education in India: Current Challenges, Issues and Remedies

G Shekar,

Introduction

Generally, we consider that the education imparted after the junior college education is termed as higher education; which is conferred on the students through the institutions of higher education. Almost all countries provide some form of education beyond secondary schooling. The institutions vary considerably in requirements for admissions in the purposes they serve. As a general rule, however, they undertake to train students for vocations, to prepare them for professions or for the study in advanced professional schools, or to give them a broad cultural background is intended to help the student become a concerned and well-informed citizen as well as to enrich his or her personal life. In the US and Canada, the word college has at least two meanings; one an independent school that offers four year courses in liberal arts leading to the bachelor's degree; and two; division or unit offering courses within a particular field or study.

A true university is a group of colleges under the same administration. Innumerable students are taking their degree and post-degree education through different universities across all over the world. When, in India, colleges for more advanced were first started, there was no difficulty in staffing them. Actually, they were first staffed locally. Obviously there was no specially literate class of Englishmen in India previous to 1854. However, the peculiarly delicate and responsible nature of educational work was not socially recognized, and the only standard of value of accepted is salary and prospectus, the less advantage terms on which 'education' men work, result in real lowering in public esteem, and this disparagement has undoubtedly exercised a somewhat depressing effect on the atmosphere of educational work. Therefore, at least, let the Indian public acknowledge what it owes to those by whose labour and devotion the educational system has been built up, and by renewed efforts, brought nearer to thoroughness and efficiency. This is said for the men of then higher educational service first, because in them, is vested a certain primacy in virtue of the qualifications demanded of them and of their relation to Government. But it is said also for all classes of educational workers; for the Provincial Service, for the Subordinate and Lower Subordinate Services, all in their places and degrees, and for the numerous workers of all grades outside Government Services in doing faithful educational service of any kind.

This paper aims to highlight the present challenges to the higher education. It also attempts to highlight theoretical and practical experiences; skill of learning in present situation. It also throws light on what the major issues in curriculum design and set up of syllabi, management of higher education, health consciousness and professional ethics and value education are.

Challenges to the Higher Education

Lack of predominance of the universities in the project of the higher education area in India, erosion of their autonomy, undermining of undergraduate education, the increasing distance between knowledge areas and the separation of universities from the real world outside and crass commercialization are some of the problems, which characterize the development of the Indian higher education system. It is significant that we develop an understanding of these issues before suggesting strategies to renovate and rejuvenate higher education in India.

Distances and Disconnects

As for invisible walls, it is often indicated that our undergraduate and graduate programmes are so 'theoretical', the implication being that they are destitute of 'practical' experiences. Without looking into familiar epistemological issues, we can say that a theory is as good as the power it has to explain the visible world. A theory is put to practice when a student attempts to use it to make sense of what he or she notices in the world. Conversely, by noticing something in the world and seeking an explanation for it, a student feels the need to have a theory. The chasm that exists between theory and practice combined with the fragmentation of the idea of knowledge leads to the confusion that our system of higher education* is suffering from. To outwit this, it would be necessary that the universities adopt a auricular approach which treats knowledge in a holistic manner and creates exciting opportunities for different kinds of interfaces between the disciplines, which is inconsiderable today in most of the universities and institutions of higher learning. It is important that universities relate to the world outside and the walls of disciplines are porous enough to let other voices be heard. It would also be necessary that the university education is treated in its perfection and subject areas have not to be designed in isolation.

Art of Learning

At present, many students coming out from their institutions of higher education have do so without achieving the kind of skills they really need to work in a real world situation. Among the drawbacks many students face are lack of ability to analyze or solve problems, relate problems to different contexts, communicate clearly and have an integrated understanding of different branches of knowledge. These problems can be addressed if the processes by which curriculum is designed and then syllabi are determined undergo improvement.

Curriculum Issues and Restructuring of Syllabus

It is necessary as to what is the objective of a university, especially at the undergraduate level, and then use the answers to develop a curriculum. Presently, the design of curriculum and syllabi is reflective of the entrenched examination system under which the student is asked to face a question paper at the end of the year, or in some universities, at the end of the semester. This archaic examination system, ostensibly used as a means of certifying the ability of students, unfortunately does not really test the kind of skills they need to be successful in either the pursuit of pure theoretical knowledge or in practical real world situations. The examination system, even in the case of the comparatively better equipped in less rigid institutions, has left quite manifestly traditional and incapable of distinguishing between different talents of students in a tangible manner. Similar to what happens at the school level; university-level evaluation practices also simply widen the scope of memory-based questioning, with tht occasional rote-based 'application' question masquerading as real-world problem solving. In doing so, they entrench the student's lack of ability to examine and understand the real world, as a result of which their engagement with people or issues remains scarce once they enter the world of work, with implications for their abilities as workers and citizens.

Management of Higher Education

The Indian higher education system is one of the largest such systems in the World. It is estimated that during the Xth Five Year Plan period (2002-07), there will be a tremendous pressure of numbers on this system and a large number of additional students will be knocking at the doors of higher education institutions in the country. There are also new challenges of management and regulation being faced by these institutions, which require serious attention, both at the institutions in the public sector and also those in the private sector now developing at a fast step. As a result of which the old structures of management established in pre-independent India and working during most of the twentieth century are now needed to undergo faster changes.

In spite of this, the demands of the society for equity and accommodation cannot be neglected any more. The new chapter under WTO where competence is the cardinal principle of achievement in global operations has made it quite clear that the country should exploit its excellent potential in higher education and training facilities and prepare itself to export the Indian brand of education to foreign countries. Policy planning and evolving strategies for this task are somewhat new for the country. But, this is an opportunity which India should not neglect, as it offers interesting possibilities to strengthen the nation's talent and resourcefulness.

Health Consciousness and Physical Fitness

Physical fitness and sports are two sides of the same coin and are mutually dependent on each other. As the famous dictum goes, mind is the key to man and eyes cannot see what mind cannot perceive. The relationship between mind and body has been acknowledged scientifically. It is generally believed that a healthy body has a healthy mind; but it could be the other way around also, i.e., a healthy mind has a healthy body. However, this requires appropriate training.

Today's education is largely academic. In real sense, this orientation is required to changer a balanced development through inculcating health conscious amongst students. This will cover the development at physical, mental and social levels. With the increasing stress on academics in the world of employment and elsewhere and the rapid progress in science and technology all over the world, parental force has been exercising academic training at the cost of health and physical fitness of the youth. It is in this context that there is now an urgent need to lay a strong foundation and strengthen physical education and sports programmes in the higher education field. This invites the integration of physical education, sports, yoga and recreation activities in the higher education system for the superficial good of the younger generation.

Ethics in Profession and Value Education

The faster developments in science and technology and the challenges of globalization are bringing some more challenges to the education system in the country. This is also the time when parental care to the children is on the wane. The adverse effects of the media on the mental development and moral values of the younger generation are indispensably being felt increasingly in all spheres of life. Gross consumerism has distorted the view of persons into one of equating possessions with richness. Exploitation of natural resources is going on without reference to sustainability. The discrepancy between the rich and the poor is growing wider, While the education system needs to keep step in step with the scientific and technological developments in terms of building the skills and knowledge, it also needs to focus attention on the more fundamental issues of the social and moral consequences of such unregulated activities. In this context, there is now a growing demand to lay greater emphasis on education to inculcate, nurture and develop values, particularly among the youth of the country.

Conclusion

Exaggerative emphasis on one at the cost of the other would be counter productive. Hence accessibility and quality upgradation are not separable and indispensable dimensions of higher education. As India is a wide and sub continental in size a population above one billion, the quantitative expansion of education (i.e., dimension accessibility) is of paramount importance to mitigate disparities across regions, gender and social strata in the field of education. This should be given due consideration.

A well-planned and structured interaction to be developed between Centres of Academic Excellence and other Universities/ Institutions; (1) While restructuring the syllabi and courses, efforts should be made to develop an optimal combination of acquisition of theoretical and practical skills. The courses should be so designed that critical reading and interpretation of classics, practical field work wherever relevant, and application of readings and other skills are given importance; (2) Quality of higher education can improve considerably through an extensive and optimal use of audio-visual technologies and Internet. The courses should be so designed to make good use of these modern developments; (3) In restructuring of syllabi, all stakeholders such as students, teachers and users of services should be involved. However, teachers should be given flexibility within the norms and benchmarks decided by the stakeholders and (4) Quality of higher education can also be improved by inducting quality oriented objectivity in merit promotions of teaching faculty. UGC, ICSSR and other research funding bodies should encourage interdisciplinary/multi-disciplinary Seminars/ Conferences/ Research projects. These bodies could allocate at least 50 per cent of their research funds for inter-disciplinary activities. UGC could also take initiatives to open Centres/Schools for promoting multi-disciplinary teaching and research.

References

1. Mayhew, Arther, H.R. James, *Development of Education System,* (ed.) Shastri Book Distributors, 2003.
2. Muzumder, N.N., *History of Education in Ancient India,* McMillan, 1917.
3. Trevelyon, C.E. *On the Education of the People of India,* Longman, Orme, Bross, Green & Lonmans, 1838.
4. Report of the Universities Commission of 1902. Howell (Arthur), Education in British India, Calcutta.

Chapter-12

Reforms in Higher Education in Telangana State

B. Shirisha,

Dr. Raja reddy,

Abstract

India must safeguard the interests of young researchers and ensure permanent appointments for temporary faculty members. The Gross Enrollment Ratio (GER) in higher education in India is very less when compared to other advanced countries. The number of institutions and enrolment in higher education continue their rapid growth, but the quality of this education remains uncertain. High selectivity of admission to these elite institutions provides a screen valued by potential employers. Domestic and foreign demand for the services of these few thousand students has created an inflated reputation of the overall quality of India's higher education. The number of such graduates remains small relative to the population and the demands of India's economy for educated manpower. Reliable estimates of value-added by higher education, beyond the screening value of admission to elite institutions, are needed to assess colleges and universities, and to guide educational policy. Graduate education - the seed farm of higher education and scholarship - continues in an alarming state of disarray with respect to both quality and quantity. Pressed by budgetary constraints, the government appears to have decided on profit-oriented privatization of higher education as the solution. Political and business classes, with significant overlap between the two, see higher education as a source of lucrative private returns on investment. There is little theoretical or empirical evidence that supports the prospects of success of a for-profit model in building quality higher education. Some recent proposals hold promise of radical reform and renovation, including regulatory restructuring. It remains unclear whether the government has the wisdom, determination, financing, and power to push reforms past the resistance from entrenched faculty and from the political and business classes.

Introduction

If India wants to transform its universities into world class institutions, it must safeguard the interests of young researchers and ensure permanent appointments for temporary faculty members. The number of institutions and enrolment in higher education continue their rapid growth, but the quality of this education remains uncertain. High selectivity of admission to these elite institutions provides a screen valued by potential employers. Domestic and foreign demand for the services of these few thousand students has created an inflated reputation of the overall quality of India's higher education. The number of such graduates remains small relative to the population and the demands of India's economy for educated manpower. Reliable estimates of value-added by higher education, beyond the screening value of admission to elite institutions, are needed to assess colleges and universities, and to guide educational policy. Graduate education - the seed farm of higher education and scholarship - continues in an alarming state of disarray with respect to both quality and quantity. Pressed by budgetary constraints, the government appears to have decided on profit-oriented privatization of higher education as the solution. Political and business classes, with significant overlap between the two, see higher education as a source of lucrative private returns on investment. There is little theoretical or empirical evidence that supports the prospects of success of a for-profit model in building quality higher education. Some recent proposals hold promise of radical reform and renovation, including regulatory restructuring. It remains unclear whether the government has the wisdom, determination, financing, and power to push reforms past the resistance from entrenched faculty and from the political and business classes.

If India wants to transform its universities into world class institutions, it must safeguard the interests of young researchers and ensure permanent appointments for temporary faculty members. The Gross Enrollment Ratio (GER) in higher education in India is very less when compared to other advanced countries. India's higher education sector is faced with twin problems: First, reforms as initiated are directionless. And second, future of researchers lies in limbo. Both of these create an adverse public perception of research and teaching. Higher Education in India is filled with low quality and high quantities.

Objectives of the study

The main objectives of the study are;

1. To study the higher education scenario.
2. To understand the issues in the higher education system.
3. To know the problems of higher education.
4. To study the reforms in higher education
5. To offer some suggestions to solve the issues of higher education.

Research Methodology

The primary data in the form of interviews and opinions of students and managements and other stakeholders is collected for the purpose of study. The secondary data is also used from the internet and other reports. The study is also conducted in emphirical method.

Limitations of the study

The study is limited to Telangana region only. There are six state universities which are implementing the state policy of higher education. Even though there is some comparison with private colleges, the study is mainly limited to Government Degree Colleges in the state. The study is also limited to reforms in Government Degree Colleges only.

The ministry of human resource development will look after the education system in India. The expenditure patter on the education is explaining the least interest on education. The expenditure on education in India is treated as waste expenditure, but it is really a good investment for future which yields up to hundred years. Even though the percentage to GDP has been increasing, it is not on par with the other countries.

Table 12.1
Public Expenditure on Education in India as percent to GDP

S.No.	*Year*	*Public Expenditure ₹ Crore)*	*% to GDP*
1	1951-52	66.46	0.64
2	1960-61	239.56	1.48
3	1970-71	892.32	2.11
4	1980-81	3884.20	2.98
5	1990-91	19615.85	3.84
6	2000-01	82486.84	4.14
7	2010-11	293478.23	4.05
8	2013-14	465142.90	4.13

Source: www.mhrd.gov.in/stat.

The Telangana State Council of Higher Education (TSCHE) was established by the Order of the State Government of Telangana according to the provisions of the AP Reorganization ACT 2014. The following table shows the list of six Telangana Universities and colleges affiliated to them.

The Telangana State Council of Higher Education is the highest body of Higher Education of the State Government. It coordinates the University Grants Commission (UGC), the State Government and the Universities. It is the general duty of the Council to determine standards in Higher Education Institutions, Research Institutions, Scientific and Technical Institutions. It streamlines the standards in accordance with the guidelines of University Grants Commission, issued from time to time. The TSCHE envisages three distinct functions (a) Planning and Coordination.

Table 12.2

No.of Colleges & Students in Telangana State in 2017-18

S.No.	*University*	*No.of Colleges*	*No.of Students*
1	Kakatiya University	766	53891
2	Mahatma Gandhi University	282	3619
3	Osmania University	930	86403
4	Palamuru University	248	17837
5	Satavahana University	291	23932
6	Telangana University	186	15155

Source: www.tsche.ac.in

Commissionerate of Collegiate Education

The main purpose of Collegiate Education is to promote Higher Education, giving special attention to the Institutes located in backward and rural areas. It aims to strengthen women education at undergraduate and post-graduate levels. It monitors the academic standards of the colleges in the interest of the students. It helps the colleges to improve infrastructure in order to maintain the quality of education. It takes important decisions regarding the academic schedules, budget approvals, academic inspections, training programmes, research provisions etc. It helps the students in their educational pursuits by offering academic guidance and by giving skill based training. It arranges campus selections for the students through TSKC.

The question that demands attention here is that since the 1960s, what (if anything) have the intellectuals, policy-makers, the Government and the society done to change the lukewarm response to research and teaching profession in general and to the humanities in particular. The failure of Indian universities to make it to the list of the top universities across the world has received a plethora of responses from our intelligentsia and the Government, but nothing substantial seems to have been done to bring the much-needed transformation in the education sector.

Most of the Indian universities are suffering from the following problems.

1. Least importance to research.
2. Vacant posts in teaching and supporting staff.
3. The Indian Universities are unable to control the brain drain.
4. Role of the Universities is to set the standards but failed to supervise in achieving.
5. Indian mindset is limited to quantity, but not in quality of education.
6. Competition from the private institutions.
7. Absentism of students and faculty.
8. Malpractices in admissions, examinations and scholarships.
9. Revamping the entire higher education system.

The Government of Telangana and the State Higher Education Council and the Commissionerate of Collegiate Education jointly take policy decisions on higher education and implement.

Reform means to change something to improve it. Changing the existing thing with an intension to improve it. The Government of Telangana introduced revolutionary reforms, immediately after formation of the new state of Telangana in 2004. Some of the reforms introduced by the Government of Telangana in the Degree Colleges are as follows;

1. Degree Online Services, Telangana (DOST).
2. Biometric Attendance.
3. Online Examination Fees.
4. Online Scholarships.
5. Using Smart Classes and E-Learning Sources.
6. Using Adhaar and Other Mobile Numbers.
7. Meeseva and Internet.
8. CBCS.
9. Semisterisation.
10. Internal Evaluation And External Evaluation.
11. Feedback From The Stake Holders.

1. **Degree Online Services, Telangana (DOST):** The entire admission process into degree colleges in the Telangana State is now possible through DOST only. The student has to register him or herself online by using adhaar and mobile number and choosing the best available course in the best college in the state. The Government through TSCHE, completes the admission process

by following all norms of reservation, metit, etc. The best applicant in the category will get admission in the best college of his preference.

2. **Biometric Attendance:** The attendance is a must for the regular students for appearing the term end examinations. At least seventy five percent of attendance is necessary for the student to appear the examinations. Further the attendance is also needed to get scholar ship. The introduction of bio-metric attendance, the attendance process became very easy.
3. **Online Examinations Fees**: Once DOST admissions are completed, the same list is forwarded to the university and the examination fee is collected based on the DOST admissions. The malpractices in admissions are controlled in this process.
4. **Online Scholarships:** The Government of Telangana is offering fee reimbursement and scholarships for almost all eligible SC, ST, BC, OC and minority students of the state through e-pass. The online processing is eradicating the manipulations and misusing the scholarships.
5. **Using Smart Classes and E-Learning Sources**: The Government introduced the smart classrooms using the technology and e-class rooms. This facility is available in many Government Degree Colleges also.
6. **Using Adhaar and Other Mobile Numbers**: Using the adhaar number and mobile number and bank account number and SSC certificate number, etc. is almost eradicating malpractices in the admission and scholar ship systems.
7. **Meeseva and Internet**: Entering into the process of DOST and e-pass and other services of the educational institutions is made easy by decentralizing the process by using Meeseva and intenet facilities. These facilities can be used by everyone and from anywhere in state.
8. **CBCS**: The old compulsory and mandatory and marks system has been replaced by Choice Based Credit System (CGCS). In the present CBCS, the student is free to select the subjects of his choice and convenient. And instead of marks, credits are being awarded.
9. **Semisterisation:** Usually the degree course is divided into three or four years. The year consists of twelve months of study. But now degree is divided into six or eight semesters. Ninety hours of

teaching is compulsory for appearing semester end examinations. Semesterization made easy for students to complete the courses.

10. **Internal Evaluation and External Evaluation**: Internal evaluation made the evaluation process more perfect. The internal evaluation is being done by the available experts knowing standards. External evaluation is made by the unknown evaluator.
11. **Feedback From The Stake Holders:** Feedback is the process of collecting the opinion of the students on the teachers and infrastructure and other things.

Findings of the study

The findings of this study are presented in the form of advantages and disadvantages in the introducing the reforms in the degree course.

Advantages of Reforms

1. DOST admission system is eradicating the malpractices in duplicate and wrong admissions.
2. Biometric attendance is making the student to be present in classroom which is compulsory for appearing the semester end examination and getting fees reimbursement.
3. Payment of Online examination fee has become convenient to the colleges by readily available nominal rolls and the students also benefited by ready lists.
4. Online scholarships is the best way to control the malpractices in scholarship and also convenient to student.
5. Using smart classes and e-learning sources increasing the scope of the subject and knowledge of the student.
6. Using Adar number, mobile number, bank account number and ssc certificate number, is the best way to control the malpractices.
7. Meeseva and internet services are making availability of online services by reducing time and money of the student by applying for admission and scholarship.
8. Choice Based Credit System (CBCS) made the subject selection easy and convenient to the student.
9. Semisterization cut down the syllabus to half for each examination which is a easy way to pass through the examination.
10. Internal evaluation is useful for knowing the talent of the student outside the examination hall. External evaluation leads to real justification for quality of the subject.

11. Feedback from the stake holders is giving the scope for re-adjustment and reinforcement.

Disadvantages of Reforms

1. DOST admission system is delaying the admission process, by extending upto three months.
2. Biometric attendance is making the waste investment in the machinery..
3. Online scholarships is the best way to managements to earn more and more.
4. In practice, it is not possible to use regularly smart classes and e-learning sources as the power problems prevail.
5. Using Adar number, mobile number, bank account number and ssc certificate number, is not so easy, as they are not tallying in most of cases.
6. Meeseva and internet services are making lot of mistakes while entering the data online while admission.
7. Choice Based Credit System (CBCS) is not possible in practice because all the colleges are not offering multiple choices to select. Only limited choices are being offered.
8. Semisterization increased the amount of examination fee paid, as the number of times is increasing.
9. Internal evaluation is leading to favouritism and failures.
10. Feedback from the stake holders is not being given proper importance.
11. Number of regular teachers should be increased.

Conclusions

1. Gross Enrollment Ratio (GER) in India should be increased. Every student in India should be given a chance to enrol in the higher education.
2. Expenditure on education should be increased to at least to 8 percent to GDP.
3. Regular feedback should be taken and it should be implemented.
4. Reforms should be student centric, which should be useful to student.
5. Reforms should not reduce the number of teachers, resources, etc.
6. Reforms should be implemented at full swing.

References

1. Reforming higher education with transperancy–University World News",www.universityworldnews.com.
2. *www.ugc.ac.in.*
3. About Department of higher education government of India, Ministry of Human resource Development". *mhrd.gov.in.*
4. Higher education in India-The Need for change, EABER". www.eaber.org..
5. www.tsche.ac.in.

Chapter-13

Reforms of Higher Education in India

Dr.G.Sreenivasulu
B.Ravi Kumar,

Abstract

Education starts with us when we start our life journey. From the very first moment, a baby steps into this world, she/he starts to learn. She/he learns to cry, to show any sort of discomfort, smiles to show his/her happiness and also learns to identify his/her mother's touch. This process continues throughout his/her life because she/he learns something new every moment of his/her life. John Dewey said: "Education is not preparation for life, education is life itself." The reform process has been in vogue since ages. The ancient universities in India were leading centres of learning in the contemporary world and attracted scholars and students from other countries. So did some famous centres of Islamic learning in the mediaeval period. But unfortunately these traditions did not survive.

Introduction

The accreditation system prevailing in various countries provides a measure of the educational quality. Through the accreditation process, an agency or its designated representative evaluates the quality of a higher education institution as a whole or of a specific educational programme in order to formally recognize it as having met certain predetermined minimal criteria or standards. The result of this process is usually the awarding of a status of recognition, and sometimes of a license to conduct educational programmes within a time-limited validity. The process can imply initial and periodic self-study and evaluation by external peers. The accreditation process generally involves three steps with specific activities: (i) a self-evaluation process conducted by the faculty, the administrators, and the staff of the institution or academic programme, resulting in a report that takes as its reference the set of standards and criteria of the accrediting body; (ii) a study visit, conducted by a team of peers, selected by the accrediting organization, which reviews the evidence, visits the premises, and interviews the academic and administrative staff, resulting in an assessment report, including a recommendation to the accrediting body; and (iii) examination of the evidence and recommendation on the basis of the given set of criteria concerning quality and resulting in a final judgment and the communication of the formal decision to the institution and other constituencies, if appropriate.

The definition of higher education includes a hierarchy of institutions and programmes. Many different kinds of university level institutions such as central universities, state universities, private universities, IITs, NITs, IIITs, IIMs, IISERs, occupy the upper end of the higher education spectrum. The various colleges offering general or specialized education, professional education, provide higher education to nearly eighty percent of students. Then, there are several other post secondary institutions such as community colleges and technical training institutions. In a sense the polytechnics and vocational institutions, which are not strictly post-secondary, are also considered as higher education.

In general our higher education system has divided these institutions and programmes into two broad categories: one for scholarly pursuits and achievements and the other for work-force requirements. It is now increasingly recognized that this dichotomy should be erased and shift away from undue emphasis on "manpoweroriented" planning (annual out-turn of graduates, growth rate, Gross Enrollment Ratio, employability etc.,) and adopt a more holistic approach to higher education at every level, not just at the university or college level only.

Universities are essentially a community of teachers and students where, in some way, all learn from one another or, at any rate, strive to do so. Their principal objective is to deepen our understanding of their role in the society and to disseminate this understanding throughout society and to apply it in the service of mankind. Yet another responsibility of the Indian universities in the present context is to strive to assist the schools in their attempts at qualitative self-improvement. For this purpose, universities should conduct experimental schools, run advanced courses for teachers in various school subjects, assume greater responsibility for the training of teachers at all levels, organize summer institutes for their in-service education, assist in the search for and development of talent, and develop new curricula, textbooks and teaching materials.

Expansion, Access and Inclusion

In the present Indian context there is a great deal of emphasis on these three aspects (besides Quality discussed later). These three issues are highly interconnected and encompass a variety of social, economic, political and cultural dimensions. For instance expansion of higher educational institutions and programmes undertaken in a random fashion does not automatically ensure access to those eligible aspiring students. Even assuming that accessibility is not a major constraint, inclusion of marginalized sections of society (Poor, First Generation Learners, Socially Backward Communities etc.,) may not be ensured. If inclusive measures and affirmative actions are enforced through legislation and persuasion, we find there is a large body of Indian opinion offering severe resistance.

Assessment of Quality

The accreditation system prevailing in various countries provides a measure of the educational quality. Through the accreditation process, an agency or its designated representative evaluates the quality of a higher education institution as a whole or of a specific educational programme in order to formally recognize it as having met certain predetermined minimal criteria or standards. The result of this process is usually the awarding of a status of recognition, and sometimes of a license to conduct educational programmes within a time-limited validity. The process can imply initial and periodic self-study and evaluation by external peers. The accreditation process generally involves three steps with specific activities: (i) a self-evaluation process conducted by the faculty, the administrators, and the staff of the institution or academic programme, resulting in a report that takes as its reference the set of standards and criteria of the accrediting body; (ii) a study visit, conducted by a team of peers, selected by the accrediting organization,which reviews the evidence, visits the premises, and interviews the academic and administrative staff, resulting in an assessment report, including a recommendation to the accrediting body; and (iii) examination of the evidence and recommendation on the basis of the given set of criteria concerning quality and resulting in a final judgment and the communication of the formal decision to the institution and other constituencies, if appropriate.

Indian Higher Education is a large system with nearly four hundred and eighty university level institutions and over twenty thousand colleges. The growth in professional institutions has also been manifold. With significant expansion of higher educational institutions, both publicly and privately funded, a mandatory accreditation system that could provide a common frame of reference for students and other stakeholders to obtain credible information on academic quality across institutions is required.

Accreditation is the principal means of quality assurance in higher education the world over and reflects the fact that in achieving recognition, the institution or programme of study is committed to external review to meet certain minimum specified standards and also to continuously seek ways in which to enhance the quality of education.

The Eleventh Plan approved by the National Development Council (NDC) provides a three point agenda in regard to accreditation, namely; introduction of a mandatory accreditation system for all higher educational institutions; creation of multiple rating agencies with a body to rate these rating agencies; department-wise ratings in addition to institutional rating.

Presently, accreditation is not mandatory and there is no law to govern the process of accreditation. There are two Central bodies involved in accreditation of institutions; the National Accreditation Assessment Council (NAAC) and the National Board of Accreditation Board (NBA). The NAAC was set up in 1994 by the University Grants Commission (UGC) to make quality an essential element through a combination of internal and external quality assessment and accreditation. The NBA was constituted by the All India Council for Technical Education (AICTE), as an autonomous Body, under section 10(u) of the AICTE Act, 1987.

Autonomy Issues

The expansion of the higher education system has brought to the fore several critical issues relating to governance of the higher educational institutions. Historically the educational institutions in India enjoyed considerable degree of autonomy vested in the heads of the institutions and the academic community guided by enlightened peers. This advantage has now been eroded substantially in the government funded as well as the private institutions.

In case of centrally funded government institutions such as IITs, IIMs, Central Universities, IISERs, NITs etc., it is reasonably certain that the interference and control of the government is minimal. Usually the governing boards and the heads of these institutions have the freedom to evolve their academic policies and strategies except in areas where it concerns the fundamental national policies (for example reservations; pay commission norms etc.). The governing boards of these institutions include just one or two officials of the Central Government. At the same time there are also several central institutions with high proportion of government official in their governing bodies where the interference effect is high and troublesome. This is particularly worrisome in the case of state-funded institutions.

Legislative Reforms

After independence the education sector (like agriculture) was in the State List of our Constitution, till the Higher Education was changed to Concurrent List through 42nd Amendment during the mid-seventies. Since then there has been continuing arguments about the implications and consequences of this change. Those who look at the positive side of the situation point out to the increased quantum of funds available to higher education in centrally funded institutions without the same degree of interference from the political or power centres as happening in the State Funded institutions (especially in the matter of appointment of Vice-Chancellors and other senior faculty members and administrators). The level of funding available to the State Institutions is considerably less. The private model of higher education has not worked well in India. The concept of Public-private partnership model has not been sufficiently evolved for operational purposes. The present initiatives of the Government of India to resolve many of the critical issues consist of creating a series of legal instruments.

Ncher Bill

An important measure awaiting political clearance of the Cabinet for introduction in the Parliament is the Bill for the Creation of the National Commission on Higher Education and Research (NCHER) (conforming to the recommendations of the Yashpal Committee Report on Renovation and Rejuvenation of Higher Education In India). This Bill addresses certain fundamental concerns in the reports of National Knowledge Commission and Yashpal Committee. These two reports draw critical attention to the fundamental academic weaknesses such as compartmentalization and fragmentation of knowledge systems, absence of innovation in learning methods, disconnect with the society and too much emphasis on multiplicity of harmful entrance and qualifying tests.They reflect concerns on the growing trend in loss of university autonomy damaging the prospect of healthy growth of spirits of enquiry, creativity, and innovation.

Four other bills approved by the Cabinet and undergoing the legislative scrutiny relate to Entry and Operation of the Foreign Institutions in India; Establishment of a National Accreditation Authority; Prevention of Malpractices; and Establishment of Educational Tribunals.

Foreign Institutions Bill

The Foreign Institutions Bill appear to have created most controversies. Unfortunately the criticisms about the Foreign Institutions Bill are based on uninformed misapprehensions. Most of the critics tend to ignore the present ground reality of more than two hundred foreign programmes offered in India in various modes. Undoubtedly majority of these are of substandard quality and value. The regrettable fact is no agency in India has an account of the number of foreign programmes, their mode of operation, nature of partnership, quality of instruction, fee structure, protection of students interest and so on. Many of them indulge in glossy and misleading advertisements enticing gullible students with false promises. Available information on them is based on tertiary sources of reports compiled by voluntary organizations.

The Accreditation Bill

The concern for quality assurance of higher education programme has been acutely felt partly because of unprecedented growth of institutions and more so because of the need to meet the ever-changing norms and standards of accreditation so that mutual recognition of programme among institutions in India or abroad is streamlined. Within a relatively short period of less than two decades, the accreditation system in India has been struggling to demonstrate their viability. It is expected that in future every educational programmes would be subjected to mandatory accreditations, unlike the voluntary process at present. In such an event, the total number of institutions and programmes that will need accreditation in a vast range of disciplines is mind-boggling. The "National Accreditation Regulatory Authority for Higher Educational Institutions Bill, 2009", provides for mandatory accreditation of all higher educational institutions through Accreditation Agencies registered under the legislation. The proposal applies to all higher educational institutions including, universities, institutions deemed to be universities, colleges, institutes, institutions of national importance established by an Act of Parliament, and their constituents, imparting higher education beyond 12 years of schooling leading to the award of a degree or a diploma, and whether through the conventional or distance education systems.

The Malpractices Bill

The malpractices occur on a large enough scale in the Indian higher education to cause major worry about its cumulative effect on the society. Many of these are wanton disregard of the existing regulations and guidelines, which have large enough loopholes. Unfortunately in quite a few instances those who are supposed to watch their proper implementation abet the irregularities. The existing set of regulations and guidelines are totally devoid of any meaningful penalties to those who flout them. They were designed some decade ago, perhaps with the assumption that those involved in educational endeavours will not resort to willful malpractices, not anticipating the entry of new class of educational entrepreneurs whose greed exceed limits of decency and propriety as seen in several of the deemed-to-be-universities, which came into existence with the connivance of power centres that are equally greedy.

Conclusion

The four bills that have been introduced in the Parliament in the middle of April and the NCHER Bill on the anvil, if enacted with whatever changes the Parliament deems fit, can provide a strong foundation to overcome the present aberrations and elevate the credibility of Indian higher educational qualifications among the community of nations. Hopefully, if the proposed legal instruments emerge through the legislative process, and perhaps go through the judicial scrutiny, and if implemented in their true letter and spirit, there will be some light at the end of the tunnel. In the meantime those who are concerned about the future of higher education in India should seek to understand the basic rationale behind these measures and help to address them in their own domains of involvement in whatever way possible. Since the nation's economic future and global stature are intricately associated with the credibility of higher education system, one can only hope that there is sufficient wisdom in the society not to let the present state of entropy to persist.

References

1. Altbach, Philip G. (2006) The Private Higher Education Revolution: An Introduction. University News. January 2-8, 2006. Vol. 44 No.01.
2. Anandakrishnan, M. (2006) Privatization of higher education: Opportunities and anomalies. 'Privatization and commercialization of higher education' organized by NIEPA , May 2, 2006., New Delhi.
3. Delors, Jacques (1996) Learning the treasure within. Report to UNESCO of the International Commission on Education for the Twenty-first Century. UNSECO Publishing, Paris.
4. MHRD (2006) Annual Report. Ministry of Human Resource Development, Department of Secondary and Higher education. Government of India. New Delhi.
5. Planning Commission (1999) Approach paper to the Tenth Five-year Plan (2002-2007). Planning Commission. New Delhi.
6. Stella, Antony (2002) External quality assurance in Indian higher education: Case study of the National Assessment and Accreditation Council (NAAC). International Institute for Educational Planning. Paris.

7. UGC (2005) Research Handbook: Towards nurturing research culture in higher education institutions in India. University Grants Commission. New Delhi.

Chapter-14

Genesis of an Ecosystem for Innovation in Research and Development

Dr. Sumit Ghosh

Abstract

For any teacher, observation and cogitation plays a pivotal role in quality research. Research is a broad term which encompasses many facets but the deterministic yardstick which explicitly makes it indispensable is that its consequences has an impact on the human life and society as a whole. Globalization. privatization and liberalization have influenced the work places especially the research and development sector. Research has become more cross-disciplinary, multi-disciplinary, interdisciplinary and transdisciplinary in nature.

A vibrant ecosystem for quality research output requires the existence of innovation. Apart from adequate infrastructural facilities, existence of a dedicated Research Cell ensures the sustenance of quantifiable research outputs and transfer of knowledge. A critical factor is dissemination of knowledge, especially theoretical and practical findings of research through various media. It not only enhances quality of research but also reinvigorates the teaching and learning process in the campus. The establishment of an Incubation Centre within the institution would help in the organization of startups, hackathons and accelerator programs. These programs will rekindle the entrepreneurial spirit among the budding researchers. Holding Intellectual Property Rights (IPR) based workshops along with industry-academia innovative practices unravel a conundrum of ideas. Linkages and Collaborations also act as support structures. Evaluator mechanisms provide the necessary checks and balances.

No country can make progress unless and until the quality of science laboratories and research acumen is strengthened. As long as academic institutions inculcate a sense of scientific temperament among staff and students, the idea of realizing innovation in research is far from realized. This paper discusses the prerequisites required to create an ecosystem for innovation in research and development (R&D) in under graduate colleges.

Introduction

Research in under graduate colleges can have a positive and encouraging influence not only on the students but also the faculty who serve as mentors. A research program which goes on par with the academic curriculum should have the essential ingredients which can lead to the holistic development of skills like working independently, analyze data and interpret results, build up confidence, experience of working in a lab and above all create a career path towards professionalism. Teaching faculty members can equally benefit by such research activities as it enhances their credibility and also provides a platform of visibility among the scientific fraternity.

Current research scenario in India

As per the data obtained from Department of Science and Technology India ranks third among the most attractive investment destinations for technology transactions in the world. Scientific publications in India ranks 6th position and ranks at 10th for patents. In context to Global Innovation Index (GII) which measures innovation and the necessary tools which will support and promote policies catering to long-term output growth, India improved its rank on the GII for the second year consecutively. From being ranked at the 81st position in 2015, India improved its ranking to 66th in 2016 and further to 60th in 2017 and 57th in 2018.

Union Government Initiatives

When we look into the figures obtained from the Central Government budget report 2018-19 the allocation to the Department of Science and Technology (DST) has been increased by 8.21 per cent to ₹5,114.78 crore as against the previous budget. The budget for the Ministry of Science and Technology, has been increased by 6.11 per cent to ₹12,322.28 crore as against the previous budget. The Department of Atomic Energy has been allocated ₹13,971.41 crore, an increase of 5.76 per cent against the previous budget. The Ministry of Earth Sciences was allocated ₹1,800 crore, which is an increase of 12.66 per cent as against the previous budget. Modern India has a strong focus on science and technology, realizing that it is a key element of economic growth.

According to the statistical data obtained from the Ministry of Human Resource Development India as a global education industry especially the sector of higher education is one of the largest networks of higher education institutions in the world with a population of about 500 million in the age bracket of 5-24 years. The education sector in India is estimated at 91.7

billion dollars in 2018 and is expected to reach 101.1 billion dollars in 2019. Number of colleges and universities in India reached 39,050 and 903, respectively in 2017-18. India had 36.64 million students enrolled in higher education in 2017-18. What could probably turn the tide in favour of India is introduction of a host of reforms and improved financial outlays which would indirectly propel and could possibly transform the country into a knowledge haven. India has signed a loan agreement with World Bank under 'Skills Acquisition and Knowledge Awareness for Livelihood Promotion' (SANKALP) Project to enhance institutional mechanisms for skills development.

Higher education scenario in India

The Union Government NITI Aayog comprehensive analysis report tells it has initiated several research popularization initiatives. In February 2018, Government of India announced grant of ₹ 1,000 crore for the second phase of Impacting Research Innovation and Technology (IMPRINT), a fund created by Department of Science and Technology and Ministry of Human Resource and Development The Government of India granted Atal Innovation Mission with ₹ 550 crore that will boost the academicians, entrepreneurs and researchers to work towards innovation. India is world's third largest technology startup hub with incorporation of 1,000 new companies in 2017. Rashtriya Uchchatar Shiksha Abhiyan (RUSA) is a Centrally Sponsored Scheme (CSS), launched in 2013 aims at providing strategic funding to eligible state higher educational institutions.

In February 2018, the Union Cabinet has approved implementation of 'Prime Minister Research Fellows (PMRF)' scheme, which will promote the mission of development through innovation, at a total cost of ₹ 1,650 crore for a period of seven years beginning 2018-19. In August 2018, Government of India launched the second phase of 'Unnat Bharat Abhiyan' which aims to link higher educational institutions in the country with at least five villages. The scheme covers 750 such institutions. The Ek Bharat Shreshtha Bharat (EBSB) campaign is undertaken by Ministry of Human Resource Development to increase engagement between states, union territories, central ministries, educational institutions and general public.

What ails Indian Higher education and research

World University Rankings show not a single university from India could make it to the list of top 275 universities in the world. Higher education system in India is the most neglected sector which inadvertently opens up a pandoras box of maladies due to which the Indian universities are not in a position to compete with other top universities in the world. An argument that is often put forth citing non-selection in the list is that the parameters and weightage of selection are adversely designed, not suitable for Indian institutes and universities as they lack facilities. This argument provided by the stereotypic mentalities question the very purpose of carrying out the ranking. One should understand that these rankings show where we are deficient and how improvements can be incorporated so that the particular university or institute can compete globally.

A survey states that only 19 per cent of engineering and 5 per cent of non-engineering graduates are employable. It has also been seen that in teachers not passion for research but urgency for climbing up the promotion ladder in their career motivates to register for Ph.D. As a result, the quality of most PhD research is sub-standard and our Indian universities have highly qualified but highly unproductive academics. Provision of creating a platform for government-industry-academia linkage is the need of the hour.

Creation of an ecosystem for innovation

Research is a broad term which encompasses many facets but the deterministic yardstick which explicitly makes it indispensable is that its consequences have an impact on the human life and society as a whole. No country can make progress unless and until the quality of science laboratories and research acumen is strengthened. Competitive accreditation and funding can be contemplated. Evaluation checks should be periodically tested. Focus should be on quality and societal impact research. A vibrant ecosystem for quality research output requires the existence of innovation. Apart from adequate infrastructural facilities, existence of a dedicated Research Cell ensures the sustenance of quantifiable research outputs and transfer of knowledge. A critical factor is dissemination of knowledge, especially theoretical and practical findings of research through various media. It not only enhances quality of research but also reinvigorates the teaching and learning process in the campus.

A good educational institution is a body of progressive teachers and thinking students who have intellectual courage. Symbiotic relationship between science and socio-economic policies is needed. Identifying promising opportunities for collaboration between industries, institutes and governments and collaboration is required. Regular dialogues between the three in the form of seminars, lectures can bring together cordial relationships. There has to be explicit recognition and valuing of employability across the curriculum. It is utmost required for inclusion of entrepreneurial activities in curriculum to nurture leadership, negotiation and confidence. Creation of diverse and regular involvement of employers and alumni in student assessments and project ideas can foster deeper understanding of sustenance.

Incubation and IPR cell

Intellectual Property Rights (IPR) based workshops need to be organized. Such workshops provide a platform where the participants learn the procedural aspects of policies and guidelines towards securing patents for their works. Protecting one's intellectual property not only provides stabilization but also a sense of generating remunerative ventures which will help to sustain further innovations and improvements. A sense of independence, collaboration and innovation is the end product. The concept of Startups, Hackathons and Accelerators are gaining momentum in the modern world of education-entrepreneurship collaboration wherein startup accelerators and incubators provide support to startups in attaining success. This is done by mentoring and guiding the startups and provide access to resources for these startups to succeed.The establishment of an Incubation Centre within the institution would help in the organization of such startups, hackathons and accelerator programs. These programs will rekindle the entrepreneurial spirit among the budding researchers.

Conclusion

No country can make progress unless and until the quality of science laboratories and research acumen is strengthened. As long as academic institutions inculcate a sense of scientific temperament among staff and students, the idea of realizing innovation in research is far from realized. Research with a humane face is the essential reality to be realized.

References

1. Department of Science and Technology, Government of India, Annual Report 2017-18, pp 112-116 (2018).
2. Government of India, Union Budget 2018-19 report, pp 434-500 (2018).
3. Ministry of Human Resource Development-UGC, Government of India, Annual Report of 2018-19, pp 243 - 316 (2018).
4. NITI Aayog Annual report 2016-17 report, Government of India, pp 845-932 (2017).
5. Times Higher Education World University Rankings 2018 report , pp 24-30 (2018).
6. QS World University Rankings 2018 report (2018), pp 62-76 (2018).
7. McKinsey Report on Employability of India's Engineers-Undergraduates, Economic Times, pp4 (2018).

Chapter-15

Role of Research in Higher Education in India

Ujjwal Ashutosh,
Sushree Sunanda Sahu,

Abstract

It is a well acknowledged fact that Research plays an important role in the economic growth of a country. Research refers to a creative work which is undertaken to in a systematic manner so as to increase one's stock of knowledge. In the context of education, it would refer to solving educational problems in a scientific and systematic way. The research scene in India is a chequered one, while the prestigious institutions and institutions of national importance are excelling in research, the mediocre and poor ones are lacking in the same. The Indian Government has taken a number of steps to promote research. The significance of research arises from its promotion of creative thinking; finding solutions to impending problems in a methodical, scientific and well-determined way; promoting further studies in the area of interest and keeping abreast with the latest developments in the selected field of study. Indian system of education is characterized by a number of constraints and research is one of the main ones. Carrying out Research in India has a number of challenges such as absence of intellectual stimulation, emphasis on rote learning, lack of scientific theory and base, inadequate data, lack of scientific knowledge, and training in Research Methodology. In the globalized world it is imperative to have knowledge driven growth powered by innovation. A number of steps could be implemented to foster research such as industry-academia collaboration, development of vocational skills, provision of more funds and inclusion of research as a criterion for faculty promotion. India has a well-acclaimed Brain Power and promotion Research will only help India move up the global intellectual ladder.

Introduction

Research assumes an essential job in the financial improvement of any nation. In reality, innovative work shapes the premise of future intensity of an economy. Sadly, investigate in India is appearing descending pattern. In this Paper an endeavour has been made to talk about the idea of research, analyze the significance of research, to address the examination scene in India, investigate the difficulties and endeavour to foresee what's to come.

Concept of Research

Research alludes to imaginative work which is attempted deliberately, so as to build the load of information of people, culture and society and further use this stock to devise new applications. In the wide sense, it covers social affair of any information, data and certainties for the progression of learning. Development can be considered as the key player of monetary development and resulting enhancement in the nature of living. In this century, there is no uncertainty about the way that India has the ability of initiating worldwide advancement, yet the unavoidable issue that rises is will Indian advanced education bolster this potential? The whole issue warrants a watchful discourse. Research in instruction alludes to taking care of instructive issues in a methodical and logical way and furthermore to comprehend, clarify and foresee human conduct in a progressively sorted out way.

Research in India

Training and education is a prime mover of the general public. So as to positively use our statistic potential, the nature of instruction together with access and value accumulates essentialness. India has the third biggest arrangement of advanced education. The general situation is that, quality does not coordinate the worldwide guidelines and there is expanded extension and criticalness for enhancing the nature of our nation's instructive foundations. The exploration situation in India depicts a chequered picture. While some driving world class organizations like the IITs and the IIMs are accomplishing what was very much arranged in their destinations others depict a grim picture as far as quality and amount of research.[1] The primary Prime Minister of free India, Shri Jawaharlal Nehru, put stock in the significance of science and instruction which would encourage a way of advancements, which thusly would help during the time spent improvement. For the most part India has developed a substantial number of amazing examination establishments which would give profitable exhortation to the arrangement creators. The institutional system for innovative work can be isolated into 2 general classes: resistance and non military personnel.

The five apex bodies which are responsible for research and development are[2]:

(a) Indian Council of Medical Research; It is the apex body for the formulation, coordination and promotion of bio medical research.

(b) Indian Council of Agricultural Research; an autonomous body which coordinates guides and manages research and education in agriculture including horticulture, fisheries and animal sciences.

(c) Indian Council for Social Science Research; It was established in 1969 by the Government of India to promote research in social sciences.

(d) Council of Scientific and Industrial Research; It was established in 1942 as an autonomous body and India's largest Research and Development organization. Its activities include various fields like aero - space engineering, structural engineering, life sciences, environment etc.

(e) Tata Institute of Fundamental Research. It is a Research institution in Mumbai dedicated to basic research in Mathematics and sciences.

Importance of Research

The importance of research can be listed out as follows[3]:

(a) Our knowledge is limited and a number of problems need to be solved in different fields of study. Very often we identify a vacuum in our knowledge and try to address it by asking related questions. Research through systematic study makes available a variety of methods which help in finding solutions.

(b) Research is regarded as an objective, methodical, well-determined scientific method of investigation. Through research a stock of the current scenario can be taken and this will guide the organizations in their decision taking of the future.

(c) We carry out our mundane daily tasks on the basis of our common sense. However, this may not be the correct approach. We will have to find out what is the best under the current situations and research serves this task the best.

(d) Another angle of research is that it helps to gather information. The findings can be recorded and then analyzed to judge the validity of the information.

(e) Research is a systematic investigator into and study of materials and sources. It helps to pursue your interests, learn something new, hone your problem solving skills and come out with results that can contribute to enhancement of knowledge.

(f) Practice of research adds depth to research papers as students are kept abreast of the latest information. Through learning from real world case studies and by seeking the guidance of faculty members help students secure up to date information. In this world of Information and Communication Technology lack of infrastructure and poor quality of digital content are grounds for concern. For making a healthy ICT environment, digitized PhD thesis, e-journals, research journals, e-books etc have to be developed.

(g) It is vital that educational institutions establish a Research Consultancy culture involving faculty, students, professionals and industry to work on a few technologies and facilitate discovery. Research should be the core area instrumental for inter-face between the academic and corporate world.

It must provide a theoretical framework that enables reassessment and refinement of current practices and thinking.[4] It empowers the faculty with in depth knowledge and instils a sense of curiosity among them. In addition it improves the consultancy capabilities of the faculty.

Challenges to Research in India

The Indian arrangement of advanced education has been confronting various difficulties. It requires real speculations in order to make HR gainful, by coupling the more established general controls of humanities, sociologies, characteristic sciences and trade, with their applications in the new economy and having satisfactory field base understanding to upgrade learning with aptitudes and create suitable frames of mind. There are a few essential issues confronting Indian advanced education at present[5]. They incorporate deficient infrastructural offices; personnel crunch; low enrolment proportion; packed classrooms; across the board topographical salary, sex and ethnic lopsided characteristics and so forth. India has a low base of analysts and the scholastic part contributes under 14 percent of the all out number of scientists. The prompt need in this setting would be, to support industry-the scholarly community joint efforts, advance coordinated efforts between the colleges and people in general specialists as additionally between the legislature and Research and Development labs and furthermore increment the number and nature of doctoral understudies. The Indian instruction framework advances repetition learning and understudies just utilize endorsed materials[6]. This pattern proceeds notwithstanding while seeking after advanced education. The examinations are more a trial of memory control as opposed to inventiveness. At the point when the stage comes to seek after further examinations and present research papers, they depict a dreary picture hampering the exploration procedure related with advanced education. As the understudies are denied of scholarly incitement encouraged by research, they miss the mark regarding precious information and abilities which are vital in their professions as well as in different everyday issues. Indeed, even the quantity of understudies seeking after research is constrained by need of time, and support. The outcome being them winding up scared, befuddled and baffled. One of the fundamental obstructions is absence of logical hypothesis. A large number of the specialists are unequipped for doing sound experimental work; information is frequently lacking and notwithstanding when accessible not benefited of; what's more the issue of bureaucratic latency is continually tormenting the framework. Regularly there is absence of logical information and preparing in Research Methodology. A large number of our scientists and aides are not sufficiently equipped to do sound exact work.

The following factors can be said to be encouraging good research:

1. A conducive environment of the institutions/universities;
2. A well-stocked library and Reference section covering books, e-books, journals, online library etc;
3. Provision of adequate infrastructural facility;
4. Existence of Research laboratories having the latest equipments;
5. Availability of adequate finance for purchase of funds;
6. Combining teaching and research related activity in the work profile of the Professors;
7. Instilling a feeling of pride and purposefulness among teachers that their major task is to transformation of the economy.

Future of Research in India

In the undeniably focused worldwide economy, it is important to have learning driven development controlled by advancements. The way to proceeded with progress for India is developing of an advanced education framework which is unrivaled in quality and which supports explore. All the time, it is the business which is the recipient of a few research endeavors and accordingly associations among industry and research foundations is critical. In the ebb and flow age where issues of research are regularly of worldwide nature dynamic collaboration with universal foundations of notoriety must be energized. Professional aptitudes ought to be accentuated. Professional preparing will assume an essential job setting up the workforce to be beneficially used to push the development procedure of the economy. There are developing enthusiasm for connecting aptitudes and advanced education segment. While making an empowering domain, note ought to be made of diminishing the showing hours, more noteworthy money related help and giving access to better framework. Granting of co-operations and empowering industry coordinated efforts will advance research. Research can be advanced by following certain rules, for example, incorporation of research as a model for personnel with the end goal of advancement, (a framework set somewhere near UGC and is as of now been trailed by associated schools and colleges); foundation of honours for recognized analysts with generous money related motivating forces; age of more noteworthy financing; enhancement of foundation; and conceivable decrease of training hours so additional time can be given to look into. India has all the capability of being an exploration centre point given her long convention of educating and famous Brain Power. The obstacles need to handled in order to simple the way to financial flourishing.

Conclusion

Research as we have seen assumes a critical job in the monetary improvement of a nation, all the more so if there should arise an occurrence of a creating nation like India. We confront various limitations, as not well loaded libraries, nonappearance of very much prepared research centres, absence of satisfactory fund, government intercession and so forth. In perspective of the way that we have an all around recognized Brain Power, the need of great importance is for developments and creations. India highly esteems creating Nobel Laureates of Indian inception. The natural abilities of our analysts must be supported and cultivated to make a check in the worldwide field. This calls for more noteworthy monetary help, right arrangement combine with chipping away at discovering answers for the weakening issues tormenting the Indian culture, in the event that we must be viewed as a noteworthy player in the worldwide world.

References

1. Chakrabarti, Alok (2007): "The Higher Education and Research in India: an Overview", Sitra Reports, Helsinki.
2. Chania, Payal, (2012, July, 4): "Importance of Research", THE HINDU
3. Dr. Mathew, P.M: "Research in India needs a major boost" – India Education Review.
4. Everitt, Richard (2014): "Understanding India: The future of higher education and opportunities for international cooperation", British Council, February.
5. "Higher Education in India: Vision 2030, FICCI, Higher Education Summit, 2013.

6. Saxena, Vandana, Kulshetra, Sanjay, and Khan Bali (2010): "Higher and Research in India", International Journal of Research and Technology, Volume 1 (1), June.
7. Singh, J.D: "Higher Education in India – Issues, Challenges and Suggestions".
8. "The future of Indian higher education and its impact on Research and innovation", A Report for the UK – India Education Research Initiative, (UKRIER).
9. Varghese, Mariamma, A, (2014, September, 23): "Indian higher education at a crossroad", DNA.

Notes

1. Choudaha, Rahul (2014-05-09). "Three Solutions for Reforming Indian Higher Education Dr Education: Global Higher Education Research". *www.dreducation.com*.
2. "*Higher Education*,(18 July 2011) National Informatics Centre, Government of India". Education.nic.in.
3. Agarwal, Pawan (2007-04-01). "Higher Education in India: Growth, Concerns and Change Agenda". *Higher Education Quarterly*. ISSN 1468-2273
4. Ranjan Ravi, Naveen (2015). "Structure and Organisation of Higher Education in India : A Macro-Perspective" (PDF). *Indian Journal of Educational Studies : An Interdisciplinary Journal*
5. Chitnis, Suma (Feb 3, 2000). "Higher Education in India". *Black Issues in Higher Education*.
6. Jayaram, N. (2007). "India". *International Handbook of Higher Education*. Springer International Handbooks of Education. Springer, Dordrecht. pp. ISBN 9781402040115.

Chapter-16

Higher Education Quality-Need of Reforms

Dr. Thanneeru Sujatha,

Abstract

Education is the basic human right for development. Education should be treated with profound seriousness is gaining knowledge, skills and academic excellence. According to John Dewey "Education is not preparation for life education is life itself". India's higher education system is the third largest in the world. The main governing body at the tertiary level is the University Grants Commission [UGC] which enforces its standards, advices the government. Over the last two decades India has remarkably transformed its higher education. The 12th plan focused in improving quality of state institution, to revamp financial aid programs, to inter link expansion, equality and excellence. The present paper is mainly focused in the higher education system, the quality of higher education system from the different stake holder's policies and reforms to increase enrollment and quality reforms by critical appraisal. The findings are drawn from the current higher education reforms gaps and lacunas. The conclusions are drawn from the findings.

Keywords: *Higher Education, Quality and Reforms.*

Higher education

In India higher education starts after the 10 + 2 which is very complex. It includes universities, colleges, polytechnics etc are in diverge streams which each stream is directly monitored by an apex body, indirectly control by ministry of Human resource development. In India there are 49 central universities maintained by union government. The engineering education and business schools are monitored and accredited by the All India Council for Technical education (AICTE), Medical education is monitored and accredited by the Medical Council of India (MCI), Agriculture education and research monitored by the Indian Council for Agricultural research, National Council for Teacher Education (NCTE) controls all the teacher training institutions in the country.

Higher education system the challenges of global competencies, equity, quality and access created a resource crunch. As a result the privatization of higher education was emerged. privatization within the government higher education institutions created the self financing courses, converting government aided private institution into private self financing institutes are emerged in higher education with and without recognition of the government. Due to this the quality of the higher education is get affected by mushrooming the privatisation of higher education. The quality of higher education is get affected by measures like high cost of education, food facility, inadequate infrastructure, exploitation, disparity in access, lack of transparency etc.

To portray the status of higher education in the country, Ministry of Human Resource Development has endeavoured to conduct a All India Survey on Higher Education (AISHE) since 2010-11. The survey is based on some quality parameters such as teachers student enrollment programs examination results education finance infrastructure and indicators of educational development such as institution density gross enrolment ratio pupil teacher ratio gender parity index.

Key results of the AISHE 2017-18

1. There are 903 universities, 39050 colleges and 10011 stand alone institutionalized on AISHE web portal out of them 882 universities, 38061 colleges and 9090 stand alone institutions have responded during the survey. 285 universities are affiliating, 343 universities are privately managed, 357 universities are located in rural areas.
2. Gross enrolment ratio(GER) in higher education in India is 25.8 percent which is calculated for 18 to 23 years of age group. GER for male population is 26.3 percent and females is 25.4 percent, for scheduled caste it is 21.8 percent and scheduled Tribes it is 15.9 percent as compared to the nation GER of 20 5.8 percent.
3. Pupil Teacher Ratio (PTR) in universities and colleges is 30 percent regular mode enrollment where as PTR for universities its constituent units is 20 for regular mode.
4. In 2017 more males received PhD degrees in the science stream overall 34000 students awarded PhD degree in 2017, 20 179 to males and 142 21 to females.
5. Gender Parity Index (GPI) A ratio of proportional representation of female and male has improved from 0.86 to 0.94 to the corresponding period.
6. While there are just 9.3 percent of colleges inclusively for girls there are 15 women exclusive universities across 10 states.

This information from AISHE will not help government map areas where there is lack of teachers but also analyse the quality of faculty employed in colleges and universities. According to the AISHE survey the quantitative improvement is observed in higher education but global rankings in world universities is under in the crisis.

UGC apex body of higher education.

UGC in the apex body along with the All India Council for Technical education, The National Council for Teachers Education and the Distance Education council, regulates universities and colleges across India. UGC was set in 1953 a statutory body through an Act of parliament in 1956. The UGC in apex regulatory body for higher education but has after become mired in tuof wars with technical education (AICTE), autonomous institutes like IIT and diploma awarding like IIMs. The UGC is responsible for providing grants to universities, colleges, researchers supposed to co-ordinate university education maintain university standards, monitoring and advising in higher education etc. By increasing number of universities the apex body UGC do not cope to maintain quality standards and monitoring in higher education institutes. The AICTE and UGC bodies the higher education are successful in developing the higher quantitatively rather than qualitatively keeping in view of recruitment faculty promoting research and to revise curriculum.

NAAC National Assessment and Accreditation Council

Quality maintenance and proportion of standards of higher education the UGC established the National Assessment and Accreditation Council (NAAC) in 1994. NAAC assessment is the combination of self evaluations and peer review based on methodology line with international trend. NAAC impact on institutions in all aspects of functioning such as pedagogical, managerial and administrative on the grounds of maintaining quality. Need based programes, Curricular reforms, student support services and learning resources were greatly improved in higher education due to NAAC impact. NAAC influences the management on same issues like faculty work load, supporting research culture motivating the faculty for development inter personal relation etc.

The impact of NAAC could also be seen in unpleasant ways that in emphasizing institutional unique ness is copied from top bracket institutions which effects the diversity among the institutions. In some times the assessment report seems to be used for purposes. That may not be appropriate to he intended out comes. Apart from the Quality consequences NAAC faces new challenges like methodological issues and implementation of polices. The impact of NAAC assessment in funding decision is also not clear and assessment in linked with basic funding (development grant) may not be appropriate. The stake holders have started expressing that more tangible out come from the NAAC on shaping funding policy. Keeping in view of aspects effects the quality indicator in higher education institutes.

Depending on the parent scenario of apex and statutory bodies of higher education need lot of reforms in the name of new regulatory bodies which enhances the quality in academic standards of higher education institutions. In earlier the UGC and other related bodies are regulated the higher education in granting funds and academic standards with the limited number of institutions. Due to the globalization, access of higher education for divergent students increases the enrolment in higher education institutions quantitatively but the quality is decreasing such as low and unskilled graduate production, low quality academic research, inadequacy infrastructure, privatization, autonomy, unskilled technical graduate production, Poor quality of curriculum, irrelevant curriculum, shortage of teaching faculty, less collaboration of higher education institutes with industries and low employability of graduates etc are engaged.

Keeping in the view of short comings from the present regulatory bodies in the realm of higher education the human resource development (HRD) ministry has prepared draft act to replace the present regulatory bodies with a new regulator for higher education in the country in an effort to improve academic standards quality in education and crack down on institutions with low academic standards. That is Higher Education Commission of India (HECI) Act 2018. Under the new law the country's apex regulator of higher education institutions will have the powers to enforce academic standards in higher education institutes. It gives authorization for granting degrees, perceive curricula and infra structure. It makes accreditation in mandatory for all institutions in higher education by 2022. This commission will be tasked with specifying learning outcomes for higher education courses and prescribe standards of teaching assessment research.

The provisions from HECI (Higher Education Commission of India).

1. It proposes to replace the (UGC) University Grants Commission
2. To provide more autonomy and facilitate holistic and harmonious growth of the higher education
3. It proposes clear separation academic and grant giving functions.
4. The academic functions include from HECI

Promoting the quality of instruction

Maintenance of academic standards

Higher Education Regulation Agency (March 2017)

1. The HEERA should be able to address the problems like infrastructural development of newly established universities and promotion of research providing fund and proper environment.
2. It should be able to create more transparency in the administrative functioning of colleges and universities without hampering their autonomy.
3. Revising curriculum periodically.
4. HEERA fulfils its role in helping socially and economically backward students. Regulating technical and non-technical institutions.

Appraisal

With close observations in the higher education present regulatory bodies, the other stake holders and the new upcoming higher education commission of India the report of All India Survey on higher education (2017),Higher Education Empowerment Regulatory Agency (HEERA) reveals that, a tremendous reforms are needed in the higher education system to raise academic standards and quality of the higher education. Due to the multiple regulators, galloping growth of education sector, privatization, low quality with deteriorating standards needs reforms in higher education system.

Reform Likely to Needed in Higher Education

1. Areas need to reform: Social Diversities Including gender and location aspects may be taken in to consideration for the references of higher education.
2. Accountability credibility remains a priority in quality of higher education should be established through quality monitoring the higher education institutes
3. Quality in teaching: National assessment and accreditation council reports that 68 percent of institutions in India are of middle or poor quality. This is due to ad-hoc appointment, low pay scale, inadequate teacher training, under graduates as teachers deteriorate the quality of higher education. This has to be regulated by rigid norms in faculty recruitment.

4. Vacancies must be fill up in institution: nearly 35 percent of professors posts and 46 percent of assistant professors posts out of total sanctioned strength remain vacant across the country. This situation need be corrected by fill up the vacancies by the qualified personnel with proper channel.
5. Financing: Enough financing is needs to raise academic standards with enough infrastructure and physical facilities.
6. Privatization: Privatization of higher education causes scanty standards and quality which leads unskilled production. This phenomena must be regulated strictly by accreditation process.
7. Curriculum: There is no correlation between the curriculum taught and industry requirements which renders graduates in unskilled.
8. Initiating foreign educational institutions: The present regulatory standards prevents the foreign education institutes in the country and it leads to lack of competitiveness in curriculum and pedagogy.
9. Over regulation by regulators: Over regulation deterred new institutions from opening campuses the legible autonomy is need to regulate the institutes to open the new campuses.
10. Academic research: The research wing in every institute must be accelerated by competent faculty in a innovative way which open new avenues of knowledge to cope with intellectual standards.
11. Political interference: Undue political interference by subjecting universities to political and partisan pressures and lack of national consenson in dealing with such situations.
12. Technology oriented facilities i.e., E-libraries, Laboratory, Computers, Net, Esat facilities Etc. Are must be provided.

The above mentioned reforms will help in improving access quality to higher education and bridge socio-economic divides across communities and ensure the quality education.

Suggestions

1. There is a need to implement creative and transformational approach From to secondary to higher education to make globally more relevant and competitive.
2. In higher education institutes industrial co-operations must be their for the improvement and design curriculum providing expert lectures, internships, live projects, career counselling and placements.

3. Higher Education Institutes exchange students, Faculty exchange programs and other collaborations with higher quality international institutes to establish quality, reputation and credibility.

Conclusion

In this paper I presented the present Situation of higher education by identifying gaps such as lack of quality research, Problems of infra structure, Shortage of faculty in the perspective of quality education. The present apex bodies like UGC, AICTE, NCTC, NAAC and other regulatory bodies approaching their own methodological way with minimal collaboration and constructive method learning a kind of deterioration in the quality of education. Privatization of higher education of produces scanty standards of quality in education. The AISHE highlights the state of higher education through several quality indicators given to the scope to develop new insights such as single regulatory body i. e. Higher education commission of India and HEERA i.e. higher Education Empowerment Regulatory body. These are mainly focussed quality in higher education institutes by raising academic standards. An appraisal of the present higher education body regulatory body monitoring keeping in view of present and upcoming of regulatory bodies. The needed reforms are highlighted in the quality perspective of higher education institutes.

References

1. All India Survey On Higher Education (2017-18).
2. All India Survey On higher Education (2016-17).
3. Ministry of Human Resources development, dpt of Higher Education New Delhi (2017).
4. Higher Education IN India –Wikipedia.
5. Insights in to Editorial reform 101:on Higher education (July-3-2016) Insights IAS.
6. Jish K. V. (2015)The role of NAAC for Quality Assurance in higher education Volume-4 issue online ISSN 2277-1182.
7. Nayanathara Narayanan (2015 April 7) Whether the UGC higher education .
8. Neelam Pandey (2018 June 28) HRD ministry, Hindusthan Times.
9. Priyanka Nagrale (2015) higher education in India Issues And challenges.
10. Rimvy Das Labanauseis, romu L Das Ginevierus (2017) Roll of stake holders leading to development of higher Education services.
11. Sampath Kumar (2012)" recent reforms in education in India achievement and unfinished tasks" IRJC Volume 1, ISSN 2277 3630.
12. Younis Ahmad Sherkh (2017) higher in India Challenges And Opportunities, Volume 8 Nos ISSN 2222-1785, Journal of education and practice.

Chapter-17

Quality Concerns in Indian Higher Education: Challenges and Opportunities

Ms. Shivani Seth,

Abstract

Education is the backbone of a nation and higher education occupies the apex of edifying pyramid. The quality of human resources normally depends upon the quality of the education in that country. Higher Education should be transformed to the needs of the time and changing global scenario. It provides an opportunity to vitally reflect upon the social, economic, cultural, moral and spiritual issues being faced by humanity. India possesses a highly developed higher education system which offers facility of education and training in almost all aspects of academic, creative and intellectual areas such as humanities, agriculture, engineering, medicine, dentistry, law, commerce and management, etc. India has world's third largest higher educational system, next to China and United States. India needs more efficient and educated people to drive our system forward. But now various indigenous institutions of international repute, have initiated providing world class higher education in India in administrative, science and technical spheres. The increasing youth population can be a great asset if potential employability is brought to fruition. Conversely, if we fail to provide education and employment, then it will open a downside gate for Indian economy. Education is an essential tool for achieving sustainability. The objective of this paper is to examine the key challenges that India is currently facing in higher education and it also focuses on those opportunities that will be created after improvement in the quality of higher education.

Keywords: *Higher Education, Education System, Universities, Quality Education, Global Scenario, Issues, Challenges, Youth Population.*

Introduction

Education is one of the basic needs for human development and to escape from poverty. It is necessary for national development and a prosperous society. That's why education has been given importance in

India since ancient times. Takshashila, Vikramshila, and Nalanda University were some world famous academic institutions, where quality laden higher education was provided. But modern education has been introduced in India since the colonial era of British. Wood's dispatch of 1854 is considered to be "The Magna Carta of English Education in India". Governor General Assent on bills in 1857 for establishment of Universities led to the establishment of Universities at Calcutta, Bombay and Madras. Thus from 1857 onwards a large number of Universities and Colleges were started in India. As of February 2017 there are 789 universities and 37,204 colleges are in India. At present India's higher education system is the world's third largest higher education system in terms of students, next to China and the United States. With the passage of time vast academics infrastructure has been developed in India, but it has fulfilled only quantitative level. If we saw the Indian higher institutions in globally acceptable qualitative standard, it's far away from achieving it.

Quality in higher education is a multi-dimensional, multilevel, and a dynamic concept. Ensuring quality in higher education is amongst the foremost challenges being faced in India today. However, Government is continuously focusing on the quality education. Still Large number of colleges and universities in India are unable to meet the minimum requirements laid down by the UGC and our universities are not in a position to mark its place among the top universities of the world.

Meaning of Quality in higher Education

Quality of higher education can be defined in multiple ways. Dimensions of higher education quality are express by quality of students, faculty credentials, academic features, and administrative supports (Akareem & Hossain, 2012; Ashraf et. al., 2009). First students' qualification and their background, according to Akareem and Hossain, (2012), contribute significantly to defining the quality of education. Individual characteristics like age, research interests, previous results, perception pattern, family background, and income are important contributors to the perception of education quality. These authors show that environmental factors such as social, economic and cultural influences can also play a vital role. Second, qualifications of teaching staff are found to be one of the most important factors affecting the perception of education quality. Third, an important aspect of education quality is identified by academic factors within the universities. Lastly, the administration system of a university will also determine how well a projected plan will be implemented to ensure the quality of education.

Quality Challenges in Indian higher Education

The overall scenario of higher education in India does not match with the global Quality standards. Hence, there is enough justification for an increased assessment of the Quality of the country's educational institutions. Traditionally, these institutions assume that Quality could be determined by their internal resources, viz., faculty with an impressive set of degrees and experience detailed at the end of the institute's admission brochure, number of books and journals in the library, an ultra-modern campus, and size of the endowment, etc., or by its definable and assessable outputs, viz., efficient use of resources, producing uniquely educated, highly satisfied and employable graduates.

The role of higher education in the emerging scenario of globalization, democratic values and competitive and knowledge based economy is very crucial and multifaceted for any country in general and in India in particular. For this, it is necessary that higher education should be qualitative as well as quantitative also. But in India there are many gaps in Indian higher education system which can create challenges in front of higher education in India. These challenges are as follows:-

- In higher education, India has a low rate of enrolment i.e. gross enrolment ratio (GER), at only 19%. As we compared to china and Brazil GER which is 26% and 36% respectively.
- NASSCOM-Mac Kinsey Report 2005 has said that not more than 15 percent of graduates of general education and 25-30 per cent of Technical Education are fit for employment.
- Indian higher education is facing with the problem of poor quality of curriculum. In most of the higher educational institutes curriculum is out-dated and irrelevant.
- Shortage of Faculty and High Student-Faculty Ratio used to see in Indian academic Institutions. In most of the state and central universities more than 30% of faculty positions are lying vacant.
- Lack of Quality Research work is also a big issue in Indian higher education. There is no shortage of funding for the top Indian Institutions such as IITs, IIMs and other institutes of national importance. However, budget for the Research is not under spent due to the insufficient good quality research work. Due to the limited focus on Research and Internationalization, very few Indian higher educational institutes are globally recognized.
- Number of Research papers published in India has increased continuously for the past few decades but reflected in low citation

impact if compared with other countries like Germany, United States, France and China.

- Presently there is a very less collaboration of higher educational institutes with industries.
- Low employability of graduates is one of the major problems in India. Only a small proportion of Indian graduates are considered employable. Placement outcome also drop significantly as we move away from the top institutes.
- Inadequate Infrastructure and Facilities is also a big problem in Indian higher education. Apart from the highly recognized higher educational institutes in India most of the colleges and universities lack in the basic and high-end research facilities. Many institutes are running without proper infrastructure and basic facilities like library, hostels, transport, sports facility etc. which is desirable to rank the quality institution.

The given points have shown the major setbacks which affect the quality in higher education. In 2007, our former Prime Minister Shri Manmohan Singh Ji has stated on our higher education.

"Our university system is, in many parts, in a state of disrepair...In almost half the districts in the country, higher education enrollments are abysmally low, almost two-third of our universities and 90 percent of our colleges are rated as below average on quality parameters... I am concerned that in many states university appointments, including that of vice-chancellors, have been politicised and have become subject to caste and communal considerations, there are complaints of favoritism and corruption."

Opportunities of Quality Higher Education in India

If Indian government and the other educational bodies such as National Assessment and Accreditation Council (NAAC), All India Council of Technical Education (AICTE), etc. focus to make sure the quality in higher education, India can achieve many opportunities such as:

- According to Indian Census report 2011, two third of Indian population are youth. This 'Demographic Dividend' can be beneficial for India, if we provide qualitative higher education to all Indian youths.
- Qualitative higher education imparts knowledge, develops the student's ability and also gives him/her a wider perspective of the world around. After getting quality higher education Indian

Diasporas can play better role in world wide. It will help Indian government to fulfill its national interest on international level.

- If demand of Indian skilled worker will increase globally, they will send more money to their Indian families as remittance. In this condition, our foreign currency reserve will also increase.
- Quality in higher education becomes input to the growth and development of industry and also seen as an opportunity to participate in the development process of the individual through a flexible education mode.
- Qualitative higher education is also essential for social cohesion and to empower the country's youth.
- Gap between demand and supply will also minimize by quality improvement in higher education.
- Education may become a source of employment and it will help eradication of poverty.
- Qualitative higher education will also help in women empowerment.

Initiatives taken by the Indian Government to Promote Quality in Indian Higher Education

- The Central Government has launched a scheme called Rashtriya Uchchtar Shiksha Abhiyan (RUSA) is an initiative which aims at providing strategic funding to eligible state higher educational institutes. The central funding is norm based and outcome dependent. The silent objectives of RUSA include improving overall quality of state institutions by ensuring conformity to prescribed norms and standards and adopting accreditation as a mandatory quality insurance framework, ensuring reforms in affiliation, academic and examination systems, ensuring adequate availability of quality faculty, creating an enabling atmosphere for research and innovation and ensuring reforms in affiliation.
- A project has been taken up to made a national digital library of eBooks on various subjects and topics and another set up through which highly qualified faculty of centrally sponsored institutions like IITs, IIMs and central universities would offer online courses free of cost.
- Another special scheme called "Udaan" for girl students has launched by the Central government. Under this scheme mentoring and scholarship will be provided to enable meritorious girl

students to transit from schools to technical education without any difficulty and also to promote teaching and learning of mathematics and science at senior secondary school level by providing free resources. The focus of the project is to overcome the low enrolment ratio of girl students in prestigious technical institutions and enable them to receive special incentives and support so that they can join these institutions and go on to take leadership roles in the future.

- Another interesting step is the launching of a mission named after freedom fighter and educationist Pandit Madan Mohan Malviya to build a strong professional cadre of teachers by addressing all the issues relating to teachers, teaching, teacher preparation, professional development, curriculum design, design and development of more effective pedagogy and better assessment and evaluation methodologies.
- The Central Government has also launched a scheme called Unnat Bharat Abhiyan for the promotion of technologies from the laboratory to the ground. Under the scheme, higher educational institutes would connect with villages in their neighborhood and address the various problems faced by them. The scheme would particularly look for the solutions for water management, organic farming, renewable energy, infrastructure and livelihood. IIT, Delhi is the coordinating institute of this scheme. About 130 villages have so far been adopted by IITs, NITs across the country under the scheme.
- Rashtriya Avishkar Abhiyan has launched to revive interest in the technology among youth through support for innovative learning based on observations and experimentation. The focus would be on learning outside the classroom through direct interaction with the environment around the educational institutions.
- Global Initiative of Academic Networks (GIAN) is a programme approved by Government of India which is aimed at tapping the talent pool of scientists and entrepreneurs internationally to encourage their engagement with the higher education institutes in India so as to augment the country's existing academic resources, accelerate the pace of quality reform and elevate India's scientific and technological capacity to global excellence. It is an attempt to fulfill the need of a scheme to garner the best international experience into our country's educational system, enable interaction of students and faculty with the best academic and industry

experts from all over the world and also share their experiences & expertise to motivate people to work on Indian problems. It is supposed to catalyse higher education institutions in the country. Initially it includes all the IITs, IIMs, central universities, IISC, IISERs, NITs and IITs.

Suggestions for Improvement in Quality of Higher Education in India

- There should be a multidisciplinary approach in higher education so that students' knowledge may not be the restricted only up to his own subjects.
- Both public and private universities and colleges must be away from the political affiliations and influences.
- Students are expecting specialized courses to be offered so that they get the latest and best in education and they are also industry ready and employable.
- Effective measures will have to be adopted to mobilize resources for higher education. There is also a need to relate the fee structure to the student's capacity to pay for the cost. So that, students at lower economic levels can be given highly subsidized and fully subsidized education.
- There is a need to implement innovative and transformational approach form primary to higher education level to make Indian educational system globally more relevant and competitive.
- Methods of higher education also have to be appropriate to the needs of learning to learn, learning to do, learning to be and learning to become.
- Student-centered education and employment of dynamic methods of education will require from teachers new attitudes and new skills.
- Colleges and Private institutes should set up Internal Quality Assurance Cell and must follow a minimum standard to give degrees. The quality assurance system must be independent of political and institutional interaction and it must have a basis in the legislation.
- Meritorious doctoral students should be recognized through teaching assistantships with stipends over and above the research fellowships Identifying talented, meritorious students and encouraging them through recognition is very important to attract students into research and teaching.

- Examination reforms, gradually shifting from the terminal, annual and semester examinations to regular and continuous assessment of student's performance in learning should be implemented
- Our university libraries have a very good collection of books, but they are all in mess. A library must be online and conducive for serious study.
- Government should promote collaboration between Indian higher education institutes and top International institutes and also generates linkage between national research laboratories and research centers of top institutions for better quality and collaborative research.
- There is a need to focus on the graduate students by providing them such courses in which they can achieve excellence, gain deeper knowledge of subject so that they will get jobs after recruitment in the companies which would reduce unnecessary rush to the higher education.
- Favoritism, money making process should be out of education system etc.
- In higher educational institutes Industrial co-operation must be there for the development of curriculum, organizing expert lectures, internships, live projects, career counseling and placements.

Conclusion

On the basis of above study we may conclude that Education is a process by which a person's body, mind and character are formed and strengthened. It is bringing of head, heart and mind together and thus enabling a person to develop an all round personality identifying the best in him or her. Higher education in India has expanded very rapidly in the last six decades after independence; yet it has so many challenges and limitations like demand-supply gap, lack of quality research, problem of infrastructure and basic facilities, shortage of faculty etc. through which quality of higher education is affected. With the rapid quantitative growth, higher education in India has not been able to attend to the core issue of quality. To make quality, and to center the future requirements in Indian higher education system, there is an urgent need to relook at the Financial Resources, Access and Equity, Quality Standards, Relevance and at the end the Responsiveness.

Bibliography

1. Agarwal, R. et al. (2014). "Higher Education and Quality Improvement: A challenge for India". Indian Journal of Applied Research Vol. 4 (10).

2. Benjamin, J. (2012). "Rejuvenation of Higher Education in India". New Delhi: Gyan Publishing House.
3. Konwar & Chakraborty. (2013). "Higher Education Scenario of the North-Eastern India". Indian journal of Research, vol.-2(3).
4. Kumar, A. & Ambrish. (2015). "Higher Education: Growth, Challenges and Opportunities". International Journal of Arts, Humanities and Management Studies, Vol. 01(2).
5. Monan. J. D. (2015). "Global Perspectives on Higher Education''. New Delhi: Atlantic Publishers & Distributors, Pvt. Ltd.
6. Nandi, R. (2014). "India's Position in the Global Community: With Respect to Higher Education Scenario". International Journal of Educational Planning & Administration, Vol. 4(1).
7. Nexus N. (2016) "Higher Education Opportunities in India", Retrieved from: http://nexusnovus.com/higher-educationopportunities-india, Jul 26, 2013 accessed on 30/07/2016.
8. Ramesh, G. (2013). "Indian Higher Education and the Challenges of Sustainability: An Analytical Note". International Journal of Social Science & Interdisciplinary Research Vol. 2(9).
9. Sunita & Mukta. (2015). "Higher Education towards 21st Century". New Delhi: Anmol Publications, Pvt. Ltd.
10. Sharma, S. & Sharma, P. (2015). "Indian Higher Education System: Challenges and Suggestions". Electronic Journal for Inclusive Education, Vol. 3 (4). Pp.3-4.

Chapter-18

Higher Education Policy in India

Dr. Kamala,

Abstract

The higher education scene in the country is set to experience a dramatic change but the ability of the state universities to cope with this change is extremely doubtful. The success of the new central universities and the proposed national universities will come about at the cost of the state universities, which cater to the majority of students in the country. This article proposes that postgraduate teaching and research in state universities will have to be taken over by the central government to ensure the survival of this important part of the higher education system. Liberalisation of higher education services in India should not be viewed from the point of view of generating revenues but as a strategy to promote the quality of its own higher education system. Further, attracting students from outside for postgraduate study and research opportunities in India will be able to fuel innovation and enterprise in the higher education system.

Keywords: *liberalization, policy reform, India, Economic, GATS, trade in services.*

Of the three factors involved in production – land, labour and capital, it is labour and more particularly the quality of labour that is the key determinant for a country's competitiveness. It is, therefore, not surprising that there is a strong correlation between endowment of skilled labour and the gross domestic product (GDP) per worker across countries. Higher education enhances a country's capacity for participation in an increasingly knowledge based world economy and has the potential to enhance economic growth and reduce poverty.

India with its huge population in the working age group and a large system of higher education has attracted world attention in recent times. There is a sense of euphoria about the Indian success in the IT services and now IT-enabled services. At a recent international exposition on trade in services, the prime minister talked about India becoming a knowledge supplier to the world. Industry leaders, on the other hand, express concerns about the severe shortages of qualified people and unacceptable attrition rates. Most countries are faced with similar problems.

Not only the developing countries, but even the advanced countries are worried about their system of higher education. While, the Europeans lament that their Universities are lagging behind those in the US, the Americans are worried that their academic leadership is threatened by complacency while the rest of the world is catching up fast.

The Chinese who expanded their system of higher education from enrolling merely a 3.82 million students in 1990 to 23 million in 2006 are now faced with massive problems of graduate unemployment.

China's National Development and Reform Commission reported that 60 per cent of China's.

Upcoming university graduates would be unable to find work

Several recent studies in India have revealed that the overall state of Indian higher education is dismal. This poses a severe constraint on the supply of qualified Manpower. While problems have been identified and solutions found, the studies have failed to map the contradictions that exist. Unfortunately, there are far more contradictions in the Indian higher education system than most countries of the world. Based on a recent comprehensive review of the Indian higher education, this article seeks to map these contradictions in Indian higher education. In the face of new developments, it provides some directions for change and suggests that people should have realistic expectations as regards public policy towards this sector. Indian higher education is riddled with many contradictions. It is both large and small. In terms of absolute enrolment (around 11 million students), it is the third largest education system in the world, but in terms of gross enrolment ratio, it is small– just around 11 percent. By taking the universities and colleges together, there are 18,000 higher education institutions in India. This is more than the rest of world taken together. Yet, the number of degree granting institutions is merely 350.

Existing Anomalies

Average enrolment in each institution is around 600. Higher education institutions in the world usually have several thousand students and many hundred teachers. Most institutions in India are very small and many too small to be viable. While undergraduate enrolment is large, enrolment in postgraduate and doctoral programmes is small. A bulk of the enrolment is in the affiliated colleges that have uniform and often outdated curriculum. Higher education courses with occupational focus form less than one-fifth of the total, while three-fourth of the students in the US pursue majors at the undergraduate level that have occupational focus. At the undergraduate level, 35 per cent enrolments in China are in engineering programmes compared to about 12 per cent in India.

While reviewing growth, one sees that over the last two decades private providers of higher education have expanded rapidly, while the number of government institutions and private-aided institutions has remained by and large the same. It is primarily the non-subsidised private institutions that have responded to the demand for new kind of knowledge and skills required in the growing Indian economy that is now closely connected with the rest of the world. A majority of the private institutions offer professional courses and their share exceeds 80 percent in many professional areas.

The small numbers of higher education institutions that are of high quality are government-funded. Their number continues to be very small, while a large expansion has been in sub-standard programmes and non-viable institutions. Industry claims that only about one-fourth of the graduates from the Indian higher education institutions are employable. As a result there are skill shortages despite large graduate unemployment.

The private organised sector in India employs around nine million people (around 2.2 per cent of the total workforce). This is so small that any expectation of it absorbing the large pool of around 3.5 million graduates coming out of the system every year is unreal. In the face of moves towards rightsizing, the public and the government sector (with 20 million people) cannot absorb many more graduates. And finally, for most jobs in the unorganised sector that employs a bulk of the Indian people, higher education qualifications are not essential. Under these circumstances, the problem of graduate unemployment will continue to persist. Higher education expansion will be dictated more by signals from the households and private demand for higher education than by the signals from the job market.

These contradictions continue. Despite very elaborate standards and the existence of many authorities responsible for maintaining standards, the overall standards of higher education have continually deteriorated, thereby reducing the value of an academic degree from India. A survey of the regulatory regimes in different countries in 2005 by The Economist pointed out that while most nations in the world are working towards relaxing norms of statutory control over higher education, India is moving in the reverse direction by imposing a more burdensome regulatory regime. Taking a cue from the US, an accreditation system has been put in place, but being voluntary with no consequences, it has failed to contain the rut in the Indian higher education.

Normally believed to be inexpensive, higher education in India is costly except in centrally funded institutions and those (that do not matter) in Bihar and Uttar Pradesh. A majority of the professional courses are offered by private institutions that depend only on fee income from the students. The government has had plans to raise fees, but the fund allocation mechanism discourages it. Despite very rigid fee caps determined by public authorities, some private unaided institutions have managed to dodge these and charge Exorbitant fees from gullible students. While, the government is concerned about the commercialisation of higher education in India, students continue to be subjected to exploitation by some unscrupulous private providers. Unfortunately students who face such problems have no recourse. Similar contradictions have been seen in public investment on higher education. The government spends merely 0.37 per cent of the country's gross domestic product (GDP) on higher education compared to 1.41 per cent in the US, 1.07 per cent in the UK. Even China spends 0.50 per cent of its GDP on higher education, considerably more than India. Only countries such as Japan and Korea, where more than 80 per cent of students are in largely unsubsidised private institutions, is government spending at a level similar to India's.

Contradictions in Policy

Not only is the level of public funding small, allocation too is skewed. A majority of the central government funding that accounts for around one-fourth of the total government funding goes to a small number of (around 130 out of 18,000) institutions in the country. Other institutions have either no government funding or have a much lower level of funding per institution and per student than the privileged few central institutions. Government funding is largely institution based and the fund allocation mechanisms obsolete, which in turn perpetuates the status quo.

Despite low spending on higher education in terms of GDP, the relative effort of the government in funding higher education in India is significantly higher than most advanced countries and China. The relative effort measured in terms of amount spent per student as a percentage of GDP per capita is 83 per cent for India, compared to 53 per cent in China, 26 per cent in the US, 31 per cent in the UK, 17 per Cent in Japan and merely 5 per cent in Korea. In the face of this reality and with competing demand from other sectors, any talk of increasing public funding for higher education to the level of around 1.5 percent is ridiculous. To reach this level, additional money required for higher education would exceed the entire subsidy bill of the government.

Private funding for higher education that is perceived to be small is as much as 50 percent in India. It exceeds private funding in most advanced countries. Despite high and increasing cost of higher education, financial support for students is almost non-existent. Only about 2 to 3 per cent students (mostly from middle income families) avail of education loans compared to 85 per cent in the UK and 77 percent in the US.

Though there are many schemes for providing financial aid to the poor students, the amount given is awfully low and procedures to secure loans are cumbersome. While, the US spends nearly $ 80 billion on higher education annually mostly in the form of student aid, India has allocated only about $ 3 million in 2005/06 for its flagship merit-cum-means scholarship scheme.

Because of its many inherent contradictions, it is not surprising that public policy on higher education in India is marred with inconsistencies. There are innumerable committees, commissions and reports and little concrete action. Public discourse is often based on rhetoric. The government is uneasy about market forces, yet it is the market forces that are increasingly shaping higher education in India. The government adopts an ambivalent stand on the growth of private institutions, yet with the interests of the ruling class and private promoters aligned with each other, private higher education continues to flourish.

The current debate on opening up the Indian higher education to foreign providers initiated by the ministry of commerce by releasing the consultation paper, 'Higher Education in India and GATS: An Opportunity' fails to capture many of the above contradictions. It seems to suggest that globally reputed institutions like Harvard, Oxford and MIT are just waiting to enter the Indian higher education sector. It goes on to say that liberalisation would increase the number of foreign students in India and retain the Indian students who go abroad thereby saving billions of dollars for India in foreign exchange. Many people take a contrary view and feel that foreign providers would hurt the political and cultural sensitivities of the people in India. It is disappointing to see that rather than drawing up a concrete road map for giving a new shape to the Indian higher education in the face of new realties, the debate in India continues to be based on its unrealistic potential and unfounded apprehensions. It needs to be realised that cross-border activities in higher education are large and growing regardless of General Agreement on Trade in Services (GATS).

The negotiations under GATS merely tend to bind the autonomous liberalisation that a country undertakes to achieve its national policy objectives. The current debate is an opportunity to define these national policy objectives in the context of an increasingly interdependent world and thereby develop a realistic plan of action. While many countries in the world have adopted pragmatic policies to serve their purposes, in India, we continue to be caught up in unnecessary debate. Singapore and Malaysia have attracted high quality higher education institutions from many advanced countries. This has augmented their domestic capacity of quality higher education serving their own citizens.

They have also been able to attract a large number of foreign students. From almost no foreign students a few years ago, Singapore and Malaysia now have over 70,000 and 30,000 foreign students respectively. China hosts more than 1, 40,000 foreign students. The number of foreign students in India continues to be in the range of 15,000 to 18,000, which in fact declined during the 1990s. The three Asian countries – Singapore, Malaysia and China – are significant global players in the cross border higher education attracting many reputed universities from advanced countries and hosting a large pool of globally mobile students. China has been gradually opening its door to foreign providers over the last decade. Today, the education authorities in China have approved proposals from more than 1,400 foreign higher education institutions to operate in China. While the main foreign motivation is commercial, the foreign institutions and governments have other motivations as well. Most of the foreign academic institutions are not the top institutions in their own countries, though Yale and Cornell in the US and several reputed Australian institutions are now working in China with a variety of motivations – including providing opportunities for their own students and faculty to learn about China because of its growing importance. There is no reason to believe that motivations would be otherwise in case of India.

Regulatory Credibility

A proper and predictable regulatory regime would see higher education facilities being set up by many foreign providers in India either on their own or in partnership with domestic providers. Though, most of these are likely to be less-reputed institutions from abroad, this would augment the capacity of the Indian higher education and may even help India to get more foreign students.

An effective system of registration has to be put in place to prevent unapproved foreign institutions from operating in India and to ensure that students are exploited. Good quality foreign institutions could also enter if proactively persuaded and facilitated. In terms of export potential, India can attract a larger number of foreign students. Higher education institutions here could also set up their campuses abroad. There are however many practical limitations and several contradictions in policy that need to be sorted out. It is however estimated that India could at best generate only about 1 to 2 per cent of the overall expenditure on higher education through export provision.

Liberalisation of higher education services in India should therefore not be viewed from the point of view of generating revenues, but as a strategy to promote the quality of its own higher education system, and as a means of creating a multicultural ambience on its campuses so as to promote diversity and international goodwill. By attracting bright students for postgraduate and research in India, it will be able to fuel innovation and enterprise in the higher education system. It is now increasingly clear that the growth on Indian higher education will be largely through private provision. Private institutions now compete with each other for students. Some of them will enter into a variety of arrangements with foreign institutions with a view to enhance their prestige and entice students.

It would be increasingly difficult for any government authority to regulate this trend. With increased and varied opportunities available within the country, many students with capacity to pay would prefer to study in India rather than go abroad to less reputed institutions. Though highly reputed institutions abroad will continue to attract both bright and fee paying students from India. Education sector and growing global interaction and interconnectedness will see several interesting developments in the cross-border activities in higher education in India. Many of these developments are inevitable and not subject to government regulation. Further, a look at the domestic higher education provision in the global context is important because of its direct link with large and growing trade in professional services. Estimated at more than $ 300 billion annually, India has a small share.

These are manpower intensive services and the changing demography suggests that India has a huge potential. According to the United Nations, over the next five years, India will contribute an additional 44 million to the global labour pool. During this time, the US workforce will expand by 10 million, Europe's will not increase and Japan's will decline by three million. In this scenario, it is important that people in India have access to high quality higher education and training system whether within the country or abroad. For the greater acceptability of the Indian graduates in the global labour markets, standards of Indian higher education have to be benchmarked with the global Standards. This would give the Indians and India a distinctive competitive edge and public policy needs to be geared to this. Unfortunately, over the last two decades, unplanned and chaotic growth of higher education has resulted in deterioration of overall standards lowering the value of an academic degree from India.

Restoring the credibility of higher education in India is therefore utmost important. For global recognition of its qualifications, India needs to work towards the harmonisation of its academic standards with internationally accepted practices. While the domestic regulation must be investment-friendly and forward-looking, the loopholes in the existing system need to be plugged to enhance the credibility of an academic qualification from India. In sum, the country requires forward looking policies on higher education. There is a need for investment both from public and private sources in Indian higher education. The private sources could even be foreign sources. The country needs an environment for more domestic as well as foreign competition.

This would require a review of the regulatory arrangements and adopting a pragmatic approach. A greater clarity is required on what serves national policy objectives best. And finally, public policy has to be rooted in the realities of Indian higher education and take into account its many contradictions. Even with all this, the expectations have to be realistic.

Beginning with the Ambani-Birla Report (2000) during the National Democratic Alliance (NDA) rule, Sam Pitroda's Knowledge Commission Report and Yashpal Committee Report on "Renovation and Rejuvenation of Higher Education" submitted during the United Progressive Alliance (UPA)-I and UPA-II governments respectively, essentially upheld and extended the neoliberal agenda in education. With a view to legitimise and intensify its neoliberal assault, the UPA government has now introduced in Parliament the following four bills:

(i) The Foreign Educational Institutions (Regulation of Entry and Operations) Bill, 2010.

(ii) The Educational Tribunals Bill, 2010.

(iii) The Prohibition of Unfair Practices in Technical Educational Institutions, Medical Educational Institutions and Universities Bill, 2010.

(iv) The National Accreditation Regulatory Authority for Higher Educational Institutions Bill, 2010.

At least two more bills in the same vein, including one on establishing the much hyped National Commission for Higher Education and Research for facilitating single-window clearance for private/foreign universities are reportedly in the offing. The government has now instituted the policy of public-private partnership (PPP) in all sectors of education – a policy designed to shift public resources to the corporate (including foreign) capital and, at the same time, allowing unregulated profiteering by hiking up fees. This neoliberal measure is also evident in the farcical Right to Education Act, 2009. We further recognise that the hidden agenda of providing low interest loans to the students is again to facilitate the growth of expensive private/foreign educational institutions, rather than to help the students. In the USA.

Entry of Foreign Universities

Another way of augmenting facilities for higher education is the entry of Universities of the UK, USA into India. They could set up branches or facilities to enable Indian students to pursue their course obviating the necessity of going abroad. In the beginning like the entry of multinationals, the entry of foreign universities was also looked at with suspicion. But now the benefits of such entry of Universities from abroad are increasingly recognized.

Not only would they augment the facilities, they would bring new and higher standards and pose a challenge to our institutions of higher education which have been suffering from stagnation. They could introduce new ideas of course content and methods. They would also stimulate research. The foreign University Bill would facilitate the process. A variant of the branches of foreign Universities is the setting up courses in Indian institutions in collaboration with foreign Universities. Everything can be said in favour of such partnership it will have a synergical effect on the progress of higher education in the country.

Conclusion

India, one of the world's largest economies, has made enormous strides in its economic and social development during the past two decades, but India can do much more to leverage its strengths in today's knowledge-based global economy. According to the National Knowledge Commission (NKC) 2006, the country needs a massive expansion of opportunities for higher education, with 1500 Universities. Nationwide, that would enable

India to attain a gross enrolment ratio of at least 15 per cent by 2015. The proportion of our population, in the age group 18-24 that enters the world of higher education is around 7 per cent, which is only one half the averages for Asia. The opportunities for higher education, in terms of the number of places in universities are simply not enough in relation to our needs. What is more the quality of higher education in most of our universities requires substantial India has about 350 universities this number is simply not enough with reference to our needs in higher education, or in comparison with china which has authorized the creation of 1250 new universities in the last three years. Yet, some of our universities are much too large, for ensuring academic standards and providing good governance.

We need to create more appropriately scaled and more nimble universities. The greatest challenge perhaps is arriving at an appropriate model that will be able to simultaneously address the questions of quality on one hand and provide access on the other. The NKC recommends that we need a much larger number of universities, say 1500 nationwide by 2015 and also smaller universities which are responsive to change and easier to manage. The NCHER should be a guardian on behalf of the universities and should protect them from encroachment by state and central government. In order for this to be possible, it is necessary that the universities and academia at large have ownerships and stakes in the proposed NCHER. It goes without saying that the governance structure in the universities needs to be a hierarchical process of a master servant relationship, where universities are perceived to be the recipients of orders from any centralized bureaucry finally, we must note that compliance and participation of state governments is essential for the effective fulfilment of this desire, this will be possible through enabling both the provisions in the NCHER bill and the regulator being the empowered authority to deal with states on matters of central funding to states in the areas related to higher education.

Reference

1. Batra, Poonam 2009 *Teacher Empowerment*; the Education Entitlement social Transformation traverse Contemporary Education Dialogue pp 121-57.
2. Behram, J.R (1974): Towards a New International Economic Order (Paris: Atlantic Institute for international Affairs), Bhattacharya, Pinaki, "The World According to GATT", Sunday Mail, Dec. 26, 1993-Jan. 1, 1994.
3. Chakravarty, Nikhil (1993): "Reflections on GATT Debate", Mainstream, Vol. 32, No.6, Dec.25.
4. Chowdhry, N.K and Aggarwal, J.C (1993): Dunkel Proposals: Implications for India and Third World (New Delhi: Shipra Publications.

5. Das, Arvind N (1993): "Why GATT has become a Four-letter word", The Times of India, December 12.
6. Datt, Ruddar and Sundharam K.P.M (2000): "Indian Economy", (New Delhi: S.Chand and Company Ltd.).
7. Debroy, Bibek (1994): "India and the GATT", Economic Growth and Social Change", March 24.(Deep and Deep).
8. Dhar, P.K (1997): Indian Economy- Its Growing Dimensions (New Delhi: Kalyani Publishers).
9. Dr. Gupta K.R. (Ed.) "GATT Accord and India – A Critical Analysis of Results of the Uruguay Round of Multilateral Trade Negotiations and their implications for India, Atlantic Publishers and Distributors, New Delhi '95.
10. Drucker, P (1986): "The Changed World Economy", Foreign Affairs, Vol 4.
11. Dubey, Muchkund (1992): "Political Economy of Uruguay Round of Trade Negotiations", Mainstream, May 30,
12. Economic Political Weekly March 27,2010 vol xlv no13
13. Edutracks May vol 9-no9 2010.
14. Eglin.M (2003): "the general Agreement on Trade in Services", (GATS) Background Note, Occasional Papers No 4, Geneva: Friend rich Ebert sifting.
15. Fisher, W. and Ponniah, T. (2004) *Another World is Possible*, London and New York: Zed Books.
16. Fredrikssen, U. (2003) GATS, Education and Teacher Union Politics, European Education Research Association Conference, Hamburg: 16-19th September. Gill, Stephen (1995) Globalisation, Market Civilisation and Disciplinary Neoliberalism. *Millenium*, 24, 2.
17. Gain, Abdul (1987): "GATT and Services Trade", Patriot, March 30.
18. Ganesan A.V (1994): "The GATT Uruguay Round Agreement – Opportunities and Challenges", Rajiv Gandhi Institute for Contemporary Studies, New Delhi.
19. Ghosh, Arun (1996): "Indian Economy under Multinational Siege", Nai Azadi Udgosh, Vol.5 No. 1.
20. Gill, Stephen (1995) Globalisation, Market Civilisation and Disciplinary Neoliberalism. *Millenium*, 24, 2.
21. Hobsbawn, E. (1994). *Age of Extremes: The Short Twentieth Century*, London: Abacus.
22. Hoekman, B. and Martin W. eds (2001): Developing Countries and the WTO, Oxford: Blackwell.
23. Hoekman, B. and Martin, W. (eds). (2001) *Developing Countries and the WTO*, Oxford: Blackwell.
24. Jayantha Bagchi (1995): "WTO (An Indian Perspective)", Eastern Law House, Pvt. Ltd., Calcutta.
25. Jayasuriya, K. (1999). The Rule of Law and Governance in the East Asian State, *Australian Journal of Asian Law*, Vol 1 (2), 107-123.
26. Kapoor, I. (2004) Deliberative democracy and the WTO, Review of International Political Economy, 11 (3), pp. 522-41.

27. Kelsey, J. (2003) *Legal Fetishism and the Contradictions of the GATS*, unpublished paper, School of Law, University of Auckland, New Zealand.
28. Knight, J. (2003). *GATS, Trade and Higher Education Perspective.*
29. Kumar, Ratnesh (2003): WTO (New Delhi: Deep and Deep).
30. Kwa. A (2002): Power Politics and the WTO, London, Zed Books.
31. Mainstream September 25 to Oct 1 2009.
32. Nicholas C. Burbules Globalization and Education –Critical Perspective 2008.
33. Parkinson, Ronald. 2003. 'Planning Ahead for Knowledge Societies'. A presentation at Education India Conference, April.
34. Pawan Agarwal Indian Higher Education Sage publications India pvt ltd 2009.
35. University News, 47 November 23-29 2009.
36. University News, 48 January 04.

Chapter-19

Higher Education in India: Issues, Concerns and New Directions

Dr. S. Venkatesh,

Abstract

Even though present include be challenge to higher education in the precedent, these nearly all fresh calls for reorganization can aggravate a primary modify in higher education. This modify may not occur as a shortest answer to call for superior lucidity and liability, but rather since of the opportunity to mirror on the point of higher education, the role of college and universities in the new millennium, and rising logical study on how people learn. These unlike literatures include not been tied as one in a way that would examine the blow of original transform from the plan level to the institutional level and to the daily live of university and university administrator, faculty and student. At the present the time have approach to make a next signal of institute structure and of brilliance in the field of teaching, study and means construction. We want higher educated citizens who be expert and who can make our wealth forward. When India can offer authority people to the surface exterior planet next we be capable of transport our country beginning a mounting country to an urban country incredibly simply and swiftly.

Introduction

Higher education in India holds immense implication for the expansion of India as a nation. The Government of India in the colobration with the State Government has brought policy initiative to golden policy frame work directorial structure and financial income, though same consequences be emerging in the area of Science and technology, here is no generally pleasure about the outcome of these situations to make the matter to focus his thought towards working on Higher education system in India with special reference to the Telangana State. Objectives of standing include discovery of block hole in the area of policies and direction with a special heart on rising standards.

The methodology basically depends on observational method. The author thoroughly from his skill, teach degree course in several college. Colleges include Government and (Autonomous) affiliated college. 'Value –for- money-audits' is ever more becoming a worry in all public military and higher education is not an omission. ever more, the scrutiny of higher education income and more so financial income be poignant beginning mere 'balancing' of book of accounts and missing documents to value for money audits. Systems of education in every parts of the world are in a state of change with increasing interest in upholding the notions of accountability, value for cash and superior admission. A transformed heart on higher education wherever university search designed for more competent system to lecture to the growing discontent by the recital of higher education systems have been feel in recent years. Reform in almost higher educational context contain be unpaid to the call for to make sure answerability, competence, managerialism as well as to take note of monetarist monetary policy which advocate commoditization of education. The strain on higher education merges themselves to inside and outer military. Outwardly, global military continue to form the higher education setting and internally, the mounting strain from a variety of stakeholders augment the drive for competence in supply operation. globally, government have occupied in frequent reform and initiative calculated to perk up cost efficacy and competence, to augment group of civic services, to turn into results-oriented and resident all ears and to stress tactical trade. School, university, and other education institution now come across remote more challenge and are subjected to extraordinary stage of outer study. Ever more, size of enlightening outcome is a heart component of assess the price accessible in one higher educational scheme. It have be argue to civic price container live describe as the donation completed in the public sector to the monetary, social and ecological well-being of culture or country, and have be usually distinct as what the public is eager to build sacrifice of currency and autonomy to get. The conjecture be base on the idea that communal price be the intervening goal of public sector behavior.

The bearing of higher education in Uganda have to game the outlook of culture and this is ever more not simply a running face but an growing anticipation from the manager of together public and private institution. This paper argue that efficient running of income will make higher education outcome as here resolve live efficient running system. supply administration in this circumstance earnings successfully and competently utilize institutional income to complete goal The paper observe that all the three key area are directly unfair by effective income running. In the circumstance of higher education, instructive institution tender military to a variety of stakeholders which necessitate a wealth of possessions. Efficient operation of cloth, being, corporeal and IT income leads to pleasing outcome and it create belief.

Management of Higher Education

The Indian higher education organization be single of the major such system in the World. It be probable that through the X Five Year map age (2002-07), here resolve live a wonderful weight of figures on this scheme and a great numeral of added student resolve be knock at the door of higher education institution in the country. present be too original challenge of running and directive being face by these institution, which necessitate somber thought, both at the institution in the communal segment and also those in the personal sector now mounting at a speedy pace. As a result, the old structure of management well-known in pre-independent India and functioning through most of the twentieth century are now requisite to feel drastic change. Also, the strain of the society for equity and accommodation cannot be neglected any more.

The novel command below WTO anywhere ability is the cardinal standard of victory in worldwide operation have made it plentifully apparent that the nation should develop its brilliant potential in higher education and guidance services and organize itself to sell overseas the Indian brand of education to distant country. Strategy setting up and embryonic strategy for this task are fairly new for the country. But, this is an occasion which cannot be missed by India, as it offer motivating promise meant for increase of the nation's flair and imagination.

The following five sub-sections cover important aspects of the deliberations, recommendations and action plans of UGC Golden Jubilee

Seminars organized at different Universities in the country:

- **Public/Private Partnership in Higher Education**, at University of Calicut, Kozhikode, Kerala;
- **Governance of higher Education**, at University of Jammu, Jammu, J&K;
- **Access and Equity in Higher Education**, at G.C.D. University, Bilaspur, Chhattisgarh;
- **Export of Higher Education**, at J.N.V. University, Jodhpur, Rajasthan and

- **Policy Planning for Higher Education** under WTO and GATT regimes at North Bengal University, Darjeeling, West-Bengal.
- Economics of Higher Education, at N. E. Hill University, Shillong, Meghalaya.

1.1 Public/Private Partnership

Indian higher education system have undergone enormous development in post-independent India with a countrywide decide to found quite a few Universities, scientific Institutes, Research Institutions and Professional / Non-professional Colleges all more than the country to produce and broadcast facts attached with the noble intention of only if trouble-free access to higher education to the frequent Indian. The Public initiative played a main and scheming role in this phase. Most of the Universities are Public institutions with power to adjust college actions on their campus as well as in their area of control through the affiliate system.

1.2 Governance

It have be experiential that strategy frame is warily designed at the level of the setting up payment, Ministry of Human Resource Development and University Grants Commission. However, the policy is not fully implementing typically since of defective running of the institution of advanced learning. The directorial organizations of the Universities, which are devising in the pre-independence period, seem to be still long-lasting. The new challenge facing the system of higher education in the country cannot be met without a total renovate of the structure of management of higher education institutions. This has become all the more necessary since of globalization, which requires aptitude, capability, make, proposal and novelty at quite a few levels.

1.3 Access and Equity

These days the world economy is experience an extraordinary modifies. New development in knowledge and technology, media revaluation and internationalization of education and the ever going up aggressive setting are revolutionizing the education scene. A pattern shift have be notice in higher education now a days, from 'national education' to 'global education', from 'one time teaching for a few' to 'life long education for all', beginning 'teacher- centric education' to 'beginner centric education'. These changes build new weight and fake clean challenge to the well-known education system and practice in the country.

1.4 Policy Planning for Export

Growing monetary mixing crosswise the World over the past decade have cast confused impact on all the area supporting human life in the mounting country, which constitute about 80 percent of the work force. The so-called structural adjustment in state policy and the new worldwide economic organize include bring about severe stress by no means professed earlier than. There are exhortations to the plan planners of higher education emanate from GATT policy made under WTO formulation e.g. withdrawal of subsidy, summary organize of the State, larger privatization and admission to company cast list, conniving of course to meet the being supply needs of the market in the tainted scenario, and confidence on self-supporting type running.

1.5 Economics of Higher Education

Admission to higher education requirements to be widen in the country, together in the proper system and from end to end other efficient inventive actions, such as a really *open* system and network of Universities. It is now vital on the part of Indian Universities to create their own income to a large extent. This could be done through several method, like raise tuition fee and collecting capitation fee, both of which having severe confines; and others like, launching course for foreign student, obtain contributions from philanthropist, etc., which encompass a good latent.

Recommendations

1. The Governmental control in the Universities has to live summary, thus that the University autonomy and responsibility are strengthening and academic decision is full on merit.
2. New method and actions of fiscal policy have to be devise and shortest intrusion of the business division in the fiscal running of Universities, which is counterproductive, must be clogged.
3. Rustic, town and gender disparity must be kept in mind by strategy maker in setting up and implement the superior education system.
4. Here must live regularity, as remote as probable, in the values of the course, academic calendar and the test system of Universities.
5. Growing of undergraduate bill to a few amount, in talk with undergraduate body and parents' organization.
6. Charge capitation bill and obtain contributions.

7. Introduction well-paid and precise course for distant students.
8. Mounting compassion and calming a prepared society of charitable.

Conclusion

No doubt accurately the three learn quite a few that the existing state of affairs of higher education in India, and the key challenge related to demand – supply gap, enrolment, privatisation etc also indicate that the circumstances of higher education subdivision is not PRAISEWORTHY. However, the key initiative form the government ride supply full solution thinking not ample, therefore the drive of public policy for higher education in India has to be to preserve the higher values of education keeping in pace with developments that gain place in the field of knowledge and technology in true method.

The identical of the debate it is experiential that policy matter are accepted away by experience of western thoughts by over stress completed to illustrate greater advantage from the development in technological world knowing the attention his focused on understanding of foundation and Directive principles of State policy. Need for the Humanization with a superior stress on equally fairness that worry the under fortunate section of the culture as well as women.

References

1. Agrawal, M, (2008): "Education in Third World and India: A Development Perspective". New Delhi, Kanishka Publication, ISBN 81-8457-023-6.
2. National Knowledge Commission, Report to the Nation 2006. New Delhi: National Knowledge Commission, 2007 (cited as NKC 2007) (http://knowledgecommission.gov.in/report2006/default.asp).
3. Uttara Dukkipati, (2010): "Higher Education in India: sustaining long term growth" South Asia Monitor, 141, 01 May.
4. All India Survey on Higher education - Pilot Report, Ministry of Human Resource Development Department of Higher Education Planning, Monitoring & Statistics Bureau, 2011.
5. Higher Education in India: Issues, Concerns and New Directions http://www.ugc.ac.in/pub/heindia.pdf.

Chapter-20

Quality of Research in Higher Education in India

Dr. Akthar Parveen,

Abstract

Research is a systematic investigation of primary and secondary sources to establish facts and reach a new conclusion. It is a careful study of a particular problem following scientific methods. Research enhances knowledge, clarifies confusion, develops a proper understanding of the subject, helps the students to learn methods and procedures create a balance between individual and collaborative work, understand the rationale. Research is important in education to contribute knowledge, for practical improvement and policy formation. The main purpose of research is to get deep into the topic so that something useful can be churned out for the welfare of humanity. But unfortunately, the research work in India is of poor quality because of many reasons. Present paper entitled "Quality of Research in Higher Education in India" aims at finding out the causes of poor quality of research in India and methods to improve the quality in Indian research.

Keywords: *Research, Quality*

Introduction

Human beings are curies by nature. They want to explore the world. Curiosity leads to knowledge, specialization and new technology. Hence research became the source of new invention and discoveries. We can say that research is curiosity codified according to the scientific method.

Research is the application of Scientific methods in the study of problems. It is more structured and systematic process of scientific analysis towards discovery and development of an organized body of knowledge. It is a planned activity to get answers to meaningful questions following a scientific approach. It is the way to find out cause and effect relationships. Research lacks bias and prejudice. It is an impartial logical analysis of facts. Research work leads to generalizations, the formation of principles and theories resulting in prediction and control of consequences.

The purpose of higher education is to prepare the learned and prepared minds for better career opportunities and carry on the research activity to add up the knowledge, make inventions and discoveries to solve the problems of the society and country at large. Unfortunately, the quality of research work in higher educational institutions is very poor. There are many factors affecting the quality of research in India. Let us observe the causes of poor quality of research in India.

Causes of the poor quality of research in India

1. The Indian education system does not emphasize creativity among the children it encourages only superficial study to pass the exam and get good marks and grades. Much emphasis is laid on stereotyped study and examinations. Creativity is snubbed in the classrooms even though the children are hyperactive.
2. There is a lot of difference between the standards of government and private schools. Government institutions lack basic amenities where most of the children with low economic standards study. Huge crowded classroom handled by a single teacher doesn't give any scope for the research-oriented education system. There is no individual attention in the classrooms. The teacher prepares the lesson keeping in view the average students neglecting highly intelligent and poor students.
3. In India, as it is developing country people link education with employment. Hence they concentrate on getting a good job with handsome salary after completing their education. Teaching and learning process is not research oriented in the schools and colleges.
4. Teachers and parents discourage questioning from infancy. Questioning is considered bad manners. Hence the children learn to obey the parents and teachers and not allowed to ask questions in the home as well as schools.
5. Students who cannot compete and clear entrance exams of professions like medicine, engineering, law etc. will join the teaching profession. The quality of students opting for teaching profession is poor. They lack motivation for the profession and lack expertise in teaching and pedagogy.
6. Students prefer teaching as there is bulk recruitment of teachers in the government sector. Most of the people consider teaching

profession is most suitable for women as they get many holidays throughout the year.

7. There are teacher educational institutions where the students join paying donations and do not attend college get the degree and join the teaching profession. people enter into teaching profession because they fail to get a job anywhere.
8. There is no authoritative body to test the efficiency of the recruited teachers in the government sector. Hence the students who get the government job feel more safe and secure. Such poor quality, inefficient teachers, lack professional commitment and they are not honest towards their profession. Hence the result is poor quality education in government schools.
9. There is no proper educational guidance in schools and colleges to guide the students for their prospective future. Only the educated parents guide their children and most of the children join courses without knowing the future prospects of their study. This leads to confusion and lack of clarity in students. Hence we see the students doing many postgraduate courses in the universities aimlessly.
10. Most of the parents discourage their children not to go for research as research is a time-consuming process. Because in India it is the parents who support the children's education. So it becomes a burden for the parents if they support the Childs education for the longer duration.
11. The students who join research with scholarships of UGC JRF consume total duration to complete their research work because the amounts they get help them to fulfill the family responsibility for the economically poor students.
12. The students who join do not have any knowledge about the process of research work. Most of the students withdraw the course when they fail to complete the work within the duration.
13. Poor economic background of the students lack financial support, family responsibilities are the major hindrances in the research
14. There are no clear cut rules and policies in the universities related to the research work. When there is any problem the authorities search for the norms and rules.
15. Most of the students are not aware of the rules and norms framed by the universities. Hence they lag behind in work without understanding the norms laid.

16. The research supervisors lack proper knowledge of the research process. They prefer topics of research of their own research but do not encourage students to go for a new area. Their improper guidance creates confusion in research scholars.
17. There is no understanding between the research supervisor and the students. Sometimes the students were unable to decide the topic of research and they conduct research on the topic decided by the research supervisor. Hence they lack proper knowledge and motivation to work.
18. Egoistic nature of the research supervisors troubles the students and there are cases of suicides even in Ph.D. scholars.
19. Research supervisors do not update their knowledge hence they stick on to the old methods which creates a knowledge gap between scholar and the research supervisor.
20. Lack of library facilities in the institutions and the universities is a major issue for poor quality in research.
21. Rules and regulations of the university control the system and hinder the process of research work.
22. The university teachers are overburdened with the workload. So they cannot devote time to research work. Lack of basic facilities in the institution also contribute to poor research work.
23. Research involves a lot of patience, hard work and a lot of time. Hence people hesitate to undertake research.
24. Most of the research work in India contributes to the knowledge but not the application part. Mostly it doesn't help to solve the societal problems in India.
25. In India people doesn't take research work seriously. They do make manipulations to get the results accordingly.
26. Most of the research scholars feel that getting a scholarship is a source of income for them to improve their life but not the research work.
27. There is no coordination between the research scholars to share knowledge and understanding.
28. There is no cooperation and coordination between the research supervisors to share experiences and knowledge. They have a passel of egos, misunderstandings, professional jealousies in educational institutions.

29. There is no tie-up of educational institutions with the industries or actual field. Hence the students lack practical exposure to the problems they have selected.
30. There is no honesty and commitment in the research scholars to conduct research work. Hence they resort to malpractice, manipulate the result, plagiarize the work of others. They want a degree for a tag rather than an achievement.

Strategies to improve the quality of research in India

Role of the schools

1. Quality of education given in private and government institutions should be the same. But the classroom strength should be restricted to 30 in each section.
2. Good infrastructural facilities in the educational institutions to provide good exposure to practical's and field work
3. Our school education system should be such that it should enhance the creativity among the children.
4. Less importance should be given to examinations, marks, and grades.
5. Delinking education with degrees and employment opportunities
6. There should be scope to express one's ideas and opinion in the classroom. Students should be given freedom of expression.
7. The curriculum should enhance curiosity and enthusiasm among the children
8. Teaching methods should be such which enhance the creativity of the children.
9. Proper guidance and counseling to the students related to various professions at the school level
10. Action research should be a compulsory part of students curriculum
11. Scholarships and stipends must be given to the children who are interested in research work.

Role of the teachers

1. Appointment of the teachers should be done through a rigorous process to choose the excellent and best teachers for the teaching profession.
2. Only those who are really interested in the teaching profession should enter into teaching.

3. Teachers should be well trained in research work after the appointment.
4. Action research should be mandatory for school teachers based on their research services should be renewed.
5. Frequent orientation must be given to in-service teachers in research latest techniques and teaching in the classroom.
6. Better laboratory facilities in the schools for research work.

Role of the Higher Educational Institutions

1. There should be clear cut policies and rules in higher educational institutions related to research.
2. All higher educational institutions must have a good library, laboratory facilities in the concern departments.
3. The library should procure the latest reference books on various subjects.
4. There should be a separate room for research scholars in the libraries with computers, Xerox machines etc.
5. The selection of research scholars in the higher education system must be based on entrance examination and merit.
6. Proper guidance and counseling must be provided to the newly joined research scholars related to the process of research, course work etc.
7. Debates, discussions must be arranged to listen to interact with each other to have intensive reading, depth of knowledge on the topic of their interest to finalize the topic of research.
8. Sufficient time should be given to the research scholar to finalize the topic of research.
9. Emphasis should be given to those topics of research which have social and utilitarian value.
10. Research advisory committees should honest judge the work of the scholars without any bias.
11. Higher educational institutions should be free with the tassel of egos, bias, prejudice and unhealthy competitions.
12. There should be mutual understanding between the research supervisor and research scholar as research is a long term activity.
13. Mutual respect, understanding, and cooperation between the faculties of higher educational institutions are essential to bring out the quality of research.

14. Mandatory orientation to the faculty of higher educational institutions related to the latest techniques in research work.

Unless we take up some serious collective measures to improve and enhance the quality of research in higher education institutions there will not be any change in states of affair. It is the need of the hour to act intelligently and change our educational system at the school level, recruiting highly committed and devoted teachers with pedagogical knowledge and professional skills who can jell well with the students understand them and provide proper guidance and be good facilitators. We need to change the role of higher education institutions from the provider of knowledge and skills to the modifier of society through research work.

Reference

1. https://www.researchgate.net/publication/282293148.
   Higher Education in India - Issues Challenges and Suggestions.
2. https://corescholar.libraries.wright.edu/cgi/viewcontent.cgi?article=1179&contex=ejie
3. https://surejob.in/higher-education-in-india-issues-and-challenges.html.
4. https://en.wikipedia.org/wiki/Higher education in India.

Chapter-21

Higher Education in India – Issues and Challenges

Dr. D. CH. Apparao,

Abstract

Knowledge is the food for man because in absence of knowledge man cannot grow his food. Education is the pond of knowledge. Education is a process in which and by which the knowledge, characters and behavior of the human being are shaped and molded. Education is lead to the enlightenment of mankind. Education is a basic pillar for human rights and democracy, sustainable development and peace; higher education in particular is necessary for solving the various problems we find as we approach the 21st century. The education system in India was first developed in the three presidencies (Bombay, Calcutta and Madras). Since we have got independence we are facing challenges to establish a great and strong education system. Various governments came and gone. Off course they tried to establish new education policies in the system but this is very sad to dictate that they were not sufficient for our country. Still we are facing lot of problems and challenges in our Education System. India recognizes that the new global scenario poses unprecedented challenges for the higher education system. India has the largest number of higher education institutions. Higher education comprises all post-secondary education, training and research guidance at education institutions such as universities that are authorized as institutions of higher education by state authorities. Higher education is extremely diverse and the challenges and issues faced by higher education institutions are just as diverse. There is an inadequate and diminishing financial support for higher education from the government and from society. We need higher educated people who are skilled and who can drive our economy forward. It is becoming important to expand higher education so that a wide range of human resources can be developed and the entire society's level of knowledge can be raised. The Government is making efforts to improve the education system in terms of various parameters like GER, quality, investments, infrastructure, etc. The major issues and challenges of education sector and the concerned issues have been properly addressed by the government to provide quality education to the stakeholders. Every year, many new colleges are being opened in almost all cities in India, but the quality education is still a long awaited dream for millions of Indian students. In this seminar paper I am trying to touch various problems and challenges exist in the Higher Education System of our country. This paper is written based on the secondary data available on various websites, published books, journals and articles.

Keywords: *Education, Higher Education, Issues and Challenges, GER (Gross Enrolment Ratio), Suggestions.*

Introduction

India's higher education system is the world's third largest in terms of students, next to China and the United States. In future, India will be one of the largest education hubs. India's Higher Education sector has witnessed a tremendous increase in the number of Universities/University level Institutions & Colleges since independence. The 'Right to Education Act' which stipulates compulsory and free education to all children within the age groups of 6-14 years, has brought about a revolution in the education system of the country with statistics revealing a staggering enrolment in schools over the last four years. The involvement of private sector in higher education has seen drastic changes in the field. Today over 60 percent of higher education institutions in India are promoted by the private sector. This has accelerated establishment of institutes which have originated over the last decade making India home to the largest number of Higher Education institutions in the world, with student enrolments at the second highest.

Meaning and Definitions of Education

According to some learned people, the word "Education" has been derived from the Latin term "Educatum" which means the act of teaching or training. A group of educationists say that it has come from another Latin word "Educare" which means "to bring up" or "to raise".

According to a few others, the word "Education" has originated from another Latin term "Educere" which means "to lead forth" or "to come out". All these meanings indicate that education seeks to nourish the good qualities in man and draw out the best in every individual. Education seeks to develop the innate inner capacities of man.

Rigved: "Education is something which makes man self-reliant and selfless".

Upanishad: "Education is for liberation".

Bhagavad Gita: "Nothing is more purifying on earth than wisdom."

Shankaracharya: "Education is the realization of self'.

Gandhi: "By education, I mean an all-round drawing out of the best in the Child and man body, mind and spirit."

Socrates: "Education means the bringing out of the ideas of universal validity which are latent in the mind of every man".

Plato: "Education is the capacity to feel pleasure and pain at the right moment. It develops in the body and in the soul of the pupil all the beauty and all the perfection which he is capable of."

Aristotle: "Education is the creation of a sound mind in a sound body. It develops man's faculty, especially his mind so that he may be able to enjoy the contemplation of supreme truth, goodness and beauty of which perfect happiness essentially consists.

Rousseau: "Education of man commences at his birth; before he can speak, before he can understand he is already instructed. Experience is the forerunner of the perfect".

Statement of the Problem

Many people are confused about the Higher Education, because there have been many changes recently, including institutions changing their names and titles and degree programs. The Higher education can be defined as a university level education. It offers a number of qualifications ranging from Higher National Diplomas and Foundation Degrees to Honors Degrees and as a further step, Postgraduate programs such as Masters Degrees and Doctorates. These are recognized throughout the world as representing specialist expertise supported by a wide range of skills that is very useful.

Importance of Higher Education

The Indian higher education system is one of the largest such systems in the World. It is estimated that during the X Five Year Plan period (2002-07), there will be a tremendous pressure of numbers on this system and a large number of additional students will be knocking at the doors of higher education institutions in the country.

Higher education is of vital importance for the country, as it is a powerful tool to build knowledge-based society of the 21st Century. With the growing size and diversity of the higher education sector particularly in terms of courses, management and geographical coverage, it has become necessary to develop a sound database on higher education.

Higher education has an important role both for the student, as an individual, and also for the society in which he lives. Higher education represents an aid for the growth and the development of the students and a key for a better life. For the society, higher education institutions can contribute to the creation of ideal citizens, who will help in keeping the society peaceful.

State of Higher Education in India

As per the latest 2011 Census (3), about 8.15 percent (68 millions) of Indians are graduates, with Union Territories of Chandigarh and Delhi topping the list with 24.65 percent and 22.56 percent of their population being graduates respectively.[4] Indian higher education system has expanded at a fast pace by adding nearly 20,000 colleges and more than 8 million students in a decade from 2000–01 to 2010–11.[5] As of 2016, India has 799 universities, with a break up of 44 central universities, 540 state universities, 122 deemed universities, 90 private universities, 5 institutions established and functioning under the State Act, and 75 Institutes of National Importance which include AIIMS, IITs, IIEST and NITs among others.[7][8] Other institutions include 39,071 colleges as Government Degree Colleges and Private Degree Colleges, including 1800 exclusive women's colleges, functioning under these universities and institutions as reported by the UGC in 2016.[6] Colleges may be Autonomous, i.e. empowered to examine their own degrees, up to PhD level in some cases, or non-autonomous, in which case their examinations are under the supervision of the university to which they are affiliated; in either case, however, degrees are awarded in the name of the university rather than the college. So this sums up the state of higher education in India.

Objectives of the Study

- To study the present position of the Higher Education in India
- To Identify the Issues and challenges of Higher Education in India
- To give suggestions to improve the Higher Education System in India

Methodology

This paper is made purely on the basis of secondary data available on various websites, published books, journals and articles available in this issue.

Issues and Challenges of Higher Education in India

➢ **Teaching Quality**

The first issue that higher education in India is facing is decreasing teaching quality. Teachers are not well trained and qualified for the job they are assigned to. Some colleges recruit young graduates as professors who have no experience or knowledge. So this is a big problem.

- **Financing**

  Financing is also an issue with higher education in India. Yes India is already spending very much on higher education and it can't spend more. However if the quality of higher education has to be improved then more financing is needed.

- **Privatization**

  Privatization is also a big problem that higher education faces. Privatization of higher education is the way to go. However just privatization is not going to solve the problem. You need to foster the culture of creativity, imagination and learning new skills in young students.

- **Quota System**

  Debating quota system is very controversial. But if you are being honest then I must tell you quota is not good for the quality of higher education. Talent and merit is more important than your identity. However quota system is still a challenge.

- **Political Factor**

  Political influence is also a bad thing and an issue with higher education. Governing bodies do not want any political influence or interference in their affairs.

- **Moral Issues**

  Younger generation is not interested in serving their country and they are more interested in just taking up a job and a hefty pay package.

- **Gap in Supply and Demand**

  India's gross enrollment rate (GER) is just 19 percent which is not good. GER is 6 percent below the world average and at least 50 percent lesser than developed world like Australia and US. This has to change if we have to really improve state of higher education in India.

- **Mushrooming of Low Quality Institutes**

  Mushrooming of low quality institutes all over the country is not good for higher education. These new colleges lack capacity and they are all about fleecing money from students and their parents. There is too much glamour and less quality of education.

- **No Project Based Learning**

  Higher education lack project based learning. Young graduates need to learn new skills especially vocational skills that can give them job. So we are not focusing on project based learning at all. Just theory is not enough; we also need practical knowledge is also.

- **Why Only Servicing Industry?**

  We are obsessed with servicing industry. We all want to get selected in campus selection so we love jobs in servicing sector only. However higher education does not solve the problem when it comes to creating jobs in manufacturing sector. That is a big problem.

- **Capacity utilization**

  Another challenge to be addressed in strengthening the Indian education system is to improve the capacity utilization. For example, a recent study on capacity utilization in India for higher education indicates that the capacity utilization in case of MBA is about 57 per cent in Maharashtra and 72 per cent in Haryana. In case of certain states, there are a lot of unfilled seats in institutions.

- **Infrastructure facilities**

  One of the factors why the capacity utilization is low in upcoming/ new institutions/colleges (both in private and public sectors) is their inability to provide necessary physical infrastructure to run the institutions. The infrastructure facilities desirable to rank the institutions of better quality include real estate, state of the art class rooms, library, hostels, furniture, sports facilities, transport, commercial buildings, etc.

- **Student-Teacher ratio**

  Another challenge for improving the Indian education system is to improve the student teacher ratio. In India, this ratio is very high as compared to certain comparable countries in the world. For example, while in developed countries this ratio stands at 11.4, in case of India, it is as high as 22.0.

- **Lack of Research or critical analysis**

  Problems solving skills are one of the most important things that are required when students complete their studies and look for jobs to earn money and build up their career. This can be learned by participating in problem solving projects with the use of creative and critical thinking. In India, despite the fact that we have the highest number of engineering graduates, still we lack technological innovation.

- **Absence of personality development program**

  Schools and colleges in India demand student's performance in terms of marks and they are not well exposed to the external world. When students complete their graduation and enter into the job market, they face problems to get a job as per their capability simply because they don't meet the criteria and skills required for the job. Companies want to hire those individuals that are aware of the course of the action.

- **Absence of Entrepreneurship development scheme**

  The majority of the students want to get a job after finishing their education. They don't like starting their own business because they are of the view that they can't become a business person and face the challenges during the circulation of their business. The absence of Entrepreneurship abilities is halting the progress of our country in several fields.

- **Outdated syllabus**

  There is an urgent need to change the present system of higher education in the country. We need to ensure quality in education as well as quantity. Students are getting the knowledge from outdated syllabus. Lots of technological and scientific improvements are taking place in India and therefore the courses are Graduate and post graduates must be updated as per the industrial and technological development.

- **No Strategy**

  There is no strategy for higher education in India. We don't have foreign students coming to the country and studying here. Government has no plan for this and this is a big challenge.

- **Poverty** can be next issue or a challenge to which our education system is facing. Nowadays the cost of getting education is very high so poor of our society find themselves lost in getting education.

- **Dearness** is another challenge for the education system. Fee of colleges and schools is rising day by day with public schools raising their fee structure in every session but the wages of laborer is not increasing at the same speed. So poor people find themselves unable in admitting their children in those schools. And government schools do not compete with the public schools or CBSE schools.

- The next challenge is our corruption which has become the right of all government officers and whole system. In many schools it is found that the fund which was sending to the school disappeared on the way.
- Next can be according to me, the issue of character of teachers. Our teacher's character is going downwards. A teacher is the only person who can change the direction of the society. He is the person who is the center point of any education system. This influences much our society than any other part of the society. This effects much our education than all the above points. But nowadays news in different form can be read in newspapers.

Suggestions Improving the System of Higher Education

- ✓ There is a need to implement innovative and transformational approach form primary to higher education level to make Indian educational system globally more relevant and competitive.
- ✓ Higher educational institutes need to improve quality and reputation.
- ✓ There should be a good infrastructure of colleges and universities which may attract the students. Government must promote collaboration between Indian higher education institutes and top International institutes and also generates linkage between national research laboratories and research centers of top institutions for better quality and collaborative research.
- ✓ There is a need to focus on the graduate students by providing them such courses in which they can achieve excellence, gain deeper knowledge of subject so that they will get jobs after recruitment in the companies which would reduce unnecessary rush to the higher education.
- ✓ Universities and colleges in both public private must be away from the political affiliations, Favouritism, money making process should be out of education system etc.
- ✓ There should be a multidisciplinary approach in higher education so that students' knowledge may not be restricted only upto his own subjects.
- ✓ Our education system should be such that it should generate enthusiasm to become a business person and it should also produce scientist, writers, thinkers, designers etc. only that India can be knowledge based economy and claim to be regarded as superpower.

- ✓ It is highly essential to start personality development program is schools and colleges to improve the education standards.
- ✓ Students must have capability to solve the problems and difficulties that the country is facing today.

Conclusion

Finally I will conclude by saying for any country both primary and higher education are needed. Primary education has its own importance just like higher education has its own importance. However higher education is very important for growing our economy. Higher education in India has many challenges and issues. We need to talk about them and highlight so that government can resolve such issues. Higher education in India has expanded very rapidly in the last six decades after independence yet it is not equally accessible to all. No doubt India is facing various challenges in higher education but to tackle these challenges and to boost higher education is utmost important. India is a country of huge human resource potential, to utilize this potential properly is the issue which needed to discuss. Opportunities are available but how to get benefits from these opportunities and how to make them accessible to others is the matter of concern. In order to sustain that rate of growth, there is need to increase the number of institutes and also the quality of higher education in India. To reach and achieve the future requirements there is an urgent need to relook at the Financial Resources, Access and Equity, Quality Standards, Relevance, infrastructure and at the end the Responsiveness.

Reference

1. What is Higher Education? http://www.wg.aegee.org/ewg/higheredu.htm [accessed 2012-3- 05].
2. www.hrmars.com/journals International Journal of Academic Research in Accounting, Finance and Management Sciences Volume 2, Special Issue 1 (2012), pp. 120-127.
3. http://aishe.gov.in.
4. *Rukmini S. (2015-08-04). "Only 8.15 percent of Indians are graduates, Census data show". The Hindu. Retrieved 2016-04-01.*
5. *"Latest Statistics on Indian Higher Education". DrEducation.com. 2012-07-17. Retrieved 2012-08-28.*
6. Jump up to:[a b c d] *"Statistics – Ministry of Human Resource Development" (PDF). mhrd.gov.in.*
7. *"Central Universities". ugc.ac.in. Retrieved 6 June 2011.*
8. *"List of State Universities"* (PDF). *27 May 2011. Retrieved 2011-06-06.*

9. Shaguri, Obadya Ray, Higher Education in India Access, Equity, Quality, EAN World Congress Scholar, Global Access to Postsecondary education, 2013.
10. Younis Ahmad Sheikh (2017) Higher Education in India: Challenges and Opportunities , Journal of Education and Practice www.iiste.org ISSN 2222-1735 Vol.8, No.1, 2017.
11. https://en.wikipedia.org/wiki/Higher education in India.

Chapter-22

Need To Encourage Intellectual Property Research in Higher Education

Dr. K. Srinivasa Raju,
Dr. D. Ashok Kumar,

Abstract

This paper explores and proffers the need for increased investments in research and development that should consequently lead to an increase in intellectual property rights. In an era when intellectual property is becoming an important aspect of a nation's economy, we highlight the fact that India's investments in intellectual property rights lags behind other countries including those which a few years ago were on par with India. It is argued that this problem has more to do with India's lack of investments in higher education and research and development. We compare the investments by China with that of India and argue that unless such investments are increased, India risks lagging behind in an increasingly knowledge economy that is globalised.

Keywords: *Higher Education, Intellectual Property, Research and Investments.*

Introduction

Intellectual property rights have been around for more than 140 years but their importance in India has grown a lot since the beginning of this century. If recent events and statements emanating from the rich countries is an indicator, their importance is set to grow further. The US President has specifically underscored the importance of protecting intellectual property in their trade policy. Hence, it is likely that in the very near future India and China will face increased pressure from other countries. Broadly, intellectual property rights (IPR) comprises of patents, trademarks, copyrights, designs, geographic indicators, new plant varieties, semi integrated circuits and biological diversity. As a generalisation, they are usually based on innovations or inventions or products related to the application of mind. There have been various international conventions and treaties that protect intellectual property starting with the "Berne Convention" in 1886. India has been a member of the various treaties that promise protection for intellectual property from a long time. It is a member of the most important such treaty, the World Intellectual Property Organisation (WIPO established in 1967, presently 191 members) which is part of the United Nations. WIPO is nodal agency that lays down procedures and coordinates intellectual property protection among members. WIPO has classified nearly 10,000 goods and services into 45 different categories called "NICE classification" so that there is uniformity of procedures for those seeking IPR registration. One advantage of being part of the international treaties is that it gives 'reciprocity' by which those filing for intellectual property in India. Due to various international treaties those filing for IPR in India can also do so in all the member countries of WIPO concurrently.

There is no doubt that awareness about intellectual property rights has come a long way since the 1990s when companies in USA tried to patent "Neem" and "Basamati". India has a long history of accepting IPR: India passed a copyright Act for the first time in 1957 and a Patents Act in 1970. These were amended at various points between 2000 and 2012, mostly to meet the requirements of the WIPO and other international treaties over the past few years. A intellectual property policy was released in 2016. Among intellectual property rights, patents are probably that aspect on which there is more awareness than other aspects. However, they are granted for new, innovative inventions which are usually relevant in the making of new products. A more relevant aspect of IPR that small businesses will find more useful are those related to Trademarks, Copyright and Designs. Copyright protects in its scope any original writings including literary works, dramatic works, musical works, artistic works, cinematograph films and sound recording. Essentially copyright registration protects the manifestation of any idea in the various tangible outcomes. Trademark registration protects any marks which have a distinctive character including those which have the name of the business or family, etc. Similarly, Designs which are novel and not known or have been displayed to the public in the past including shapes, patterns, ornaments, composition of lines, colours or combination of those which are unique in 2D or 3D format can be protected. However, design registration does not protect any technical features; it protects only those which are appealing to the naked eye and those which are not a trademark or those which have already been copyrighted.

IPR in India: story so far

Though the importance of IPR has grown in the past two decades, they are nowhere as important as they are in the more advanced countries such as USA, Japan or South Korea. A US report pointed out that in 2016, Intellectual Property intensive industries employed about 4.5 crores people or about 30 percent of all employed in USA and contributed about 45 percent of the total value addition in the US economy. More importantly, the average worker in an intellectual property industry earns 46 percent more than other workers. The total exports by IP intensive industries in USA was nearly US$1 trillion in 2015. American companies earn more nearly ₹8 lakh crores annually (about US$120 billion) by way of licensing intellectual property to companies in other countries. Thus, investing in intellectual property rights not only helps the businesses but also those who work in those industries and the country in the form of increased economic activity and the collection of taxes.

IP is increasingly becoming important in countries like India and China. The size of the Indian market means that increasingly foreign companies are looking at India. Government data points out that till 31 March 2017, 33788 international applications have been filed for copyrights in India using the WIPO process. A commonly misunderstood aspect of IPR is that it is only useful for the larger companies and not for the smaller companies. At the outset it is important to note that patent, copyright, trademark or design registrations are not only for companies. Even individual and small business can use the internet or submit a hardcopy to register their trademarks, copyrights, patents or designs. IPR can be of great help to the smaller companies if they are able to plan their strategy and think with a long-term perspective. Businesses and innovative individuals often think that investing in IPR is a wasteful expenditure. If they want to benefit this mindset has to change and they should approach IPR as a long-term investment in the future. It is because they lack this mindset that often small business and even innovative individuals to find that their designs or ideas to be copied/plagiarised. There is no doubt that the larger companies frequently use IPR to protect and expand their business due to their ability to marshal resources. IPR is especially important for artisans and other small business owners like jewellers, painters and others to register their intellectual property. Registration will allow them to block others from misusing or copying their work. In case of very innovative ideas or works, it may even be possible to force those interested in using the work by paying a license fees for the use of their products and ideas. They are especially important since India has innumerable small business, some of them unregistered and working in the villages or semi-urban areas but have been in business for decades and are well known in the region or even across a particular state. Hence, these small businesses and individuals need to cautious and see to it that they do not face the risk that at some point in future, someone else may find it profitable to register the intellectual property in their own name. In the worst case scenario, such stealing of intellectual property may even lead to the original owner having to either paying a license fees or being dragged into costly litigation.

Table: Overview of major IPR filings in India

	Filed/Applications Received			*Examined*			*Granted/Registered*		
	2010-11	**2015-16**	**2016-17**	**2010-11**	**2015-16**	**2016-17**	**2010-11**	**2015-16**	**2016-17**
Patents	39400	46904	45444	11208	16851	28967	7509	6326	9847
Trademarks	179317	283060	278170	205065	267861	532230	115472	65045	250070
Copyrights	NA	14812	16617	NA	9325	16584	NA	4505	3596
Designs	7589	11108	10213	6277	9426	11940	9206	7904	8276
GI	27	17	32	NA	NA	NA	29	26	34

Annual Report, 2017-18, Department of Industrial Policy and Promotion, p.108-115

Long, Difficult Road Ahead

One reason why IPR has been slow in gaining a foothold is that for a very long time we have been accustomed to thinking that everything will be provided free of cost by the government. Hence, there are low levels of awareness. This is further aggravated by the Central government which has done very little to promote their increased adoption except to an extent in the case of patents. Government's lack of vision and efforts to increase awareness has not helped matters. This lack of vision and plan to expand awareness is hindering further progress despite the existence of various concessions including subsidy in fees payable for start-up and small companies. A good way to encourage such IPR is for the state governments to encourage their micro, small and medium businesses (MSMEs) to file for such intellectual property by offering subsidy. At present government bodies spend a lot of money chasing richer industrialists for investments but often ignore such long-term beneficial measures.

An issue that has constrains a larger number of people is that filing for patents has to be through the regional offices located in the four metro cities of New Delhi, Mumbai, Chennai and Kolkata. There is an urgent need to expand the network of offices and establish registration offices in all the capital cities and even larger cities across the country. This will invariably help in the filing of IPR. Another issue that plagues the filing of IPR is that there are very few accredited facilitators who can help file them on behalf of those wanting to do so. The government appoints facilitators for expediating the process. Unfortunately, there are too few of them in a vast country like India: at the end of December 2017 there were 423 facilitators in patents and designs and 596 in the case of trademarks. This is a case of too few considering that there are about 6 crores business enterprises in India. A good way by which the Central government expand awareness is by taking the help of state level and especially district level reach of the industries department in a state. These district level or state level bodies like industries departments, industrial investment and infrastructure development (IICs) can start another section that helps complete various compliance and registration filing requirements. That would help a number of small businesses. Industrial investment and infrastructure development need not always mean encouraging large industries only.

Higher Education and R&D Investment

One of the problem is that, unlike China we are not investing in Research and Development. The gross expenditure on R&D has increased from ₹ 24, 117.24 crores in 2004-05 to ₹ 85,326.10 crores in 2014-15. It is estimated to be ₹ 94,516.45 crores in 2015-16 and ₹ 1,04,864.03 crores in 2016-17[1]. We need not mislead ourselves into complacency by thinking that this is a big jump because that decade was also the period when the Indian economy also grew substantially. However these statistics mask the true lack of investment. According to UNESO Statistics, China's investment in R&D as a percentage of GDP increased from 0.56 percent to 2.07 percent from 1996 – 2016; in contrast India's spending has stagnated at 0.63 percent of GDP[2] over the past few years. An area for concern should be that our Gross Expenditure on R&D (GERD) is mainly driven by the Government sector - mostly of the Central Government which contributes about 45.1 percent, while State Governments contribute 7.4 percent, Higher Education 3.9 percent and Public Sector Industries 5.5 percent with Private Sector Industries contributing 38.1 percent during 2014-15. Among the G-20 countries, India is the only country where R&D spending by the government exceeds more than 50 percent while businesses and university system spends the least. In all the other major countries it is businesses that spend most of the money: in USA 72 percent; Germany 68 percent; China 77 percent; South Korea 78 percent; UK 66 percent; Russian Federation 59 percent while in India it is 44 percent.This is in contrast to most of the other countries where government spending on R&D usually varies from 7-15 percent while that of the businesses is 50 percent or more and very high in a few countries like Japan (78 percent), South Korea (78 percent), China (77 percent), USA (72 percent), UK (66 percent). Similarly, investments by Higher educational institutions is about 4 percent in India which is by far one of the lowest in the world especially among countries like Canada (40 percent), Australia (30 percent), Italy (29 percent), Spain (28 percent), UK (26 percent) and even Mexico (26 percent).

The lack of investments in R&D is a direct consequence of the problem of availability of quality human resources, especially in the higher education system. A large part of our education system is not sufficiently productive to support the cutting edge research and development to keep pace in a rapidly changing world. This is despite the huge size. A 2016 OCED study pointed out that India produces the fourth largest number of PhD students in a year[3] – about 24,300 in 2014 against 67,449 in US, 28,147 in Germany and 25,020 in UK[4]. Unfortunately, there is a lot to be desired in case of quality of such students.

Conclusion

In the context of the above discussion, it is important to note that India has not invested sufficient amounts in Research and Development, especially in the sphere of R&D spending in Higher education. Unless India invests more in R&D, we risk being left out in an increasingly knowledge society. There is an urgent need to recalibrate our higher education system and offer special benefits for investments in intellectual property. The earlier we begin in our endeavour the better it is.

Reference

1. Annual Report 2017-18, Department of Industrial Policy and Promotion, Government of India, New Delhi
2. OECD Science, Technology and Innovation Outlook 2016, OECD Publishing, (https://dx.doi.org/10.1787/sti_in_outlook-2016-en)
3. Research and Development Statistics at a Glance, 2017-18, Department of Science and Technology, Government of India, New Delhi.
4. Brito, Jerry (2012), Eds, Copyright Unbalanced: From Incentive to Excess, MercatusCenter at George Mason University: Arlington
5. Drahos, Peter (1996). A Philosophy of Intellectual Property, Dartmouth: Aldershot.
6. Flew, Terry, Leisten, Susanna H., & Hearn, Gregory N. (2006).Alternative syst ems for Intellectual Property in the digital age. In: Servaes, Jan & Thomas, Pradip (Eds.) Intellectual Property Rights Communication in Asia: Conflicti ng Traditions. SAGE Publications: New Delhi, pp. 226240.
7. Horten, Monica (2013). A Copyright Masquerade, Zed Books: London Hughes, Justin (1988). The Philosophy of Intellectual Property, 77 Geo. L.J. 287, Retreioved from http://www.justinhughes.net/docs/a-ip01.pdf.
8. Murphy, D.J. (2012). Are intellectual property rights compatible with Rawlsian principles of justice?Ethics and Information Technology, 14 (2), pp.109-121.

9. Wang, Chunyan (2008). Creative Commons License: An Alternative Solution to Copyright in the New Media Arena, In: Fitzgerald, B., Gao, F., O'Brien, D, &Xiaoxiang Shi, S. (Eds), Copyright Law, Digital Content and the Internet in the Asia Pacific, Sydney University Press; Sydney.

Notes

1. http://www.nstmis-dst.org/Statistics-Glance-2017-18.pdf.
2. https://data.worldbank.org/indicator/GB.XPD.RSDV.GD.ZS.
3. https://read.oecd-ilibrary.org/science-and-technology/oecd-science-technology-and-innovation-outlook-2016 sti in outlook-2016-en#page149.
4. https://www.weforum.org/agenda/2017/02/countries-with-most-doctoral-graduates/.

Chapter-23

Research Ethics in Social Science

Dr. Jagdish Buwade

Abstract

Research ethics is an analysis of ethical issues that are raised when people or animals are involved as participants in research. Social science research has long been concerned with ethical issues. Social science investigates complex issues which involve cultural, legal, economic (Freed-Taylor, 1994). It is important to adhere to ethical principles in order to protect the dignity, rights and welfare of research participants. The Aim of this paper is to demonstrate the importance and need of ethical issues in social science.

Keywords: *Research, Ethics, Social Science*

Introduction

Research is a systematic, socially organized quest for new and better insight. 'Research ethics' refers to a complex set of values, standards and institutional schemes that help constitute and regulate scientific activity. Ethical issues are becoming a crucial element in social research. It is compulsory for a social researcher conducting research involving humans to apply for ethical clearance. *Research:* Research is a systematic, socially organized quest for new and better insight. The word *research* is derived from the Middle French "*recherche*", which means "to go about seeking", the term itself being derived from the Old French term "*recerchier*" a compound word from "re-" + "   cerchier", or "sercher", meaning 'search. *Definition of Research:* Research is a process of steps used to collect and analyze information to increase our understanding of a topic or issue". It consists of three steps: pose a question, collect data to answer the question, and present an answer to the question. *Ethics:* Ethics is based on well-founded standards of right and wrong that prescribe what humans ought to do, usually in terms of rights, obligations, benefits to society, fairness, or specific virtues. The English word "ethics" is derived from the Ancient Greek word *ethikos* meaning "relating to one's character", which itself comes from the root word *ethos* meaning "character, moral nature". This was borrowed into Latin as *ethica* and then into French as *ethique*, from which it was borrowed into English.

Definition of Ethics: "Ethics is the discipline dealing with what is good and bad and with moral duty and obligation". *Research Ethics*: 'Research ethics' refers to a complex set of values, standards and institutional schemes that help constitute and regulate scientific activity without harming anyone in the process.

Social science research has long been concerned with ethical issues. Social science investigates complex issues which involve cultural, legal, economic, and political phenomena. This complexity means that social science research must concern itself with "moral integrity" to ensure that research process and findings are "trustworthy" and valid. Research involving human subjects is required to show respect for ethical issues by obtaining approval from the institution's Human Research Ethics Committee (HREC) prior to commencement. University policies on research ethics state that all research involving human subjects must comply with the Statement on Ethical Conduct in Human Research. The aim of the paper is to demonstrate the importance and need of ethical issues in social science.

Importance of Research Ethics in Social Science

Research ethics played an important role in social science research activities as, It is a reflection of respect for those who 'take part' in research, It ensures no unreasonable, unsafe or thoughtless demands are made by researchers and It has a professional requirement for practitioners in some disciplines e.g. Psychology and many other Heaths professional.

Need of social Research Ethics

These are the major needs of social research ethics: To protect human participants, To ensure that research is conducted in a way that serves interests of individuals, groups and/or society as a whole and To examine specific research activities and projects for their ethical soundness, looking at issues such as the management of risk, protection of confidentiality and the process of informed consent.

Research Ethics in Social Science

These following are the major research ethics concerns in social science are given below:

- **Human Dignities:** Researchers must base their work on a fundamental respect for human dignity. Researchers must protect personal integrity, preserve individual freedom and self-determination, respect privacy and family life, and safeguard against harm and unreasonable strain.
- **Consent and Obligation to Notify:** When a research project deals with personal data, researchers are obliged to inform the participants or subjects of research and to obtain their consent.
- **Deception:** Research deception involves an intentional misrepresentation of facts related to the purpose, nature, or consequences of an investigation. Researcher should not involve in this misconduct.
- **Privacy:** Researchers must respect the participants' autonomy, integrity, freedom and right ofco -determination.
- **Confidentiality:** Researcher should protect confidential communications, such as papers or grants submitted for publication, personnel records, trade or secrets, and patient records.
- **Responsibility for Avoiding Harm:** Researchers are responsible for ensuring that participants are not exposed to serious physical harm or other severe or unreasonable strain as result of the research
- **Justice** (Fairness): This principle implies that everyone should be treated fairly and equally.
- **Reporting Results to Participants:** Researchers have a special obligation to report results back to the participants in a comprehensible and acceptable manner.
- **Respect for Vulnerable Groups:** Researchers have a special responsibility to respect the interests of vulnerable groups throughout the entire research process. Individuals who belong to disadvantaged groups may not want to be the subjects of research for fear of being viewed by the general public in an unfavorable light. In such cases, researchers must place particular emphasis on the requirements regarding information and consent.
- **Animal Care:** Show proper respect and care for animals when using them in research. Do not conduct unnecessary or poorly designed animal experiments.
- **Respect for Intellectual Property:** Honor patents, copyrights, and other forms of intellectual property. Do not use unpublished data, methods, or results without permission. Give credit where credit is due. Never plagiarize.

- **Ethics among Researchers**: Authorship and Ownership data, Publication Rights should be clearly mention. Researchers must observe good publication practice, respect the contributions of other researchers, and observe recognized standards of authorship and cooperation.
- **Plagiarism:** Plagiarism is unacceptable and constitutes a serious breach of recognized norms of research ethics.
- **Inducements, Financial Benefits, And Financial Costs:** It is considered ethically acceptable and appropriate to reimburse individuals for any costs associated with participation in research, including transportation, child care, or lost wages.

Conclusion

This article provides an insight into the debate concerning ethical issues in social science research. The results of findings based on data gathered unethically could lead to harm, possible conflicts and enormous dilemmas as such; it is considered good practice for social science research project to fully comply with ethical standards.

References

1. *"Research"*. Merriam Webster (*https://www.merriam-webster.com/*). Merriam-Webster, Incorporated. *Retrieved 20 May 2018*.
2. Creswell, J. W. (2008). Educational Research: Planning, conducting, and evaluating quantitative and qualitative research (3rd ed.). Upper Saddle River: Pearson.
3. An Intermediate Greek-English Lexicon. 1889.
4. Merriam Webster dictionary(onlinehttps://www.merriam-webster.com/
5. Freed-Taylor, M. (1994). Ethical considerations in European cross- national research. *International Social Science Journal*, No. 142, pp.523-532.
6. Biber, H. (2005). The Ethics of Social Research, Longman, London. *Merriam Webster dictionary*.

Chapter-24

Higher Education in India-issues, challenges and suggestions

T. Kalpana,

Abstract

Higher education in India has grown exponentially in recent years. A survey by the All India Survey on Higher Education published in July this year shows that the gross enrolment ratio (GER) was 25.8 percent in 2017-18, up from 10 percent in 2004-05. GER is the ratio (expressed as percentage), of the total enrolment within a country in a specific level of education, regardless of age, to the population in the official age group corresponding to this level of education.

Although there have been challenges to higher education in the past, these most recent calls for reform may provoke a fundamental change in higher education. This change may not occur as a direct response to calls for greater transparency and accountability, but rather because of the opportunity to reflect on the purpose of higher education, the role of colleges and universities in the new millennium, and emerging scientific research on how people learn. These disparate literatures have not been tied together in a way that would examine the impact of fundamental change from the policy level to the institutional level and to the everyday lives of college and university administrators, faculty and students. Now the time has come to create a second wave of institution building and of excellence in the fields of education, research and capability building. We need higher educated people who are skilled and who can drive our economy forward. When India can provide skilled people to the outside world then we can transfer our country from a developing nation to a developed nation very easily and quickly.

Introduction

Education is a social process. The form and content of education of any age and society are products of society-education dialectics. Education, particularly higher education, as the instrument of the individual, societal and economic transformation in India became well recognized in the second half of the twentieth century. Since independence in 1947, there have been larger investments in higher education, with the concomitant increase in the number of students who opt for higher education. The transformation of Indian education system from the ancient gurukula system to today's virtual learning system is a reflection of the changing social context. The new social realities, particularly the interplay between democratization of education, emergence of knowledge society and globalization, greatly influence the educational processes in all societies (UNESCO, 2002).

India's higher education system is the world's third largest in terms of students, next to China and the United States. Unlike China, however, India has the advantage of English being the primary language of higher education and research. India educates approximately 11 per cent of its youth in higher education as compared to 20 per cent in China. The main governing body at the tertiary level is the University Grants Commission (India), which enforces its standards, advises the government, and helps coordinate between the centre and the state. Universities and its constituent colleges are the main institutes of higher education in India. At present in 2011, there are 227 government-recognized Universities in India. Out of them 20 are central universities, 109 are deemed universities and 11 are Open Universities and rest are state universities. Most of these universities in India have affiliating colleges where undergraduate courses are being taught. However Jawaharlal University is a remarkable exception to this rule. According to the Department of higher Education government of India, 16,885 colleges, including 1800 exclusive women's colleges functioning under these universities and institutions and there are 4.57 lakh teachers and 99.54 lakh students in various higher education institutes in India. Apart from these higher education institutes there are several private institutes in India that offer various professional courses in India. Distance learning is also a feature of the Indian higher education system.

Issues in Indian Higher Education

As India strives to compete in a globalised economy in areas that require highly trained professionals, the quality of higher education becomes increasingly important. So far, India's large, educated population base and its reservoir of at least moderately well-trained university graduates have aided the country in moving ahead, but the competition is fierce; from China in particular. Other countries are also upgrading higher education with the aim of building world class universities. Even the small top tier of higher education faces serious problems. Many IIT graduates, well trained in technology, have chosen not to contribute their skills to the burgeoning technology sector in India; perhaps half leave the country immediately upon graduation to pursue advanced studies abroad, and most do not return. A stunning 86 per cent of Indian students in the fields of science and technology who obtain degrees in the United States do not return home immediately following their graduation. A body of dedicated and able teachers work at the IITs and IIMs, but the lure of jobs abroad and in the private sector makes it increasingly difficult to lure the best and brightest to the academic profession.

The growth of higher education in India has been largely guided by the serviceable prerequisite of the economy. After independence, the role of the state in planning out a development path and also in building higher education institutions was guided by mutuality of purpose. Most observers of higher education in India feel that performance of higher education institutions has been less than satisfactory in terms of access, equity and quality. Now there is an urgent need to work for the development of the educational sector to meet the need of the emerging opportunities, increasing younger generation population and challenges of the 21st century.

Challenges of higher education in India

Since we have got independence we are facing challenges to establish a great and strong education system. Various governments came and gone. Off course they tried to establish new education policies in the system but this is very sad to dictate that they were not sufficient for our country. Still we are facing lot of problems and challenges in our Education System. India recognises that the new global scenario poses unprecedented challenges for the higher education system. The University Grants Commission has appropriately stated that a whole range of skills will be demanded from the graduates of humanities, social sciences, natural sciences and commerce, as well as from the various professional disciplines such as agriculture, law, management, medicine or engineering.

India can no longer continue the model of general education as it has been persisting in for the large bulk of the student population. Rather, it requires a major investment to make human resource productive by coupling the older general disciplines of humanities, social sciences, natural sciences and commerce to their applications in the new economy and having adequate field based experience to enhance knowledge with skills and develop appropriate attitudes.

There are many basic problems facing higher education in India today. These include inadequate infrastructure and facilities, large vacancies in faculty positions and poor faculty thereof, low student enrolment rate, outmoded teaching methods, declining research standards, unmotivated students, overcrowded classrooms and widespread geographic income, gender, and ethnic imbalances. Apart from concerns relating to deteriorating standards, there is reported exploitation of students by many private providers. Ensuring equitable access to quality higher education for students coming from poor families is a major challenge. Students from poor background are put to further disadvantage since they are not academically prepared to crack highly competitive entrance examinations that have bias towards urban elite and rich students having access to private tuitions and coaching. Education in basic sciences and subjects that are not market friendly has suffered.

There are so many people in various parts of country which are still out of reach. This is when we have emphasized more on our education programs and made our system reachable to all areas. Government has to rethink on these areas to implement more on the policies. Money also plays a vital role for the education system which needs to unique for all globally recognized syllabus and curricula. Take a look on our constitution which says that this is the responsibility of central and state government to build good education system. For that we need to have funds. But despite there was a large expenditure on the funds every year on Education where the fund goes and our system remains intact.

Central government prepares policies and plan while responsibility of State government is run those policies on ground. The standard education facilities are higher in the states which are much rich. There is a need to change such defects from the country education system which only can be influenced by increasing funding and providing better facilities to students. But we know there is always increase in the fund for the education system but never implemented in that area. So we have to work in this area. Government tries to make different policies which are implemented but quality never checked. Majority of fund goes in the pockets of officials working for this. There is a vast need to improve the quality and standards.

The time now is to modernize our education system so that our country can get much more technically graduated people which can help our country to developed state. Today's youth always try to go foreign for his higher education as they have much better facilities and quality of their system. Can't we get that quality here itself? We have to stop this brain drainage so as avoid students to run away from country. Our governments trying for various challenges faced but no one is doing well for that. Government came and goes but system remains intact.

Higher education is extremely diverse and the challenges and issues faced by higher education institutions are just as diverse. The process of education is not merely digesting books. It is also about doing several co-curricular and extra-curricular activities that give a broader meaning to life in general and education in particular. I believe that opportunities for such holistic development are not enough in India. Facilities for the same are lacking or not easily accessible in India. Even where facilities exist, there is a lack of information about the same.

Suggestions on the road to recovery for quality of higher education.

There are some suggestions and Expectations from Government, Industry, Educational Institutions, Parents and Students for improving quality of higher education:

Moving towards an innovative Society- As we move towards an innovative society, every human action will necessitate contributions from experts, and this will place the complete sector of higher education in sharp focal point. Although the priorities, which are being assigned today to the task of Education for All, will continue to be preponderant, the country will have to prepare itself to invest more and more on higher education and, simultaneously, measures will have to be taken to refine, diversify and upgrade higher education and research programmes.

Innovative Practices- The new technologies offer enormous opportunities for progress in all walks of life. It offers opportunities for economic growth and political stability, improved health, better service delivery, improved learning and socio-cultural advances. Though efforts are required to improve the country's innovative capacity, yet the efforts should be to construct on the existing strengths in light of new understanding of the research-innovation-growth linkage.

Correlation between Industries and Academic institutions- the present society needs the correlation between industries and academic institutions in terms of ensuring Industrial growth and enhancement of Academic skills in tune with the present modern civil society. This relationship ensures employability of skilled academia and it also facilitates good employability at global level.

Establishment of Public Private Partnership-PPP is most essential to bring in quality in the higher education system. Governments can ensure PPP through an appropriate policy. University Grants Commission and Ministry of HRD should play a major role in developing a purposeful interface between the Universities, Industries and National Research

Laboratories (NRLs) as a step towards PPP. Funding to NRLs by the government should ensure the involvement of institutions of higher education engaged in research activities to facilitate availability of latest sophisticated equipment. There has been some effort both by the government and the private education institutions to develop the teaching staff at various levels. However, this needs to be intensified with appropriate attention to all the aspects related in order to prepare quality and sufficient number of educational staff. Such efforts need a very serious structuring for the research base institutions. We have to be optimistic that private-public partnership and the Industry interface will take place in the field of education at all levels, and particularly in the backward regions, which is the need of the hour. To achieve excellence, we thus need to create a real partnership between government, educators and industry–Partnerships that can provide our high-tech industries with skilled workers who meet the standards of their industry.

To formulate Need Based Job-Oriented Courses-All round development of personality is the purpose of education. But the present day education is neither imparting true knowledge of life and nor improving the talent of a student by which one can achieve laurels in the field one is interested. So, combination of arts subjects and computer science and science and humanities or literature should be introduced so that such courses could be useful for the students to do jobs after recruitment in some companies which would reduce unnecessary rush to higher education. The programme must be focused on graduate studies and research and developing strategies and mechanisms for the rapid and efficient transfer of knowledge and for its application to specific national and local conditions and needs. Meritorious doctoral students should be recognized through teaching assistantships with stipends over and above the research fellowships. Finally, based on knowledge only vision of the future life and work can be had; based on this vision only a broad ambition can be fixed for oneself; and based on this ambition only one can lead interesting life doing satisfying job to do remarkable achievements in some field in the world.

Towards a New Educational vision-India realizes, like other nations of the world, that humanity stands today at the head of a new age of a large synthesis of knowledge, and that the East and the West have to collaborate in bringing about concerted action for universal upliftment, and lasting peace and unity. In this new age, great cultural achievements of the past have to be recovered and enriched in the context of the contemporary advancement so that humanity can successfully meet the evolutionary and revolutionary challenges and bring about a new type of humanity and society marked by integrated powers of physical, emotional, dynamic, intellectual, ethical, aesthetic and spiritual potentialities.

Quality improvement and World Class Education: Quality depends on its all functions and activities: teaching and academic programs, research and scholarship, staffing, students, building, facilities, equipments, services to the community and the academic environment. It also requires that higher education should be characterized by its international dimensions: exchange of knowledge, interactive networking, mobility of teachers and students and international research projects, while taking into account the national cultural values and circumstances. India should aspire for the international standard in education. Many national universities like in the USA, UK, Australia, etc. allow studies in higher education for foreign students in their countries and through correspondence courses as well. In the same way India Universities of world class education can also offer courses of studies to foreign students taking advantage of the globalization process. To achieve that goal it should adopt uniform international syllabus in its educational institutions.

Conclusion

After independence, there has been tremendous increase in institutions of higher learning in all disciplines. But with the quantitative growth has it been able to attend to the core issue of quality. India is today one of the fastest developing countries of the world with the annual growth rate going above 9 percent. In order to sustain that rate of growth, there is need to increase the number of institutes and also the quality of higher education in India. To reach and achieve the future requirements there is an urgent need to relook at the Financial Resources, Access and Equity, Quality Standards, Relevance and at the end the Responsiveness.

To attain and sustain national, regional or international quality, certain components are particularly relevant, notably careful selection of staff and continuous staff development, in particular through the promotion of appropriate programs for academic development, including teaching/learning methodology and mobility between countries, between higher education institutions and the world of work, as well as student mobility within and between countries. Internal self-evaluation and external review must be conducted openly by independent specialists, if possible with international experts.

References

1. Anandakrishnan, M. (2006) Privatization of higher education: Opportunities and anomalies. 'Privatization and commercialization of higher education' organized by NIEPA, May 2, 2006., New Delhi.
2. MHRD (2006) Annual Report. Ministry of Human Resource Development, Department of Secondary and Higher education. Government of India. New Delhi.
3. Planning Commission (1999) Approach paper to the Tenth Five-year Plan (2002-2007). Planning Commission. New Delhi.
4. UGC (2005) Research Handbook: Towards nurturing research culture in higher education institutions in India. University Grants Commission. New Delhi.
5. Agarwal, Pawan (2006) Higher Education in India: The Need for Change (ICIER Working Paper No. 180). New Delhi: Indian Council for Research on International Economic Relations, (http://www.icrier.org/publication/working papers 180. html).
6. Jandhyala B.G. Tilak, Absence of Policy and Perspective in Higher Education. Economic and Political Weekly Vol. 39, No. 21 (May 22, 2004), 2159-2164.
7. Higher Education in India: Issues, Concerns and New Direction http:// www.ugc.ac.in/pub/heindia. pdf.

Chapter-25

Accessibility of Higher Education through ICT

Dr. M. RAVI BABU,

Abstract

Globalization and technological changes have created a new global economy powered by technology, fueled by information and driven by knowledge. ICT is that technology which uses the information to meet human need or purposes including processing and exchanging. These technologies include computers, the internet, broadcasting technologies (radio and television) and telephony. ICT can affect the delivery of education and enable wider access to the same. In addition, it will increase flexibility so that learners can access the education regardless of time and geographical barriers. It can influence the way students are taught and how they learn. It would enable development of collaborative skills as well as knowledge creation skills. This in turn would better prepare the learners for lifelong learning as well as to join the industry. It can improve the quality of learning and thus contribute to the economy. Similarly wider availability of best practices and best course material in education, which can be shared by means of ICT, can foster better teaching. However there exist some risks and drawbacks with introducing ICT in education which have to be mitigated. Successful implementation of ICT to lead change is more about influencing and empowering teachers and supporting them in their engagement with students in learning rather than acquiring computer skills and obtaining software and equipment. Also proper controls and licensing should be ensured so that accountability, quality assurance, accreditation and consumer protection are taken care of. ICT enabled education will ultimately lead to the democratization of education. This paper discusses the few key issues in enhancing the quality and accessibility of higher education through the usage of ICT.

Keywords: *ICT, Technology, Internet, Higher Education.*

Introduction

'The future lies in the marriage of education and technology.'

(Blair, 1995)

Communication and information are at the very heart of the educational process. Information and communications technology (ICT) is an extended term for information technology (IT) which stresses the role of unified communications and the integration of telecommunications (telephone lines and wireless signals), computers as well as necessary enterprise software, middleware, storage, and audio-visual systems, which enable users to access, store, transmit, and manipulate information. In modern society ICT is ever-present, with over three billion people having access to the Internet. With approximately 8 out of 10 Internet users owning a Smartphone, information and data are increasing by leaps and bounds. This rapid growth, especially in developing countries, has led ICT to become a keystone of everyday life, in which life without some facet of technology renders most of clerical, work and routine tasks dysfunctional. The most recent authoritative data, released in 2014, shows "that Internet use continues to grow steadily, at 6.6 percent globally in 2014 (3.3 percent in developed countries, 8.7 percent in the developing world); the number of Internet users in developing countries has doubled in five years (2009-2014), with two thirds of all people online now living in the developing world."

Information and communication technology (ICT) is a force that has changed many aspects of the way we live. If one was to compare such fields as medicine, tourism, travel business, law, banking, engineering and architecture, the impact of ICT across the past two or three decades has been enormous. The way these fields operate today is vastly different from the ways they operated in the past. Today technology has emerged, strengthened and encouraged moves to adopt ICTs into classrooms and learning settings. These have included a growing need to explore efficiencies in terms of program delivery, the opportunities for flexible delivery provided by ICTs. The capacity of technology to provide support for customized educational programs to meet the needs of individual learners and the growing use of the Internet and WWW as tools for information access and communication.

Contributions of ICT

- Easy access to huge amount of information.
- Quick and reliable process of all kinds of data.
- Communication channels (on/off line)
- Data Storing
- Programming of computer tasks
- Interactivity
- Digitalization of all kind of information

Cross Cutting Applications of ICT in Education

ICTs open up new horizons for progress and the exchange of knowledge, education and training, and for the promotion of creativity and intercultural dialogue. The opportunities to accomplish UNESCO's core missions - to promote "the free exchange of ideas and knowledge" and to "maintain, increase and diffuse knowledge" - have possibly never been greater. Education, science, and culture are at the heart of the trend towards a knowledge society as are the media and information; thus all UNESCO sectors have a role to play in this process. The goal of this cross-cutting strategy is to show how UNESCO intends to provide a coordinated response, based on an interdisciplinary approach.

- The application of remote sensing for integrated management
- Developing open learning communities
- Higher education, open and distance knowledge base for decision makers
- ICT-based training in basic education for social development

In the 21st century, these factors and many others are bringing strong forces to bear on the adoption of ICTs in education and contemporary trends suggest we will soon see large scale changes in the way education is planned and delivered as a consequence of the opportunities and affordances of ICT. This paper seeks to explore the likely changes we will see in education as ICT acts as a powerful agent to change many of the educational practices to which we have become accustomed. In particular, the paper will explore the impact both current and emerging information and communication technologies will be likely to have in coming years on *what* is learned, *when* and *where* learning will take place and *how* the learning will occur.

ICT can be used as a tool in the process of education in the following ways:

- Informative tool: It provides vast amount of data in various formats such as audio, video, documents.
- Situating tool: It creates situations, which the student experiences in real life. Thus, simulation and virtual reality is possible.
- Constructive tool: To manipulate the data and generate analysis.
- Communicative tool: It can be used to remove communication barriers such as that of space and time (Lim and Chai, 2004).

E learning has the following advantages:

- Eliminating time barriers in education for learners as well as teachers

- ❖ Eliminating geographical barriers as learners can log on from any place
- ❖ Asynchronous interaction is made possible leading to thoughtful and creative interaction
- ❖ Enhanced group collaboration made possible via ICT
- ❖ New educational approaches can be used.
- ❖ It can provide speedy dissemination of education to target disadvantaged groups
- ❖ It offers the combination of education while balancing family and work life
- ❖ It enhances the international dimension of educational services
- ❖ It allows for just in time and just enough education for employees in organizations
- ❖ It can also be used for non-formal education like health campaigns and literacy campaigns

Integrating ICT in Higher Education: Advantages & Usage

- ❖ Empowerment in Learning
- ❖ Allows Effective Collaboration
- ❖ Allows Effective Networking
- ❖ Allows easy sharing of Resources
- ❖ Effective accessibility to Resources
- ❖ Ubiquitous Education

The emergence of ICTs as learning technologies has coincided with a growing awareness and recognition of alternative theories for learning. The theories of learning that hold the greatest way, today those are based on constructivist principles. These principles posit that learning is achieved by the active construction of knowledge supported by various perspectives within meaningful contexts. In constructivist theories, social interactions are seen to play a critical role in the processes of learning and cognition. In the past, the conventional process of teaching has revolved around teachers planning and leading students through a series of instructional sequences to achieve a desired learning outcome. Typically these forms of teaching have revolved around the planned transmission of a body of knowledge followed by some forms of interaction with the content as a means to consolidate the knowledge acquisition. Contemporary learning theory is based on the notion that learning is an active process of constructing knowledge rather than acquiring knowledge and that instruction is the process by which this knowledge construction is supported rather than a process of knowledge transmission.The strengths of constructivism lie in its emphasis on learning as a process of personal understanding and the development of meaning in ways which are active and interpretative. Learning approaches using contemporary ICTs provide many opportunities for constructivist learning through their provision and support for resource-based, student centered settings and by enabling learning to be related to context and to practice.

Challenges Ahead

- Modern ICT enabled innovative education technologies should be adopted to enhance higher learning.
- Teachers must try to integrate the ICT tools in their pedagogy as a facilitator, allowing student to construct their own learning, rather than rote memorizing the learning material.
- Gender disparities should be reduced.
- Monitoring and evaluation of programs should be conducted to meet the objective of lifelong learning.
- More emphasis should be given on follow up studies and remedial teaching.

Conclusion

ICT has fundamentally changed the practices and procedures of nearly all forms of endeavor within business and governance. Within education, ICT has begun to have a presence but the impact has not been as extensive as in other fields. Education is a very socially oriented activity and quality education has traditionally been associated with strong teachers having high degrees of personal contact with learners. The use of ICT in education lends itself to more studentcentered learning settings and often this creates some tensions for some teachers and students. But with the world moving rapidly into digital media and information, the role of ICT in education is becoming more and more important and this importance will continue to grow and develop in the 21st century. The role of ICT in transforming teaching and learning and seeks to explore how this will impact on the way programs will be offered and delivered in the universities and colleges of the future.The rise of IT sector and engineering education in India has boxed students into linear path without giving them a chance to explore and discover their passions. Concerted and collaborative efforts are needed in broaden student choices through liberal arts education. Today there is a need to revive the Higher Education in India in terms of access, equity and quality.

References:

1. Agarwal, P. (2006), 'Higher education in India: the need for a change', Indian Council for Research on International Economic Relations.
2. Amutabi, M. N. & Oketch, M. O. (2003), 'Experimenting in distance education: the African Virtual University (AVU) and the paradox of the World Bank in Kenya', *International Journal of Educational Development* 23(1), 57-73.
3. Bhattacharya, I. & Sharma, K. (2007), 'India in the knowledge economy – an electronic paradigm'. *International Journal of Educational Management.* Volume 21 No. 6, pp. 543-568.
4. Boucher, A., Davis, N.E., Dillon, P. Hobbs, P. & Tearle P. (1997) *Information Technology Assisted Teaching and Learning in Higher Education.* HEFCE Research Series. Higher Education Funding Council for England, Bristol.
5. Brown, A. & Davis, N.E. (eds) (2004) Digital technology, communities and education. World Yearbook in Education 2004. Routledge, London.
6. Collis, B. & Wende, M. van (eds) (2002) *Models of technology and change in higher education. An international comparative survey on the current and future use of ICT in higher education.* EDEN [http://www.eden.bme.hu/contents/dissemination/bulletin.html]
7. ICT. https://en.wikipedia.org/wiki/Information and communications technology.
8. IITE UNESCO (2000) *Analytical survey of distance education for the Information Society: policies, pedagogy and professional development.* UNESCO Institute for Information Technologies in Education, Moscow. [http://ww.iite.ru].
9. Johnson, D.L. & Maddux, C.D. (eds) (2003) *Technology in education. A twenty year retrospective.* The Hayworth Press, Binghampton, NY.
10. Mann, D., Shakeshaft, C., Becker, J., & Kottkamp, R. (1999) *West Virginia story: Achievement gains for a statewide comprehensive instructional technology program.* Milken Exchange on Educational Technology, Milken Family Foundation, Santa Monica, CA.
11. Partnership for 21st Century Skills (2003). *Learning for the 21st century.* Author, Washington DC. [http://www.21stcenturyskills.org].
12. Roblyer, M.D. & Marshall, J.C. (2003) Predicting success of virtual high school students: Preliminary results form an educational success prediction instrument. *Journal of Research on Technology and Education*, 35, 2, 241-255.
13. Solomon, G., Allen, N.J., & Resta P. (eds) (2003) *Toward digital equity: Bridging the divide.* Allyn & Bacon, Boston.

Chapter-26

Reforms in Quality of Higher Education

Reddeppa Tagadi,

Abstract

As one of three fundamental principles of India's higher education quality has been sloganizing in post-independent and being used to organize higher education system along with two other principles of expansion and equity. It is said that quality is all about realization of objectives of higher education and its stakeholders which required policies attentions across all aspects in all types of education. This paper says that quality in India's higher education is multidimensional, competitive and conflictive in matter of its reportage in the policy documents, and put attempts to study two contrast set of factors based reforms, related to academic which attaining improvements and governance which attaining complete overhaul, undertaken to ensure quality in the higher education on different higher education aspects of teaching and learning and research, innovation, social justice, information and communication and technology, regulation, methodologies, ties with foreign countries and MOUs and recent initiatives. It highlighted issues with these policies and said that these policies lacked social relevance. It is also noted that since these policies have single mandate orientation with the centralized directions, particularly governance related schemes; they are not meeting specific vision and objectives of different higher learning institutions. This paper is also mentioning that new methodologies developed to rank institutions have inadequate rural and social conception.

Introduction

As our national leaders realized complexities in system, along with the importance of higher education in national development, they sloganized the three fundamental principles of expansion, equity and excellence to cover whole system, which are reflection of higher education system problems to be solved and objectives of higher education to be served and national needs to be meet, as an integument to restructure, consolidate and evolve higher education to suit the modernized and self-reliant independent India. Though the talk about quality in higher education has been there from the time of British Raj and echoed in the government policy documents after independence, they got prioritized and found the place in policy circle education in mid-eighties. Despite the conflict between the three fundamental concepts, policymaker intervened to ensure quality with number reforms by translating national educational policy-1986 and program of action-1992s recommendations in the 1900s and 2000s and entrusted the UGC to undertake the responsibility to implement all measurements.

Protecting university education from degeneration and erosion of quality was far most concern than the expansion of higher education (Indian higher education report-2015, pg-43). India has addressed contentious trilemma, how to reconcile scale, costs, and quality, by focusing on scale and costs with the quality the inevitable causality (Kapoor & Mehta-2017). A conflict between the urge for expansion and the need for quality has rendered more complex the task of reorganization of university education (Report of the review of first five year plan-1957). At the policy level, Quality in higher education is contested concept, and it has the conflict with the expansion particularly and equity and the discourse in different dossiers on this aspect also rendered diverse views. There are two different types of approaches for quality as per commissions and committees, before 2000 and after 2000. The University Education Commission-1948-49 and education Commission-1966-68 favored to quality maintenance in the disadvantage of expansion and batted for selective admission on per availability of facilities. Challenge of education document-1985 and NEP-1986 favored to consolidation rather than expansion. But the government approach to quality changed from the advent of the 21st century as committees and commission like Ambani-Birla committee-2000, NKC-2006, and Narayana Murthy committee-2012 favored for expansion education opportunities with maintaining quality. Even in the 21st century, there are policy documents like Yashpal committee which favored for quality over the expansion. But it is interesting to see that while NKC batted for expansion of system, it sees that quality, expansion, and equity are separable and says that they do not go hand in hand, but in contrast, Yashpal committee, despite its stand for non-expansion of system, sees quality, expansion, and equity are non-separable and says that they go hand in hand. This has highlighted ambiguous recommendations of committee and commission and the struggle between expansion and quality making whole reorganization higher education system of India very complicated.

Reforms for Quality enhancement involve with the institutions and aspects of system Indian higher education. These reforms range from higher technical institutions, research institutions, general universities, disciplines, colleges, state universities and deemed to be universities and distance learning institutions, researchers and scholars along with aspects of higher education like governance, research and innovation, teaching and learning process, ICT and funding and fellowships etc. with intentions of ensuring expansion, equity, excellence, empowerment, engagement and ethics.

The UGC as an autonomous body has been undertaking schemes for the improvement of quality through giving directions and funding other regulations. UGC has been using the 12B condition providing funding to universities and colleges. To improve infrastructures and basic facilities in the central and state universities under section 2(f) and 12(b) and deemed to be universities, general development assistance to central, state and deemed to be universities and this scheme also merged with development grants, One time catch up grant to non-12b state universities under 2(f) and 12(b) schemes funded by the state governments, Operation faculty recharge, Scheme of enhancing faculty resources of universities, Rajiv Gandhi chairs in universities, academic staff college, special assistance program, CPE in particular areas, area study centers in universities, UPE, Computer centers in universities, UGC-INFONET connectivity program, UGC-INFONET digital library consortium, promotion of yoga education and incentives for resources mobilization development assistance for up gradation of existing and new management departments. Although these schemes are concentrated on augmenting overall quality, they were primarily concentrated on teaching and learning process and research, infrastructure development, ICT, socio-economic development, and public policy. The finance allotted to universities under their schemes is high compared with colleges receiving under their schemes (UGC-2011).

The UGC has undertaken Schemes particularly to improve quality in the colleges. The important one is developments grants to colleges which are merged scheme of 14 other developmental schemes to development infrastructure and other developmental activities. One time catch grant to uncovered (non 12b) colleges, development assistance to colleges for construction of buildings, construction of women hostel for colleges, establishment of new degree colleges in educationally backward districts, faculty development program for colleges, organizing seminars, conference and workshops , CPE, instrumentation maintenance facility in the colleges, establishing and up gradation of UGC network resources center in colleges and jubilee centenary grants to colleges. Creation and expansion of infrastructure academically and physically and creation and enhancing of even educational ambiance are the main agenda behind schemes for colleges.

Interestingly some schemes take the age of colleges in awarding (UGC-2011).

The UGC also applied some schemes for both universities and colleges. Providing additional assistance to universities and 5,500 colleges already covered under section 12(b) of UGC act 1956, development of women studies in Indian universities and colleges, capacity building for women managers in higher education, special cells for SC/ST in universities, DTBU, grant-in-aid-institutions and IUCs receiving central assistance, innovative and emerging areas, setting media centers and affiliated media centers, carrier orientated courses in universities and colleges, IQAC in higher educational institutions, E-content development, strengthening humanities and social science teaching and research capacity, fellowships like research fellowships in humanities and social sciences, development of sports infrastructure and equipment, guidelines for universities, research institutions and colleges on usage of radioactive and other hazardous materials, epoch-making social thinkers of India, human rights and value education, lifelong learning and extension. They were centered on teaching and learning process, research mostly. Expanding study area base and opportunities and maintain gender parity are other aspects got attention under these schemes (UGC-2011).

In the area of quality enhancement, Indian higher education has seen such an innovative policy developments in the 12th five-year plan. Under the 12th five year plan, number decisions made to take for facilitation of quality and excellence. Making accreditation mandatory for institutions and programs, mandatory teacher and student ration and lifting ban teacher recruitment, developments in ASCs, faculty and students mobility among institutions and states, facilitation of international students, developments in assessment process, participatory teaching and learning process, establishing schools in specific area of knowledge, national educational resources portal, strengthening ICT facilities, flexible and de-bureaucratized organization of the higher education institutions, structural amendments to regulating bodies, development autonomous college system, converting self-financed courses to government approved courses and collaboration and coordination between inside and outside institutions, encouraging multi-disciplinary studies, business connections and intellectual property rights, research in state universities and colleges, increasing funding under schemes, curbing plagiarism, fellowships and encouragements for universities and other institutions to maximum utilization of research facilities in the national laboratories and institutions and establishment of Navratna universities (UGC-2011). In recent years, the government implemented path-breaking schemes like RUSA, MOOCs, and IMPRINT, GIAN and PMMMNMT, etc.

There is a selection process followed in awarding schemes involved by the expert committee visiting and also there is mid-term reviewing. The schemes are particularly related to academic domain have limited operation tenure, and there is the possibility of revision and extension. Limited institutions awarded based on the standard by using Section 12(b) and section 2 (f) of UGC 1956 Act as criteria for selection of institutions and neglecting other institutions which are not part of these UGC sections. These schemes also are not removing corruption in academics. The schemes also failed in reflecting broad objectives of higher education. All these programs highlight regional gaps, institutional imbalance, thematic focus, standardized problem and gaps in money allocations. Under the scheme of special assistance program, institutions are being supported under three different levels of DSA which is supporting 89 departments, DRS supporting 712 departments and CSA supporting departments 142, in total UGC supporting departments 943, purely promote research in all domains of knowledge. Under these schemes interestingly state universities are hugely getting benefitted and central universities and deemed to be universities stand next. The scheme dispersal in different state institutions is also uneven, even online of different programs. In some states like Jammu Kashmir and Madhya Pradesh under CAS and Assam and Jharkhand under DSA, institutions have not got this scheme status, while in some states like Andhra Pradesh and West Bengal, institutions got the huge number of slots as others states like Jharkhand and Uttarakhand got the low number of slots. Schemes like UPE allocated to only limited institutions, number of 15 in 10 states that to schemes focused areas mostly reserved to science and technology-based disciplines and also schemes like CPEPA, reserved to 23 particular areas and centers spread over in 13 states. Under the scheme of major and minor research projects, UGC supported 987 major research projects and 7501 minor research projects in the universities and colleges with miniscule money of 61.86 crores and these projects dispersal uneven in state wise. Even though the UGC has launched CPE for colleges, the scheme reached out was very limited, out thousands of colleges only 284 colleges got selected, and also unevenly distributed among the states. UGCs faculty development programs are also disbursed unevenly among the states (UGC-2013).

Enhancing the quality of an expanding and diverse system has become the major challenge facing most of the countries across the globe (India higher education report-2017). An ideal quality higher education system is which win fully combined with expansion, diversity, and equity. In India, higher education cannot be seen as interested field of elite as people from downtrodden sections like SC, ST, OBC, Minorities, and women popping up, particularly after the 1990s, who need special arrangements to perform well in higher education, due to their socio-economic, cultural regional and language-based study experiences and also they are first generation learners. By keeping it in mind, to develop professionalism and academic eminence in universities and colleges, UGC has intervened with different schemes for development of teaching and research, advanced studies and learning process, but these schemes mostly about to encourage talent of the institution's stakeholders and compensation for social inequity. Post graduate merit scholarship for university rank holders at undergraduate level, research fellowship in science for meritorious students, JRF in science, humanities and social science, engineering and technology, JRF research associateship for foreign national, fellowships to MPhil and PhD scholars in central universities, Dr. S. Radhakrishna post-doctoral fellowship for humanities and social science including languages, Dr. D.S. Kothari postdoctoral fellowship in science, medical science and engineering science, PDF to women candidates, post-graduate Indira Gandhi scholarship single girl child, RGNF for SC/ST students, PDF for SC/ST, PDF for Women, emeritus fellowship, special honorarium for teachers who are part of science academy's, research award, major research project, minor research project, incentives for teachers based organization for organization of various academic and research activities, travel grant schemes for college teachers, librarians, V/Cs and others, appointment and honorarium of guest and part-time teachers. These schemes are proven that quality goes in hand in hand with expansion and equity. These schemes reflects society requirements of Social inequalities and backwardness, skill development for employment needs, sophistication of society, usage of science and technology, etc., but important schemes are not inclusive as they specified with institutions, subjects, and stakeholders and also they have subjected to standards on limited operational tenure (UGC-2011 and UGC-2013).

In this process of increasing quality by sharing educational expertise and opportunities of higher education with other countries, the Indian government joined hands with other nations like France, USA, and the UK. Singh and Obama, 21st-century knowledge initiative, is the collaboration of USA and India to promote partnership between both countries in higher learning and research in the area of development studies like energy, sustainable development, and climate change and environmental studies, education and community development, innovation, and urban and rural development. With the United Kingdom, India had initiated a scheme called UK-India education and research initiative to foster educational institutions relationships between two countries. Under this scheme, UGC has undertaken 20 projects related to sustainable development and science topics. UGC give awards like research awards to teachers, Kothari fellowship in SET, Raman fellowships for PDF scholars in the USA and non-net fellowships and Fellow of different academia. In 2016, BRIC had issued New Delhi declaration on education which aims of ensuring the inclusive, equitable and quality education at all level of education in member countries. In 2018, India had entered into MOU with government of France to facilitate mutual recognition of educational qualifications and periods of study undertaken by students in dully approved and recognized institutions of both countries along with it both countries facilitated 15 more MOUs between the institutions of both countries in areas of higher education, research, innovation and faculty exchange, etc. (UGC-2013).

Despite there is minuscule attention for innovation culture in HEIs in national scientific policies and education policies, as the third generation university activity, innovation occupies an essential part of academic culture. As delivering justice to the poor and making them prosper is a vital agenda of development of innovation culture, it becomes the mandate for policymakers to involve higher learning institutions in the national culture of innovation. The government of India has initiated schemes to augment culture of innovation in higher learning institutions. MIC or MHRD innovation cell is established for systematic promotion the innovation culture in HEIs through the boosting, inspiring and cultivating young students to new ideas in their developmental years through the network of innovative clubs which are intended to form the basic framework for structure, formation and smooth running of innovation cells. MHRD also launched another scheme called Atal Ranking of institutions on innovation achievements-ARIIA, is also formed methodology to rank HEIs as per institutions innovation attainments with indicators, Smart India Hackathon-2019(SIH) is also launched by the Indian government at the national level, and it would provide a platform for students to solve daily problems with innovative ideas with working with NGOs, and other public and private organizations.

National student startup policy started with the aim of promoting student-driven innovation and startups. Ensuring quality is one of important agenda of UGC from a long time. Under regulating bodies UGC and AICTE, there are two kinds of agencies for the quality assessment and accreditation in India, and there are NAAC which assess and accredit higher learning institutions and NBA which engage in specialized accreditation technical institutions. There is another ranking body called NBICAR which is participating in specialized accreditation in agriculture institutions. There are other statutory bodies like BCI, DCI, PCI and MCI which recognize courses and programs and play the pivotal role in ensuring of quality in programs and institutions. For those institutions which are affiliated to universities, affiliating universities maintain quality.

These are all ranks giving bodies, except statutory bodies, and work for restoring accountability and transparency of higher education institutions. These institutions are given ranking to education institutions by following the set of parameters which reflect all aspects of higher education. Since the ranks given by these institutions are considered as the matter of reputation, money collection, faculty, and student mustering, and provision of the data and information of institutions, nationally and internationally, they gained prominence in country's higher education system.

Formation of methodologies or framework, like National Institution Ranking Framework, Swacch Campus Ranking and Atal Ranking of Institutions on Innovation Achievements, to rank the higher education institutions as per their realities is another important step in restoring quality in institutions and prepare them for global rankings. Yashpal committee highlighted the problem with criteria setups and asked it to be including native sensibilities and realities. Unfortunately, these parameters belonged to the methodologies and regulating bodies are lacking these broad institutional own goals and broad education aims as they restricted to the academic excellence mostly. There are no parameters of NIRF to assess national and socio-cultural provisions and responsibilities of the institutions. Nationalism, national integration and unity and other aims and values and morals and religion and student learning of how to live in society are missing from. Rural area has specific needs like cultivation, handicraft works and other livelihood needs and amenities to meet by HEIs. But parameters have no scope for these to be assessed. Though these methodologies and parameters are being directed to rank state education institutions, they are not evaluating the state governments who are playing the prime role in the uplifting higher education sector. Every institution has a specific objective, despite their nature and status. Even NAAC and methodologies have not had scope for assessing their objectives. ARIIA parameters purely promote marketization and commerciality in the HEIs. It treated innovation as commerciality and ignored socio-scientific conception of innovation and responsible research and innovation. It is not having scope for citizen science, socialization of innovation and innovations in social science. Teaching and learning process with changes in the curriculum of institutions to support innovation in science and technology and marketization and commerciality.

Conclusion

There have been some interesting changes in higher education policy making with abducting policy making sites, delaying legislation actions, involving bureaucrats, repetitive and incoherent protections by commissions and making schemes promotion of private interests which have the negative impact on quality enhancement in higher education. It is unfortunate to see schemes like IOE, Graded Autonomy and tripartite memoranda understanding and proposal of higher education financing agency intended to promote commercialization and privatization. As prevention of wastage and make huge young population valuable for national development depends on quality higher education with expansion and equity, governments must put all needy efforts to fill lacunas in the schemes and reorient them to meet the needs of stakeholders.

Reference

1. Auroshree,-2018: ARIIA Launched to Foster the Culture of Innovations in Higher Educational Institutions. https: //bolg.scconline.com.
2. Auroshree-2018: Cabinet Approves the Agreement with France to Facilitate Mutual Recognition of Academic Qualification. https: //bolg.scconline.com.
3. UGC (2011): UGC Interventions Towards Quality Enhancement in Higher Education: the Compendium of the Scheme, New Delhi.
4. UGC (2013): Indian Higher Education-Quest for Excellence: A Compendium of Flag-ship Programs of UGC. New Delhi.
5. UGC (2011): Inclusive and Qualitative Expansion of Higher Education: 12th Five-Year Plan, 2012-2017, page no; 87-103, New Delhi.
6. Devesh Kapur, Pratap Bhanu Mehta ed. Navigating the Labyrinth: Perspectives on India Higher Education. Hyderabad: orient blackswan, 2017, page no. 7-20.
7. MHRD (2018): The Government has Taken up Far-reaching Education Reforms to Improve Quality and Access to Education, PIB, GOI, New Delhi.
8. N.V Varghese, Garima Malik ed. India Higher Education Report 2015. New Delhi: Routledge, 2016, part-1.
9. N.V Varghese, Pachauri Anupam, Mandal Sayantan, ed. India Higher Education Report 2017: Teaching, Learning, and Quality in Higher Education. New Delhi: Sage, 2018, 1-12.
10. Pal, Yash (2009); Report of the Committee to Advice on Renovation and Rejuvenation of Higher Education. https://www.aicte-india.org, page no.26-28.
11. Rajalakshmi T.K, Perils of Privatization, Frontline, August 04-17, 2018.
12. Saba-2016: New Delhi Declaration on Education Adopted by BRICS Minister of Education. https://bolg.scconline.com.

Chapter-27

Research Ecosystem and Plagarisum

Sathyanarayana G,

Abstract

The aim of this paper is to propose a new theoretical perspective and a conceptual model to build a sustainable research ecosystem in universities. A thriving university research ecosystem leads to consistency, efficiency and sufficiency in research output. The ideas proposed in this paper are in the growing stage and in the emerging market context. Future research is suggested to Operationalise and validate the proposed framework in both developing and developed nation context. Over the past decades, plagiarism has been classified as a multi-layer phenomenon of dishonesty that occurs in higher education. A number of research papers have identified a host of factors such as gender, socialisation, efficiency gain, motivation for study, methodological uncertainties or easy access to electronic information via the Internet and new technologies, as reasons driving plagiarism. The paper at hand examines whether such factors are still effective factors influencing plagiarism. A quantitative paper-and-pencil survey was carried out in 2017/ 2018 academic year, with a sample of 485 students from higher education institutions. The major findings of this research reveal that easy access to information-communication technologies and the Web is the main reason driving plagiarism. In that regard, there are no significant differences between students in terms of personal factors such as gender, motivation for study, and socialisation. In this sense, digitalisation and the Web outrank national borders.

Keywords: *Research, Research Ecosystem, Plagiarism*

Introduction

"If you want to build a world-class city, build a great university. Great research universities are engines for progress individual and societal. They create knowledge, explore new possibility, and educate students and other stakeholders. Universities extend our understanding of particular disciplines and, through basic research, provide the foundation for transformative advances. These improvements may include next-generation products, such as pharmaceuticals that target serious disease, or superior processes, like better logistics to deliver supplies or humanitarian aid. training good members of society" through the refinement, development, and expression of their opinions. When it works well, this process consolidates what's best about the received wisdom, and yet is unafraid to challenge status quo thinking when it falls short. Such challenges, after all, can generate bold ideas and new models, which then may lead to break through that solve urgent social problems.

Systems Thinking

It takes a robust ecosystem to succeed. Each of us is involved in an ecosystem — more than one, really, since we all are part of dynamic relationships in our personal and professional lives. These relationships frame our decisions and inform our options. We're subject to influences and obligations: our spouse, family, finances, and jobs are usually among our top priorities. Balanced attention to each aspect of our lives brings fulfillment; imbalance in one area can affect the whole.

- Creative and motivated talent: A world-class faculty is manifestly the foundational element, since thought leadership is at the core of research and teaching. At a university, talent does not stop at the faculty but includes great students, post-docs, and research staff. Recruitment and retention of talent is vital for every business, and a research university is no different. As in other businesses, universities leverage world-class talent to attract additional exemplary talent. The very best faculty not only are un intimidated by those who some say are better, but they strive to recruit colleagues who are even better than themselves. They know that this talent makes the entire research enterprise thrive, even their own, and allows everyone within it to pursue new ideas with greater potential impact. But talent alone is insufficient.
- The university's original core facility was a library: every faculty member could not possibly buy every book needed to conduct great research, so they turned to the library as an essential resource. Similarly, today, not every faculty member can buy and maintain each piece of scientific instrumentation or every IT system necessary to conduct research. This is especially the case with very expensive tools that path breaking research now often requires. Core facilities bring these resources, and the expertise to use them, into reach.

- Administrative support: The research environment has become more complex and regulated. Faculty need experts to help them navigate that complexity and, significantly, to allow faculty to remain focused on what they do best — teaching and research. Building a strong, efficient administrative ecosystem is vital. While administrators do not directly drive classroom teaching or produce new research knowledge, they do perform a catalytic function and support those who are in the frontlines of discovery. As such, they are very much a part of the team producing discovery.
- Collaborations: A university is a knowledge hub, but one with many connections around campus and to the world beyond. Candidly, not all the talent necessary for new discoveries can or should be found locally. Researchers need a way to collaborate within their university and with colleagues at other institutions. These relationships are especially crucial as new fields develop at the intersection of existing ones, prompting novel discovery opportunities. Collaborations also inspire greater research relevance, enabling more knowledge transfer from the laboratory bench to society. A great research university enables and encourages the development of those collaborations that drive new discoveries.
- An entrepreneurial environment: It was once enough for academics to publish their findings and let society take the next steps. While that model will always be the foundation for academic scholarship, universities are finding that supporting a more direct outlet for discovery is essential. Too often, good ideas stalled at publication and went unimplemented. Increasingly, our faculty, post-docs, and students want to drive the next steps of taking a discovery directly to society. It is now essential that universities have an entrepreneurial environment to advance innovations.
- Financial resources. Research is expensive. Research is often a "long game," one measured in decades, not years or fiscal quarters. That's why long-term financial support and excellent fiscal management are vital to the discovery ecosystem. Faculty generate much of their own funding — for instance, through grants — but not all of it. Some of those resources must come from other places. The university itself and incredibly supportive donors are two major other sources.

The research ecosystem drives the discovery side of a research university. It can be framed simply, but keeping harmony among the parts is challenging: if one component becomes "overgrown," which can happen simply through success, another component suffers due to lack of resources. By neglecting one part of the system, we hobble the entire enterprise, limiting growth and impact. Great research universities continuously monitor and proactively adjust the entire network of resource relationships, identifying needs, measuring results, and assessing opportunities for high-impact growth. It takes an ecosystem to propel discovery; it takes diligence to sustain the ecosystem. Universities with robust ecosystems drive progress for their own stakeholders and for society.

Across various disciplines there has been an increased call to focus on the relationship between university research, its productivity and stakeholder's involvement. The importance of research lies in the fact that research is the foundation for knowledge that has made innovation and application possibly resulting in benefits for the society at large (Marginson, 2009). It is also true that all research does not lead to immediate gains and in reality some of it does not lead to any measurable outcome but it is the inquisitive spirit of mankind that expresses itself through research. This gives rise to some interesting questions such as what it takes to produce high quality research, how various stakeholders interact with each other and what could be the possible measures to increase research productivity.

Objectives

1. To find out the factors influencing plagiarism and research ecosystem.
2. To know the factors influencing plagiarism connected with specific areas of study (technical sciences, social sciences, natural sciences)?
3. To assess the students' motivation factors influencing plagiarism

Advent of Research Universities

Today research has become an important function of the university system although its roots can be traced back to the beginning of the 19th century research is of ultimate importance for all universities as the status of universities is based on the research quality and productivity. Many authors have defined research in many ways as regards to the discipline and form in question.

Research is primarily defined in different ways by various disciplines and can take many forms. A broad definition of research by Shuttle worth (2008) suggests that research includes any gathering of data, information and facts for the advancement of knowledge.

Another definition by Creswell (2002) states that "research is a process of steps used to collect and analyze information to increase our understanding of a topic or issue". It consists of three steps: pose a question, collect data to answer the question, and present an answer to the question.

The aim of these universities is to bring research to the core of the university system and apply that research to national economic development. It all started in the later part of the 19th century with the onset of the direct service to society mainly in agriculture and industry to the objectives of research universities. This brought universities to the limelight and since then universities have been contributing to the society more directly through research and development in almost all countries worldwide

The University Research System Over a period of time, universities world over have developed indigenous science and technology system. The science and technology system comprises of resources available to the university like finance, governance or administrative, human, intellectual, and physical capital that acts as inputs to the productivity through research, education, training, and socialization generating intellectual and human outputs.

According to Frischmann (2008), the system comprises of:

I. Human Capital: Faculty, Researchers, Students, Administrators, Technicians etc;

II. Governance Capital: Rules, Norms, Policies;

III. Physical Capital: Land, Facilities and Equipment;

IV. Intellectual Capital: Knowledge, Information, Ideas; and

I. Financial Capital: Research Grant, Funding etc. Each of these resources is integral to the system.

The elements of this system, combined within a university structure, together act as valuable inputs in reaching the desired goals of universities like facilitation of research, dissemination of knowledge through education, imparting training and acting for the betterment of the society at large. University science and technology research systems, like any other system, are invaluable to the society because of the economic activity they generate in addition to the knowledge base that they create for the society. In fact the contributions of the research systems are in the value that is imbibed in final output (Frischmann, 2005). The research results produced by these systems mostly contribute to industrial and social needs by facilitating the production of various private or public goods. The results derived from research not only vary in specifications but also in terms of its use and application to reach desired outcomes towards the benefit of the society (Reichman and Uhlir, 2003). Allocation of the infrastructural capital of the universities is not a conscious decision to exploit the market potential of research results. (Auerswald and Branscom, 2003). Therefore, the majority of the research and development activities resulting in results have not been towards market oriented research. Of course, this is not to say that university research systems have not contributed by way of conducting commercial research or that research results have never been used commercially but rather that this area has not been an area of priority to the universities (Henderson, Jaffe and Trajtenberg, 1998).

Historically speaking, as regards to the industry or its need in terms of industry orientation, universities have not allocated enough resources. But the trends are changing with changing times. In the same way, for a good part of the last century public funding for research in universities have not been towards finding solutions for specific problems of the commercial segment of the To solve the problems of insufficient research and underutilization of research results by the industry, a re-look at the age old concept of production and utilization of intellectual property was required (Kieff, 2001). An identification of major facilitators of research in universities thus becomes pertinent.

Defining University Research Ecosystem

University Research Ecosystem (URE) can be basically understood as a community of researchers which interacts with one another, their environment and other stakeholders interested in their respective areas of research in such a way that knowledge is transferred between them and system-level processes emerge. For a research ecosystem to evolve, sharing of knowledge is a must as it works like essential abiotic components of a biological ecosystem. Research ecosystem can be better understood if we analyze it by two views: stakeholder view and process view.

Stakeholders view as collection of interaction of individuals and institutions. The key stakeholders of a research ecosystem of an institution are their faculty, doctoral students, research associates and postgraduate students. Burrows (1999) called these stakeholders, facilitators which included regulatory powers, teaching staff, administrative personnel, competitors, donors, governmental organizations, and various partners among others. Here, it should also be noted that research in isolation is not possible in new age and knowledge economy. Cut throat completion, changing technology and other resource constraints define the context which calls for collaboration with external institutions, industry, central or state government. For research ecosystem to survive, each and every stakeholder has to play a critical and responsible role.

Stakeholder View of Research Ecosystem Research Ecosystem Faculty Research Associates Funding Agencies State Government, Central government Industry External Institutes Post Graduate Students Doctoral Students.

The different processes which help the stakeholders of the research ecosystem to share and transfer knowledge among them.

The process view is characterized by the processes that can guide a university research ecosystem if managed carefully. These include regular brainstorming in seminars, workshops, conferences and online forums and informal gatherings as well. Technology being a major factor in almost every walk of life cannot be ignored in creation of a research ecosystem. Leveraging on technology available, a library information system and an academic information system can be developed by the institutes to give access to journals, books and audio and video archives as well as making forums and notice boards, etc. Figure 2: Process View of Research Ecosystem Research Ecosystem Research Review Seminars Research Training Seminars Workshops Academic Information System Library Information System Online Research Forums Journals and book publications Conferences Doctoral Summer Schools sustainable research ecosystem is a system that survives, functions, and updates itself over time; a system in which research community can continue to interact, share, and transfer the knowledge; which can guide the upcoming generations of researchers on its own. Research ecosystems are not static. The properties of a research ecosystem are governed by four dynamic elements or interactive controls: regional research culture, research resource management, research stakeholders, and disturbance regime. These interactive controls are constrained by four external factors: global research culture, global research community, and time. interactive controls must be conserved to sustain a research ecosystem. A new research ecosystem with different properties will evolve with the major changes in any interactive controls. Though each interactive control may change over the time, these controls operate within bounds represented by unique research ecosystem in a way that large changes in interactive controls are prevent Research Culture (National/ Regional/ Institutional) Research culture is the interactive control that most strongly governs the structure and research productivity of a research ecosystem. The key ingredients of the research cultures are: trust, collaboration, cooperation, and motivation. Trust is necessary for the stakeholders to interact and share their research ideas without fearing of theft of the same with a hope that they will get honest feedbacks from others. Trust will make the foundation for the research stakeholders to collaborate and cooperate for the greater interest of research community and society at large. Collaboration and cooperation amongst similar as well as cross disciplinary stakeholders will increase the research productivity of ecosystem and effectiveness of the research ecosystem processes. Motivation such as rewards, acknowledgements, promotions, incentives will lead to the greater interests of the Research Ecosystem Processes National/Reg ional /Institutional research Culture Disturbance Regime Research resource management/ Knowledge management Research stakeholders Global Research Culture Time Global Research Community Society researchers and other stakeholders to concentrate towards the quality research that in turns results into the synchronization among the research stake holders and creation of sustainable research ecosystem. Sharing of knowledge plays a vital role in attaining the sustainability for a research ecosystem. However current studies show that for sharing the knowledge trust, cooperation, collaboration and motivation is required.

Conclusions

In contrast to a number of preliminary studies, the major findings of this research paper indicate that new technologies and the Web have a strong and significant influence on plagiarism, whereas in this specific context gender and socialisation factors do not play a significant role. Since the majority of the students in our study believe that new technologies and the Web have a strong influence on plagiarism, we can assume that technological progress and globalisation has started breaking down national frontiers and crossing cultural boundaries. These findings have also created the impression that at universities the gender gap is not predominant in all areas as it might be in society. This paper started with an aim to develop a new understanding of producing high quality research through the development of a unique perspective of creation of research ecosystem and plagarisum. We expect that research based on this perspective would immensely benefit the research both as a practice and process in institutes of higher learning in emerging markets like India. Firstly, it is expected that such research would provide valuable input towards the creation of such sustaining ecosystems of research, on the basis of features operationalized and described in this conceptual paper. The insights generated here would therefore contribute to the existing models and frameworks that very few institutes follow. New as well as existing institutes can take these inputs to co-create an ecosystem of learning. The future research initiatives need to carefully analyze the dual perspective of research as well as the teaching in the universities same can be studied from the knowledge sharing point of view.

References

1. Altbach, P. G., &Salmi, J. (Eds.). (2011). The road to academic excellence: The making of world-class research universities. World Bank Publications. Marginson, S. (2009). Open source knowledge and university rankings. Thesis Eleven, 96(1), 9-39.
2. Shuttleworth, M. (2008).Definition of research. Experiment Resources.
3. Wang YM. University student online plagiarism. International Journal on E-learning. 2008; 7(4): 743– 757.
4. Altbach, P. G. (2008). The complex roles of universities in the period of globalization.
5. Das, S. (2007). The Higher Education in India and the Challenge of Globalisation. Social Scientist, 47-67.
6. Frischmann, B. M. (2005). An economic theory of infrastructure and commons management. Minnesota Law Review, 89, 917-1030.
7. Creswell, J. W. (2002). Educational research: Planning, conducting, and evaluating quantitative. Prentice Hall.
8. Wong, K. Y., & Aspinwall, E. (2004). Knowledge Management Implementation Frameworks: A Review. Knowledge and Process Management,

Chapter- 28

Current Status and Problems of Higher Education Among Tribals in Telangana State

D. Shiva,

Abstract

Better education is necessary for socio-economic development of the Scheduled Tribes. It develops their confidence and helps to build the personality of a person. School education plays a great role in Tribal's life. The whole education has been divided into three divisions such as the primary education, secondary education and Higher Secondary education. All the divisions of education have their own importance and benefits. Primary education prepares the base which helps throughout the life, secondary education prepares the path for further study and higher secondary education prepares the ultimate path of the future and whole life. The present study is on Higher Education status and problems among tribals with literacy Rate, Gross Enrollment, Pupil Teacher Ratio and Growth of Universities in Telangana State. The analysis is based on secondary data.

***Keywords**: Higher Education, Tribals, Status, Importance, Enrollment.*

Introduction

Education is one of the essential requirements for man-making and nation building. It is indispensible for development of human resources. Education imparts knowledge, skills, and character. Education is a determinant of the social, economic, cultural and political development of a region. Literacy determines the standard of living, levels of income, fertility and mortality, social status, economic growth etc.

The state of Telangana emerged as the 29th state in the Indian Union as per the Andhra Pradesh Reorganization Act, 2014 of Parliament, which received the assent of the President of India on the 1st March, 2014 and came into existence with effect from 2nd June, 2014.

Telangana is one of the States having large tracts of hilly and agency areas and sizeable scheduled tribe population. According to 2011 census, the scheduled tribe population is 31.78 lakhs constituting 9.08 percent in the total population of the state. Out of total 50, 24,104 lakhs of total scheduled tribe population of the state 25, 48,295 lacks are male and 24,75,809 lakhs are female. In Telangana Tribal literacy 49.80 percent, male literacy 61.02 percent and female literacy 40.64 percent.

The state of Telangana has been satisfactorily fulfilling the education in terms of access, equity and excellence, the three tenets of Higher Education. The central universities and institutions of the state are catering to the needs of the cosmopolitan populations and multiple branches of learning. The geographical distribution of Higher Education institutions is based on the district as a unit in order to cater to the needs of urban, rural and tribal populations. In addition to the conventional courses and institutions, the health, language, culture, agriculture and gender issues are prioritized to establish universities and institutions.

In India, literacy and human development are keys to any quantitative social change and those two factors influence demographic behaviour. The educational system in India is the second largest in the world. All India Survey on Higher Education 2015-16 covers entire Higher Education Institutions in the country. Institutions are categorized in 3 broad Categories; University, College and Stand-Alone Institutions. There are 799 Universities, 39071 colleges and 11923 Stand Alone Institutions listed on AISHE web portal and out of them 754 Universities, 33903 Colleges and 7154 Stand Alone Institutions have responded during the survey. 268 Universities are affiliating i.e. having Colleges. 277 Universities are privately managed. 14 Universities are exclusively for women, 4 in Rajasthan, 2 in Tamil Nadu & 1 each in Andhra Pradesh, Assam, Delhi, Haryana, Karnataka, Maharashtra, Uttarkhand and West Bengal. In addition to 1 Central Open University, 13 State Open Universities and 1 State Private Open University, there are 118 Dual mode Universities, which offer education through distance mode also and the maximum (19) of them are located in Tamil Nadu. There are 459 General, 101 Technical, 64 Agriculture & Allied, 50 Medical, 20 Law, 11 Sanskrit and 7 Language Universities. Total enrollment in higher education has been estimated to be 34.6 million with 18.6 million boys and 16 million girls. Girls constitute 46.2 percent of the total enrollment. Gross Enrollment Ratio (GER) in Higher education in India is 24.5 percent as on 2015-16.

The Ministry of Tribal Affairs is implementing the education-oriented schemes which include Pre Matric Scholarships & Post-Matric Scholarship for ST students, Hostels for ST girls and boys, Establishment of Ashram School in Tribal Sub-Plan Areas, Up gradation of Merit through coaching and remedial classes, Rajiv Gandhi National Fellowship for ST students, Top Class Education for ST students and National Overseas Scholarship for ST students to improve the literacy level of students belonging to the Scheduled Tribe communities, besides usual reservation for ST students. These are supplementary to the efforts made by other Ministries. Telangana government offers for tribal students such as, Integrated Hostels, Ashram Schools, College of Teacher Education, Coaching and Allied, Ambedkar Overseas Vidya Nidhi for SC,ST, FAST (Financial assistance for students of Telangana): Tuition Fee & Post-Matric Scholarships, Residential Schools for Tribals (Gurukulam) etc.

Objectives

- It is an attempt to understand current status of higher education among Tribals in Telangana
- The study aims at understanding the problems of higher education among scheduled tribes.
- To assess the educational gaps and suggest suitable remedial measures for improvement of tribals education.

Methodology

The present study is based on secondary data. The sources of secondary data are the published and unpublished sources. Data from secondary sources were gathered from books, articles, journals, published reports, and Government documents.

Present Scenario in Higher Education institutions of Telangana State

Telangana as a major education hub augurs well for the proposed Telangana State. The state has quite a few technical institutes, management colleges, universities and research centers. Apart from Osmania University, the oldest and largest university in the State, the state has three central universities, including the top-ranked University of Hyderabad. The Maulana Abul Kalam Azad National Urdu University and English and Foreign Languages University make Telangana strong in specialised education as well.

Telangana now houses many institutes of global repute such as the Centre for Cellular and Molecular Biology, Indian Institute of Chemical Technology and the National Remote Sensing Agency, and a host of defence laboratories, and space institutes. The ICICI Knowledge Park and the Shapoorji Pallonji Biotech Park offers lot of scope for research and entrepreneurship development, National Institute of Technology in Warangal, as well as the Kakatiya University, can be catalysts to growth. Similarly, the IIT Medak and IIIT in Basar in Nizamabad district, they have attracted considerable talent and they spread of education in the state.

The state capital city and surrounding areas are home to a mix of top business and engineering institutes. The Indian School of Business, Indian Institute of Technology, Tata Institute of Social Science Research, Tata Institute of Fundamental Research, Birla Institute of Technology & Sciences, Narsee Monjee, and ICFAI would continue to drive human resource development and knowledge base in Telangana State. In addition, over 250 private engineering colleges, medical colleges and nearly 50 business schools have sprung up in Telangana.

The core point of Higher Education is a University system, wherein the Under Graduate and Post Graduate courses are offered for the award of Degrees. Knowledge on several subjects like arts, humanities, social sciences, law, sciences, technology, engineering etc. are imparted through coursework. However, in recent years a few branches of knowledge have been the main focus for some of the universities; thereby specialized and technological universities have emerged. The affiliating character of several universities is responsible for offering UG courses through colleges located in its jurisdictional area. Designing courses and their combinations, syllabus formulation, conducting examination, awarding degrees and diplomas are the main tasks of a university system.

Table-28.1 Growth of Universities in Telangana State
Universities Growth of the Universities – Year

Universities	*Growth of the Universities – Year*									
	1970	**1980**	**1990**	**2000**	**2005**	**2006**	**2007**	**2008**	**2009**	**2014**
State Universities	1	3	6	6	6	7	8	12	12	16
Central Universities	0	2	2	3	3	3	3	3	3	3
Deemed Universities	0	0	0	1	1	1	1	1	2	2
State/Central level Inst.	0	0	1	1	2	2	2	3	3	3
Total	1	5	9	11	12	13	14	18	20	24

Source: - TSCHE Statistical Booklet 2015

Table -28.1 explains that only one of the Osmania University was established before 1970 in the state, in 1980 five universities have increased, at present 2 Deemed Universities, 3 central universities and 16 state universities are there, total 24 universities in Telangana State. The state universities are playing a major role in imparting higher education in Telangana State.

Table-28.2 Category Wise Enrollment during Last 5 years in Telangana State

Years	*All Categories*			*Tribals*		
	Male	*Female*	*Total*	*Male*	*Female*	*Total*
2015-16	795790	678445	1474234	71184	53411	124595
2014-15	803391	675697	1479088	72774	51503	124277
2013-14	800353	669131	1469484	67475	47844	115319
2012-13	773110	609027	1382137	61041	41127	102168

Source: AISHE 2015-16

Table-28.2 explains the enrollment data from the year 2015-16 shows that there are 14, 74, 234, students for all programmes, whereas in 2012-13 the number was 13, 82,137. The number 92,097 students have actually increased for enrollment in all categories and Tribal students enrollment in the year 2015-16 shows that are 1,24,595 students for all programmes, whereas in 2012-13 the number was 1,02,168. The number 22,427 students have actually increased for enrollment in Tribals. It is a good sign of awareness about higher education among Tribals. The government is still going ahead with its claims of on the strength of the quality of its higher education.

Table- 28.3 Pupil Teacher Ratio during last 5 years in Telangana State

	All Institution		*University & College*		*University & its Constituent Units*	
	Regular & Distance Mode	*Regular Mode*	*Regular & Distance Mode*	*Regular Mode*	*Regular & Distance Mode*	*Regular Mode*
2015-16	16	14	16	14	67	15
2014-15	16	14	16	14	68	14
2013-14	18	16	18	16	80	14
2012-13	17	14	17	14	78	15

Source: AISHE 2015-16

Table-28.3 explains during the year 2012-13, the Pupil -Teacher Ratio (PTR) of all institution Regular & Distance Mode was 1:17, regular mode 1:14; the same ratio in university and colleges. University and its constituent units Regular & Distance Mode was 1:78, regular mode 1: 15. In 2015-16, this Regular & Distance Mode ratio decreased to 1:16, regular mode is same, university and colleges Regular & Distance Mode ratio decreased to 1:16 regular mode is same and universities and its constituent unit's ratio decreased to 1:67 and regular mode is same. Compare from 2012-13 to 2015-16, regular& distance mode ratio is decreased, but the regular mode of all Institution, University & College, University & its Constituent Units of the pupil and teacher ratio is constant. It is observed that Regular & Distance mode of University & its Constituent unit's pupil teacher ratio is high, so that it is to be decreased to have more interaction between student and teacher.

Table 28.4 Literacy rate of Scheduled Tribals Population and Gap in Literacy rate 1991-2011

	Literacy Rate 1991		*Gap in Literacy Rate*	*Literacy Rate 2001*		*Gap in Literacy Rate*	*Literacy Rate 2011*		*Gap in Literacy Rate*
	All	*ST*		*All*	*ST*		*All*	*ST*	
Telangana	----	----	----	----	----	----	66.5	49.5	17
Combined AP	44.1	17.2	26.9	60.5	37	23.4	----	----	----
India	52.2	29.6	22.6	64.8	47.1	17.7	74.04	59	14

Source: Statistical profile of scheduled Tribals in India 2013, Census of India 2011.

Table-28.4 explains it is crystal clear that the literacy rate for the total population in 2011.Telangana literacy rate 66.5 percent for the period 2011, whereas the literacy rate among the scheduled tribes has 49.5 percent. In the same time, it is also observed that the gap between ST and All groups is quite high that is 17, so here it is the matter of concern how this will be minimized in the next decade. It is mainly due to the economic condition of their parents, present attitude and social factors for more gap between STs and All groups.

Problems of Tribal Education

Some of the following issues and challenges facing by the tribals for Higher education:

Poverty: - Scheduled tribe students will not continue their higher education because of severe poverty; similarly most of the parents force their children to go to work at an early age to meet their basic amenities. It is mainly because of their utter poverty. The family background is the main cause for lagging behind in higher education.

The Medium of language: - Language is one of the important constraints of tribal children which prevents them access to education.

Financial problem: - The economic condition of tribal people is so poor that they do not desire to spare their children or their labour power and allow them to attend schools.

Family environment: - Tribals family environment is mainly responsible for their dropout in the early level of education.

Inferiority feeling: - Tribals are living in Forest area they unable to interact with other people and they feeling shy and inferiority, in that reason tribe people will not go for higher education.

Parents want to work in early age: - As education does not yield any immediate economic return, the tribal parents prefer to engage their children in remunerative employment which supplements the family income.

They have no interest in education: Naturally, tribals are doing hunting, forest product collection and agriculture their children's also following them they do not interest in education.

Lack of proper guidance: - In the tribal areas nobody is educated so they don't know education uses and values.

The Location of the Village: - The physical barriers create a hindrance for the children of a tribal village to attend the school in a neighboring village. Too long college from their villages in those cases they do not attend regularly.

Teachers Problem In tribal villages: - villagers have virtually no relationship with the teachers. Teachers do not get any accommodation facility in the village, which makes them irregular which hampers the normal routine of a school. Further, the apathetic attitude of the villagers and the appointment of untrained teachers in tribal areas diminish the values of education.

Lack of proper monitoring: - Proper monitoring is hindered by poor coordination between the Tribal Welfare Department and School Education Department.

Suggestions

Education is an important avenue for upgrading the economic and social status of marginalized communities in the society. It's essential for backward communities like SCs and STs. The Government has considered the students, community leaders and authors, suggestions at the time of formulation of the policies.

The government must establish Tribal residential colleges and universities, some tribal members as faculty wherever possible. This will certainly bring confidence and also motivate the tribal students to get enrolled in the school and keep on continuing.

The premier institutions like IITs and IIMs are to reach out to tribals if they fail to turn up. There should not be any discriminatory treatment at such institutes, even if they joined. In view of all these conditions, priority must be given to the sector wise plans and its implementations for the betterment of the tribal children.

The inclusion of local culture, folklore, and history to the curriculum can help building confidence among the tribal students, and this approach may help in increasing their enrollment and retention at the college level since music and dance are the essential aspects of their cultural life. Therefore, storytelling, theatre, painting, music, and dance performances should be promoted at schools and college level. Similarly, sports like archery, football, and other popular local sports are extremely beneficial remedies for dropouts; it should be promoted.

The tribal literature and ethnology constitute the invaluable indigenous knowledge. It should be documented, researched, and promoted. For developing a better understanding of the tribal cultures and their promotion, there should be an adequate number of cultural research and educational centers in tribal regions. An important step in this direction is to teach tribal history and culture at schools and colleges to both tribal and non-tribal children. It would indirectly help to overcome the paucity of teachers in tribal areas.

This emphasis should be given on priority basis for the promotion of education. Necessary infrastructure and the appointment of teacher belonging to the community should be encouraged. If no such teacher is available, others with a positive attitude and understanding about tribal community should be employed in the area and responsibility may be laid down to teachers for enrollment of all students. Adult literacy programmes should be promoted to bring the illiterate persons who have dropped out or never enrolled for schooling.

The schooling facility must be provided on demand of community and enough community mentors must be mobilized to spontaneously come forward to run and manage the school.

The children should be provided text books in their own language in initial stages of their schooling and gradually they should be exposed to standard textbooks in state language at a later stage.

The textbooks should have local specific contents, contexts and narration by which the students can relate learning to their real life situation.

Teaching is imparted in tribals' local language and official language at least up graduation level. Educated tribal youth are given employment as teachers, wherever possible.

Curricula for Meta skill up gradation are to include aspects of tribal games and sports, archery, identification of plants of medicinal value, crafts art and culture, folk dance and folk songs, folk paintings etc.

Moreover the education administrators should be more responsive and responsible to the education of the students. Continuous monitoring of educational institutions (Academic and administrative) would definitely render insights to the functional problems and its solution at the earliest.

Conclusion

According to above study more higher education institutions are available in Telangana state. Enrollment of tribal students in higher education is increased when compared with all categories. Literacy gap also decreased between ST and All categories. There is a decline in the percentage of dropouts and out of school children among the tribals, but to further reduce the number of dropouts, the curriculum should be prepared in their local language. There can be the mid-day meal, night school, adult education centers to be established. Moreover, it is necessary to encourage research, vocational courses to provide high-quality education. It is equally important to improve the quality of college education at the undergraduate level, which will have a direct impact on the quality and caliber of students opting for entry into institutions of excellence in higher education.

References

1. Butt, T. I. and Gupta, R. (2014) – "Tribal Population and Development Policies in the Himalayan State of Jammu and Kashmir: A Critical Analysis", International Journal of Humanities and Social Science Invention, Volume 3 Issue 1, Pp. 18-26.
2. Dutta (Dasgupta), S. and Sivaramakrishnan, L. (2013) – "Disparity in the Literacy Level among the Scheduled and Non-Scheduled Population: Indian Scenario in the 21st Century", Trans. Inst. Indian Geographers, Vol. 35, No. 2, Pp. 187-200.
3. Adivasi, vol.50, No.1, June and December 2010, Education for tribes of India", Journal of SC and ST Research and Training Institute.
4. Lal, M. (2005), Education-The Inclusive Growth Strategy for the economically and socially disadvantaged in the Society.

5. Jayaswal, M., Sinha, S.K., Kumari, K. and Arora, A. (2003), Parental Support and Academic Achievement in Tribal School Students of Jharkhand, Journal of All India Association for Educational Research, September, Vol. 15, No.3, Pp: 9-16.
6. Sujatha, k. (2002) Education among Scheduled Tribes. In Govinda, R. (ed.), India Education Report: A profile of Basic Education. New Delhi: Oxford University press.
7. Ambasht NK (2001). Tribal Education: Problems and Issues. New Delhi,
8. Agarwal A (2000). "A study of some Educational Problems of Scheduled Caste Students.", Indian J. Educ. Res. Configuration 19(1):37-41
9. Lansky, M. 1997. "Child Labour: How the Challenge is Being Met." International Labour Review, 136(2): 233-257.
10. Sharma RK (1995).Tribal Education in India. The Progress of Education 69(8):161.
11. Sujatha K (1987). Education of the Forgotten Children of the Forests: A Case Study of Yenadi Tribe, New Delhi, Konark Publishers.
12. Rathnaiah EV (1977). Structural Constraints in Tribal Education. Sterling Publishers Pvt. Ltd, New Delhi.
13. Dr.V.B.Shastry, Tribal Education; 'Policy Promises and Performances', an article published in Dimensions of Tribal Education in Orissa, SC ST Research and Training Institute.
14. Statistical profile of scheduled Tribals in India 2013, planning, monitoring and statistics division, Department of Secondary and Higher Education, Ministry of Human Resource Development, Government of India 2016, New Delhi.
15. Census Report of (2011),Office of the Registrar General & Census Commissioner, Ministry of Home Affairs, Government of India
16. All India Survey on Higher Education 2015-16, Telangana State council for higher education Statistical Booklet 2015.
17. National Policy on Education 1986 with modifications in1992, Publications of SCST Research Institute, India

Chapter-29

Implications for Higher Education in India

Dr. J.Ratna Prabhakar,

Abstract

Globalisation has had a profound impact on the changing landscape of higher education around the world. India aspires to build a knowledge-based society that critically values research and scholarship through publications as a central component of University development. International collaborations and global initiatives are critical for developing academic standards and research capacities within our Universities. While there are significant milestones that the post-independent India has achieved in various sectors both in the economy and society, transformational reforms relating to higher education is an urgent need of the hour. The Times Higher Education World University Rankings 2011-12 glaringly demonstrates that not a single university from India is ranked as one of the world's top 200 universities, while universities in other parts of the world including in China and East Asia have a number of Universities that have made great achievements in the last few decades. The criteria for these rankings are: teaching (30 percent); research (30 percent); citations (30 percent); industry income (2.5 percent); and international outlook (7.5 percent). It is clear that research and the impact of research alone constitute 60 percent of the weightage for determining the rankings. International collaborations are central to developing research agenda not only in terms of the thematic framework for research, but also for understanding the best practices of research capacities that prevail in different parts of the world. It needs to be noted that collaborative research between scholars from different institutions is a well-established phenomenon that prevails in most of the top universities. Increasingly, there is a strong commitment in pursuing research with an international and comparative dimension. There are a number of issues that affect the world at large and there is a strong need for developing research collaborations between universities in India and other parts of the world. Pursuing such research partnerships in the form of international collaborations between faculty members from two or more institutions, or research centres help in fulfilling the research objectives.

Keywords: *higher education, planning, administration, Collaboration.*

Introduction

The phenomenon of globalization, which transformed world trade, communications and economic relations in the latter part of the 20th Century, is having a similarly profound effect on education at the start of the 21st. Student options for higher education, in particular, are no longer constrained by national boundaries. For the first time in history, large segments of the world's student population truly have access to a "global marketplace" of higher education. Globalization is a process, which has affected many areas of human life, one of those being education. In the twentieth century, many developing countries have experienced growth in the educational facilities available to them due to the entry of institutions from the west. Some believe that this process is an invaluable opportunity for the people of the developing countries to raise their skills and standards of education.

Others fear that it is merely a modern version of cultural imperialism that will lead to the creation of a universal, ultimately western society. No human activity has remained unaffected by globalization and education is no exception. It brings education to the front lines. In the prevailing discourse, education is expected to be the major tool for incorporation into the 'knowledge society' and the technological economy. In educational terms, there is a growing understanding that the neoliberal version of globalization, particularly as implemented (and ideologically defended) by bilateral, multilateral, and international organizations, is reflected in an educational agenda that privileges, if not directly imposes, particular policies for evaluation, financing, assessment, standards, teacher training, curriculum, instruction, and testing. In the face of such pressures, more study is needed about local responses to defend public education against the introduction of pure market mechanisms to regulate educational exchanges and other policies that seek to reduce state sponsorship and financing and to impose management and efficiency models borrowed from the business sector as a framework for educational decision-making. Is it possible, to give general answers to the question of how globalization is affecting educational policy and practice in India and worldwide? We believe that there can be no single answer; national and local economic, political, and cultural changes are affected by, and actively responding to, globalizing trends within a broad range of patterns. Indeed, because education is one of the central arenas in which these adaptations and responses occur, it will be one of the most myriad of institutional contexts. Hence, the answers developed will require a careful analysis of trends in education, including:

- The currently popular policy "buzz words" (privatization, choice, and decentralization of educational systems) that dive policy formation in education and prevailing research agendas based in rational organization and management theories.

- The role of national and international organizations in education, including teacher unions, parent organizations, and social movements.
- The new scholarship on race, class, gender, and the state in education (hence concerns about multiculturalism and the question of identity in education), critical race theory, feminism, post colonialism, diasporas communities and new social movements. The current globalization of higher education creates both challenges and opportunities. The relationship between universities education and globalization gives special attention. Education will be the answer to many problems raised by globalization. Educational goals are seen to be an area of great concern in the era of globalization. It is here that universities play a crucially important role, to create better society. It is impossible to ignore the global; universities need to reflect on the impact of globalization. They must engage with the issues of globalization, both theoretically as analysts and researchers, and practically as academic workers involved in an increasingly globalised enterprise. The likelihood of entry of foreign universities into India is an inevitable consequence of globalization. Top class foreign universities are anticipated to add prestige to India's higher education. The expectation is that foreign universities will bring much needed capacity and new ideas on higher education management, curriculum, teaching methods and research, together with investment. Though fear has been expressed that only commercial institutions will come to India and that Oxford and Cambridge will shy away, my guess is that top class universities will come to India, not to make profit, but to profit from the vast intellectual resources of the country. The foreign universities bill has adequate safeguards against throwing open our higher education to fortune seekers and unscrupulous business interests.

International Influences in Indian Higher Education

If one scans the horizon of Indian higher education institutions today, the legacy of prior waves of international, if not global, influence can be seen in virtually every field. India hosts a wide variety of pre-Independence missionary institutions – colleges founded in the late 19th and early 20th Centuries by foreign missionaries of different faiths. St. Joseph's College Trichy, St. Xavier's Chennai, Christian Medical College Vellore, St. John

College Agra, Isabella Thoburn College Lucknow, etc. In the post-Independence era, the Indian Institutes of Technology, consciously patterned after the Massachusetts Institute of Technology in the U.S., received substantial overseas help right from the outset. With support from four donor nations, the five IITs benefited from guest faculty from outside of India, the ability to send Indian faculty for training abroad, and contributions of modern laboratory equipment and facilities. Similar international links were established by the Indian Institutes of Management: IIM-Ahmadabad, for example, still maintains strong connections with the Harvard Business School. Perhaps the most recent innovation in Indian higher education, the Indira Gandhi National Open University (together with similar, state sponsored Open Universities), drew heavily on the UK experience with distance education and the Open University concept.

Impact of Globalization on Higher Education

The challenge of higher education is to make full use of the opportunities that globalization has provided. First and foremost, the marvels of technology must be fully and profitably deployed. In India, Internet connectivity for university students is still inadequate. But the massive increase in cell phones, which are becoming more and more versatile, may be the answer to India's connectivity crisis. Once full connectivity is accomplished, the students can be liberated from the classrooms and allowed to find and create knowledge. The Universities will simply have to devise a means by which it can be established that the knowledge attained is genuine and accurate and that it is relevant to the needs of the countries concerned. Different students in the same class may diversify themselves and enrich different branches of knowledge. The impact of globalization on higher education may be summarized in the following ways:

- Increasing interest of parents to get their children admitted to foreign educational institutions will cost us precious foreign exchange.
- Sometimes there is also the possibility of sub-standard courses being offered to the students, which may lead to cheating of innocent citizens of India.
- It will lead to the creation of three different classes of graduates – those educations in foreign universities, those from costly private domestic institutions, and those from economically weaker sections studying in government funded institutions. This will only lead to social tensions.
- In view of the nature of the globalised higher education, the commoditization of Indian higher education is bound to have an

adverse effect on our culture, the ethos of social welfare and even the quality of Indian education system.

One impact of globalization on education is the urgency to develop a skilled work force at all levels to meet the demands of increasing business environment. Instead of its traditional role of providing education as a welfare measure, the state is required to facilitate privatization and deregulation in education, particularly as the quality of education provided by the state institutions has been rather poor. This is by no means undesirable, as privatization of education has helped to increase quantity as well as quality. Profiteering is a negative factor, but its evil is often offset by the timely and efficient utilization of human talent to develop competitiveness worldwide. Indians seeking employment and competing successfully is no recent phenomenon. Globalization has merely hastened the pace of migration and created better placements worldwide. As the private sector's contribution in higher education in India is gaining in strength, India cannot take recourse to article 1.3 of the GATS that allows exemption for services provided by the government. In order to cope with the western countries, the measures required include the adoption of a credit based semester system with continuous internal evaluation. A cafeteria type option to the students for the course to be offered and facilitates of credit transfer. A majority of conventional universities in India are far behind, at least in non-professional courses. As the UGC, AICTE (All India Council of Technical Education) and other controlling agencies are not in a position to intervenes effectively and control the foreign educational institutions, the government of India has set up a committee under the NAAC, under its chairman Ram Takwale, to monitor the applying foreign universities. At present 150 foreign universities (50 from UK, 45 from Australia. 30 from USA and the rest from Canada and other European countries that have been operating in India. The UGC has decided to invite proposals from institutions that are keen on "exporting Indian education" to foreign learners under a "Study India Programme". A recent study shows that one in every 10 students studying in the US was an Indian, while less than 0.6 percent of American Students were receiving educational credit for studying in India. The government of India has recognized these dangerous phenomena and belatedly started the process of constituting a Committee for the Promotion of Indian Education Abroad under the Ministry of Human Resources Development, department of education.

During 2001, there were 54,664 Indian students in the United States alone, with the total number abroad exceeding 10 lakhs. In contrast, there were only 7,791 foreigner students in India, mainly from the developing countries like Bangladesh and countries of South and East Asia. Globalization and commercialization of education has thus become a reality and, India being a signatory to the WTO as also to the WATS, we have to be very much cautious about the functioning of the foreign educational institutions.

Looking Ahead: Pathways to a Global Future

Even an extreme optimist cannot help but be disheartened by the many problems confronting the Indian higher education system – a vast and unwieldy system comprised of some 300 universities and deemed universities, more than 10,000 colleges and some 6.5 million students. The situation is further complicated by the rigidities of India's centralized higher education bureaucracy, the political pressures on higher education institutions and the growing problem of corruption in various aspects of university life (e.g., admissions, examinations, promotions). In such a beleaguered system, how can internationalization efforts possibly be effective? If India has to emerge as preferred location for higher education in the globalizing world it will have to develop a national policy to address the challenges of sub-standard quality, ineffective systems of monitoring and control, red-tapism in growth and development and political interference. Three pathways offer some hope and promise for the future.

The first path is labeled policy reform. It includes opening up space for private universities, easing or eliminating research restrictions on foreign scholars and graduate students, and encouraging ''foreign collaboration'' in the university sector in the same way such joint ventures now exist in private industry. Stronger partnerships need to be developed between Indian universities and universities in other countries. A second pathway for Indian internationalists has to do with partnerships. In fields such as engineering, management and computer sciences, for example, industry-university collaborations can yield significant benefits for both sides. A more systematic focus on institutional partnerships could also become part of India's approach to bi-lateral scholarly exchange programs. The final pathway focuses on innovation and leadership, two qualities in greatest need within Indian higher education today. Innovation can take a variety of forms, ranging from the use of internet technology to develop joint on-line courses between Indian and foreign universities to institutional innovations like the recent initiative by SNDT Women's University to establish an overseas branch campus for women students in the Gulf region. Successful innovation does not take place without leadership. For India to broaden and expand its place in the global marketplace of higher education will require bold and innovative leadership by university Vice-chancellors, political leaders, administrators and policy makers at the central and state levels. The need of the hour is not to fight the onset of globalization, but to turn the challenges into opportunities. The best revenge against the forces that cannot be stopped is turning them to our advantage. Education is one area where it can be done effectively. Some of the measures suggested by experts to accomplish this are: Liberalize and deregulate the education system, De-license higher education, confer institutional autonomy and decentralize syllabus design Change the role of Governments into facilitation and supervision through adequate regulatory measures Upgrade teacher training, infrastructure and syllabus.

Conclusion

There is now increasing global competition for the best and brightest students, as more and more countries recognize the economic potential of higher education as a service export sector and India is not an exception. The major concern of globalization has been "how to fulfill the national objective of equality?" Interaction is expected to improve the quality of education and performance evaluation at all levels of education which is giving more avenues to the private education and in turn affecting the equity consideration. Changes in Indian education system that pervasive the core appears to remain the same only the notion of change and the rate at which it takes place varies virtually and spatially and in field operations. Globalization of higher education may help India to take advantage of opportunities in the new global environment. With foresight, skill and determination, today's leaders of Indian universities have it within their power to craft a different kind of globalization, one which affirms and values cultural difference and encourages greater mobility for all students. The world of higher education in the 21st century can truly be a border-less world of knowledge and ideas which will yield reciprocal benefits for all nations. There is no single, simple path for reaching this new global future, but instead, multiple pathways that lead toward "a world in one nest".

References

1. Assocham–Icrier, Joint Conference on Globalization and Higher Education in India, November 1-2, 2006, New Delhi. Draft Report of Working Group on Higher Education for the XI Plan, Planning Commission, Government of India (2007).
2. Gaynor, N. (2010). Globalizing higher education: Challenges and contradictions in policy & practice; A development Education Review, Vol.II Higher Education and Globalization, 23rd Convocation Address by Dr. Panjab Singh, Oct. 14 2008,

3. Mishra, J. K., Abidi, N. and Sharma, R. (2008). Indian Higher Education: Global Challenges and Local Issues. JBS Working Paper Series.
4. Safaya, R. (2002). Current problems in Indian Education, Dhanpat Rai Publishing Co: New Delhi.
5. Scott, P. (1998). Classification, Internationalization and Globalization, in P. Scott (ed.), The Globalization of Higher Education, The Society for Research into Higher Education/Open University Press, Buckingham, pp. 108- 129.
6. Sharma, V. (2007). Indian Higher Education: Commodification and foreign direct investment. The Marxist, Vol.XXIII, No. 02.
7. Takwale, R. (2002). Presidential Address on 'Convergence of Educational Modes – An Opportunity for Evolving New Paradigm of Education' at the IDEA 2002 Conference held at University of Jammu, Jammu, during 1-3 March 2002.
8. Teichler, U. (2004), .The Changing Debate on Internationalization of Higher Education. Higher Education, Vol. 48, pp. 5-26.
9. Tilak, J.B.G. (2002). Education and Globalization: The changing concerns in Economics of Indian Education. Perspectives in Education, Vol. 17, Special Issue pp. 05-08.
10. Valimaa, J. (2004). Nationalization, Localization and Globalization in Higher Education. Higher Education, Vol. 48, pp. 27-54.

Chapter-30

Reforms of Higher Education

Baby Kumari,

Abstract

Higher Education has played important role in development of all the Nations. Economic and cultural globalisation has ushered in a new era in higher education. Higher Education was always more internationally open rather than the other sectors because of its immersion in diverse knowledge and which never seems to be a higher respect for juridical boundaries. Education is key elements in the formation of knowledge .The superior wise technology highly came up crossed the all borders between entire world and all the small or bigger communities. Now a day all the higher educational institutes' often see themselves as the whole objects of globalisation. In this paper, I studies all the reforms of higher education as well as the impact of globalisation on higher education.

Introduction

In terms of Social and Economic perspective higher education plays an important role in the production, development and distribution of national income. The planning and reform of higher education is a difficult process in any country. The fact that India has been totally unsuccessful in its efforts to control its burgeoning higher education system is, in comparative terms, not especially unusual. India is particularly important Third World case because it is among the earliest to have developed its universities and colleges and because it now has the largest academic system in Third World. It can provide lesson to other Third counties and at the same time an international dimension may shed light on India's own experience with growth, change and reform in higher education.

Globalization is the process of interaction and integration among people, companies and government worldwide. As the result of globalization, higher education is becoming a marketable commodity. The increasing need to set up a chain of education institute which are accredited, globally, acceptable, has led to gradual privatization of higher education. gloalization has also affected the education, policies and higher education in India. (Giddens, 1996).

Methodology

This paper is secondary data based on qualitative review of literature which has been collected from books, magazines, journals. Explanatory research methodology is also been used in this research paper.

Importance of the study : Higher education in India plays key role for the social, economic and political development. This paper focuses on the vocationalization and reforms of higher education in Global sphere, which provides the way for the government to implement programmes, policies and development activities for the higher education.

Objectives of the study

a. To study the higher education with the special reference to globalization.
b. To study the vocationalization of higher Education.

Framework of Higher Education in India

The present format of higher education in India was started in 1857 with the inception of university in the three presidency town. At present, India possess a highly developed higher education system which offers facility of education and training in almost all aspects of human's creative and intellectual and social sciences, engineering, medicine, dentistry, agriculture, education, law, commerce and management, music and performing arts, national and foreign languages, culture, communication etc, For smooth conduction of higher education in India we have the following framework:-

1. Academic Framework

- **Under graduation level:-** After 12 years of schooling education bachelors degree is offered in two streams-liberal i.e. three years of degree course in arts, science and commerce and professional course i.e. agriculture engineering, medicine, pharmacy.
- **Postgraduate level-** Masters Degree is normally of two years duration in both the liberal and professional course.
- **Research programmer-** A research programmer i.e. M.Philand PhD is taken after completion of master degree.

- **Diploma**-Diploma course are also available at the UG and g level.

2. **Institutional Framework:** The degree and diploma awarding institutions in India for higher education are Central Universities, State Universities, Deemed Universities, Private Universities, Open Universities and Institutes of National Importance.
3. **Regulatory Framework:** The institutions imparting higher education at different levels are regulated by University Grants Commission (UGC), All India Council of Technical Education (AICTE), Medical Council of India (MCI), and India Council for Agriculture Research (ICAR).

Globalization and its Impact on Higher Education in India

Globalization has a multidimensional impact on the system of higher education in India. It has underlined the need for reforms in the educational system with particular reference to the wider utilization of information technology, giving productivity dimension to education and emphasis on its research and development activities because education is an important investment in building human capital. The higher education system in India suffers from acute paucity of funds, lack of autonomy, burden of affiliation. On the other hand the effect of globalization on education brings rapid developments in technology, communication and knowledge economy. (Bhoite, 2009).

- **Privatization of higher education**- There has been an increasing trend towards privatization of higher education in India. The quality and content of the education are industry oriented due to privatization. In this day age of globalization and privatization with competition and to meet the new challenges of the 21st century higher education should be radically transformed. India is required to set up a chain of educational institutions which are accredited, globally acceptable. We should also keep in mind that quality can come only from quality teachers and quality infrastructure, under quality leadership.
- **Globalization and economic reforms** in India have yielded significant changes in the role of state and restructuring of social welfares education, employment, and agriculture and health system. In higher education it was always the monopoly of middle class and elite groups of the society.
- **Commercialization**- Impact of globalization is commercialization of higher education due to which self-financing courses have been introduced which has deprived many from getting higher education

especially in countries like India where illiteracy still prevails and education is a dream to many. The existing policy of globalization of higher education is motivated by profits rather than social justice or the policy of the government. Its goals therefore are to meet the demands of the market.

- **Women education**- Women literacy rate has grown over the three decades. Women education plays a very important role in the overall development of the country and improving the quality of life at home and outside.
- **Teacher's education**- In the global society today the aspects of rapid change, lifelong learning, flexible routes of learning and the use of technology have a major impact on all the areas of teacher education. Major steps to be taken qualitative expansion, value based, competency based and ICT based teaching learning.
- **Knowledge**- The impact of globalization on higher education is the transition to a knowledge society towards universities as knowledge-centers.
- **Skill**- Higher education is seeking ways to meet the demands and challenges put forth by globalization. Higher education today is expected to produce skilled and trained workforce who can compete in this global market.
- **Entry of Foreign Universities**- Foreign Direct Investment (FDI) is important tool of globalization. As government lack of funds FDI is allowed into higher education. The foreign universities is expected to bring the quality infrastructure in teaching, research as well as physical infrastructure This will attract large scale foreign investments into India and also to an extent reverse brain drain. However, the government will have to create a level playing field for all institutions and also ensure that other factors are considered. Their entry should also increase the qualities in research areas and so on, rather than focus on undergraduate programs.
- **Education policies**- Globalization also impact the education policies on higher education in India. In the last two decades Indian government has formed various committees, commission and also different kinds of economic bodies came to existence like NAAC.
- **Communication**- The effects of globalization one ducation bring rapid developments in technology and communications. It changes the role of students and teachers and producing a shift in society

from industrialization towards an information-based society.

- **E-learning**- People with disability get benefit from globalization only if they endowed with knowledge, skills, capabilities and rights needed to pursue their basic livelihoods. The introduction of technology into the classroom is changing the nature of delivering education to students is gradually giving way to a new form of electronic literacy , more programs and education materials are made available in electronic form, teachers are preparing materials in electronic form; and students are generating papers, assignments and projects in electronic form. Video projection screens, books with storage device servers and CD rooms as well as the emergence of on-line digital libraries are now replacing blackboards. Even exams and grades are gradually becoming available through electronic means and notebooks are starting to give way to laptops. Also, students can be examined through computer managed learning systems and do tutorial exercises on a computer rather than in a classroom. these are main impact on higher education. (Naik 2015).

Vocationalization of Higher Education

During the pre-independence period no progress was made in the field of vocationalization. After independence in spite of various efforts, vocationalization of education has not been satisfactory, The National Policy on education (1986) has, therefore, very rightly observed ," The introduction of systematic, well planned and rigorously implemented programme of vocational education is crucial in the proposed recognization, These elements are meant to enhance individual employability, to reduce the mismatch between the demand and supply of skilled manpower, to provide an alternative for those pursuing higher education without particular interest or purpose. Vocationalization means learning of skill and some related skilled by studying technologies, applied science and other practical activities, The UNESCO (1974) defined vocationalization "comprehensive term embracing those aspects of the educational process involving, in addition to general education, the studying of technologies and related sciences and the acquisition of practical skills, attitude, understanding and knowledge relating to occupations in various sectors of economic and social life. Such an education would be an integral parts of general education and a means of preparing".

Needs and Importance: Vocationalization of education makes it possible for an individual to get a job or be his own master by either starting a new production activity or a service which may satisfy felt need of community. It makes education more relevant and meaningful to student and accelerate the pace of progress adequately. Mahatma Gandhi also viewed education as a means of all-round development of the personality and desired that craft or manual work should occupy a central position in the system of education which was called by him as Basic Education.

The Ministry of Human Resource Development , Govt. of Indian and NCERT having been fully aware of the implications of vocationalization have laid stress on diversification at the secondary stage, particular at +2 or higher secondary level. In the development countries like India where industrial and agriculture production is gathering momentum, where sciences as well as technology have opened new vistas and where trade and commerce are expanding rapidly, vocationalization of education has been extremely important. It is required for optimizing the utilization of manpower resources and improving potentially of individuals for increasing production and improving service at various levels and quarters. The following needs can be taken care of through vocationalization of education. Vocational awareness and readiness should permeate the entire school curriculum in order to relater education of life, needs and aspirations of pupils and national productivity. (Mishra, 2006).

Strategies and Methodology: The National Review Committee (1978) and the Working Group on vocationalization of Education, 1976 are unanimous in the recommendations for preparation and implementation of the vocation plans .**The following guidelines were suggested for effective implementation** :

- The former has suggested two streams as given by the NCERT in its national document there are: first is General Education Spectrum. And second is Vocationalization Education Spectrum.
- The pattern of vocationalization courses recommended by the Review Committee was following:

Courses	Time Allocation
Language	15 percent
General Foundation Courses	15 percent
Elective Subjects	70 percent

- 70 percent of the weekly hours of instruction was allocated to the teaching of vocational selected subjects with 50 percent of practical works.
- Different board based vocational courses linked to agriculture and industry and other allied field were suggested by Review

Committee.

- Counseling and placement officers particularly in rural areas to start with should be appointed to advise student on the choice of elective subjects.
- models were recommended in the offering selective subjects by the schools.

  Those offering only General Education Spectrum and its selective subjects.

  - Those offering only vocation Education Spectrum and its selecting subjects.
  - Those offering both General Education and Vocational Education Courses and their selective subjects.

Conclusion

This research paper is brief profile of India's higher education. We can say that Higher Education is key of success. This research paper is brief profile of India's higher education. There are some suggestions for improving the quality of higher education:

- To Development Quality of higher Education.
- To increase Quantity of Universities.
- To Examination Reforms.
- To High - tech Libraries.
- To promote Innovative practices.
- To increase activeness of government.

Reference

1. Salmi, J. (1991). *'The Higher Education crisis in Developing countries'*, The World Bank.
2. Mishra, S. (2006).' *UGC and Higher Education System in India',* Book Enclave Pulication, Jaipur.
3. Maeginson, S. and Wende. M. (2007). *'Globalization and Higher Education',*. OECD (paris).
4. Varghese, N. V. (2013).' Globalization and Education : A study of selected countries in Africa', *International Institute for educational planning*. 334, 1-28.
5. Kogan, M. Bauer. M, Bleiklie (eds). (2014)' Transforming Higher Education: A comparative study': 25-28.
6. Naik,P.(2015).'Globalization and its Impact on Hiher Education in

India',*International Journal of Humanities and Management Science* (IJHMS),Vol. 3: 414-417.

7. Shikh,Y.A.(2017).'The higgher education in India: challangges & opportunities' ,*Journal of Education and practice*.Vol-1:11-15.
8. https://www.researchgate.net/publication/282293148_Higher_Education in India Issues Challenges and Suggestions.
9. https://www.globalslaveryindex.org/2018/findings/country-studies/india/.
10. http://www.iiep.unesco.org/en/reforms-revive-higher-education-india.
11. https://translate.googleuesercontent.com/translate c?depth = 2&hl = hi&nv = 1 & prev = search&rurl=translate.google.com&sl=en&sp=nmt4&u=http://www.research gate.net/publication/282293148 Higher Education in India. Issues Challenges and Suggestions &xid =17259, 15700023, 15700122, 15700124, 15700186, 15700191, 15700201, 15700237, 15700242, 15700248 &usg =ALk Jrhh Qz X4 A FxL2TDirfJGOG7QiQVmQxg.

Chapter-31

Reforms in Higher Education in India: Prospects and Challenges

Dr. S. Chandra Shekar,

Abstract

The image of higher education in India is to know the country's human resources probable to its fullest through equality and calculation. The higher education part, in existing decades, have experiential a amazing rise in quite a few skin tone such as its institutional skill, enrolment, teacher-student relative, etc. The immediate augment of the higher education understanding at the like case have move a few applicable focus linked to equality, ability, brilliancy and entrance to higher education in the country. The present article focus on issue of concern to take care of by the stakeholders in the state as well as the international level. The study is also single in the sense that it brings about superior kind of the present state in the higher education organization in the country and its pattern of increase given the opportunity and challenge to the system under reflection. The at hand study throw a rewarding approaching on finance scheme and enrolment aspects of higher education in India.

Introduction

The system of higher education now accessible in India was first fixed by the British ruler in the mid-19th century to serve up the royally fiscal, political and administrative benefit, and in particular, to unite and keep their governance in the country. It was innate by the state manager after independence (in 1947) as a colonial legacy, and has been expanded phenomenally during the last five decades. The massive system of higher education in India consists of 214 (198 state and 16 central) universities, 38 institutions 'deemed-to-be universities,' 11 institutes of national importance, 9,703 colleges, and 887 polytechnics. The system now employs 321,000 teachers and caters to 6,755,000 students.

Serious appraisal undertake by the legislative committee and indepen dent academicians have dyed the crisis confront the system: 'over-production of "educated" persons; growing educated job loss; waning of student inspiration; increasing strife and rowdiness on the campus; frequent collapse of administration; deterioration of values; and above all, the demoralizing effect of the unimportance and futility of most of what is being done.' While the politicians and policy makers have often vocal about the need for radical renovation of the system, what have been achieve in reality is only moderate reformism.

Management of Higher Education

The Indian higher education system is one of the largest such system in the World. It is probable that during the X Five Year Plan period (2002-07), there will be a wonderful pressure of statistics on this system and a large number of extra students will be knocking at the door of higher education institutions in the country. There are also new challenge of management and directive being faced by these institutions, which require serious attention, both at the institutions in the public sector and also those in the private sector now growing at a fast pace. As a result, the old structures of management reputable in pre-independent India and working during most of the twentieth century are now required to undergo severe changes. Besides, the strain of the society for equity and lodging cannot be abandoned any more. The following important reform and recommendation.

The goal of the higher education, for that matter any education system of any country is development with inclusion, ensure quality and applicable education.

1. To meet this challenge, there is a need for policy to identify the jet issue drawn in, to build up on the earlier policies, and to take a step ahead.
2. India's huge pool of young people might be considered its biggest strength. Unfortunately, India is far from having its act together when it comes to figuring out how to educate these young people.
3. Government data suggests that only one out of every seven children born in India goes to college. What's more, the nation suffers from both a crippling number, as well as a quality, challenge when it comes to higher education.

Challenges in Higher Education in India

On the eve of 69th year of independence still our education system has not been urban fully. We are not able to list a lone university in top 100 university of the world. Different government changed during these six decades. They tried to boost the education system and implement different education policy but they were not plenty to put an example for the universe. UGC is endlessly working and focus on quality education in higher education sector. Still we are facing lot of harms and challenge in our education system. Some of the basic challenge in higher education system in India is discuss below:

1. **Enrolment:** The Gross Enrolment Ratio (GER) of India in higher education is only 15% which is quite low as compare to the urban as well as, other mounting countries. With the increase of enrolments at school level, the supply of higher education institutes is insufficient to meet the mounting command in the country.
2. **Equity:** There is no equity in GER among different sect of the society. According to earlier studies the GER in higher education in India amid male and female vary to a greater extent. There are area variation too some states have high GER while as some is rather at the rear the national GER which mirror a major imbalance within the higher education scheme.
3. **Quality:** Quality in higher education is a multi-dimensional, multilevel, and an active concept. Ensure excellence in higher education is amongst the primary challenge being faced in India today. However, Government is endlessly focused on the quality education. Still Large number of college and universities in India are powerless to meet the minimum necessities laid down by the UGC and our university is not in a position to mark its place among the top university of the world.
4. **Infrastructure:** Poor transportation is another challenge to the higher education system of India particularly the institutes run by the free sector suffer from poor physical military and infrastructure. There are large numbers of college which are functioning on second or third floor of the construction on ground or first floor there exist readymade hosieries or photocopy shops.
5. **Political interference:** Most of the educational Institutions are down by the political best, which are playing key role in governing body of the Universities. They are using the not guilty students for their self-seeking earnings. Students organize campaign, forget their own objectives and begin to develop their career in policy.
6. **Faculty:** Faculty scarcity and the inability of the state educational system to draw and retain well-qualified teachers cover are posing

challenge to quality education for many years. great facts of NET / PhD candidates are unemployed even there are lot of vacancies in higher education, these worthy candidate are then applying in other department which is a major blow to the higher education system.

7. **Accreditation:** As per the data provide by the NAAC, as of June 2010, "not even 25% of the total higher education institution in the country be accredited. And among folks accredited, only 30% of the university and 45% of the college be found to be of quality to be rank at 'A' level".
8. **Research and Innovation:** Here is very ostensible scholar in our country whose script is cited by famed western author. There is not enough heart on study in higher education institutes. There are deficient income and services, as well as, limited statistics of quality faculty to counsel student. Most of the study scholars are without fellowship or not getting their fellowship on time which directly or indirectly affect their research. Besides, Indian Higher education institution is poorly connected to research center. So, this is another area of face to the higher education in India.
9. **Structure of higher education:** Organization of the Indian learning face challenge of over-centralization, bureaucratic structure and require of responsibility, simplicity, and professionalism. As an outcome of raise in number of joined colleges and student, the burden of administrative function of universities has appreciably increased and the heart heart on academic and study is weak.

Measures needed to improve innovation in universities:-

Study cannot be enhanced only by adjustable universities, as an alternative they need pains to generate enable impression for which it is vital to scholarship more self-sufficiency, improved backing and new instrument to order labor ethic.

1. New proposal like Hackathon, curriculum improvement, anytime anyplace education from end to end SWAYAM, teacher teaching be all intended at civilizing superiority. These need to be successfully implemented.
2. As India needs to transform its university into world class institution, it must maintain the welfare of young researchers and thousands of impermanent faculty member by expedite the lasting travels in a time-bound frame and transparent mode.

3. Institute world-class multidisciplinary study university.
4. generate a master map for each state and combination land
5. Both positions must institution an included higher education master plan to supply an excellent education for all its populace.
6. Be a focus for the top and the brightest flair to be power member

Reforms to the higher education

1. **Reforms to expand the system:** India's higher education subdivision have stimulated beginning at age of unhurried increase and low gross enrolment ratio (GERs) to an era of record development. Over the past 15 years, student enrolment has quadrupled to reach 34 million with a GER of 24 percent in 2015-2016. The size of India's education arrangement has now surpassed the United States, attractive the world's second leading past China.
2. **Reforms to improve quality:** India well-known outer superiority declaration agency and inner superiority declaration mechanism to improve higher education superiority. Though authorization is compulsory to find community backing, a mass of personal higher education institutions immobile stay non-accredited.
3. **Reforms to enhance relevance:** regardless of the sector's increase, a lot of employer in India has lost self-confidence in the superiority of the experience award by the country's university. It is question whether this university offers the skills and competencies to its alumnae as expected in the labour market. In order to regain the consistency and improve the bearing of university education, India is now in the course of mounting a National Higher Education Qualification Frame (NHEQF), which is focus on learning outcome, employability skills and competencies. This follows the 2013 growth of a state skills condition frame (NSQF).
4. **Looking to the future:** The massification of higher education is accompany by a widen of region gap, persist social inequality and commercialization of the sector. The test now is to talk to the issue of equity and range to provide reasonable, quality higher education in a period of market-led reform. It is probable that the national policy on learning now in expansion resolve expectantly lecture to a few of this concern.

Conclusion

Education is a procedure by which a person's corpse, mind and quality be bent and strengthen. It is bring of skull, mind and intellect jointly and consequently enable a self to build up an all around character identify the finest in him or her. Higher education in India encompasses extended incredibly quickly in the last six decades after self-rule yet it is not equally available to all. India is today one of the best ever mounting country of the world with the yearly increase rate departing above 9%. Still a large section of the populace remnants uninformed and a large number of children's do not get even main education. This is not only disqualified a great piece of the populace beginning causal to the expansion of the country entirely but it have as well prohibited them from utilize the payback of whatever expansion have taken place for the profit of the people. No doubt India is facing a range of challenge in higher education but to tackle these challenge and to boost higher education be highest vital. India is a country of enormous human resource latent, to utilize this latent right is the matter which desirable to argue.

References

1. Brener ND, Kann L, Smith TK. Reliability and validity of the School Health Policies and Programs Study 2000 questionnaires. J Sch Health. 2003;73(1).
2. Dowda M, Sallis JF, McKenzie TL, Rosengard P, Kohl HW. Evaluating the sustainability of SPARK physical education: a case study of translating research into practice. Res Q Exerc Sport. 2005;76(1).
3. Fairclough SJ, Stratton G. Effects of a physical education intervention to improve student activity levels. Phys Educ Sport Pedagog. 2006;11(1).
4. Humbert ML, Chad KE, Bruner MW, et al. Using a naturalistic ecological approach to examine the factors influencing youth physical activity across grades 7 to 12. Health Educ Behav. 2008;35(2).
5. Kann L, Brener ND, Wechsler H. Overview and summary: school health policies and programs study 2006. J Sch Health. 2007.
6. McKenzie TL, Kahan D. Physical activity, public health, and elementary schools. Elem Sch J. 2008;108(3).
7. Nader PR, Bradley RH, Houts RM, McRitchie SL, O'Brien M. Moderate-to-vigorous physical activity from ages 9 to 15 years. J Am Med Assoc. 2008;300(3).
8. Rowe PJ, Schuldheisz JM, vanderMars H. Validation of SOFIT for measuring physical activity of first- to eighth-grade students. Pediatr Exerc Sci. 1997;9(2).
9. SHPPS 2006: School Health Policies and Programs Study. In: State-Level School Health Policies and Practices. A State-by-State Summary from the School Health Policies and Programs Study 2006. DoHaH Services., editor. Centers for Disease Control and Prevention; Atlanta, GA: 2007.

Chapter-32

A Qualitative Study to Improve the Quality of Higher Education by Promoting Research and Innovation

Naghma Shahida,
Asma,

Abstract

Nation requires higher educated citizens having skills and can capable to drive economy of nation forward. When India becomes able to provide intellectual people to the outside world then higher education can contribute to transform our country from a developing nation to a developed nation very easily and quickly. Innovation's in higher education in all aspect is very important because it address several interrelated terms implementation, creativity and novelty that inform a product and process in higher education which helps to achieve quality in education system. In this era significant changes in research and teaching influences and innovative approaches also contribute in theory and practice. The development of research on the correlation between higher education, government and different institutions together with the new concept of knowledge develops a trans-disciplinary, socially, spatially distributed and deeply contextualized approach to maintain relevance of higher education in global world. Various universities and colleges will need to careful plan and preparation for their respective identities in order to survive the competition and institutions have to improve the quality of their services. Innovations, researches and best practices serve to enhance quality and add value. This study was conducted on a sample of 50 government and private college teachers of various discipline selected from the Darbhanga district of Bihar. The objective of this study was to know the strategies for development of quality in higher education by promoting innovation and research. The researcher administered a self-constructed structured Interview schedule based on 10 questions for data collection and the gathered information was analyzed through qualitative method. The analysis of the data gives interesting results regarding the various strategies like Exploratory Learning, Collaborative Learning, Critical Thinking, Examination Reform,

Faculty Peer Review, Seminar and workshop, International Education, Learning Communities, Science Reforms, Service Learning, Student Peer Teaching, Technology and Undergraduate Research. This study is very much relevant because it reveals the innovation and significant researches for improvement in higher education for the teachers, parents, policymakers and administrators of higher education.

Keyword: *- Higher Education, Quality, Innovative strategies, Research*

Introduction

Education is a very essential aspect for the progress of a nation. We should make it appropriate according to the contemporary demand and progressive scenario of the world. Education gives an opportunity to resolve upon the social, economic, cultural, and moral issues facing by human being. India needs to emphasize on education system for more educated and efficient person to drive our country. In the world, there are so many Indian who well known for their abilities and skills. To develop India as a digital nation or to become a successful partner in global development, India has to strengthen higher education through research and innovation.

Higher Education

India is developing country and to achieve our national goal we have to promote our higher education system. The middle class in India are continuously grow (approximately 200 million people) has led to increased demand for higher education and we know that this demand met by the Indian Higher Education system is not possible. Although the government is planning to establish new universities and colleges in future, these are not being enough to provide places for all students who seek higher education. Nowadays, Higher Education faces a wide range of challenges related with the arrival of new demands. Students and academics are growing the association and role of research and innovation which is in debate sustained by accountability standards, funding constraints and ranking imposition. India's higher education system is the world's third largest in terms of students, next to China and the United States. Unlike China, however, India has the advantage of English being the primary language of higher education and research. India educates approximately 11 per cent of its youth in higher education as compared to 20 per cent in China. At present in 2011, there are 227 government - recognized Universities in India. Out of them 20 are central universities, 109 are deemed universities and 11 are Open Universities and rest are state universities.

Quality of Higher Education

Quality in higher education is a very subjective and complex concept, to explain quality there are so many ways, many theories, models and performance indicators used to try to quantify and assess quality. According to this vision of the world, quality is not a really serious matter, since the price of any product will automatically reflect its quality. Three main key aspects of quality in higher education are the adequate availability of best faculty, optimum quantity of infrastructure and resources and availability of third aspect quality assurance system. We have been observing that while majority of students in higher education go to state universities and colleges, they lack optimum resources in terms of manpower and infrastructure. Five issues are there quantity/quality; privatization, staffing, regulation and studying abroad form the core on the state and the prospects of higher education in India. Students are the primary stakeholder in an educational setup and it is strongly supported by many researchers. The simplest is that stakeholders expect from students to learn knowledge and skills that directly contribute to their ability to be more productive; both parties to the transaction, students and teachers, may be using an education as an ability to take a long term view of future investments.

Research in Higher Education

The higher education sector in India spends 4.1 percent of country's research fund. In India, higher education is in the affiliated colleges which are 22000 in number. They have no Professor; not even Assistant professors necessarily. Ninety percent (90 percent) of our undergraduate students and 66 percent of our postgraduate students; and 84 percent of our faculty in higher education are in the affiliated colleges. There is no research in the affiliated colleges; this means that in the field of higher education 84 percent of faculties members do not do research. They are not expected to do research and only 16 percent of the faculty in higher education is expected to do research in the country. The Indian higher education system should spend more money for research and motivate students and faculty of university and working in affiliated colleges.

Overall, in the past four decades research on the links between the roles of teaching, learning and research in higher education has evolved from a more narrow approach focused on the statistical relationships between teaching and research quality using the individual academic perspective through quantitative/qualitative methodology based on the study of a wider range of research and settings (Jenkins 2005). The pattern teaching and research are organized within departments and institutions are also an important factor to study the extent of internal effort to develop policies and strategies to promote the quality.

At this level, the emphasis is on the organization of subjects for teaching and for research and its variations in the way relations are conceptualized and transacted. These variations are framed according to nature of knowledge, the different forms of pedagogy and curricula, and the effect of professional planning and student interests on the content and practices of the subject.

The continuous progress of science and the application of technology attract the attention of technical education, both vocational and professional, and it constitutes the foundation for the development of innovation in higher education. Concentrated efforts are desirable to tap the potentials of alternative methods of knowledge transaction including television, information communication technology (ICT), self-learning, and internet based courses. India should enter on a massive digital program to convert the whole higher educational curriculum into a multimedia, web-based format and to establish accredited levels for recognition of distance educational courses. The demand of higher education cannot be fulfilled by the Government alone. It needs the participation of the Government, the private sectors and perhaps selective participation of foreign universities. We should have free mindset and take a positive attitude, taking into consideration the fact that a great revolution is taking place in higher education in the world. Finally, there is an urgent for more and better innovative practices both to improve the quality of higher education and to increase the number of students who complete their studies.

Most of the universities and colleges in India where innovative strategies are used apart from these higher education institutes there are several private institutes in India that offer various innovative practices in India. At present, the world class institutions in India are mainly limited. Most of the Indian colleges and universities lack in high end innovative facilities. Under investment in libraries, information technology, laboratories and classrooms makes it very difficult to provide top quality instruction or engage in innovative way of teaching learning. This gap has to be bridged if all stakeholders want to speed up our path towards innovation. The time now is to modernize our education system so that our nation can get much more technically educated people which can help our country to developed state.

The Present Study

The present study was conducted in Darbhanga city of Bihar, which contains two universities and so many government colleges. Some government colleges of Darbhanga city are using innovative strategies in higher education that's why this study was conducted at Darbhanga city with the following objectives.

Objectives of the study

The study has the following objectives:

1. To find out the strategies to improve the quality in higher education by promoting innovation.
2. To know the strategies to improve the quality of higher education by promoting research.

Methods and Participants

A sample of 50 respondents was selected from Universities and college teachers in Darbhanga city of Bihar. In sample, 25 were university teachers and 25 were college teachers. All respondents were selected through purposive sampling technique. The researcher were administered a self-constructed open-ended-questionnaire and the data was analysed through qualitative method.

Finding of the Study

After analyzing the data, the investigator found that there are various strategies suggested by university and college teacher which helps in development of quality in higher education through promoting innovation and research are presented below:

Research to Promote Higher Education

Suggestions for improving quality of higher education by promoting research:

Develop research society: - According to college teachers social development will require contributions from experts, and this will place the entire sector of higher education in sharp focus. Although today the prior task of the country will have to plan itself to invest more on higher education and, simultaneously, research will have to be taken to refine, diversify and uplift higher education, policies and programmes.

Provide incentives to Teachers and Researchers - Teachers and research scholar are expecting specialized courses to be offered so that they get the latest and best in research methodology and become employable. Doctoral and Diploma courses in research need to be made more attractive to facilitate specialized skills being offered to students. Incentives should be provide to researchers and teacher to make these areas more attractive for the younger generation.

Researches on Innovative Practices – Teachers opined that innovation in system provide more opportunities for progress in all aspects of life. Though abilities are needed to improve the higher education innovative capacity, yet the efforts should be to build on the existing strengths in light of new understanding of the research and innovation growth linkage. It offers opportunities for economic growth, improved learning, improved health, better service delivery and socio - cultural advances.

Use of unconventional resources – University teachers were of the opinion that decline in educational funding in the plan periods has resulted in serious effects on standards of higher education due to decline in available resources. Effective research approaches will have to be adopted to mobilize resources for higher education.

Education and Dynamic Methods – College teachers believed that approach of teaching in higher education also have to be appropriate to the needs of learning to learn, learning to do, learning to be and learning to become. Methods of teaching through lectures will make stress on self-study, thus personal interaction between teachers and pupils, and dynamic sessions of seminars and workshops should be explored through various researches in higher education will have to be required on a vast scale.

International Cooperation – According to the faculties universities in India have been a primary path for the improvement and transmission of knowledge. Researches on international cooperation are very important for the increase in development of nation and communication with the global village.

Action Research for Improving Quality - Government and administrative stakeholders should be conducted once in year in universities or colleges by research scholars and external experts for ensuring quality in all determinants of academic activities. Universities and colleges should realize the need for quality education and come forward with action research plan.

Research on Privatization- Respondents told the researcher that in reality whole population of India are not educated. So, researches in this area enlighten the standard of education as first priority for improvement and should be provided to the majority by the sincere authorities thus privatization of higher education is absolutely necessary in our country like India as government alone is helpless to do so.

Undergraduate Research: - Supervisors opined that undergraduate' students those who recently shift toward first and second year are involved in faculty research in a similar fashion like research scholar assistants. Students & Faculty Supervisor of under graduate researchers must encourage participating in research work.

Innovation in higher education to promote quality

Suggestions for improving quality of higher education by promoting innovation:

Active Learning: - Respondent responded that faculty utilizes strategies such as the students ask and develop questions related to the lecture material being reviewed. Students, faculty and pedagogical reformer move away from memorization of theories and facts to use and apply knowledge.

Collaborative Learning: - Most of the faculties focus on Group discussion and active project work with course material should be emphasized. Faculty shift from "instructor to guide" thus respondents respond that higher education include multiple new assumptions about learning like learning is an active, constructive process, diversity of learner, learning depends on context and learning is inherently social.

Cooperative Education: - The teachers replied that development of interpersonal skills is as important as the learning itself. Learning to cooperate is key concept in high quality work and peer process skills development. Higher education must teach students to work well with interdependency in group setting.

Cultural Pluralism: - Reform aimed at supporting students to learn and respect other cultures also aimed at helping other institutions which create communities where diversity is valued and accepted. Respondents viewed as an essential component of maintaining justice, democracy and economic empowerment. Students, Faculty, & Institution of higher education have to Shift syllabi and focus on inclusion of multiple perspectives.

Examination Reform: - Respondents told that to promote quality and excellence in higher education academics and administration should take and adopt in respect of semester system, choice-based credit system, curriculum development, admission procedure and reform in examination system with innovative strategies with the use of educational technology.

International Education: - According to faculties students must train as compare to global demand by establish a world view, know international curriculum, and be able to take part in international affairs and join international competition particularly. This can be possible by international exchanges and collaboration with well known colleges, educational and science research institutions.

Science Reforms: - Faculties of higher education also believe that focus on interdisciplinary teaching and curriculum is meant to enhance students understanding of linkage between various ways of looking towards global village through different disciplinary lens. There is an innovative approach like examples and process other than only memorizing facts.

Service learning: - Faculties responds that service learning utilizes experiences and practice to teach students in areas that may be difficult to teach through abstract reasoning such as empathy. Integrating outside experience into the classroom helps in understanding the concepts in concrete way.

Student Peer teaching: - Faculties opined that in peer teaching students feel more comfortable taking educational risks as students' shares ideas with each other rather than in front of the teachers initially. Students & Curriculum teaching role is extended from faculty member to students.

High-tech Libraries –In Indian university libraries have a very good collection of books, but they are not systematic. Few libraries must be online and conducive for study of research scholar. Respondents told that Indian higher education should concentrate more on providing hi-tech libraries which is comparable to that of global standards.

Conclusion

The purpose of education is not to produce "literate" individual at one string by putting all information and knowledge into course at one time but on the other hand, it is to take the individual to provide what further information and knowledge students' wants for future career. If higher education follow this innovative approach and research it is to be considered that only important content is not to be loaded as the curriculum but to systematize it in such a way that different requirements and needs of the higher education students calling are provided in the process of lifelong education. The development of research on the correlation between higher education, government and different institutions together with the new concept of knowledge develops a trans-disciplinary, socially, spatially distributed and deeply contextualized approach to maintain relevance of higher education in global world. Various universities and colleges will need to careful plan and preparation for their respective identities in order to survive the competition and institutions have to improve the quality of their services. Innovations, researches and best practices serve to enhance quality and add value. Higher education institutions and its stakeholders should try to provide innovative academics and research approaches between who assesses and who is assessed.

Reference

1. Ana Paula Cabral, & Isabel Huet. (2011*). Research in Higher Education: the role of teaching and student learning*. International Conference on Education and Educational Psychology (ICEEPSY 2011). Procedia - Social and Behavioral Sciences 29 (2011) 91 – 97
2. David Andrew Turner . (2011). *Quality in Higher Education*. Sense Publishers. ISBN: 978-94-6091-682-3
3. Dr. T. Sreenivas, & N. Suresh Babu. (july-2015). *Higher education in India– Quality perspective.* International Journal of Advanced Research in Management and Social Sciences. ISSN: 2278 - 623 6. Vol. 4, No. 7
4. Kirti Matliw. (2016). *Present Scenario of Higher Education in India*. Conference Paper citations reads 2,892 1, Journal of Youngish Teachers' Interaction Forum. ISSN- 2395-6437 Retrieved from: https://www .researchgate.net /publication/ 314216861
5. The Role of Higher Education in Society: Quality and Pertinence. 2nd UNESCO - Non - Governmental organizations. (8 -11 April 1991). Collective Consultation on Higher Education Paris.
6. Tapio Varis. (oct-2007). *New technologies and innovation in higher education and regional development.* Revista de University y Sociedad del Conocimiento.vol. 4, issn 1698-580x.

Chapter-33

Information and Communication Technologies (ICTS): Means to Quality Higher Education in Kashmir

Ferooz Akram
Ravees Ahmad

Abstract

In the present scenario, we are in a digital era. It is difficult to think of any event in our day to day life without using Information and Communication Technologies. Information and Communication Technologies (ICTs) have a greater significance in revolutionizing the modern information society. Present-day schools and classrooms are no exceptions. Education is a very socially oriented activity and quality in education has usually remained a debatable problem since ancient times. The role of ICTs in stimulating quality in higher education can never be ignored. The use of ICTs in education advances itself to more student-centered learning. It is evident that an upsurge in the use of ICT in education with integrating technology to the curriculum has a noteworthy and positive impact on student's achievement. It is obvious that the students who are continuously exposed to technology have enhanced 'knowledge', presentation skills, innovative competencies, and are ready to put more efforts into learning as compared to their counterparts. The proposed study is meant for investigating the present higher education system of Kashmir and to provide possible suggestions to integrate ICTs in education with the intension to enhance the practices that are directly or indirectly concerned with teaching and learning process. The study is based on data collected from different higher educational institutions of Kashmir using different tools like Checklist, observations, Questionnaire, and other tools and techniques.

Keywords: *ICTs, Quality Education, Teaching and learning process.*

Introduction

India's higher education system is the third largest in the world, next to the United States and China. About 8.15 percent (68 millions) of Indians are graduates ***(Census 2011)***. The Higher education systems of India have grown-up rapidly in last few decades. This expansion has led to degraded quality higher education. This impetus continued due to instantaneous advancements in different fields which eventually lead to the prolonged demand of skilled and competent manpower in this globalized society (*Ajit Mondal 2012)*.

Information and communication technology (ICT) has transformed different aspects of life. The introduction of ICT in the higher education institutions has thoughtful implications, especially concerned with key issues of access, equity, management, efficiency, pedagogy and quality. ICT provides lot of improvements at Schools, Colleges, Universities, workplace, home and in every aspect of our day to day lives. The International Telecommunication Union (ITU) stated that "The key to the information society is universal access to ICTs. Everybody should have equal opportunity to be a part of the digital world and nobody should be starved of to get the probable benefits of Information and Communication Technologies (ICTs) ***(Ashok Kumar Veerasamy 2012)***. The primary goal of higher education Institution is to provide quality higher education for students, and research work. ICTs plays significant role in bringing quality in higher education. Therefore Information communication technology (ICT) has positive influence in higher education directly or indirectly. Now a days, ICT is becoming a means for medium of instruction in higher education Institutions.***(Musa Dima Genemo 2016)*** In higher education Institution of developed countries, ICTs are being used as medium of instruction by using multimedia, video lecture, E-Learning and other ICT are used as medium of instruction in the class room settings. The main benefit of ICTs is that it solves the communication gap between different higher education Institutions and integrating ICTs in classroom settings helps both students and teachers to bring improvement in teaching learning process, research, and self-study.

Purpose of the Study

The main purpose of the proposed study is to investigate the impact of Information Communication Technology (ICTs) on Higher Education Students of Kashmir valley especially rural and urban Degree Colleges of Kashmir valley. Under the proposed study the fallowing objectives have been framed and will be specifically, investigated;

(1) To investigate and compare the use of Information Communication Technology (ICTs) among urban and rural degree College students of Kashmir valley.

(2) To investigate the impact of Information Communication Technology (ICTs) on the academic achievement of urban and rural degree College students of Kashmir valley.

(3) To provide some possible suggestions to strengthen the integration of Information Communication Technology (ICTs) in degree Colleges.

Research Questions

In the proposed study, the following research questions were formulated.

(1) How far does the urban and rural degree College Students of Kashmir valley use ICTs in their studies?

(2) How far does ICTs impact the academic achievement of urban and rural degree College Students of Kashmir valley?

(3) How far does urban and rural degree college students differ in using ICTs in their respective areas?

Methodology

The methodology for the said study was equipped with proper procedures in order to properly fit the study, so that to reach the goals for which the study was intended to reach. To get the probable results, proper quantitative tools and techniques were used for data collection such as check-list and questionnaires. The Data collected through questionnaire permits the researcher to go through objective analysis. Under such type of study the researcher can accessibly reach the probable statistical findings. The data collected from the research tools were analysed properly by using different types of software like SPSS and Minitab, so that to quantify the results appropriately and to put it in the form of columns and tables that would helpfully enhance and encompass the research analysis. The proposed study is free from personal bias, since, the analysis is based on statistical analysis of data which enhances the validity and reliability of the study. The study has been undertaken in Kashmir Division of Jammu and Kashmir State. The main focus of the study is to find out the access of ICTs over different colleges of Kashmir and compare the accessibility between urban and rural colleges and its impact on their teaching learning process.

Tool construction

The check-list and Questionnaire was developed after thorough literature review, and by taking help of previous research tools. Both Questionnaire and interview schedule comprises of close ended questions.

A separate Questionnaire was constructed for both teachers and students in order get the probable results for the proposed study.

Data collection and Sample

The sample for the proposed study was selected from 6 degree colleges of Kashmir division by using the technique of Stratified Random Sampling. Firstly a list of total number of degree colleges was prepared and then 6 colleges were selected from each strata using Stratified Random Sampling technique i.e., 3 degree colleges from urban areas and 3 degree colleges from rural areas. Six (6) degree colleges were selected for the proposed study, including three (3) urban degree colleges and three (3) rural degree colleges from each one of the six (6) colleges, a sample of twenty five (25) students and ten (10) teachers were taken. Thus the total sample comprised of 150 students and 60 teachers. After the sample was selected, the data was collected by using tools.

Data Analysis

The data collected using different tools was subjected to rigorous statistical analysis. The data analysis has been done using various tools and software like SPSS and minitab. The mean and percentages were computed on the collected data. Content analysis were used for analysis of data collected through open ended questions. The t-test was used for comparing the use of ICT among rural and urban degree college.

Descriptive analysis

Table 33.1: Showing the use of ICTs among Urban and Rural Degree College Students of Kashmir division.

	Group	*N*	*Mean*	*Std. Deviation*	*t-value*	*Level of Sig.*
Use of ICT	Rural	150	7.94	2.407	12.94	Sig. at 0.01 level
	Urban	150	11.10	3.018		

The data presented in table 33.1 reveals that there is a significant difference between rural (M= 7.94; SD = 2.407) and Urban (M= 11.10; SD =3.018) degree college students on use of ICT services dimension. The calculated t-value 12.94 which exceeds the table value is significant at 0.01 level (e" 2.59). The mean score indicates that urban students have more use of ICT services dimension than rural students. Hence one of the objective of our study is realized.

Table 33.2: showing the relationship between ICT literacy and academic achievement of rural and urban degree college students of Kashmir division.

Group	*Academic Achievement*	*N*	*Mean ICT Literacy*
Urban	0-50%	44	11.67
	50-70%	74	13.23
	70% and above	32	15.26
	Total	**150**	
Rural	0-50%	73	7.24
	50-70%	58	48.89
	70% and above	19	9.71
	Total	**150**	

The table 33.2 specifies the relation between academic achievements and ICT literacy of Urban and Rural degree college students of Kashmir division. The relation between ICT literacy and academic achievement of 150 Urban college students presented in the table 33.2, depicts that 44 students have mean score of 11.67 in ICT literacy and the academic achievement of 0-50 percent, 74 students have mean score of 13.23 in ICT literacy and the academic achievement of 50-70 percent and 32 students have mean score of 15.26 In ICT literacy and the academic achievement of 70 percent above. While as the relation between ICT literacy and academic achievement of 150 Rural college students presented in the table 33.2 represents that 73 students have mean score of 7.24 in ICT literacy and the academic achievement of 0-50 percent, 58 students have mean score of 8.89 in ICT literacy and the academic achievement of 50-70 percent and 19

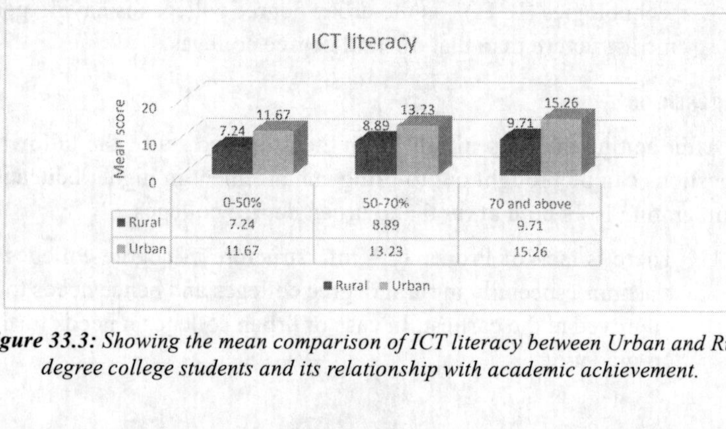

Figure 33.3: *Showing the mean comparison of ICT literacy between Urban and Rural degree college students and its relationship with academic achievement.*

students have mean score of 9.71 in ICT literacy and the academic achievement of 70 percent above. The above table 33.2 helps us to achieve another objective of the study.

Results

1. **Access to ICTs for urban and rural college students of Kashmir**

   The outcomes of the study depicts clearly that there is a significant difference between the rural and urban degree college students regarding the use of information and communication technologies (ICTs).Theme an usage of ICTs among rural and urban degree college students shows significant difference at 0.01 level of significance. The findings of the research can be justified on the basis of many other researchers conducted that supplement the outcomes of the present study. The study also depicts that that rural degree college of Kashmir have a very meager infrastructure available for ICTs as compared to urban degree colleges of Kashmir, it can also be said that infrastructure in the urban degree colleges of Kashmir is not up to mark.

2. **Impact of Information Communication Technology (ICTs) on academic achievement of urban and rural degree college students of Kashmir.**

   The Proposed study depicts that in both rural and urban degree colleges, those students who use more ICTs have better academic achievement than those who use less ICTs. Table 33.2 clearly indicates that there is a positive correlation between ICT literacy and academic achievement of degree college students. The study reveals that the students of urban degree college students have higher academic achievement than rural degree colleges because of difference in access to information and communication technologies (ICTs) , as the urban degree colleges is having good infrastructure than that of rural degree colleges.

Suggestions

After getting the deep insight from the proposed study, the fallowing suggestions can be brought out to bring enhancement in higher education by integrating ICTs both at rural and urban degree colleges.

1. There is lack of Proper ICT infrastructure in degree colleges of Kashmir especially in rural degree colleges and hence needs to be improved at the earliest. In case of urban colleges it needs further up-gradation.

2. Degree college students especially from rural colleges should provide suitable training for ICT facilities in their colleges so that the students may likely to get attracted towards ICT which may ultimately enhance their academic achievement.
3. The study also suggests that the degree colleges should provide free workshops and seminars to students regarding the benefits of ICTs in Higher education.

Conclusion

The findings of the present study shall brings us to deep insight that ICTs play an uncharacteristic role in higher education institutions especially in degree colleges of Kashmir. The study also depicts that there is significant difference between the access and infrastructure of urban and rural degree colleges of Kashmir. The study shall prompt the administration at college level and other stakeholders who are involved in administration of these higher education institutions in order to frame sound policies for the integration and implementation of ICTs in higher education institutions and to bridge the gap of access and infrastructure between urban and rural degree colleges.

References

1. Adel ben youssef, mounir dahmani (27 Jan 2014) the impact of ICT on student performance in higher education: direct effects, indirect effects and organisational change
2. Ashok Kumar Veerasamy (2012) Impact of ICTs on society-Higher Education Students in South-East Asia
3. Chandra Shekhar Singh (sept 2017) Impact of information and communication technologies on higher education in India J. E. Lawrence, "Examining the factors that influence ICT adoption in SMEs: a research preliminary findings," *International Journal of Technology Diffusion (IJTD)*, vol. 6, no. 4, pp. 40–57, 2015.
4. Esen, B. K., & Gundogdu, M. (2010). The Relationship between Internet Addiction, peer pressure and perceived social support among adolescents. The International Journal of Educational Researchers, 2(1), 29-36.
5. hadiya habib (4 December 2017)Role of Ict in higher education
6. Mishra, S. and R. C. Sharma 2005. Development of e-Learning in India. University News, 43(11), March 14 – 20, 2005.
7. Musa Dima Genemo (2016) The Impact of ICT on Higher Education Institutions in Ethiopia.
8. Onyia, mary n. (*October 2013*) the impact of ict on university students' academic studies.

9. UNESCO. (2003), "Manual for Pilot Testing the Use of Indicators to Assess Impact of ICT Use in Education". http://www.unescobkk.org/education/ict/resource.
10. Uttam Kr Pegu .2014. Information and Communication technology in Higher Education in India: Challenges and opportunities. International journal of Information and Communication Technology, 4 (5) pp 513-518.
11. Youssef, B., A., & Dahmani, M. (2008). Student's performances and ICTs, *University and Knowledge Society Journal* (*RUSC)*, March 2008, 45-56.
12. Yusuf, M. O., & Afolabi, A. O. (2010). Effects of computer assisted instruction (cai) on secondary school students' performance in biology. *The Turkish Online Journal of Educational Technology, 9*(1): 626.

Chapter-34

Quality, Content and Context in Higher Education

Joginapallyramesh,

Abstract

Education is one of the significant factors instrumental to the development of a country. It should be transformed to the needs of the time and changing scenario of the world. It provides an opportunity to critically reflect upon the social, economic, cultural, moral and spiritual issues facing humanity. India needs more efficient and educated people to drive our economy forward. There are many Indian around the corner who known for their capabilities and skills. To develop India as an education hub or to become a prosperous partner in global economy, India has to qualitatively strengthen education in general and higher education with research and development in particular. This paper is mainly focused on the overall performance of higher education system in India. We try to find out the initiatives taken by the government to raise level of education system. This paper aims to identify emerging issues and challenges in the field of Higher Education in India. Finally the paper concludes here is need of plans requires solutions that combine, employers and youth need of Expectations of from various stakeholders Students, Industry, Educational Institutions, Parents and Government.

Keywords: *Higher Education, Financing, Issues, challenges*

Introduction

Higher education is very important for a developing country like India and it is encouraging to increasing human development. Higher education in India has experienced phenomenal expansion since independence. India has produced scientists, engineers, technologists, doctors, teachers and managers who are in great demand all over the world. Now it is one of the top ten countries in our industrial and technological capacity, because of the significant contribution of manpower and tools provided by higher education, especially, technical education. India has already entered into the era of knowledge explosion. It has proved its tremendous potential by its performance in reflect on the critical social, cultural, moral, economic and spiritual issues facing humanity. Higher education provides specialized knowledge and skilled persons for national development. In next few decades, India will have world's largest set of young people. While the correlation between people and higher education is not up to the mark. The increasing youth population can be a great asset if potential employability is brought to fruition. Conversely, if we fail to provide education and employment then it will open a downside gate for Indian economy. Education is an essential tool for achieving sustainability. The Education Commission 1964-66 described the role of education in social and economic transformation through a statement- the density of a nation is shaped in its class rooms. Education creates human capital which is the core of economic progress and assumes that the externalities generated by human capital are the source of self sustaining economic process.

Emerging Issues in quality

The role of higher education in the emerging scenario of knowledge economy is very crucial and multifaceted for any country in general and India in particular. There are many basic problems faced by higher education system in India. These include Lower level of teaching quality, Financing of higher education, More concentrated on theories and rather than practical knowledge, Traditional methods of teaching, Privatization, Inadequate facilities and infrastructure Quota system.

- Lower level of teaching quality: Our education system is torture by issues of quality in many of its institutions and universities. Many of the issues like lack of faculty, poor quality teaching, Traditional teaching methods, outdated and rigid curricula and pedagogy, lack of accountability and quality assurance and separation of research and teaching are raise questions on Indian education system.
- Financing of higher education: One of the most important things that have to be noticed is the issue of financial constraints regarding higher education before the government. Expenditure on education in common and on higher education in particular by the government, is one of the parameters to judge the quality in education for at all nation. The State Government have already been spending 20-30 per cent of its revenue budget on education. It cannot afford to spend more. In India, higher education has received less attention in terms of public spending than other

levels. It is not feasible for India to make massive state investments in research and development that produced research led universities in the west such as MIT, University of California, Berkeley in the US or University of Cambridge in Britain. More concentrated on theories and rather than practical knowledge: Indian education system is more focused on theoretical knowledge rather than practical knowledge. In many jobs there is also a minimum requirement of percentage which is high.

- Traditional methods of teaching: Professors still stick to those older methods of teaching like board, marker. They don't like to make use of audio visual aids in teaching. Also they are not up to date with the information available and what global industry demands.
- Privatization: In the present scenario, privatization of higher education is apparently a fledgling but welcome trend and is essential to maintain creativity, adaptability and quality. The economic trail of liberalization and globalization demands it. In India both public and private institutions operate simultaneously. Approximately 50 per cent of the higher education in India is imparted through private institutions, mainly unaided involving high cost. However, the situation is not so simple. Private providers, in the interest of maximizing profit, have every incentive to 'minimize costs' by compromising on the quality of education provided in their institutions. Last but not least, quality of teaching staff is one of the considerable issues for higher education sector to sustain in the future. Earlier, they were committed to their students to their subjects and to their profession. Today, high salaries are available but the commitment is less. Thus, it is the need of the hour to free the higher education system from unnecessary constraints and political interference.
- Inadequate facilities and infrastructure: In India, many of the universities don't have adequate infrastructure or facilities to teach students. Even many private universities are running courses without classrooms. Internet and Wi-Fi facility is still out of reach of many students.
- *Quota system:* Bringing the reservation and quota system for different categories in education lost its quality. Even deserving candidates of general categories are ignored and on quota we have to select other person from reserved category even though he is not suitable.

Content and Context

The system of Indian Higher education is the second largest in the world which fulfils the educational requirements of millions of students who come from different sections of the society since it is the student community that can help to generate healthy academic atmosphere in institutions of higher learning. No doubt that India faces today a number of problems pertaining to poverty unemployment disappearance of moral and spiritual values. But in the last few decades a countrywide problems/ challenges have emerged in Higher Education system in India they are discussed as under.

- Our heterogeneous education system, based on geographical, rural-urban, rich-poor set up have posed in great challenge for the educational institutions. Varieties of colleges, universities, technical institutions have produced and different types and quality of Education. Some of them are really imparting qualitative education although a few others are doing the dirtiest job. Thanks to UGC, for publishing the list of such a fake Universities and Institutions indulging in educational malpractices.
- Interference of political factors: Most of the Institutions, imparting education (Aided-non-aided) are owned by the dominant political leaders, now playing key role in governing bodies of the Universities. They have established their own youth cells and encourage students' organization on political basis. They exploit the students' energy for their political purposes. The students forget their own objectives and begin to develop their career in politics.
- Economic Difficulties: Is one of the most troublesome changes that the present higher education system has imposed on the communities? The numbers of students are coming from the ordinary classes; many of them are unable to provide the minimum necessities of life for themselves. Economic miseries have grown due to the increasing prizes, habits of wasting money on luxuries, increasing population, scarcity of food supply, corruption, selfish etc. students hold part time jobs in order to pay for the their educational expenses and should divide their attention between a job and College/University education. Near about seventy five percent of the total students community today, have been facing the financial problems. Earn while learn scheme cannot adequately support student to face economic challenges.

- Lack of Moral values: Rapid growth of science and technology and subsequent industrialization has caused a great and danger to our old moral and values. The younger generation's dissatisfaction and revolt is the outcome of a decaying system of values.

Suggestions for improving quality of higher education:

There are some suggestions and Expectations from Government, Industry, Educational Institutions, Parents and Students for improving quality of higher education.

- Student-Centred Education and Dynamic Methods-Methods of higher education also have to be appropriate to the needs of learning to learn, learning to do, learning to be and learning to become. Student-centred education and employment of dynamic methods of education will require from teachers new attitudes and new skills. Methods of teaching through lectures will have to subordinate to the methods that will lay stress on self-study, personal consultation between teachers and pupils, and dynamic sessions of seminars and workshops. Methods of distance education will have to be employed on a vast scale.
- Examination Reforms- Examination reforms, gradually shifting from the terminal, annual and semester examinations to regular and continuous assessment of student's performance in learning must be implemented.
- International Cooperation-Universities in India have been a primary conduit for the advancement and transmission of knowledge through traditional functions such as research, innovation, teaching, human resource development, and continuing education. International cooperation is gaining importance as yet another function. With the increased development of transport and communication, the global village is witnessing a growing emphasis on international cooperation and action to find satisfactory solutions to problems that have global dimensions and higher education is one of them.
- To increase Quantity of Universities- We need more universities because we are more in number and present number of universities is too less. On 13th June, 2005 Government of India constituted a high level advisory body known as National Knowledge Commission (NKC) to advise the PM about the state of education in India and measures needed to reform this sector. It was headed by Sam Pitroda and submitted its report in November 2007. NKC

has recommended setting up of 1500 universities by 2015 so that gross enrolment ratio increases to 15 percent. It has also called for establishing an Independent Regulatory Authority for Higher Education (IRAHE) to monitor the quality of overall higher education in India.

- Cross Culture Programmes- After education, tour to every the places in India and world as far as possible with the cooperation of government is necessary so that one can understand about people, culture, arts, literature, religions, technological developments and progress of human society in the world.
- Action Plan for Improving Quality- Academic and administrative audit must be conducted once in three years in colleges by external experts for ensuring quality in all aspects of academic activities. The self-finance colleges must come forward for accreditation and fulfil the requirements of accreditation. Universities and colleges should realise the need for quality education and come forward with action plan for improving quality in higher educational institutions.
- World Class Education- Indian government is not giving priority to the development of Standard in education. India must aspire for the international standard in education. Many national universities like in the USA, UK, Australia, etc. allow studies in higher education for foreign students in their countries and through correspondence courses as well. In the same way India Universities of world class education can also offer courses of studies to foreign students taking advantage of the globalization process. To achieve that goal it must adopt uniform international syllabus in its educational institutions.
- Personality Development- Finally, education must be for the flowering of personality but not for the suppression of creativity or natural skill. In the globalized world opportunity for the educated people are naturally ample in scope. As a result business process outsourcing (BPO) activities have increased competition in the world trade leading towards the production of quality goods and their easy availability everywhere in the world market. That is the way the world can be developed for peace, prosperity and progress by able and skilful men.
- High-tech Libraries-Our university libraries have a very good collection of books, but they are all in mess. A library must be online and conducive for serious study. Indian universities should

concentrate more on providing quality education which is comparable to that of international standards.

Conclusion

- In concluding words, we can say that over the period of time, growth have been take place in higher education in terms of institutions, enrolments etc. but it is not sufficient. Indian economy is facing various challenges regarding higher education, which need to overcome through appropriate policy formation and their effective implementation.
- Higher education in India plays many roles. It is of extraordinary importance to many and reforms are often seen as significant threats to specific, social arrangements that provide benefits to powerful groups.
- The politics is the result and most often the changes are not implemented language has been a similar issues in which government attempted to solve in difficult social and political problem through policy relating to higher education.
- To conclude, Higher education in India is an extraordinarily important part of modern Indian society and it is intertwined in the political and social systems of the society. It is in need of change, development and important. In order to effectively plan for reforms and improvement, it is necessary to have in realistic perceptions of what is possible and what is not.

References

1. Agarwal R et al. Higher Education and Quality Improvement: A challenge for India. Indian Journal of Applied Research 2014; 4(10).
2. Mishra Sharda, (2006). UGC and Higher Education System in India. Book Enclave, Jaipur.302006.
3. Arunachalam P. Higher Education Sector in India: Issues and Imperatives. Journal of Global Econom 2010; 6(4).
4. Padhi, S.K. (2011), 'Issues, Challenges and Reforms in Higher Education for a Knowledge Society,'.
5. Higher Education in India: Issues, Concerns and New Directions http://www.ugc.ac.in/pub/heindia.pdf.
6. Ramesh G. Indian Higher Education and the Challenges of Sustainability: An Analytical Note. International Journal of Social Science & Interdisciplinary Research 2013; 2(9).
7. Chronicle of Higher Education, various issues (cited as CHE) (http://chronicle.com/).

8. British council report. Understanding India: The future of higher education and opportunities for international cooperation, 2014.
9. Bhatia K, Dash MK. National Knowledge Commission-A Step towards India's higher Education Reforms on India's Higher Education. International Research Journal of Finance and Economic 2010; 53: 46.
10. University Grants Commission (UGC) released a report "Higher education in India at a glance.

Chapter-35

Issues and Challenges – Higher Education in India

Ravi Kaka,

Abstract

Although there have been challenges to higher education in the past, these most recent calls for reform may provoke a fundamental change in higher education. This change may not occur as a direct response to calls for greater transparency and accountability, but rather because of the opportunity to reflect on the purpose of higher education, the role of colleges and universities in the new millennium, and emerging scientific research on how people learn. These disparate literatures have not been tied together in a way that would examine the impact of fundamental change from the policy level to the institutional level and to the everyday lives of college and university administrators, faculty and students. Now the time has come to create a second wave of institution building and of excellence in the fields of education, research and capability building. We need higher educated people who are skilled and who can drive our economy forward. When India can provide skilled people to the outside world then we can transfer our country from a developing nation to a developed nation very easily and quickly.

Keywords: *Higher Education, Issues, Challenges.*

Introduction

India's higher education system is the world's third largest in terms of students, next to China and the United States. Unlike China, however, India has the advantage of English being the primary language of higher education and research. India educates approximately 11 per cent of its youth in higher education as compared to 20 per cent in China. The main governing body at the tertiary level is the University Grants Commission (India), which enforces its standards, advises the government, and helps coordinate between the centre and the state. Universities and its constituent colleges are the main institutes of higher education in India. At present in 2011, there are

227 government-recognized Universities in India. Out of them 20 are central universities, 109 are deemed universities and 11 are Open Universities and rest are state universities. Most of these universities in India have affiliating colleges where undergraduate courses are being taught. However Jawaharlal University is a remarkable exception to this rule. According to the Department of higher Education government of India, 16,885 colleges, including 1800 exclusive women's colleges functioning under these universities and institutions and there are 4.57 lakh teachers and 99.54 lakh students in various higher education institutes in India. Apart from these higher education institutes there are several private institutes in India that offer various professional courses in India. Distance learning is also a feature of the Indian higher education system.

Some institutions of India, such as the Indian Institutes of technology (IITs), have been globally acclaimed for their standard of education. The IITs enroll about 8000 students annually and the alumni have contributed to both the growth of the private sector and the public sectors of India. However, India has failed to produce world class universities like Harvard and Cambridge. According to the London Times Higher Education (2009)-Quacquarelli Symonds (QS) World University rankings, no Indian university features among the first 100. But universities in East Asia have been included in the first hundred. Hong Kong has three, ranked at 24, 35 and 46; Singapore two ranked at 30 and 73; South Korea two ranked at 47 and 69 and Taiwan one in the 95th position. Notably, China's Tsinghua University and Peking University are ranked at 49 and 52 respectively. There is no Indian university in the rankings from 100 to 200. It is only when one moves on to the next 100 that we find the Indian Institute of Technology, Kanpur at 237; IIT Madras at 284 and the University of Delhi at 291.

A recent evaluation of universities and research institutes all over the world, conducted by a Shanghai university, has not a single Indian university in the world's top 300 while China has six. The Indian Institute of Science, Bangalore, comes in somewhere in the top 400 and IIT, Kharagpur, makes an appearance after that. Yet this decisive edge also has its shortcomings. Besides top rated universities which provide highly competitive world class education to their pupil, India is also home to many universities which have been founded with the sole objective of making easy money. UGC and other Regulatory authorities have been trying very hard to extirpate the menace of private universities which are running courses without any affiliation or recognition. Students from rural and semi urban background often fall prey to these institutes and colleges. Today, Knowledge is power. The more knowledge one has, the more empowered one is. According to the University Grants Commission (UGC), India needs 1500 more universities with adequate research facilities by the end of the year 2015 in order to compete in the global market.

The overall scenario of higher education in India does not match with the global Quality standards. Hence, there is enough justification for an increased assessment of the Quality of the country's educational institutions. Traditionally, these institutions assumed that Quality could be determined by their internal resources, viz., faculty with an impressive set of degrees and experience detailed at the end of the institute's admission brochure, number of books and journals in the library, an ultra-modern campus, and size of the endowment, etc., or by its definable and assessable outputs, viz., efficient use of resources, producing uniquely educated, highly satisfied and employable graduates. Critical appraisals undertaken by the governmental committees and independent academicians have highlighted the crisis confronting the system: 'increasing educated unemployment; weakening of student motivation; increasing unrest and indiscipline on the campuses; frequent collapse of administration; deterioration of standards; and above all, the demoralizing effect of the irrelevance and purposelessness of most of what is being done.' While the politicians and policy makers have often spoken about the need for radical reconstruction of the system, what has been achieved in reality is only moderate reformism.

After recording growth rate of around 9 percent for the three consecutive years, India is now considered to be one of the most promising economies of the world. While, higher education gives India an edge in the world economy as evident from the availability of the skilled manpower, and research scholars working abroad, unemployment, illiteracy and relative poverty continue to be the major deterrents to realize her potential in human resources. The taskforce constituted by World Bank and UNESCO during 2000 has also observed that higher education helps increase wages and productivity that directly enrich individuals and society. The prospects and development in the higher education sector in India needs a critical examination in a rapidly globalising world. Expansion, inclusion and excellence were the three objectives of higher education policy of Government of India. The government had taken many steps to increase student enrollment in higher education and quality improvement in higher educational institutions.

Critical issues in Indian higher education

As India strives to compete in a globalised economy in areas that require highly trained professionals, the quality of higher education becomes increasingly important. So far, India's large, educated population base and its reservoir of at least moderately well-trained university graduates have aided the country in moving ahead, but the competition is fierce; from China in particular. Other countries are also upgrading higher education with the aim of building world class universities. Even the small top tier of higher education faces serious problems. Many IIT graduates, well trained in technology, have chosen not to contribute their skills to the burgeoning technology sector in India; perhaps half leave the country immediately upon graduation to pursue advanced studies abroad, and most do not return. A stunning 86 per cent of Indian students in the fields of science and technology who obtain degrees in the United States do not return home immediately following their graduation. A body of dedicated and able teachers work at the IITs and IIMs, but the lure of jobs abroad and in the private sector makes it increasingly difficult to lure the best and brightest to the academic profession.

According to a study only 25% of engineering graduates are directly employable (Infosys, an IT giant, last year sorted through 1.3 million applicants only to find that around two percent were qualified for jobs.) Quality of education delivered in most institutions is very poor. While India has some institutions of global repute delivering quality education, such as (Indian Institute of Management) IIMs and (Indian Institute of Technology) IITs, we do not have enough of them. It has very narrow range of course options that are offered and education is a seller's market, where is no scope of incentive to provide quality education. There is clearly a lack of educated educators and teaching is not an attractive profession. It's a last choice in terms of career. Number of Ph.D.s produced each year is very low and those required by academia is far higher. In fact, at many institutions fresh graduates are employed to teach, leading to poor quality of classroom instruction. Most of the education institutions esp. in states such as Maharashtra and states in South India are owned by politicians. This Education system which is highly regulated by the government has been set up to benefit politicians.

Challenges of present higher educational system in India

Since we have got independence we are facing challenges to establish a great and strong education system. Various governments came and gone. Off course they tried to establish new education policies in the system but this is very sad to dictate that they were not sufficient for our country. Still we are facing lot of problems and challenges in our Education System. India recognises that the new global scenario poses unprecedented challenges for the higher education system. The University Grants Commission has appropriately stated that a whole range of skills will be demanded from the graduates of humanities, social sciences, natural sciences and commerce, as well as from the various professional disciplines such as agriculture, law, management, medicine or engineering. India can no longer continue the model of general education as it has been persisting in for the large bulk of the student population. Rather, it requires a major investment to make human resource productive by coupling the older general disciplines of humanities, social sciences, natural sciences and commerce to their applications in the new economy and having adequate field based experience to enhance knowledge with skills and develop appropriate attitudes. Responding to these emerging needs, the UGC stated: "The University has a crucial role to play in promoting social change. It must make an impact on the community if it is to retain its legitimacy and gain public support". It seeks to do so by a new emphasis on community based programmes and work on social issues. Concepts of access, equity, relevance and quality can be operationalised only if the system is both effective and efficient. Hence, the management of higher education and the total networking of the system has become an important issue for effective management. The shift can occur only through a systemic approach to change as also the development of its human resource, and networking the system through information and communication technology.

Research in higher education institutions is at its lowest ebb. There is an inadequate and diminishing financial support for higher education from the government and from society. Many colleges established in rural areas are non-viable, are under-enrolled and have extremely poor infrastructure and facilities with just a few teachers. A series of judicial interventions over the last two decades and knee-jerk reaction of the government – both at the centre and state level and the regulatory bodies without proper understanding of the emerging market structure of higher education in India has further added confusion to the higher education landscape in the country. There is an absence of a well-informed reform agenda for higher education in the country. A few efforts made now and then are not rooted in the new global realties based on competition and increased mobility of students and workforce.

Conclusion

After independence, there has been tremendous increase in institutions of higher learning in all disciplines. But with the quantitative growth has it been able to attend to the core issue of quality. India is today one of the fastest developing countries of the world with the annual growth rate going above 9%. In order to sustain that rate of growth, there is need to increase the number of institutes and also the quality of higher education in India. To reach and achieve the future requirements there is an urgent need to relook at the Financial Resources, Access and Equity, Quality Standards, Relevance and at the end the Responsiveness. To attain and sustain national, regional or international quality, certain components are particularly relevant, notably careful selection of staff and continuous staff development, in particular through the promotion of appropriate programs for academic development, including teaching/learning methodology and mobility between countries, between higher education institutions and the world of work, as well as student mobility within and between countries. Internal self-evaluation and external review must be conducted openly by independent specialists, if possible with international experts. Report of the National Knowledge Commission if implemented can help boost education sector in India. We are moving towards an era which would be defined by the parameters of knowledge and wisdom. India in order to become a developed nation by 2020 and knowledge power by 2015. The decisions that are going to be taken on these are likely to hold the key to India's future as a center of knowledge production. We need higher educated people who are skilled and who can drive our economy forward. When India can provide skilled people to the outside world then we can transfer our country from a developing nation to a developed nation very easily and quickly.

References

1. Altbach, Philip G. (2006) The Private Higher Education Revolution: An Introduction. • University News. January 2-8, 2006. Vol. 44 No.01.
2. Anandakrishnan, M. (2006) Privatization of higher education: Opportunities and anomalies. 'Privatization and commercialization of higher education' organized by NIEPA , May 2, 2006., New Delhi
3. Delors, Jacques (1996) Learning the treasure within. Report to UNESCO of the International Commission on Education for the Twenty-first Century. UNSECO Publishing, Paris.
4. MHRD (2006) Annual Report. Ministry of Human Resource Development, Department of Secondary and Higher education. Government of India. New Delhi.
5. Planning Commission (1999) Approach paper to the Tenth Five-year Plan (2002- · 2007). Planning Commission. New Delhi.
6. Stella, Antony (2002) External quality assurance in Indian higher education: Case study of the National Assessment and Accreditation Council (NAAC). International Institute for Educational Planning. Paris.

7. UGC (2005) Research Handbook: Towards nurturing research culture in higher education institutions in India. University Grants Commission. New Delhi.
8. Jandhyala B.G. Tilak, Absence of Policy and Perspective in Higher Education. Economic and Political Weekly Vol. 39, No. 21 (May 22, 2004), 2159-2164 (http://www.epw.org.in/epw/uploads/articles/7650.pdf)
9. Higher Education in India: Issues, Concerns and New Directions http://www.ugc.ac.in/pub/heindia.pdf.
10. Higher education in India and Yashpal Committee recommendations http://www.jnu.ac.in/Yash Pal Committee.pdf.April 18, 2009, available on 25.1.2011.

Chapter-36

Improving Quality and Research in Higher Education-A Case Study Analysis

Dr.P.Srinivasa sastry
Ananth Narayan Tripurari

Abstract

This paper is a survey on the Research Trends in Implementing Data Science Technology for Improving Quality and Research in Higher Education of Education Sector in which contentsrelating to Artificial Intelligence are discussed.

Keywords: *Neural Networks, Data science, Artificial Intelligence.*

Introduction

NEURAL NETWORKS are mathematical models originally inspired by biological processes in the human brain. They are constructed from a number of simple processing elements interconnected by weighted pathways to form networks. Each element computes its output as a nonlinear function of the weighted input when combined in to networks. These processing elements can implement arbitrarily complex, non linear networks which can be used to solve classification, prediction, and optimization problems.

NEURAL NETWORK DIAGRAM

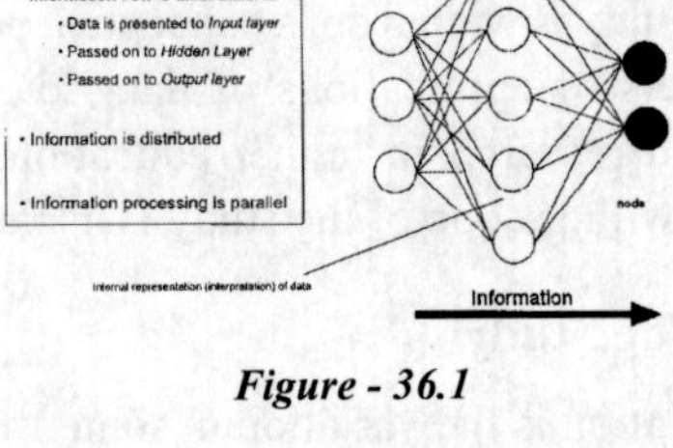

Figure - 36.1

I. Neural networks

Definitions of Neural Networks

A Neural Network is massively parallel distributed processor that has a natural propensity for storing experiential knowledge and making it available for use. It resembles the brain in two respects:

1. Knowledge is acquired by the Network through a learning process.
2. Interneuron connection strengths known as synaptic weights are used to store the knowledge.

The operation of Neural Networks is controlled by three properties

1. The pattern of its interconnections, architecture.
2. Method of determining and updating the weights on the interconnections, training.
3. The function that determines the output of each individual neuron, activation or transfer function.

II. Objective of The Study

To study the importance Research trends in implementing Data Science technology for improving quality and research in higher education of education sector.

5. Hypothesis of The Study

H1 : There is considerable impact of the data science technology for improving quality and research in higher education of education sector.

6. Research Methodology

This study is based on both primary data and secondary data. Primary data is from questionnaire responses. Secondary data is from journals, various articles, books etc. As the study deals with factors like the data science technology for improving quality and research in higher education.

7. Scope of The Study

The scope of the study is wide from a conceptual point of view because it covers major aspects of applications of data science technology for improving quality and research in higher education. However from an empirical point of view the scope of the study is narrow.

7.1. Limitation of The Study

The primary limitation is the variation in some variables

8. Analysis of The Study: Swot

Analysis on research trends in implementing data science technology for improving quality and research in higher education of education sector.

Strengths

Government support of open data and open science. The young people involved.

The commercial world is engaging at the pre competitive stage People feel good about working for the common good.

Weakness

Need for better search. overcoming the cultural gap economics entrenched business models. The current way we evaluate academic value. clear delineation between what belongs in the public domain and what represents IP. Double standard regarding openness.

Opportunities

Openness is a gateway to much more.

The 6 finalists you have seen today real opportunities to change the public health agenda and accelerate discovery. Willingness to move from individual to team science.

AMP emergence of open platforms. Mechanisms for giving people credit for being open. Community efforts as drivers.

Threats

Incentives/Rewards. Roll back of government initiatives. Closure of the network-not the internet per se but the data and knowledge layers on top. Inability to push back on centralization will banks Anglo global is not global,global -good hand.

Data Analysis of Research Trends In Implementing Data Science Technology for Improving Quality And Research in Higher Education of Education Sector.

1. Are you aware of Data science technology ?

Answers	*Total Respondents*	*Total Percentage%*
Yes	43	86%
No	3	6%
Neutral	4	8%
Total	50	100%

Data analysis: In my analysis it is found that for the question are you aware of data science technology gave a positive response with the answer of yes with 86 percent.

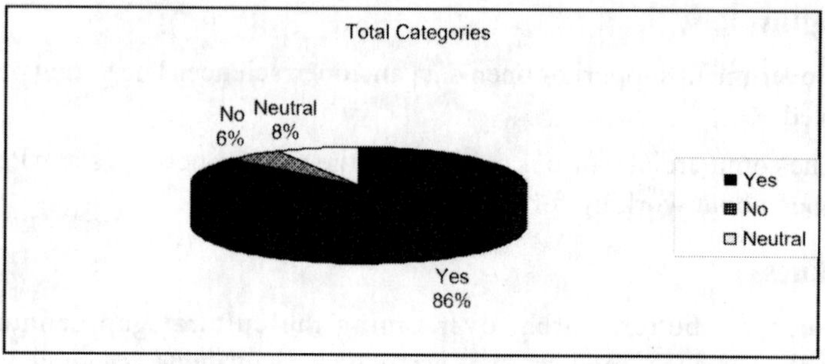

Interpretation: From the response of various sectors of respondents it is clear that majority of the respondents are aware of data science technology.

2. Are you aware of Machine learning & Deep learning?

Answers	*Total Respondents*	*Total Percentage%*
Yes	33	66%
No	7	14%
Neutral	10	20%
Total	50	100%

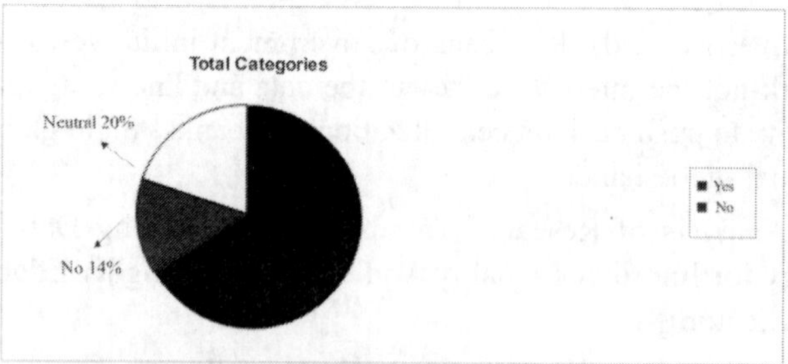

Data analysis: In my analysis it is found that for the question are you aware of Machine learning & Deep learning gave a positive response with the answer of yes with 66 percent.

Interpretation: From the response of various sectors of respondents it is clear that majority of respondents are aware of Machine learning & Deep learning.

3. Data science technology can be used for improving quality and research in higher education?

Answers	*Total Respondents*	*Total Percentage%*
Yes	28	56%
No	9	18%
Neutral	13	26%
Total	50	100%

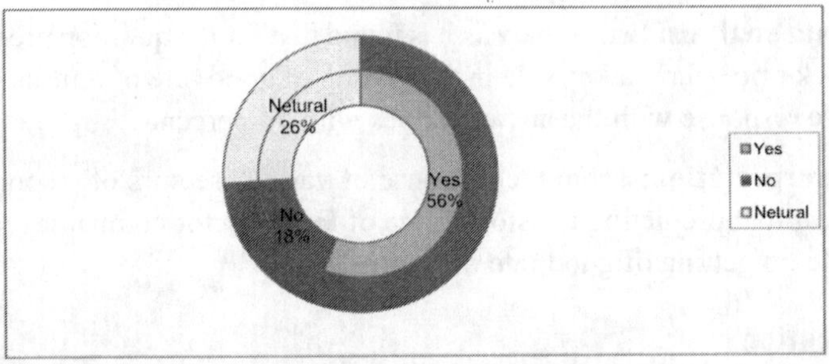

Data analysis: In my analysis it is found that for the question game theory applications are used to Neural Networks in predicting stock price gave a positive response with the answer of yes with 56 percent.

Interpretation: From the response of various sectors of respondents it is clear that Data science technology can be used for improving quality quality and research in higher education.

4. We can analyze by using data science technology for improving quality and research in higher education ?

Answers	*Total Respondents*	*Total Percentage%*
Yes	29	58%
No	11	22%
Neutral	10	20%
Total	50	100%

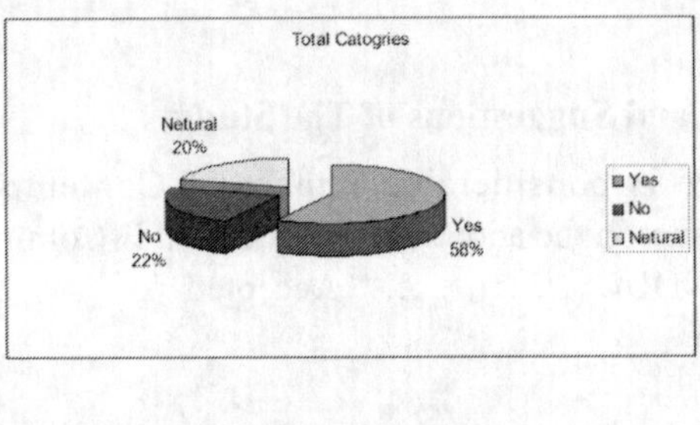

Data analysis: In my analysis it is found that for the question we can predict stock prices by Neural Networks gave a positive response with the answer of yes with 58 percent.

Interpretation: From the response of various sectors of respondents it is clear that we can predict stock prices by Neural Networks of Hotel sector companies.

5. Using data science technology for improving quality and research in higher education ` plays a key role in getting of good results?

Data analysis: In my analysis it is found that for the question predicting the stock price plays a key role in the getting of good rate of returns gave a positive response with the answer of yes with 74 percent.

Interpretation: From the response of various sectors of respondents it is clear that predicting the stock price of Hotel sector companies plays a key role .in getting of good rate of returns.

Implications

The study provides insights for investors and traders to comprehend the concept of a commensurate rate of return they can secure by operating in the stock markets. The quality of prediction concept therefore holds relevance in the stock markets.

9. Conclusions

H1: There is considerable improvement in the rate of return by minimizing the risk and maximizing the profit using Game theory to Neural Networks in predicting the Stock price of Hotel sector companies ——— Accepted

Each of the concepts discussed about Game theory and Neural Networks in this paper is of research based and it can be further elaborated in separate studies. Thus, the discussions in this paper are preliminary and do addresses only the basic structures and further work that can be carried out.

Results

9. Conclusions and Suggestions of The Study

H1 : There is considerable impact of Contemporary business management issues in the adoption of digitalized E-Commerce services by consumers in INDIA. ....Accepted.

Each of the concept discussed about issues in Ecommerce services by consumers in India in this paper is of research based and it can be further elaborated in separate studies.

References

1. E. Turban, J. Lee, D. King and H.M. Chung, Electronic Commerce: A Managerial Perspective. Prentice Hall, 1999.
2 P. Timers, Electronic Commerce – Strategies and Models for Business to Business.

Chapter-37

Student Based Financial Support System in Higher Education: Challenges in Implementation of Centrally Sponsored Schemes

Dr. Vetukuri P. S. Raju,

Abstract

One of the core ideas of Higher education in the twenty-first century India is the transmission and transformation of India through education. As higher education has been considered a significant factor in human development, it has its implications among the poor and disadvantaged sections in India. The State has organized a wide range of self-evolved strategies and transforming mechanisms to reach-out the unreached and impoverished, largely through a number of incentives and self-developing programmes attempting and making a crucial paradigm shift. Even though higher education seems to be an inaccessible commodity of the deprived, the proliferative principle of inclusiveness among the educationists, philanthropists, etc., resuscitates tens of thousands of students to avail college and University education at an affordable cost. The accessibility and enhancing and retaining all college-going students to successfully complete graduation have become pertinent and imperative. The higher education policy also would be of inclusive, liberal, scientific and knowledge-oriented, where the transformation of society, particularly through modern education is to be imminent, when students from the underprivileged are to be well-equipped with a strong desire to learn new subjects and explicit their willingness to explore the opportunities to new frontiers of knowledge.

Arguably, at the outset, this paper discusses on the innovative schemes offered by the Government of India to the meritorious students belonging to the underprivileged sections of our society for higher education which has its imperceptible implications. The impressive way through which the new incentives and other scholarship schemes for higher education in India are initiated, conceptualized and implemented, resuscitates the underprivileged students in one way or the other. The paper highlights the issues and challenges in implementation of centrally sponsored scholarship/incentive schemes in higher education that the schemes such as, Central Sector Scheme of Scholarship for College and University students (CSSSCU), Prime Minister's Special Scholarship Scheme for Jammu & Kashmir (SSSJK) and Central Scheme to provide Interest Subsidy (CSIS) on Education Loan, which are considered to be hallmarks in the annals of higher education in India, consequently, have undaunted and effervescent efforts on those students who avail and accomplish in their mission of completing higher education at large.

Introduction

The marginalized and depressed classes in India have been undergoing unprecedented difficulties to achieve higher education for centuries, as they are oppressed and their rights for an education is either denied or they are notified as ineligible. A scholarship is a form of financial aid awarded to meritorious students so that they can meet the cost and financial expenses of studying in some of the top educational institutions and universities of the world. Almost every country has various types of scholarships on offer for students and the eligibility criterion for each scholarship varies from institution to institution. Both the Government and Non-Government educational institutions provide financial assistance to students in form of scholarships in India. With the help of scholarships and schemes, students can continue their studies without putting too much monetary burden on their families.

Ever since the educational policies of India have recently focused on improving accountability and incentives of public providers for actual learning outcomes, often with school-based rewards programs for high performers. The programmes and practices, which have become prominent among such efforts, providing incentives to students of government and government recognised higher education institutions that propels to achieve learning at specified higher levels of degrees.

In the past decade, there has been an increasing recognition of the importance of education for social welfare and national economic growth and, subsequently, there has been a large push to increase enrolment and learning in colleges and universities. Until recently, interventions to improve higher education have typically taken the form of supply-side reforms, such as improvements in infrastructure, materials, or teachers. Over the past decade, policy attention has shifted towards demand-side interventions, which either lower the costs or increase the immediate benefits that households face when deciding to educate their children. One common demand-side intervention is to offer cash rewards or other incentives to households, usually to the parents, when their children attend or perform well in school. Implicit in the design of these interventions is the idea that rewarding the parents, rather than the children, produces the best results. However, there is limited evidence on whether it is more effective to target parents or children. If parents do not place a high value on learning or if they are unable to fully motivate their children, then incentives provided to children could result in better outcomes than incentives provided to parents.

The higher education policy also would be of inclusive, liberal, and accommodative of higher level of scientific and knowledge-oriented society, where the transformation of society, particularly Indian society through modern education is to be imminent, and researchers and teachers are to be well-equipped with a strong desire to learn new subjects and explicit their willingness to explore the opportunities to new frontiers of knowledge. The tedious efforts among the public and private agencies to make higher education accessible made some implications in the past. This paper argues that though higher education seems to be an inaccessible commodity of the disprivileged, the proliferative principles of inclusiveness among the educationists, philanthropists, etc., thousands of students are still accessing the college and University education at an affordable cost.

The scholarship is to be awarded for studies in India in a government or private college/university, including such residential institutes of the Government and eligible private institutes selected and notified in a transparent manner by the State Government/Union Territory Administration concerned. It will also cover technical and vocational courses in Industrial Training Institutes/ Industrial Training Centres affiliated with the National Council for Vocational Training (NCVT).

Objectives

Higher education has become even more diverse through the establishment of new higher education policy providers and the establishment of government schemes as scholarships or fellowships become an indomitable and important experience for the university students.

The higher education policy of a nation must have proliferative principles of inclusiveness among teachers, scholars and research scientists from different universities and Institutes, with in-depth knowledge and understanding of their concerned subjects, generate new knowledge by publishing commendable books and articles, produce outstanding students, and contribute immensely for the growth of a nation and to make an egalitarian society.

The schemes for awarding scholarships to meritorious students belonging to economically weaker sections of minority community so as to provide them better opportunities for higher education, increase their rate of attainment in higher education and enhance their employability.

Pertinent to the selection criteria of the fellowship recipients in getting the fund and how they receive and utilize in their academic career at the college/university, and to identify that in what way the students have been benefitted.

Methodology

The incentive and scholarship schemes established by the government, becomes paramount importance when it is implemented for the welfare and improvement of students. The study envisages the perspectives collected from the data available with the MHRD, Government of India on the number of students received and benefitted from these schemes. Whereas, the study also brings out the students involvement and achievement, which is found to be more important than any other factor and that perpetuates among the poor children to propel themselves towards reaching the goal of scoring more and also enrolling themselves for higher education in various sectors, and even to the level of reaching the highest degrees of research. Survey method is preferred for this, as students who are getting the possibility of availing the scholarship are scattered in all States of India and reaching out all of them is found to be a paramount task. While analyzing the students, their class of study, background, the parents and their perceptions, their annual income, education, occupation etc., were considered to be given utmost importance.

The incentives of the government of India and its implications among the recipients of the scholarships and stipends are to be studied in the light of feedbacks from the students as well as parents. The data received has become very significant for this research because it is to be interpreted to identify the beneficiaries, who all have an important role in assessing the experience of the boys and girls, parents and institutions after the implementation of the schemes at the institution level. The interpretation may also identify how far the schemes are successful among the students who are hailing from the depressed sections and their financial backgrounds to investigate whether the support could be taken for granted by these students gradually for improving themselves in their respective fields. The study significantly points out the fact that the states have strong and impinging experiences among the students, particularly belonging to SC, ST and Backward families, including girls, who have been undergoing tremendous problems and find it difficult to complete the collegiate education as proper help and guidance are not given to them.

Student Based Financial Support System in Higher Education

Jandhyala Tilak, while referring the higher education scenario in early 1980s pointed out, higher education is financed in India largely by the government, and the long term trends in financing show that higher education is increasingly becoming a state funded activity. In the absence of a private university that time, a large number of private colleges, most of which were 'privately managed but publicly funded', 80-90 per cent of their recurrent budgets was provided by the government. He further argued, from the point of view of finance, efficiency and equity, the private sector's contribution to educational development was almost negligible (Tilak, 1992).

Even though there are many important student based schemes or fellowships for the higher education in India, this paper is confined with mainly three schemes, such as, Central Scheme to provide Interest Subsidy (CSIS) on Education Loan, Special Scholarship Scheme for Jammu & Kashmir (SSSJK), Central Sector Scheme of Scholarship for College and University students (CSSSCU) etc., which are considered to be hallmarks in the annals of higher education in India. Consequently these schemes which are unparallel to other schemes of the previous years, marveled and precipitate new forms of support and encouragement to those students who are aspiring to reach higher echelons of education at large. Claiming that many developing countries such as India, have been examining alternative methods of financing higher education, Tilak argues, the 1963-launched National Loan Scholarship scheme programme in India has been identified for marginal improvement and also made little contribution to either the efficiency or equity of higher education in India (Tilak, 1992: 392). There are some norms and regulations stipulated by the MHRD for the submission of application, based on the allotment of quota and other formalities, which are prescribed in the brochures of the ministry proceedings and websites.

Central Scheme to Provide Interest Subsidy (CSIS) on Education Loan

One of the other prominent schemes – Central Scheme to provide Interest Subsidy (CSIS) on Education Loan was introduced by the Government of India with an objective to ensure that nobody is denied Professional education because he or she is poor. The scheme is to provide 'interest subsidy' for the period of moratorium on Educational Loans taken by students from Economically Weaker Sections (EWS) from scheduled banks under the Educational Loan Scheme to pursue Technical and Professional Education studies in India. The eligible students are entitled for full interest subsidy during the period of moratorium i.e., Course Period plus one year or six months after getting job, whichever is earlier, on loans taken by students belonging to Economically Weaker Sections with an annual gross parental family income upper limit of ₹ 4.5 lacs per year (from all sources).

The Government of India has now approved a scheme to provide full interest subsidy during the period of moratorium i.e., Course Period plus one year or six months after getting job, whichever is earlier, on loans taken by students belonging to Economically Weaker Sections from scheduled banks under the Educational Loan scheme of the Indian Banks' Association, for pursuing any of the approved courses of studies in technical and professional streams, from recognised institutions in India. The nomenclature of the Scheme would be "Central Scheme to provide Interest Subsidy (CSIS) for the period of moratorium on Educational Loans taken by students from Economically Weaker Sections from scheduled banks under the Educational Loan Scheme of the Indian Banks' Association to pursue Technical Professional Education studies in India."

The schemes, particularly central scheme to provide interest Subsidy for the period of moratorium on Educational Loans taken by students from Economically Weaker Sections from scheduled banks under the Educational Loan Scheme of the Indian Banks' Association to pursue Technical Professional Education studies in India, that enables the scholars to complete their courses on time without difficulties.

One of the major concerns of the Government is to ensure that nobody is denied Professional education because he or she is poor. The Indian Banks' Association (IBA) had formulated a comprehensive model educational loan scheme for adoption by all Banks aimed at providing financial support from the banking system to deserving/meritorious students for pursuing higher education in India and abroad.

The main purpose of offering the education loan to those students who aspire for higher education is to pay the course fees, purchase of books, equipments, instruments, uniform, payment of hostel fees, examination fees and study tours for studies in India. The eligibility of a student to avail the loan scholarship is based on the admissions at the professional courses like Engineering, Medical, Agriculture, Veterinary, Law, Dental, Computer, Management, etc. According to the plan envisaged by the government of

India, the loan amount funded to any student who is continuing his/her course in India is maximum ₹10.00 lacs.

Table 37.1: No of students and Amount of Interest Subsidy Benefitted in India

Period	*Interest Subsidy*	
	No. of Accounts	*Amount (₹ in crores)*
2009-10	618860	282.04
2010-11	838655	685.37
2011-12	698316	853.84
Total	2155831	1821.25

Source: Canara Bank Data

The table above clearly states that from 2009-10 to 2011-12 the Department of Higher Education, MHRD has disbursed ₹ 1821.25 crores Interest Subsidy loan to student belong to different states in India.

Special Scholarship Scheme for Jammu & Kashmir Students

The northern most state of India has been identified to be one of the most backward states in India regarding higher education. Even though the State is responsible for taking the initiatives for establishing more institutions for higher education, the difficulties of the state are inadequately addressed, so good initiatives are not properly addressed. The special scheme for Jammu & Kashmir – Prime Minister's Special Scholarship Scheme for Jammu & Kashmir (SSSJK), was set up under the aegis of the Prime Minister in 2010 in the context of enhancing employment opportunity in J&K and to formulate job plan involving the public and private sector. According to the plan an expert group was constituted, and it recommended offering 5000 scholarships, per annum, over the next five years, to encourage the youth of J&K to pursue higher studies outside the State of J&K.

In 2010, an Expert Group was set up by the Prime Minister in the context of enhancing employment opportunity in J&K and to formulate job plan involving the public and private sector. Among the key recommendations of the Expert Group, one was to offer 5000 scholarships, per annum, over the next five years, to encourage the youth of J&K to pursue higher studies outside the State of J&K. An outlay of ₹1200 crore was recommended for this initiative over the next five years. This scheme is being implemented from 2011-12.

Under the Scheme, the students belonging to the State of Jammu & Kashmir, who have passed the Class XII or equivalent exam through the State Board of Jammu & Kashmir or from the Central Board of Secondary

Education (CBSE) affiliated schools located in Jammu & Kashmir, and pursuing general degree courses, engineering and medical studies in Colleges/Institutes located outside the State of Jammu & Kashmir, are eligible for scholarship provided their parental income is less than ₹6.00 lakh per annum.

The Scheme aims to provide tuition fees, hostel fees, cost of books and other incidental charges to students. Five thousand fresh scholarships are available every year, of which 4500 scholarships are for general degree courses, 250 for engineering and 250 for medical studies. The scheme is being implemented through a web portal of All India Council for Technical Education (AICTE).

An Inter-Ministerial Committee (IMC) under the Chairmanship of Secretary (HE) regularly monitors the implementation of the Special Scholarship Scheme for J&K Students. The Committee has Adviser (PAMD), Planning Commission and representative of Department of Expenditure as Members and representatives of the Ministries of Social Justice and Empowerment, Tribal Affairs, Home Affairs, Health & Education and so on. A monitoring mechanism shall be evolved by the Ministry of HRD to monitor the benefits accruing to different categories of loanees, such as Scheduled Castes (SCs), Scheduled Tribes (STs), Minorities, disabled, including women candidates and their achievements in their respective field after receiving the scholarship.

Table 37.2: Caste wise eligible students for scholarship

Category	*2012-13*	*2013-14*	*2014-15*
General	13	1409	0
OBC	1	1	2
Other	3315	0	0
Schedule Caste	83	183	146
Schedule Tribe	150	205	82
Open	0	1461	0
Open (PH)	0	6	0
SEBC	0	480	301
SEBC (PH)	0	2	0
Gujjar & Backward	0	0	1
Null	0	0	1
Open (OP)	0	0	1566
Resident of Backward Area	0	0	3
Total	3562	3747	2102

Source: MHRD, Govt. of India

Interestingly, the scholarship schemes which have been sponsored by the government of India for the betterment of students of J & K, who are doing their courses in different parts of India in other states, but helped centrally, are using this golden opportunity fervently with good spirits. Equally, it is to be noted that, the distribution of the awards also have good merits, as the scholarships have been given to the students belonging to general, Other Backward Classes (OBCs), Scheduled Castes (SCs), Scheduled Tribes (STs), SEBC, Gujjars & Backwards, including the minorities, particularly Muslims, Kashmir Pandits and so on. Even though all caste have been represented in this process, certain ups and downs also could be seen, as the number of scholarships issued in 2012-13 for others is 3315, which is much beyond the level of distribution of other categories. Meanwhile, the SCs and STs are given their share comparatively well, as in 2012-13, the SC students were offered 83 scholarships, whereas the STs bagged 150; in 1013-14, SC students were offered 183 scholarships, whereas the STs bagged 205; and in 2014-15, 146 SC students and 46 ST students were benefitted. The following table (Table 37.3) delineated the J&K students who are availing scholarships and staying in other states of India.

Table 37.3: Course wise no. of students in different states

State	*2012-13*				*2013-14*				*2014-15*			
	Engg.	*Medi*	*Gen*	*Total*	*Engg.*	*Medi*	*Gen*	*Total*	*Engg.*	*Medi*	*Gen*	*Total*
Andhra Pradesh	0	0	0	0	3	0	0	3	15	0	2	17
Bihar	0	1	0	1	0	2	0	2	3	0	8	11
Chandigarh	2	1	0	3	1	1	1	3	3	0	2	5
Chhattisgarh	0	0	0	0	0	0	0	0	10	0	2	12
Delhi	1	2	17	20	8	12	0	20	12	0	45	57
Goa	0	0	0	0	1	0	0	1	4	0	6	10
Gujarat	7	2	0	9	9	0	1	10	54	0	33	87
Haryana	59	1	20	80	73	2	28	103	156	0	59	215
Himachal Pradesh	7	3	4	14	14	3	4	21	22	0	25	47
Jammu & Kashmir	0	0	0	0	0	1	0	1	0	0	0	0
Jharkhand	1	4	0	5	1	1	0	2	6	1	1	8
Karnataka	9	3	1	13	10	1	17	28	153	1	97	251
Kerala	0	0	0	0	0	0	0	0	12	0	13	25
Madhya Pradesh	3	2	1	6	7	1	1	9	22	0	23	45
Maharashtra	25	4	8	37	28	0	3	31	180	0	58	238
Manipur	0	0	0	0	0	0	0	0	1	0	0	1
Meghalaya	0	0	0	0	0	0	0	0	0	0	2	2
Odisha	2	0	0	2	1	0	0	1	2	0	2	4

(Contd...)

Pondicherry	0	0	0	0	0	0	0	0	2	0	1	3
Punjab	43	2	6	51	59	1	27	87	111	0	81	192
Rajasthan	13	7	14	34	28	6	21	55	140	7	47	194
Sikkim	0	0	0	0	0	0	0	0	1	0	0	1
Tamil Nadu	1	0	0	1	4	0	1	5	49	0	38	87
Uttar Pradesh	18	12	16	46	42	10	21	73	151	2	110	263
Uttarakhand	9	0	1	10	10	0	8	18	32	0	18	50
West Bengal	1	0	2	3	3	0	0	3	8	0	16	24
All India	201	44	90	335	302	41	133	476	1149	11	689	1849

Source: MHRD, Govt. of India

Central Scheme of Scholarship for College and University Students

The National Merit Scholarship Scheme, the objective of which was to provide financial assistance to meritorious students studying from Class XI to Post- Graduation level in Government Schools/Colleges and Universities has been discontinued with effect from April 1, 2007. However, a new Central Sector Scheme of Scholarship for College and University Students has been introduced during XI Five Year Plan. The objective of the scheme is to provide financial assistance to meritorious students from poor families to meet a part of their day-to-day expenses while pursuing higher studies.

The 'Central Sector Scheme of Scholarship for College and University students' is a centrally-sponsored scheme, introduced during XI Five Year Plan, to provide financial assistance to students from poor families to meet a part of their day-to-day expenses while pursuing higher studies. 82000 fresh scholarships (41000 for boys and 41000 for girls) for graduate/post-graduate studies in colleges and universities and for professional courses, such as Medical, Engineering, etc. are awarded annually to the meritorious students on the basis of the results of senior secondary examination. The number of scholarships allotted to the different Boards is to be distributed amongst pass out of the Science, Commerce and Humanities streams of the Boards in the ratio of 3:2:1. The eligible allotted students are given ₹ 1000/- at Graduation level for the first three years of College and University courses and ₹ 2000/- per month at Post-Graduation level, where as students pursuing professional courses would get ₹ 2000/- per month in the 4th and 5th year provided their parent's annual income is less than ₹ 6 lakhs. The scholarships would be paid for 10 months in an academic year and is subject to annual renewal based on some conditions to both 'general' and 'reserved'.

The scholarships are awarded on the basis of the results of senior secondary examination. 82000 fresh scholarships per annum (41000 for boys and 41000 for girls) for graduate/post-graduate studies in colleges and universities and for professional courses, such as Medical, Engineering, etc. could be provided. The total number of scholarships has been divided amongst the State Boards based on the State's population in the age group of 18-25 years, after segregating share of Central Board of Secondary Education (CBSE) and Council for the Indian School Certificate Examination (CISCE) on the basis of number of students passing out from various Boards in the country. The number of scholarships allotted to the Boards is to be distributed amongst pass out of the Science, Commerce and Humanities streams of the Boards in the ratio of 3:2:1. Students who are above 80th percentile of successful candidates in the relevant stream for a particular Board of Examination, in class XII of 10+2 pattern or equivalent and having family income of less than ₹ 6 lakhs per annum, pursuing regular courses (not correspondence or distance mode) from recognized educational institutions and not availing of any other scholarship scheme, would be eligible for consideration under this Scheme. This is applicable to all categories of students both 'general' and 'reserved.'

The rate of scholarship are ₹ 1000/- at Graduation level for the first three years of College and University courses and ₹ 2000/- per month at Post-Graduation level. Students pursuing professional courses would get ₹ 2000/- per month in the 4thand 5th year. The scholarships would be paid for 10 months in an academic year. This is subject to annual renewal on the basis of stringent criteria.

Scholarship will be paid to the selected students directly by the Central Government through a Bank Account opened by them for the purpose in a designated Bank. Based on the eligibility certificate presented by the awardees, the designate bank(s) shall open account for all such merit scholars and ensure timely credit and maintain a proper database of the account numbers of the students receiving the scholarship. Where the branch of the bank is not available, the bank will issue co-branded ATM cards to the awardees, so that they can draw scholarship from any ATM without any charges. This will include flexibility of withdrawal of scholarship by the awardees through ATM of all nationalized banks, and its subsidiaries. The payment of scholarship will start from the month the admission is obtained.

The Central Sector Scheme of Scholarship for College and University Students is covered under the Direct Benefit Transfer (DBT). Under DBT Programme of the Government of India, scholarships are disbursed directly into the bank accounts of the beneficiaries. For smooth operation of the DBT, the Central Plan Scheme Monitoring System (CPSMS) has been devised. The CPSMS is a Web Based Transaction System, which facilitates Aadhaar Payment Bridge (APB) and Electronic Clearance Service (ECS) / National Electronic Clearing Service (NECS) /National Electronic Funds Transfer (NEFT) based payments.

Table 37.4: Number of Scholarships to States/UT under the Scheme of Scholarship to University / College Students

State	*No. of Scholarship Fresh 2012-13*
Andhra Pradesh	5405
Assam	470
Bihar	0
Chhattisgarh	518
Goa	66
Gujarat	3125
Haryana	1590
Himachal Pradesh	320
J&K	746
Jharkhand	5
Karnataka	4144
Kerala	2324
Maharashtra	2901
Madhya Pradesh	2769
Manipur	12
Meghalaya	33
Mizoram	4
Nagaland	0
Orissa	1777
Punjab	1304
Rajasthan	3978
Tamil Nadu	1883
Tripura	236
Uttar Pradesh	2687
Uttarakhand	444
West Bengal	2407
Pondicherry	78

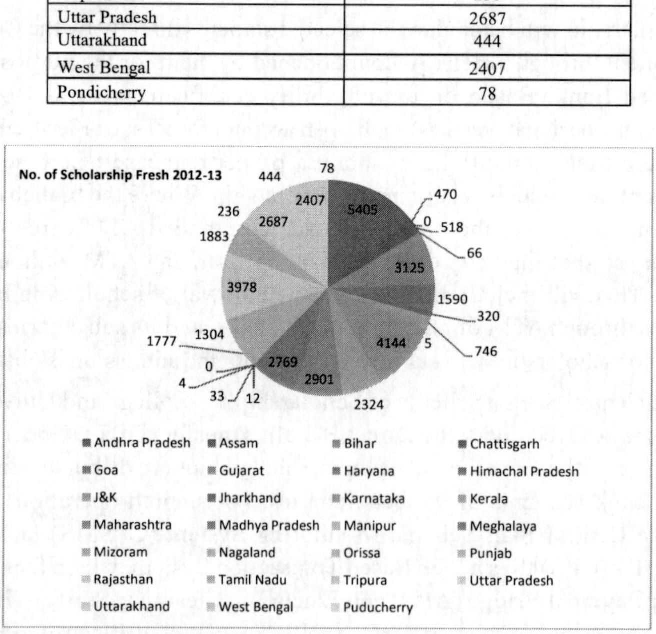

Source: MHRD, Govt. of India

Chart 37.1: Number of Fresh Scholarships in 2012-13

Table 37.5: Central Sector Scheme of Scholarship for College and University Students

Central Sector Scheme of Scholarship for College and University Students, (as on 17.07.2014)				
Sr. No.	***State***	***Quota (per year)***	***No. of Scholarship Fresh 2012-13***	***No. of Scholarship Fresh 2013-14***
1	CBSE	6853	3728	4385
2	1CSE	577	0	0
3	Andhra Pradesh	6097	5405	5921
4	Assam	2002	470	1022
5	Bihar	5624	0	0
6	Chattisgarh	1387	518	928
7	Goa	113	66	98
8	Gujarat	3944	3125	2713
9	Haryana	1591	1590	1591
10	Himachal Pradesh	461	320	226
11	J&K	768	746	742
12	Jharkhand	1878	5	0
13	Karnataka	4237	4144	0
14	Kerala	2324	2324	2309
15	Maharashtra	7417	2901	2256
16	Madhya Pradesh	4299	2769	3945
17	Manipur	181	12	181
18	Meghalaya	166	33	49
19	Mizoram	75	4	0
20	Nagaland	176	no	0
21	Orissa	2736	1777	2322
22	Punjab	1902	1304	1813
23	Rajasthan	3978	3978	3108
24	Tamil Nadu	4883	1883	4883
25	Tripura	236	236	236
26	Uttar Pradesh	11460	2687	4673
27	Uttarakhand	616	444	603
28	West Bengal	5941	2407	0
29	Puducherry	78	78	78
	Total:-	82000	43064	44082
Note:- (i) * under CBSE the quota earmarked for Arunachal Pradesh, Delhi, Sikkim, A&N, Chandigarh, Dadra & Nagar Haveli, Daman & Diu, and Lakshadweep are included				

Table 37. 6: Central Sector Scheme of Scholarship for College and University Students, (as on 17.07.2014)

Central Sector Scheme of Scholarship for College and University Students, (as on 17.07.2014)				
Sr. No.	***State***	***Quota (per year)***	***No. of Scholarship Fresh 2012-13***	***No. of Scholarship Fresh 2013-14***
1	CBSE	6853	3728	4385
2	ICSE	577	0	0
3	All States	82000	42954	44082

Source: MHRD, Govt. of India

The Central Sector Scheme of Scholarship for College and University Students, are entitled through, CBSE, ICSE and other bodies, which are entitled to carrying out these scholarship schemes in accordance with their allotted capacity. The CBSE has been allotted 6853, 3728 4385. The Indian Certificate of School Education (ICSE), one of the charismatic boards of India, has been allotted a total of 577 scholarships. Andhra Pradesh and Maharashtra are the two states, are getting more scholarships as compared to other states in India. The scholarships for higher education, allotted to students from poor and underprivileged backgrounds, benefit the level playing fields to those states, where no scholarship has been allotted.

Table 37.7: Central Sector Scheme of Scholarship for College and University Students, (as on 17.07.2014)

Central Sector Scheme of Scholarship for College and University Students, (as on 17.07.2014)				
Sr. No.	***State***	***Quota (per year)***	***No. of Scholarship Fresh 2012-13***	***No. of Scholarship Fresh 2013-14***
	Total	74570	39226	39697

Source: MHRD, Govt. of India

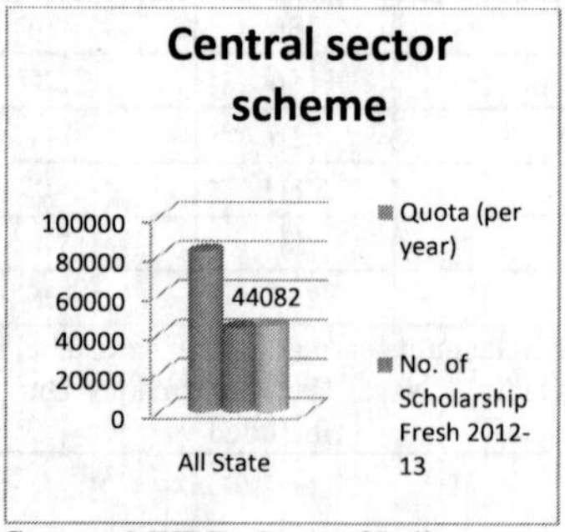

Source: MHRD, Govt. of India

Chart 37.2: Number of Fresh Scholarships in 2012-13

The above table and graph ideally show the Central Sector Scheme of Scholarship given to College and University Students, as on 17.07.2014. During 2012-13, 39226 Scholarships have been sanctioned and disbursed, meanwhile in 2013-14, 39697 scholarships are issued to the beneficiaries.

Concluding Remarks

The paper identifies the fact that the new approach of the State to garner full participation among the people groups to represent in higher education by attaining the targets set by our country for participation in higher education. This requires significant increases in participation by under-represented groups. While there have been very welcome improvements in participation, there are still some substantial challenges to be faced by the State. The key challenge would now be to develop integrated approaches to underperformance in higher education.

Educational disadvantage in some areas is complex and multi-faceted and the policy is to be designed accordingly for getting proper responses. Obviously, it has been observed that no agency or institution can work alone to achieve equity of access to higher education of the students/citizens. The higher education system is to be prioritised over the action plan of the State, and that will be to enhance co-operation across government departments, relevant agencies and all levels of education in order to achieve a more accessible and flexible higher education system.

Higher education will become even more diverse in the future through the establishment of new higher education providers and the creation of various consortia and partnerships between universities for research and/or teaching purposes will be benefitted into tens of thousands of students. The higher education policy of a nation must have proliferative principles of inclusiveness among teachers, scholars and research scientists from different universities and Institutes, with in-depth knowledge and understanding of their concerned subjects, generate new knowledge by publishing commendable books and articles, produce outstanding students, contribute immensely for the growth of a nation and to make an egalitarian society.

The study demonstrates that most socio-economic groups have been benefitting from the general expansion of higher-education opportunities but inequalities still persist. The traditional target groups of semi-skilled and unskilled manual workers remain significantly below national averages and the non-manual group currently derives least benefit from higher education.

While progress in widening participation across the full spectrum of people will be supported and evaluated, it is crucial that the national targets for accommodating the groups identified above on the basis of their continuing low levels of participation in higher education.

Even though the incentive/scholarship programmes is a heart-warming for the students who have been studying in colleges and universities, the process of implementation of the scholarship seemed to be mind-boggling. The scheme also brings some impediments often in the process of sanctioning and disbursement as the amount given is delayed. The underprivileged sections of our society, which have been passing through under tremendous implications of inability and infringements to send their students to colleges will get a boast up through these scholarships and also their children will be benefitted by getting proper systematic college education, so that it will make a new history in the annals of Indian higher education.

References

1. Adhikari, L.R. (1992), "Fundamentals of Labour Economics", McGraw-Hill, New York NY
2. All India Council for Technical Education (AICTE), secondary data from 2012-13 to 2014-15
3. Chitnis, Suma (1999) "The Transformation of an Imperial Colony into an Advanced Nation: India in Comparative Perspective" in Higher Education in the 21st Century: Global Challenge and National Response, Altbach, Philip G. and Patti McGill Peterson, eds., IIE Research Report Number Twenty-nine.
4. Indian Bank Association, Mumbai. (2008). *Circular on Education Loans.*
5. Maiti, Prasenjit (2001) "World view: Expansion without funding", The Times Higher Education Supplement, October 5, 2001.
6. Ministry of Human Resource Development (2013), Department of Higher Education, Revised Guidelines for the Special Scholarship Scheme for Jammu and Kashmir, New Delhi.
7. Ministry of Human Resource and Development (MHRD), Department of Higher Education. (2007). *Guidelines for the Scheme of Scholarship for the College and University Students.*
8. Raju, Vetukuri P.S (2015) Prime Minister's Special Scholarship Scheme for Jammu & Kashmir: An Evaluation, NUEPA, New Delhi (Unpublished research report)
9. Raju, Vetukuri P.S (2016) An Evaluation Study of Central Sector Scheme of Scholarship for College and University Students, NUEPA, New Delhi (Unpublished research report)
10. Tilak, Jandhyala B.G. (1997) The dilemma of reforms in financing higher education in India, Higher Education Policy, Volume 10, No. 1.

11. Tilak, Jandhyala B.G. (1992) 'Rural-Urban inequalities in eduation: A study on returns to education, human capital information and earnings differentiation,' pp. 89, 394-396, Promethus, New Delhi.
12. Tilak, Jandhyala B. G. and N. V. Varghese (1991) 'Higher Education in India', Higher Education, Vol. 21, No. 1, Higher Education in Developing Countries, pp. 83-101, Kluwer Academic Publishers, Netherland.
13. Tilak, Jandhyala B. G. (2002). "Student loans in financing higher education in India," *Higher Education*, Kluwer Academic Publishers, (23), 389-404.
14. Varghese, N.V. (2015) Challenges of Massification of Higher education in India, CPRHE Research paper 1, NUEPA, New Delhi.

Chapter-38

Rusa in Higher Education in West Bengal- A Study

Arnab Chowdhury,
Jayanta Mete Professor,

Abstract

The last decade has witnessed that education sector has dominated economic planning in all over developing countries of the world. During this time, the countries transformed from developing to advanced economies due to strategic planning and a larger vision that correlated economic development to transformation in the education sector, in particular Higher Education and Research, to become globally competitive. Despite many new National Missions/Programs and reforms agenda, by both the central and state governments with private sector intervention, the higher education sector is in a state of complete flux in India. While we have tremendously enhanced capacity, we lag in quality, given inadequate autonomy to our Universities. Centralized control and a standardized approach remains at the heart of regulations (FICCI, 2013).

This paper, newly explains about the Rashtriya Uchchatar Shiksha Abhiyan (RUSA)/National Higher Education Mission, a Centrally Sponsored Scheme (CSS) for reforming the State Higher Education System in India. The end part of the title also portrays the economic impact of the scheme on the current Higher Education System of WEST BENGAL in the Eastern States of India.

Keywords: *Higher Education, RUSA Preparation, RUSA Approval, RUSA Implementation, RUSA in India and WEST BENGAL, National Mission Authority, PAB, TSG, SHEC, SHEP, Higher Education System in WEST BENGAL, MSHEC, MSHEP.*

1. Introduction

"By 2030, India will be amongst the youngest nations in the world. With nearly 140 million people in the college-going age group, one in every four graduates in the world will be a product of the Indian Higher Education System." **-FICCI**

Beforeexploring¯RASHTRIYAUCHCHATARSHIKSHAABHIYAN(RUSA)/ NATIONALHIGHEREDUCATION

MISSION % 2013 across the country it is enough to remember that ***"Live as if you were to die tomorrow. Learn as if you were to live forever."* %Mahatma Gandhi**[2]

UNESCO Institute for Statistics (UIS) has forwarded that Asia's spectacular rise in enrolment rates in Higher Education over the past 20 years has been the subject of many reports published all over the world. It draws an attention to the result of high birth rates, increasing school participation rates, increasing demand of the society and economy for specialised human resources, and the perceived importance of advanced education in subsequent life opportunities (e.g. ADB, 2011; World Bank, 2012). Over the past four decades, global higher education enrollment increased from 32.6 million in 1970 to 182.2 million students in 2011, 46% of which was in the East and South Asia region in 2011 (UIS, 2013). This phenomenal expansion was fueled by a convergence of demographic trends, public preferences, policy decisions and external economic circumstances (ADB, 2011). Among the key factors driving this growth were higher participation rates in basic education and higher progression rates in primary and secondary schools. More students were entering and graduating from Secondary School and seeking to continue their education. To accommodate these enrolment increases, Higher Education Systems have had to expand out' by constructing new universities, hiring new faculty members, diversifying delivery mechanisms, and allowing and encouraging the entry of private higher education providers (UIS, 2014).

Higher Education, thus, has expanded rapidly in recent ages reflecting the growing importance of the sector in promoting economic growth. The sector has introduced various reforms to align itself more closely with the market. Most of these have been influenced by the concept of new public management', which implies a lesser reliance on the State and a greater reliance on markets (IIEP, 2014).Reforms in higher education reflect the increasing importance and use of knowledge in production, and the role of Higher Education Institutions (HEIs) in training for the production, transmission, and use of knowledge. Reforms in higher education in the Commonwealth of Independent States (CIS) were intended to reposition and facilitate the transition from a centrally planned to a market economy. Higher education reforms in countries in Africa occurred mostly in response to a decline in the public financing of higher education. All these reforms centre on the idea of cost-recovery measures and indicate a clear shift in the provision and management of higher education from state to market. This implies a reduced reliance on the state for funding and control and a shift towards market processes. Thus, resulted in substantial changes in the way activities are organized and managed in institutions of higher education. Governance structures and management practices at the system and institution levels have been modified in response to these changes introduced at the national level. This has had a wide effect on the relative distribution of responsibilities for the management of higher education systems. In spite of this, the state continues to play a role, providing a framework for other non-state actors to intervene – in essence, steering from a distance (Varghese, 2009).

The transition from State to market in higher education was frequently mediated through higher education institutions. Many governments transferred part of their authority and responsibility to institutions of higher education in the form of increased institutional autonomy. This led to a shift from the state control model to a state supervision model of higher education management (OECD, 2003). In order to mediate effectively between the Ministry and higher education institutions, many countries have created established Ministries of Higher Education, National Quality Assurance Agencies and quality monitoring mechanisms, buffer institutions such as National Commissions for Higher Education, National Commission for Higher Education and Research (NCHER), the setting up of a National Accreditation Agency, and the admittance of foreign educational institutions and so on (Varghese, 2014).

In India, all States and Union Territories across the country, this, in turn, have also required that the Higher Education Systems expand up'. The Ministry of Human Resource Development (MHRD), therefore, is launching an umbrella scheme of RUSA as a flagship program of 12th Plan for reforming the State Higher Education System in India. Do you want to know how RUSA impacts on the current State Higher Education System of WEST BENGAL?

2. Objective

1. To study Rusa Preparation for HEI_S
2. TO study RUSA approval for HEI_S
3. TO study RUSA implementation for HEI_S
4. TO outline RUSA scenario for HEI_S in West Bengal

3. Rusapreparation

Human resources are the top determinant of the overall development of the World. To impart education is the greatest charity and the key to knowledge of the future humanity. We all know that the main in use dies, the moment we stop learning (UGC, 2003) and also generally agrees to the moment we cease to learn and to grow, we die (Bookrags, 2014). Without doubt, education is the blood and soul of human power in the remaining 21stCentury. Higher education is a key area to maintain a country's competitiveness in the global economy (UNESCO, 2011). Here, we can solve the problem and get the light that" ***The educated differ from the uneducated as much as the living differ from the dead."*** –**Aristotle**[3]

For India, International Labour Organisation (ILO), further estimates that by 2020, it will have 116 million workers in the age group of 20-24 years as against 94 million in China. In addition to this, the average age of Indian population by 2020 will be 29 while many developed countries will be in early or late 40s (MHRD, 2013). This advantage of demographic dividend helps in creating enough sustainable job opportunities to prevent socio-economic complications arising out of a large unemployable young population within India.

Successful population policy, thus, lies on the top priority of a country and is also directly linked to its successful education policy which forms the bedrock of all fields of national development— political, economic, technical, scientific, social and environmental.Success in raising literacy rates and school enrollment rates while reducing drop-out rates, especially for women, are closely correlated with the delayed onset of marriage and child birth, improved mortality for both mothers and children, and reduction in family size. Greater coverage and better quality education at all levels from basic literacy to hi-tech science and technology is the essential prerequisite for raising agricultural productivity and industrial quality, spurring growth of India's budding IT and biotechnology sectors, stimulating growth of manufactured and service exports, improving health and nutrition, domestic stability and quality of governance (GoI, 2002). Hence, the importance of education can hardly, be overemphasized. To impart education, the best is to establish a school (UGC, 2003).

4. Rusaapproval

The current policy and programs for the development of higher education in India is completely governed by the–National Policy on Education of 1986 (as modified in1992) and its Programme of Action adopted in 1992, based on two land mark basic frame work reports namely, the–University Education Commission Report of 1948-49 (popularly known as the Radhakrishnan Commission Report), and the–Education Commission Report of 1964-66, (popularly known as the Kothari Commission Report). But, it was openly appealed that–*Our university system is, in many parts, in a state of disrepair.....In almost half the districts in the country, higher education enrollments are abysmally low, almost two-third of our universities and 90 per cent of our colleges are rated as below average on quality parameters.....I am concerned that in many states' university appointments, including that of vice-chancellors, have been politicized and have become subject to caste and communal considerations and there are complaints of favoritism and corruption.* –**Manmohan Singh, Former PM,GoI**[4]

The National System of Qualifications in the Indian context comprises of School Education, Vocational Education and Higher Education. The School education comprises of twelve years of schooling subdivided into Primary, Elementary, Secondary and Senior Secondary levels. Such types of schools are largely governed by the National Curriculum Framework (NCF) and are by and large uniform across the country. The system of Vocational Education, aimed at skill development and employability, which has so far been overlapping across the school and higher education and largely seen as terminal, is now being sought to be streamlined through a National Vocational Education Qualification Framework (NVEQF) recently notified by the MHRD (CABE, 2013).

The 10th Plan (2002-07) provided a the basis for Higher Education System in India and the system is now accelerating itself in 12th Plan (2012-17) to face the challenges of the 21st Century. The preparation for the 11th Plan began in 2007. We all know that the Plan is also named asan¯ Education Plan tusher in the¯Second Wave of development of higher education (UGC, 2013). Beside, many progressive steps are also taken in 12th, 13th and 14th Five Year Plans respectively. It has accelerated to the target and help to produce one-fourth of all graduates in the World by the system. India, thus, becomes the single largest benefactor of global talent and it seems to have indeed entered a golden age for higher education (Vision, 2030).

Amendment of the Constitution of India, 2002 to make elementary education a justiciable Fundamental Right emphasis ingon the¯ Universalization of Elementary Education (UEE) guided by five parameters was the main focus of 10th Five Year Plan of India. Universal Access, Universal Enrollment, Universal Retention, Universal Achievement, and Equity are the targeted parameters. Besides, many major important schemes for elementary education sector were included, viz., Sarva Shiksha Abhiyan (SSA), District Primary Education Programme (DPEP), National Programme of Nutritional Support to Primary Education, commonly known as Mid-Day Meal Scheme (MDMS), Teacher Education Scheme, Kasturba Gandhi BalikaVidyalaya Scheme (KGBVS), etc. (GoI, 2002;2005).

Faster and inclusive growth were main objectives; and expansion, inclusion, and excellence along with equity and quality are the watchwords of the education sector in the 11th Education Plan. The share of this sector in total plan outlay increased to 19.4% from mere 6.7% of the last Plan, of which 30% was earmarked for higher education. This was a nine- fold increase over the 10th Plan, viz. ₹ 84,943 crores against ₹ 9,500 crores (GoI, 2008). This Plan, therefore, placed great emphasis on expanding access to education at all the three levels%elementary education, secondary education, and higher education%and also on improving the quality of education. The Right to Education (RTE) Act and Saakshar Bharat became operational in 2009 (GoI, 2011).There has been massive improvement both in regard to enrollment and in reduction of dropout rates. The major achievement is that most of children are now in the school. It is proof that for the age group 6-14 years in all of rural India, the percentage of children who are not enrolled in school has dropped from 6.6 per cent in 2005 to 3.5 per cent in 2010. The proportion of girls in the age group 11-14 years who were out of school has also declined from 11.2 per cent in 2005 to 5.9 per cent in 2010. However, the absolute numbers of children who are out of school remains large (ASER, 2010). In addition, six Centrally Sponsored Schemes (CSS) were launched at the end of the Plan: (i) Rashtriya Madhyamik Shiksha Abhiyan (RMSA) (ii) setting up of model schools; (iii) setting up girls‘ hostels in secondary and senior secondary schools; (iv) National Scheme of Incentive to Girls for Secondary Education (NSIGSE); (v) Inclusive Education for the Disabled at the Secondary Stage (IEDSS); and (vi) National Meritcum-Means Scholarship scheme (NMMS). The ongoing scheme of ICT in Schools was alsorevised.

For the development of higher education, the 11th Plan also focused on many strategies — providing equitable access, improving quality and standards; evaluation and accreditation; expansion and strengthening of infrastructure, networking and digitization, research and development; and strengthening of the open and distance education system and of research institutions. Restructuring and reforming the higher education system to improve accessibility and quality of services offered through greater autonomy and more participative governance were also key elements of the 11thPlan's strategy. During this period, India, thus, moved from an-elite system of higher education to a-mass system when the Gross Enrolment Ratio (GER) crossed the threshold of 15%. However, the GER at 19.4% still remained below the world average of 29% (GoI, 2011). This increase in GER has, naturally, been accompanied by an increase in the number of higher education institutions serving the population (MHRD, 2013). Today, India has successfully created one of the biggest higher education systems in the world comprising 700 universities and 35,539 colleges. However, Indian education system faces problems and issues that originate from disparities and developmental models adopted (UGC, 2012). Despite higher levels of enrollment at all levels of education, and a massive increase in physical infrastructure, the value added by formal education is still weak. Poor quality of education resulting in weak learning outcomes at each stage of education is the central challenge facing by the Indian education sector today. It is proof that not even one Indian university figures in the latest list of 200 universities in the world (GoI, 2012).

The current 12th Plan commenced at a time when global second financial crisis occurred in 2011-12. Faster, more inclusive and sustainable growth are its main objectives. The Plan outlined three targets reflecting the vision of rapid, sustainable and more inclusive growth for education sector: To mean Years of Schooling to increase to seven years by the end of the Plan; To enhance access to higher education by creating two million additional seats for each age cohort aligned to the skill needs of the economy; and To eliminate gender and social gap in school enrollment (that is, between girls and boys, and between SCs, STs, Muslims and the rest of the population) by the end of the Plan.

In order to materialize a "quantum jump" in achieving the triple objectives of access and expansion, equity and inclusion, and quality and excellence, with an emphasis on consolidation and optimal use of infrastructure, the 12th Plan provides a good foundation for future higher education system of India because it included the provision of flexi funds of 1, 10,700 crore for the development of higher education in the country. The Plan also proposed a comprehensive Plan for the development of State Higher Education System by focusing on four major areas: (i) State universities and colleges including polytechnics; (ii) Equity initiatives including student financial support; (iii) Central universities and institutions; and (iv) Research and innovation initiatives (GoI, 2012).

The success of (SSA), (DPEP), (MDMS), (KGBVS), (NSIGSE), (IEDSS) (RTE), (NMMS), Saakshar Bharat, (RMSA) and ICT in Schools and the consequent improvement in transition rates increased the number of students that would opt for higher education and thus, it made a strong case for enhancement of financial support for expansion, upgradation and quality improvement of higher education system. Such enhancement can bring about balanced growth of new institutions, based on spatial and need-based planning. This, in turn, can help absorb the ever increasing number of students completing the higher secondary level (MHRD, 2013). Quality, therefore, becomes a critical priority area for ensuring sustainability. Several initiatives (Report of the All India Survey on Higher Education (AISHE), Report of the Nation Knowledge Commission (NKC), Report of the Committee to Advise on Renovation and Rejuvenation of Higher Education, Proposal of National Quality Renaissance Initiative (NQRI) by NAAC (National Assessment and Accreditation Council); the Conclave of Vice-Chancellors and other Forums of Educationists) are lined up to achieve excellence for increasing both the capacity and quality of higher education system. An umbrella scheme of RUSA was launched to address the needs of State institutions so as to strengthen them and enhance their quality in the 12thPlan. RUSA will also address a major challenge on regional imbalances in higher education (MHRD, 2013).

5. Rusaimplementation

Proper, successful and excellent education system helps achieve huge challenges in demographic advantage nations in the world. Not only makes a man a perfect gentleman, education also arms him to meet all the situations in life. It is said that it is not ease but effort, not facility but difficulty that makes a man. Education, thus, helps a man to develop a balanced personality (Shamim, 2003). It also plays a fundamental role in the development of a nation as it enables achievement of individual capabilities, which, in turn, helps a nation reach its national goals (UGC, 2013). Higher education, therefore, is critical for developing a modern economy, a just society and a vibrant polity. It equips young people with skills relevant for the labour market and the opportunity for social mobility. It provides people already in employment with skills to negotiate rapidly evolving career requirements. It prepares all to be responsible citizens who value a democratic and pluralistic society. Thus, the nation creates an intellectual repository of human capital to meet the country's needs and shapes of its future. Indeed, higher education is the principal site at which our national goals, developmental priorities and civic values can be examined and refined (GoI, 2012). Now, India is just at the situation. The Government is also taking high initiatives in coming Plans for the development of education sector to achieve bigger challenges in the remaining period of the 21st Century. All citizens, therefore, should remember that "*Education is the manifestation of perfection already existing in man.*" –**Swami Vivekananda**[5]

The Central Advisory Board on Education (CABE), the highest advisory body of the Government of India (GoI) in education on policy matters, in its meeting held on 08.11.2012 gave in-principle approval to RUSA. Subsequently, it was included in the list of 66 schemes approved by the Cabinet on 20.06.2013, as part of the restructured CSSs for implementation in the 12th Plan. The Expenditure Finance Committee (EFC) appraised the Scheme on 11th September, 2013 and recommended it for approval. Finally, with the approval of the Cabinet Committee on Economic Affairs (CCEA) on 3rd October, 2013, the Rashtriya Uchchatar Shiksha Abhiyan (RUSA)/ National Higher Education Mission became the final tier of the CSSs of the MHRD, which began with SSA and graduated subsequently to RMSA. Reforming to improve access, equity and quality of the State Higher Education System in the country is RUSA's main objective. The primary components of RUSA includes creation of new institutions, expansion of existing institutions, infrastructural upgradation, establishing of bodies such as State Higher Education Councils (SHECs), accreditation agencies, sectoral, affiliation, academic, examination reforms etc. It will be spread over the 12th (2012-17) and 13th (2017-22) plans periods. Many authorities and experts describe about RUSA. Combining the literatures, some facts of RUSA are given below:

1. RUSA is an umbrella scheme operated in mission mode that would subsume other existing similar CSSs in the State Higher Education Sector. The funding to States is made on the basis of State Higher Education Plans outlining the States' strategy to address issues of equity, access and excellence in higher education. All funding under RUSA are norm based and future grants would be performance based and outcome dependent. Commitment by States and institutions to certain academic, administrative and governance reforms will be a precondition for receiving funding under RUSA. Centre-State funding would be in the ratio of 90:10 for North-Eastern States, Sikkim, J&K, Himachal Pradesh and Uttarakhand and 65:35 for other States and Union Territories. Support would be extended to only government and government aided institutions.
2. In order to facilitate the successful implementation of the scheme, the Government of India has set up a National Mission Authority for RUSA in the MHRD (Department of Higher Education). The

Mission Authority will be an independent and autonomous wing of the MHRD (Department of Higher Education).

3. The National Mission Authority on RUSA is ordered to be constituted with the following compositions:

I	Union Human Resource Minister	Chairperson
II	Secretary, Department of Higher Education, Ministry of Human Resource Development	Vice-Chairperson
III	Chairperson, UGC	Co Vice-Chairperson
IV	Member, Planning Commission (in charge of higher education)	Member
V	Chairperson, AICTE	Member
VI	Chairpersons of the State Higher Education Councils	Members
VII	Prof. Pankaj Chandra, former Director-IIM, Banglore	Member
VIII	Shri AjitRangnekar, Dean, Indian School of Business	Member
IX	Prof. Deepak Pental, former Vice-Chancellor – Delhi University	Member
X	Financial Advisor to MHRD	Member
XI	Chairperson, Medical Council of India or representative	Member
XII	Chairperson, Bar Council of India or representative	Member
XIII	Secretary, Department of Agriculture, Govt. of India or representative not below the rank of Joint Secretary	Member
XIV	Secretary, Department of Culture, Govt. of India or representative not below the rank of Joint Secretary	Member
XV	Secretary, Department of Health, Govt. of India or representative not below the rank of Joint Secretary	Member
XVI	Secretary, Department of S&T, Govt. of India or representative not below the rank of Joint Secretary	Member
XVII	Secretary, Department of Sports, Govt. of India or representative not below the rank of Joint Secretary	Member
XVIII	Representative of Ministry of Finance, Govt. of India	Member
XIX	Joint Secretary (HE) & National Mission Director	Member Secretary

Source: http://mhrd.gov.in/rusa

4. The RUSA National Mission Authority will be empowered to fix and alter the programmatic norms within the overall framework of the scheme from time to time. It will delineate the overall policy and planning and will be empowered to make necessary changes in planning, implementation, monitoring and evaluation parameters so as to enable the National and State level implementing bodies to implement the Scheme efficiently and effectively so that gains from RUSA are maximised. It will review functioning of Project Approval Board (PAB) and allocate funds to the Board for release to States. It may commission policy reform, thematic and evaluation studies and review the same. The RUSA National Mission Authority shall meet once in six months at such time and place as may be fixed by the Chairperson.

PAB would undertake detailed evaluation of the State Higher Education Plans submitted by the States. Based on such evaluation, these plans would be approved by the PAB and funds released to States as pernorms. During the course of such evaluation the PAB may suggest certain changes to these plans in which case the States would carry out the necessary changes and resubmit the same to PAB for consideration and evaluation. The PAB and other national implementing bodies would be assisted by a Technical Support Group (TSG) established for providing professional, strategic, logistic and other support as may be required for implementing the project.

5. The PAB is hereby constituted with the following compositions:

I	Secretary, Higher Education, MHRD	Chairperson
II	Chairperson, UGC	Co-Chairman
III	Chairperson, AICTE	Member
IV	Secretary, UGC	Member
V	Chairperson, State Higher Education Council (of the concerned State whose plans are to be considered)	Member
VI	Secretary, Higher Education of the State concerned	Member
VII	Secretary, Technical Education of the State concerned	Member
VIII	Prof. Shailendra Mehta, Visiting Professor, IIM- Ahmedabad	Member
IX	Prof. B. Venkatesh Kumar, Professor & Chairperson, Centre for Governance and Public Policy, TISS	Member
X	Financial Advisor in MHRD	Member
XI	Advisor (Higher Education), Planning Commission	Member
XII	Joint Secretary (HE) & National Mission Director	Member – Convener

Source: http://mhrd.gov.in/rusa

6. RUSA structure is divided into three levels. The levels and their institutional structure are shown in the following table:

NATIONAL LEVEL	➢ RUSA Mission Authority ➢ Project Approval Board(PAB) ➢ Technical Support Group(TSG) ➢ Project Directorate (in MHRD)
STATE LEVEL	➢ State Higher Education Council(SHEC) ➢ Project Directorate (in State Government) ➢ Technical Support Group(State)
INSTITUTIONAL LEVEL	➢ Board of Governors ➢ Project Monitoring Unit

Source: http://mhrd.gov.in/rusa

7. Rusa In West Bengal

Over the years Government of WEST BENGAL (GoM) have not been able to allocate enough funds to its higher education sector; these scanty funds are finely spread as a result of being shared amongst many institutions. Plan expenditure on higher education sector is almost stagnant. As a result, the quality of infrastructure and teaching in the State Higher Education Institutions (HEIs) is far below the acceptable levels. Shortage of funds and procedural bottlenecks cause vacancies in faculty positions and also compel the state public institutions to look for alternate funding options (MHRD, 2013). Good faculty quality and availability comes from the quality of teaching, research output and general management but these areas have also been exceptionally neglected in the State Higher Education System of WEST BENGAL. Beside, student teacher ratio is also very low. At this time, I want to follow the landmark judgment "*Teachers are like foster parents to the students. Can we afford to place the future of the country in hands of these hired teachers?*"–**Supreme Court, GoI**[6]

The year 2013 is the landmark in the history of higher education in WEST BENGAL. GoM started reformation of higher education sector to participate in the schemes of RUSA since February, 2013 in particular. The WEST BENGAL State Higher Education Council (MSHEC), therefore, was set up by the Department of Higher & Technical Education on 28thOctober, 2013. The Council was created by an executive order. Its composition and roles are as required under RUSA. Process for enactment of the MSHEC through State Assembly started and will be enacted within two years as stipulated in the RUSA Guidelines. Meetings of the MSHEC held as per necessity and for due consultation in preparation of the State Higher Education Plan (SHEP) and other Plans under RUSA as well as for other important matters pertaining to Higher & Technical Education Sector in the State. After this, Department of Higher & Technical Education participated on the first meeting of the RUSA Project Approval Board (PAB) held on 6thNovember, 2013 under the Chairmanship of Shri. Ashok Thakur, Secretary Higher Education, MHRD and presented a report of the SHEP to the meeting. Appraisal note of the WEST BENGAL State Higher Education Plan (MSHEP) was released on the 3rdmeeting of the PAB on the 13th May, 2014. Analysis and findings of the appraisal note of the SHEP and the changing trends in higher education system of WEST BENGAL are discussed below:

For participating the schemes of the RUSA, all necessary actions have been taken for assessment and accreditation by all 28 Govt. Colleges and 12 Aided Colleges in the State as per the UGC (Mandatory Assessment and Accreditation of Higher Educational Institutions) Regulations, 2012. The provisions for the State Share Funds for RUSA has also been duly included in the State Budget for the current year 2014-15 and the trends of expenditure for higher education sector in the State from 2011-2014 is tabulated as follows:

Expenditure	*2011-2012*	*2012-2013*	*2013-2014*
Plan	₹1,762 lakhs	₹1,700 lakhs	₹3,148 lakhs
Non-Plan	₹12,181 lakhs	₹11,861 lakhs	₹13,450 lakhs
RUSA (Preparatory Grant)	Nil	Nil	₹270 lakhs
Total	₹13,943 lakhs	₹13,561 lakhs	₹16,868 lakhs

Source: http://mhrd.gov.in/rusa

The MSHEP consists of various proposals for reformation of the higher education sector in WEST BENGAL. Before submitting it to the PAB, the Technical Support Group (TSG) rechecked it for recommendation and finally approved by the PAB. The following table shows comparison of funds for reformation of the State Higher Education Sector asked by the GoM in the Current Annual Plan (2014-15) and its approval of the PAB of RUSA in lakhs:

Faculty Recruitment Support is proposed as Priority No. 04 Faculty Recruitment Support is proposed as Priority No. 04 by the MSHEP to facilitate faculty recruitment for the Cluster colleges in the New State University being set up. The State has committed to take over the liability of faculty positions at end of the scheme and seeks relaxation on the student teacher ratio which is 26:1. The State has submitted a detailed plan for hiring of Assistant Professors/Equivalent cadre of candidate in different Post Graduate Departments along with their salary component. The total proposed amount for the 12thPlan Period is ₹2175 lakhs and the fund sought for 2014-15 is ₹435 lakhs. The TSG recommends allocating the total amount of ₹435 lakhs but the PAB did not approve the grant in view of the fact that the current student teacher ratio in this State is 45:1 which is above the programmatic norm of 20:1. The following table shows the estimation of the Faculty Recruitment Support Grant to University Post Graduate Department (₹ Lakhs):

The MSHEP also proposed 4 New Model Degree Colleges (MDC) as a Priority No. 05 and recommended it by TSG but did not approved by the PAB. Since, no District in WEST BENGAL falls in the Educational Backward Districts (EBDs) category as notified by the UGC, funds sought under this cannot be considered. Now, further approval of Mission Authority of RUSA is waiting forit.

Sl.No	Component	Total funds asked for by the states				Funding abstract as approved by PAB			
		XII Plan		2014-15		Total Outlay	2014-15	Physical Quantity	Remarks
		Physical	Financial	Physical	Financial				
1.	Creation of Universities by way of Upgradation of existing Autonomous Colleges	0	0	0	0	0	0	0	Nil
2.	Creation of Universities by conversion of colleges in a cluster	1	5,500.73	1	2,500	5,500	2,500	1	Conditional Upon adherence to future commitments (refer RUSA guidelines) and submission of DPR
3.	Infrastructure Grants to Universities	0	0	0	0	0	0	0	Nil
4.	New Model Colleges (General)	4	4,800	0	0	0	0	0	Not Approved
5.	Upgradation of existing Degree Colleges to Model Degree colleges	0	0	0	0	0	0	0	Nil
6.	New Colleges (Professional)	3	7,569.72	3	1,000	2,500	1,300	1	Conditional, Upon submission of DPR
7.	Infrastructure Grants to Colleges	30	6,000	30	3,000	4,000	2,000	20	Approved list of Govt. Colleges
8.	Research, Innovation and quality improvement	12	12,000	12	5,760	0	0	0	Not Approved

(Contd...)

9.	Equity Initiatives	40	500	40	80	0	0	0	Not Approved
10.	Faculty Recruitment Support	75	2,175	75	435	0	0	0	Not Approved
11.	Faculty Improvement	For the entire state	1,000	For the entire state	1,000	0	0	0	Not Approved
12.	Vocationalisation of Higher Education	40	1,500	40	80	1,500	0.80	40	Approved
13.	Leadership Development of Educational Administrators	For the entire state	934	For the entire state	00	0	0	0	Not Approved
14.	Institutional Restructuring and reforms	For the entire state	1,000	For the entire state	300	0	0	0	Not Approved
15.	Capacity Building and preparation, Data Collection and Planning	For the entire state	500	For the entire state	300	0	0	0	Not Approved
16.	Management Information System	For the entire state	200	For the entire state	100	0	0	0	Not Approved
17.	Support to Polytechnics	1	100	1	100	0	0	0	Not Approved
18.	Management Monitoring Evaluation and Research	For the entire state	1000	For the entire state	300	0	0	0	Not Approved

Name of the University Post graduate department in descending order of importance	*2014-15*	*2015-16*	*2016-17*	*2017-18*	*2018-19*	*Total*
Physics	17.40	17.40	17.40	17.40	17.40	87.00
Mathematics	17.40	17.40	17.40	17.40	17.40	87.00
Chemistry	17.40	17.40	17.40	17.40	17.40	87.00
Geology	17.40	17.40	17.40	17.40	17.40	87.00
Computer Science	17.40	17.40	17.40	17.40	17.40	87.00
Environmental Science	17.40	17.40	17.40	17.40	17.40	87.00
Electronics	17.40	17.40	17.40	17.40	17.40	87.00
Biotech	17.40	17.40	17.40	17.40	17.40	87.00
Food Technology	17.40	17.40	17.40	17.40	17.40	87.00
Anthropology	17.40	17.40	17.40	17.40	17.40	87.00
Botany	17.40	17.40	17.40	17.40	17.40	87.00
Mathematics	17.40	17.40	17.40	17.40	17.40	87.00
Zoology	17.40	17.40	17.40	17.40	17.40	87.00
M.Ed.	17.40	17.40	17.40	17.40	17.40	87.00
L.L.M.	17.40	17.40	17.40	17.40	17.40	87.00
Physical Education, Health & Sports	17.40	17.40	17.40	17.40	17.40	87.00
English	17.40	17.40	17.40	17.40	17.40	87.00
Management Studies	17.40	17.40	17.40	17.40	17.40	87.00
Economics	17.40	17.40	17.40	17.40	17.40	87.00
Psychology	17.40	17.40	17.40	17.40	17.40	87.00
Statistics	17.40	17.40	17.40	17.40	17.40	87.00
Linguistics	17.40	17.40	17.40	17.40	17.40	87.00
Library Science	17.40	17.40	17.40	17.40	17.40	87.00
Education	17.40	17.40	17.40	17.40	17.40	87.00
Juridical Science	17.40	17.40	17.40	17.40	17.40	87.00

Source: http://mhrd.gov.in/rusa

The MSHEP comprises many other proposals namely Research, Innovation and Quality Improvement for College and University; Equity Initiatives; Faculty Improvement; Leadership Development; Institutional Restructuring and Reforms; Capacity Building and Preparation, Data Collection and Planning; Management Information System (MIS); Support to Polytechnics; and Management Monitoring Evaluation and Research (MMER). All these components are recommended but did not approved by the PAB.

8. Conclusion

The demand for higher education has been accelerating in the worldwide since last decades. Today, higher education becomes a critical input in human resource development and is essential for the country's economic growth.India is also expanding its higher education system by launching a new CSS % Rashtriya Uchchatar Shiksha Abhiyan (RUSA)/National Higher Education Mission. This is for the first time since independence that Higher Education is being expanded in a mission mode which will particularly benefit State Universities and Colleges. This scheme is key to reformation of State Higher Education System in the country including WEST BENGAL which is one of the North-East State of India.

In WEST BENGAL, most of the Colleges are understaffed with inadequate Teaching Faculty. But the enrollment of students had increased from 12,152 in 2008-09 to 41,608 in 2012-13 and the total enrollment was 123,497 in 2012-13. However, the sanctioned posts of College Teachers have stagnated at 1264 since the last 20 years, which has vacancy of 301 posts at present. As per the mandate of the UGC/WEST BENGAL University, there is a need for 2130 posts of Govt. College Teachers which necessitates creation of 866 posts. The State Govt. has been unable to increase the no. of posts so far due to its acute financial constraints. All unemployment qualified citizens for these vacant posts in this small State are dreaming that RUSA will help the State in tackling such crucial issues.

References

1. ASER (2010).Annual Status of Education Report 2010. http://www. asercentre. org/Annual/Status/of/Education/ Report/The/Annual/p/80.html.
2. Bookrags (2014). http://www.bookrags.com/essay-2005/9/2/203158/4914/.
3. Federation of Indian Chambers of Commerce and Industry (FICCI). 2013. Higher Education in India: Vision 2030 (New Delhi). http://www.ey.com/IN/en/ Industries/India-sectors/Education/EY-Higher-education-in-India-Vision- 2030.
4. ILO (2011). Equality at work: The continuing challenge - Global Report under the follow-up to the ILO Declaration on Fundamental Principles and Rights at Work http://www.ilo.org/declaration/ info/publications/elimination of discrimination /WCMS 166583/lang—en/index.htm.
5. GoI (2002). Report of the Committee on India Vision 2020. New Delhi: Planning Commission. http://planningcommission.nic.in/reports/publications/index. php? repts=pub.
6. GoI (2002). 10th Five Year Plan (2002-2007). New Delhi: Planning Commission. http://planning commission.nic.in/plans/planrel/five yr/default.html.
7. GoI (2005). Mid -Term Appraisal of the Tenth Five Year Plan (2002-2007)- English. New Delhi:Planning Commission.http://planning commission.nic.in/ plans/mta/midterm/cont eng1.htm.
8. GoI (2008). Twelfth Five Year Plan 2012-17. New Delhi: Oxford University Press. http://planningcommission.nic.in/plans/planrel/fiveyr/welcome. html.

9. GoI (2011). Mid Term Appraisal for Eleventh Five Year Plan 2007-2012: New Delhi: Oxford University Press. http://planningcommission.nic.in/plans/mta/11th_mta/MTA.html.
10. GoI(2013).Twelfth Five Year Plan(2012–2017): Faster, More Inclusive and Sustainable Growth. New Delhi: Sage Publication. http://planning commission.nic.in/plans/planrel/fiveyr/welcome.html.
11. ILO (2014). Transforming Economies: Making industrial policy work for growth, jobs and development:http://www.ilo.org/global/publications/ilo-bookstore/order-online/books/WCMS 242878/lang—en/index.htm.

Chapter-39

Financing Higher Education

S. C. Bhandari, CEO,

Abstract

Education is the life-blood of the country. It should be sponsored by the government by providing adequate funds for its healthy growth. The union and the state governments do allocated funds for the higher education, but not in the desired quantum. The GER is increasing year by year and more and more children are being brought in the main stream of education. There is a substantial growth of private sector in the field of education. However, the financial scarcity is the main constraint due to which access, equity and quality in education suffers. An attempt has been made in this paper to highlight the important aspects of the topic under discussion.

Keywords: *Higher Education, Sources of Finance, Government Alloca-tion of Funds, Provision of Funds during the Plan Period, Participation of Public Sector and Private Sector in Education*

Introduction

Sufficient financial resources are necessary for the healthy growth of educational sector. Expenditure on education is an investment in human beings and results in all round progress of the nation. Public spending on education should be a national priority. Education assumes a great importance in a country like India in ensuring equity and quality in education. Education is a basic human right and cannot be denied. But despite the best efforts, it still remains a neglected sector. The Kothari Commission, 1966 had fixed a target of investing 6 per cent of Gross National Product (GNP) on education by the public exchequer by 1986. But till 2018, the target is still elusive. Currently, India spends 4.54 per cent of GDP on education. A developed country like Denmark spent 7.8 per cent of its GNP in 2008 and a developing country like South Africa spent 5.6 per cent of its GDP in the same year. In their comparison, India spent only 3.2 per cent in that year.

Table 1 - Government Expenditure on Education (percent of GDP)*

Year	2000	2005	2010	2011	2012	2013	2012-17
%	4.4	3.2	3.4	3.8	3.9	3.8	3.8

****Source:*** UNDP- Human Development Report 2018

During the pre-globalisation period i.e., before 1990-91, total government expenditure on education increased by five times from ₹ 3884.20 crore in 1980-81 to ₹ 19615.85 crore in 1990-91. During the post-globalisation period, total government expenditure on education was ₹ 22393.69 crore in 1991-92, which increased to ₹ 242504.82 crore in 2009-10, by eleven times. *(Source: 1. Handbook of Statistics, 2012-13, Reserve Bank of India. 2. Analysis of Budgeted Expenditure on Education published by D/o Secondary and Higher Education. New Delhi, Various Issues)* Further, even at this low level, only 1/10th of the total percentage is being spent on higher education. Therefore, it has been very difficult to provide higher education to a large number of people and to speak about the quality of education is a cry in the wilderness. Therefore, the government should generate more resources and allocate them for financing education, in general, and then transferring a major part in favour of higher education, in particular.

Table 2 - Trends of Government Expenditure on Higher Educationas Percent of GDP

Year	***Government Expenditure on Higher Education as % of GDP***
1980-81	0.31
1985-86	0.38
1990-91	0.43
1994-95	0.36
1999-00	0.47
2004-05	0.31
2009-10	0.41
2017	0.38

Source: 1. National Informatics Centre, Budgetary Resources for Education, Department of Education, MHRD, GOI, New Delhi, (1995),
2. Analysis of Budgeted Expenditure on Education, MHRD, Various Issues.
3. Handbook of Statistics, 2011-12 & 2012-13, Reserve Bank of India.

Expansion of Education in India

In terms of its size and diversity, India with its 864 universities, 40026 colleges and 11669 Stand Alone Institutions (2016-17) is the third largest education system in the world, next only to China and the United States.

Table 3 – No. of Universities and Colleges in India*

Year	*Universities*	*Colleges*	*Stand Alone Institutions*
2012-13	667	35525	11565
2013-14	723	36634	11664
2014-15	760	38498	12276
2015-16	799	39071	11923
2016-17	864	40026	11669

***Source:** UGC

With growth in the number of universities and colleges, the total enrolment is also going up. More and more resources are required to be provided to this growing population of students.

Table 4 - Total Enrolment of Students in India (in millions)*

	Male	*Female*	*Total*
2012-13	16.7	13.5	30.1
2013-14	17.5	14.8	32.3
2014-15	17.9	15.4	33.3
2015-16	18.6	16.0	34.6
2016-17	19.0	16.7	35.7

****Source:*** AISHE portal, 5th Jan 2018

But the enrolment ratio in India is still below the world average with a Gross Enrolment Ratio (GER) of 26.87 percent (2015) for 18-23 years of age group.The GER is envisaged to be 30 percent by 2020 in 12th plan period.

Table 5 - GER (percent) in Selected Countries (2015)*

Pakistan	9.93
Indonesia	24.25
India	26.87
China	43.39
Thailand	48.86
USA	85.86

****Source:*** UNESCO, 21-11-2017

GER is gradually picking up in various states in the country and thereby the financial responsibility of the government is also increasing. However, the state governments are finding it difficult to raise their outlay on education proportionately.

Table 6 - GER (percent) in Selected States*

	2012-13	*2013-14*	*2014-15*	*2015-16*	*2016-17*
Bihar	13.1	13.0	12.9	14.3	14.4
Odisha	16.3	16.4	17.5	19.6	21.0
Tamil Nadu	42.0	43.0	44.8	44.3	46.9
Maharashtra	22.9	26.3	27.9	29.9	30.2
U.P.	19.5	21.6	22.1	24.5	24.9

*Source: AISHE portal, 5th Jan 2018

Sources of Funds for Higher Education in India

The sources of finance for higher education can be broadly classified into governmental sources and non-governmental sources. The governmental sources include contribution from the central government and the state governments. The non-governmental sources include student fees, funds, voluntary donations and endowments, etc.

In case of public sector and aided institutions in private sector, the main source of finance is state and central government grants. Since independence, the country has witnessed unprecedented expansion in the higher education system. But commensurate financial aid from government at, the central or the state level, is not forthcoming. Thus, many universities are finding it difficult to meet essential expenditure on account of payment of salaries, maintenance of buildings, purchase of books, journals, equipments etc. The universities are starved of funds and educational research is suffering.

Universities have become examination conducting centres rather than research promotion centres. In case of un-aided institutions in private sector, fee collection from students is the main source. In several states, salary and non-salary expenditure is reimbursed by the government to aided institutions in private sector. The quantum of grant varies from state to state. In Maharashtra, 100 percent salary grant is released to the aided institutions, and only a part of non-salary expenditure is met by it, that too sporadically and irregularly. Both these models suffer from inadequacy. Government funding is declining further and further. Private institutions are finding it difficult to manage due to limitations on charging higher fee. The main issue with majority of the institutions, especially with private sector, is mobilization of funds for maintenance of quality service as well as growth. The scarcity of resources continues to haunt the institutions.

The inability of government to shoulder the responsibility of education has resulted in the retarded growth of private sector institutions. The private sector has to manage the institutions on their own without relying on government aid. Thus, the educational sector has been divided into two segments. On the one hand, there are aided institutions getting government grants and on the other hand, the unaided institutions devoid of it and starving. After independence, during Pandit Jawaharlal Nehru's regime, India adopted a path of socialistic pattern of society. The aim was to bridge the gap between the 'haves' and 'have nots'. But the present government has deviated from that path and is creating two islands, one for the rich and the other for the poor. The privately managed institutions find it difficult to make the both ends meet. They are not able to employ fully qualified staff or pay adequate salary. Education is available to 'classes' and not the 'masses'. As a result, the quality, access and equity in education is suffering.

Plan and Non-plan expenditure on Higher Education

Government expenditure on higher education consists of plan and non-plan expenditure. Plan expenditure is less than 30 per cent of the total government expenditure on higher education. Whenever adjustment is required, the plan expenditure is the first victim because it is easier to cut it. The non-plan expenditure is difficult to curtail because a major chunk of non-plan expenditure is incurred of the payment of salaries to the existing staff.

Higher Education and Five Year Plans

In the first five year plan, 9 per cent of the total plan resources to education were allocated to university education. It was 11 per cent in the tenth plan period.

Table 7 - Allocation of Plan Expenditure on Higher Education in Five Year Plans

Five Year Plan	*Plan Expenditure on Higher Education (Rs in crore)*	*Plan Expenditure on Higher Education (%)*
1	14	9
2	48	18
3	87	15
4	195	25
5	205	22
6	530	18
7	1201	14
8	1516	7
9	4350	8
10	4799	11

Source: Planning Commission

An outlay ₹ 1,10,700 crore for higher education is proposed for the Twelfth Plan. This is merely 30 per cent more than the outlay in the Eleventh Plan, even though it is more than two and a half times the actual expenditure in the Eleventh Plan. Such a significant increase is justified because of the increasing demand for quality higher education driven by improved schooling coupled with the shortfall in spending during the Eleventh Plan.

The Twelfth Plan will build on the momentum generated during the Eleventh Plan and continue the focus on the 'Three Es'—expansion, equity and excellence. (*Source: Planning Commission*) However, the Plan proposes a paradigm change in the way we achieve such goals—through three new principles.

Expansion

1. Expand access by scaling up capacity in existing institutions rather than increasing the number of institutions, with the exception of new institutions needed to address critical regional and social gaps.
2. Create a system of institutional differentiation and distinctiveness to cater to a diverse body of students and the varied needs of employers.
3. Use the transformative potential of new technologies to improve quality, reduce costs, improve processes and efficiency and reach a larger body of students, while promoting efficient and transparent governance and raising the quality of teaching and research.

Equity

Provide significant increase in budgetary support for equity-related measures through targeted, integrated and effective equity-related schemes, which will replace the existing maze of multiple and diffused small outlay schemes.

Excellence

1. Foster a shift from an input-centric and credential-based pedagogical approach to a learner-centric and learning-outcome based approach to improve the quality of teaching and research.
2. Ensure availability, recruitment and retention of qualified people to meet the growing need for quality faculty; upgrade the skills of existing faculty; and, build synergies between teaching and research to promote excellence in both.

3. Facilitate translation of academic research into innovations for practical use in society and economy and foster entrepreneurship that creates wealth and public goods.
4. Promote internationalisation by encouraging and supporting institutions and their faculty to engage more deeply with institutions and faculty around the world in areas ranging from teaching–learning to research and outreach.
5. Create and facilitate alliances, networks, clusters, and consortia of academic institutions amongst themselves and with research institutions and industry to accelerate the process of knowledge development by better resource utilisation and by complementing mutual expertise.

Conclusion

Let us hope that the growth of education is not retarded for want of funds. The government should treat education as a priority sector and allocate more funds to this sector. If the country wants to progress, investment in man power is essential. World class educational institutions cannot be created in financial vacuum. Moreover, it is also to be seen that education does not remain a bastion of the classes but, in a country like India, it is within the reach of the poor too.

Reference

1. UNDP- Human Development Report 2018
2. National Informatics Centre, Budgetary Resources for Education, Department of Education, MHRD, GOI, New Delhi, (1995),
3. Analysis of Budgeted Expenditure on Education, MHRD, Various Issues.
4. Handbook of Statistics, 2011-12 & 2012-13, Reserve Bank of India.
5. UGC
6. AISHE portal, 5th Jan 2018
7. UNESCO portal, 21-11-2017
8. Planning Commission
9. Different web sites

Chapter-40

Professional Ethics: Predicament in Higher Education

Dr. P. Venu Gopal,

Abstract

The literature about professional is deficient that attempts to intensify thoughts pertinent to an ethical code, which needs to cultivate professionalism among teachers. The quality of the services of the teaching profession influences the nation and its citizens, teachers shall exert every effort to maintain and raise professional standards, to promote a climate that encourages the exercise of professional judgment, and to achieve conditions that attract persons worthy of trust to careers in education. The teacher stands for as a righteous and a virtuous stature for moral influence and abides accountability to make sense of transformation of the society. Teachers are vested by the public with trust and responsibility, together with an expectation that they will help prepare students for life in society in the broadest sense and so, ethics outlines the profession and considered to be an integral part of the teaching profession. The paper, in this light, shall discuss the crisis of professional ethics and the importance of various aspects of work ethics in higher education. It also highlights that teachers need to be sensitized for ethical contemplation involved in the teaching profession for effective and quality educational organisations in the contemporary context.

***Keywords**: Professional ethics, globalisation, code of conduct, educational institutions.*

Introduction

Education is considered as a powerful agency, which is instrumental in bringing about the desired changes in the socio-cultural life of the nation. Education is not knowledge alone, but also the capacity to utilise it. The quality of education depends upon the ability it imparts to make proper use of learning. Importance of education has been recognised for centuries by all societies in the world, but it has got special attention in the modern age.

Education can rarely free itself from social and cultural norms and has to relate it to the ferments within the society. It has to deal with, transmit the cultural heritage and the tradition as a prime mover of change. The status of the teacher reflects the socio-cultural ethos of a society and code of ethics enables to set out the ideals and responsibilities of the profession as what and how teachers are supposed to perform. The human being is, moving rapidly towards its formation of one world family and the people of one part of the world cannot remain indifferent to what is happening elsewhere. Earlier, we had more or less static society and a static outlook. Our goal was to make our children good citizens who would be physically and mentally fit to move in the world and serve our society and country as well. It is not that these needs have been out of place now. Nonetheless, new responsibilities have been vested and the world situation has changed to such an enormous extent that we are now required to revise the whole perspective. All these require a complete and total change in the outlook of a man, a transformation of character and a sincere, real respect for the values of universal brotherhood and unity of man irrespective of caste, colour, race, religion, region and class. Students must be taught to be a universal man who can cross the walls of social or national egocentric existence and look upon humanity as tied by the bonds of unity, justice and brotherhood. The current generation is not being educated in that manner, although we have been encountered several times about the goals of education, such as; individual, social, national and international development. Now, one has to proceed differently, thinking above than just self-development, but time is demanding for global thinking, global competition and global goals as well.

The quality of education depends upon the ability it imparts to make proper use of learning. The most essential domain for the quality of higher education institutions is the set of beliefs and moral standards about the rules of right conduct or practice that becomes professional ethics when carrying out professional practice of teachers in educational settings. It becomes incredibly important to discuss about 'ethics' prior to have an argument about professional ethics. Generally, 'Ethics' has been defined as the science of morals or moral principles. The term 'ethics', derived from the Greek word, ethos (character), refer to the philosophical science that deals with the rightness and wrongness of human actions. Ethics convey the rules of right conduct or practice, especially the ethical standards of a profession. The ethics provides people in the organization with a standard of what is right in a particular context, but sometimes people lack the skills and knowledge required to make effective and high quality ethical decisions.

These beliefs help to shape the character of the people in that society, teaching them what is good or bad.

The ethics of a professional group refer to the essential values, principles and kinds of behaviour that are thought appropriate to the profession. When we discuss about ethics in teaching profession, it implies the meaning of the task of a teacher inside and outside the classroom and also a kind of value judgment which is realised by the teacher towards the teaching profession. Professional ethics of teachers can be understood by the normative moral values directed by the governing authority and self judgment of the individual in order to perform his/her duty and responsibility in the profession with full accountability.

Prominence of Professional Ethics in Teaching as a Profession

A code of ethics is nothing but a kind of mission statement for human beings to live by; similarly ethics for teachers is nothing but a kind of mission statement for learners and teaching learning activities to be performed by the teachers. The organisation seeks to establish congruence between the social values associated with or implied by their activities and the norms of their acceptable behavior in the larger social system of which they are a part (Allen, 2003). It flows out of the overriding necessity to ensure that any given task is undertaken and completed in conformity with the principles of accountability, equity, propriety, prudence, decency, morality, honesty, integrity and transparency. Teaching does make moral demands on the teacher, specifically evident in teachers' relationships with a number of stakeholders (Sockett, 1993). Ethics is ultimately a matter of conscience for the individual and professional ethics concerns one's conduct of behaviour and practice when carrying out professional work (Scriven, 2006). Ethics implies knowledge of these basic principles and responsibility to make the appropriate choice when necessary. Ethics has several attributes, and are also considered synonymous with the expression of norms, and values, something to do with a sense of right or wrong (Enderle, 2007).

The Professional Code of Conduct provides the text for teachers that allowed them to respond to questions and problems, and to redefine relations with different stakeholders in education. Professional Code of Ethics makes common and collective claims in so far as they construct a set of uniform guidelines for teachers that articulate what it means to be a teacher in the current context. Although many professional organisations have adopted formal and well-established codes of ethics, the academic profession has not, is being emphasised by Felicio and Pieniad (1999). Durkhiem (1956) recognised the importance of Education for the preparation of individuals who will assume responsibility for society and emphasized on inculcating a certain number of physical, intellectual and moral states is similar to the current focus on the lack of ethical training in higher education. Ahmed Commission Report (1985) has suggested some recommendations such as; pursuit of excellence and relevance for curricula, enforcement of minimum standards, autonomy and linkages with community, resources and management of education, living and working conditions of teachers, work culture and environment all which substantiate in building up the professional ethics and values in education set up. In the era of globalisation, part of the reform movement has focused on quality education for all students, and most reform is framed in terms of better outcomes for students (A. Hargreaves and Evans, 1997).

Wallerstein (1991) suggests that cultural practices and the shared premises of the cultural attributes of, these practices are often shared subconsciously between classes and thus elude discussion. The UGC (1988) adopted the code of professional ethics for university and college teachers on the recommendations of the Task Force it had constituted for the purpose. The code has been placed under seven sections, namely, teachers and their responsibilities; teachers and their students; teachers and colleagues; teachers and authorities; teachers and non teaching staff; teachers and guardians; teachers and society. *The National Policy on Education* (1986) stated that professional organizations of teachers shall develop a code of professional ethics and shall also see to its observance. The central thesis about the ethical claims of teaching concerning the causal relationship between the moral claims of teachers and the influences on their students. For Socket (1996), the concept of professional virtue underpins the development of the profession. If taken further, the virtue extends into teachers' dealings the important function of transmitting the knowledge which provides access to practice of many professions.

Crisis of Professional Ethics in Higher Education

The notion of how societies change and development are not new in the present discourse, but it is started from ancient time and still going on right up to the modern period. There have always been ideas and theories about how societies change and develop. Teachers in such concerns become the central agent for change. There is a lack of accountability of teachers in higher education and teachers is not acquainted with the existence of a Code of Conduct in higher education. Professional Code of Ethics makes common and collective claims in so far as they construct a set of uniform guidelines for teachers that articulate what it means to be a teacher in the current context. In making these claims, attention is given both to external demands, for example, the demands of different stakeholders, and to internal demands, such as the need for ongoing conversations about what it means to be a teacher. The ethical guidelines aim to unpack the notion of ethical behaviour and move towards greater precision in making visible professional obligations.

The Code of Ethics forms the beginnings of defining teachers' identity, according to teachers. Shils (1983) states that the academic profession has done very little to disseminate a set of guiding principles which should govern the role in the internal conduct of Universities and its participation in the public sphere. The teacher symbolises as a principled figure, assigned as with moral authority, able to make sense of change, and in doing so, can help students to make sense of change. The code addresses teachers' social agency and political commitment. It answers the challenge for teachers' unions to move forward and outward into global and local communities in search of the common good that addresses social and educational needs for all. University's autonomy and academic freedom are very important concerns in all the activities and rests on a certain legal traditions and requires the emergence of a modern society, moreover there is no profession which is exempt from fundamental ethical obligations. Scott (2002) argues that the important organisational values are five basically as honest communication, respect for property, respect for religion, and respect for justice which allow parallel constructs at individual and organisational level.

Academic profession has not received adequate attention and has been captured in negative terms, but the professional responsibility includes a distinctive positive dimension, so there is a special reason to value a profession as the profession contributes to human excellence and is solely committed to enlarge the power and influence of reasoned discourse (Baumgarten, 1982). By reaching out to global organisations that have used teacher ethics as a way to unite the profession at the global level, teaching fraternity can align themselves to powerful coalitions that give greater capacity for teachers to empower their own profession and be a force in determining what it means to be a teacher in the new century. According to Abbott (1983), the five basic properties of professional ethics include universal distribution, enforceable visibility, and allowance for individuality, collegial obligations, as well as alignment with recognized status, also states that both intra-and extra-professional status needs to be taken into account when forging professional ethics. These properties present the basis for a collective agreement about teachers' ethical obligations. Rather than promoting ethical teaching as a personal obligation and preference, ethical deliberations, taking into account the types of properties suggested by Abbott, become part of the negotiations in defining the profession. The code of ethics stresses the public duties and moral commitment of teachers as public employees entrusted by society.

Higher education has witnessed massive change for restructuring and reforming institutions with the passage of time in the last few decades. In the era of change, higher education has been facing value paucity due to increasing influences of global and commercial orientation in this sector. Such changes in new world order also influence the culture and traditions which largely depends on capability, skill and talent as much as it depends on practice of such knowledge. Higher Education is often conceived in terms of broadening its knowledge to extended stakeholders i.e. the society, keeping in mind the harmonious nature, values and morality between institution and society. So, ethical considerations and values are presumed to be imperative for the effective and efficient internal coordination of the university. It is crucial to identify the problems and address the fundamental reality to begin to discern between substantial and insubstantial aspects required to promote the moral principles in academia.

Conclusion

General observation and text also suggest that teachers are failing in their services, not because they are deficient in command of subject matter, but for the reason that they lack adequate understanding of their students and are so unskillful in their efforts within the complex processes of interpersonal relationships. The most essential domain for the quality of educational institutions is the set of beliefs and moral standards about the rules of right conduct or practice that becomes professional ethics when carrying out professional practice of teachers in educational settings. This trust requires teachers to adhere to a moral code of conduct where true professionalism is guided by high ethical standards. As evident professional ethics deal not only with conduct but also with motives and character. Ethics constitute a higher standard of moral and values which are quite individual in nature than just rules, regulations and laws.

The literature about professional is deficient that attempts to intensify thoughts pertinent to an ethical code, which needs to cultivate professionalism among teachers. The quality of the services of the teaching profession influences the nation and its citizens, teachers shall exert every effort to maintain and raise professional standards, to promote a climate that encourages the exercise of professional judgment, and to achieve conditions that attract persons worthy of trust to careers in education. Quality enhancement in higher education is a deliberate process of change that leads to improvement and teachers are the only agents who can bring about the significant changes in the quality upgradation of educational institutions. Consequently, it can be said that professional values, ethics and quality are inseparable since these are embedded into every aspect of teaching. Hence, it can be concluded that teachers need to come to a sensitive wakefulness of ethical contemplation involved in teaching profession for effective and quality educational organisations.

References

1. Allen, O.K. (2003). Organizational Climate and strategic change in higher education: organizational insecurity higher education. Vol. 46, No.3. I
2. Abbot, A. (1983). Professional Ethics. American Journal of Sociology, Vol. 88, No.5.
3. Baumgarten E. (1982). Ethics in the Academic Profession: A Socratic View, *Journal of Higher Education* , Vol. 53, No.5.
4. Durkheim, E. (1956). Education And Sociology, Translated With An Introduction By Sherwood D. Fox. Glencoeil: The Free Press.
5. Felicio, D.M. and J. Pieniad (1999). Ethics in Higher Education: Red Flags and Grey Areas, Vol 9, No. 1.
6. Hargreaves, D. H. (2000). The production, mediation and use of professional knowledge among teachers and doctors: A comparative analysis. Paris: OECD.
7. National Commission of Teachers In Higher Education) 1986), Ahmed Commission Report, New Delhi: University Grants Commission.
8. Scriven, M., (2006). Professonal Ethics. *The Journal of Higher Education,* Ethics and the Academic Profession, Vol 5, No.9.
9. Soltis. J. F. (1986). Teaching Professional Ethics. *Journal Of Teacher Education.* Vol. 37, No.3.
10. Sockett, H. (1996). The Moral Base for Teacher Professionalism. New York: Teachers College Press.
11. Shills, E. (1983), The Academic Ethic, Minerva, Vol.97, No.104.
12. Scott, E.D., (2002). Organizational Moral Values. *Business Ethics Quarterly.* Vol. 12(1).
13. Wallerstein, I. (1991). The Heritage of Sociology: The Promise of Social Science. *Current Sociology,* Vol. 47, No. 1.

Chapter-41

Contemporary Issues in Higher Education- Liberalization Privatization, Globalisation

Priyanka Mokale,

Abstract

Talking about the Contemporary issues in Higher education the under the name of public private partnership government is doing the privatization of education. The government largely spends on the underlying assumption that a few high quality graduates are adequate for rapid economic growth. J.B.G. Tilak states how heavy reliance on the private sector is a poor strategy, reflecting that the state is "weak" in controlling the market forces and is reluctant to prioritise public higher education. The mushrooming private sector has allowed the government to shift its costs to families through fees and loans. This shift signifies a big ideological shift. The government largely spends on a few high-quality elite institutions based on the. Tilak describes it as "state opportunism", which may have an ideological element, but demonstrates itself to be the "pragmatic" path of raising funds from non-governmental resources.

Globalization and its Impact on Higher Education in India

Globalization has a multidimensional impact on the system of higher education in India. The higher education system in India suffers from acute paucity of funds, lack of autonomy, burden of affiliation. On the other hand the effect of globalization on education brings rapid developments in technology, communication and knowledge economy.

1. Globalization and economic reforms In India have yielded significant changes in the role of state and restructuring of social welfares education. In higher education it was always the monopoly of middle class and elite groups of the society.

2. Privatization of higher education. There has been an increasing trend towards privatization of higher education in India. In this day age of globalization and privatization with competition and to meet the new challenges of the 21st century higher education should be radically transformed.
3. Women education Women literacy rate has grown over the three decades. Women education plays a very important role in the overall development of the country and improving the quality of life at home and outside.
4. Commercialization Impact of globalization is commercialization of higher education due to which self-financing courses have been introduced which has deprived many from getting higher education especially in countries like India where illiteracy still prevails and education is a dream to many.
5. Teacher education Today the aspects of rapid change, lifelong learning, flexible routes of learning and the use of technology have a major impact on all the areas of teacher education. Major steps to be taken qualitative expansion, value based, competency based and ICT based teaching learning.
6. Knowledge: Because of globalization the accessing of knowledge become easy fast and anytime of the all over world .
7. Skill: Higher education is seeking ways to meet the demands and challenges put forth by globalization. Higher education today is expected to produce skilled and trained workforce who can compete in this global market.
8. Education policies Globalization impacts the education policies on higher education in India. In the last two decades Indian government has formed various committees, commission and also different kinds of economic bodies came to existence like NAAC.
9. Entry of Foreign Universities Foreign Direct Investment (FDI) is important tool of globalization. As government lack of funds FDI is allowed into higher education. The foreign universities are expected to bring the quality infrastructure in teaching, research as well as physical infrastructure. This will attract large scale foreign investments into India and also to an extent reverse brain drain.
10. E-learning People with disability get benefit from globalization only if they endowed with knowledge, skills, capabilities and rights needed to pursue their basic livelihoods. The introduction

of technology into the classroom is changing the nature of delivering education to students is gradually giving way to a new form of electronic literacy , more programs and education materials are made available in electronic form, teachers are preparing materials in electronic form; and students are generating papers, assignments and projects in electronic form. Video projection screens, books

With storage device servers and CD rooms as well as the emergence of on-line digital libraries are now replacing blackboards.

How Globalisation affecting the higher Education in current Era:

Education became a Business Indian educational system is full of culture, tradition, factors relating to Dharma, Spiritualism. Education was considered as a path for salivation. Globalization has made education a business process, by way of entry of foreign universities, privatization of education which leads to multi-dollar business.

- Global Competition International universities and other educational institutions stand for global competition. And they aim to provide quality education with world norms; they are away from local needs like basic education, agriculture, handlooms, etc. Indian educational institution which is bonded with cultural propagation, transmission, will find tough to compete with foreign universities.
- Delinking Between Education and Employment Due to globalization in education, the number of unemployed youths is increasing. Getting certificate is easy, the young graduates are getting frustrated as their education of poorly linked with employment opportunities, service sectors etc.

Dewan, Anjali (2012) Globalization, Higher Education and the Changing Status of Indian Women- An Appraisal of the Emerging Issues and Challenges. Globalization has brought in a number of changes in the world today changing it into a global market. The direct nexus between the industry, corporate world and higher education has brought a transformation in the skills required for various jobs. Natural and Pure Sciences are not considered supreme anymore. Applied Sciences and professional skills are much more in demand now. The new developments have led to the de-evaluation of the subjects in the fields of Humanities and Social Sciences. Women used to take admission in the Colleges in General Education, Arts or in Humanities in the early 1990's. The trend is very much different now. Feminist perspectives on women's educational qualifications have expressed their concern on their under participation, underachievement and underrepresentation. A focused vision is required which will reach out to more women by encompassing the issues of access to and equity with respect to education of women in the higher education sector.

Conclusion

Therefore it is found the Because of Liberalisation there is easily we can contact to the world and world come closer means contact with world become easy then in this process of globalisation occur. Impact of globalisation goes on living standard, food habit and most importantly on Education. So because of globalisation the privatisation started in the education sector also. Because of privatisation Education become one type of business market where student parents are the customer and private institute with big donations become a producer /owner. So those are rich they can afford, survive in this environment by paying money. But what about the poor, weaker section, disadvantaged group, how can they manage in this LPG era of higher education that is the big question mark?

References

1. Private Sector Participation in Indian Higher Education: FICCI Higher Education Summit 2011, Retrieved January 14, 2012, from.
2. http://www.ey.com/Publication/vwLAssets/Private sector participation in Indian higher education/$FILE/Private sector participation in Indian higher education.pdf.
3. Dewan, Anjali (2012) Globalization, Higher Education and the Changing Status of Indian Women- An Appraisal of the Emerging Issues and Challenges accessed on January 20, 2013 http://scholarly-journals.com/sje/April/ Anjali.pdf.

Chapter-42

Education System: Role of Stakeholders, Impact on Nations Growth– A Case Study on South Korean Higher Education System

K. Prabhu Sahai,
L. N. Gupta

Abstract

Education system has become subtle, commercial, brain drain is order of the day, ratio of graduates and their employability is very low, even enrollment in higher education is not encouraging, bridging the gap between University and Industry is not answered, in this scenario a nation has done exceptionally well to raise its standards and quality of education, the skills of students are exceeding the average skills of OECD Nations, its education policy or system is proving to be worth and adoptable. In South Korea more than 95 percent of eighteen-year-old children graduate from high schools, and more than 70 percent of them advance to higher education institutions. Awareness among parents, Responsible nature of Educational Institutions, and Government Strict Norms for Control are the reasons for success of the system.

Keywords: *Education system, Society role, Nation role, 21st Century skills, OECD*

Introduction

Overcoming a long history of Japanese rule and a devastating war, the small Republic of South Korea (just 45 million people) has achieved transformations that took centuries in most nations in the West. With its push toward heavy industry — steel, construction, ship building, automobiles - and a substantial investment in high technology, South Korea has surpassed regional rivals such as Taiwan and has gone on to challenge both Japan and the U.S. at the heart of this remarkable achievement is Korea's education system, which has been the major source of trained labour in the various fields and at skill levels needed for economic development.

South Korea's quality education system rests on four pillars: (1) putting education at the center of a long-term development strategy, (2) getting the right people to become teachers, (3) developing these people into effective instructors, and (4) prioritizing information and communications technology in education.

Background

Korea's education system underwent a tremendous expansion since the end of the Korean War. In 1945, Korea had an estimated adult literacy rate of only 22 percent. Less than 2 percent of the population was enrolled in higher education. Today, the country has achieved universal adult literacy, estimated to range between 98 and 100 percent, and the tertiary gross enrolment ratio stands at a lofty 93 percent (2015).

In the 1950s, elementary education was made compulsory for all children, which led to the Universalization of elementary education by the 1960s. Beginning in 1985, the length of compulsory education was then extended by another three years, and all children in Korea are now mandated to stay in school until the end of grade nine (age 15). As of 2014, 98 percent of Koreans went on to upper-secondary and completed high school at minimum.

The education zeal of the South Korean people has increased due to the policy of respect for learning and the doctrine of seeking for social success. The tradition of Confucian education, which is the pursuit for the enhancement of socio-economic position limited to the privileged class, after liberation from the Japanese, however, awakened the latent educational fever with the current of democratization in higher education. Furthermore, during the 1980s, moral cultivation and social success-oriented thought, which were regarded as the purpose of Confucian education in the traditional times, were upsided toward an emphasis on the instrumental values of education, the pursuit of socioeconomic progress, along with the current of western pragmatic materialism.

South Korea—the Republic of Korea—is the most educated country in the world. According to the Organization for Economic Cooperation and Development (OECD), 70 percent of 24- to 35-year-olds in the nation of 51.5 million people have completed some form of tertiary education—the highest percentage worldwide and more than 20 percentage points above comparable attainment rates in the United States. Korea also has a top-quality school system when measured by student performance in standardized tests: The country consistently ranks among the best-performing countries in the OECD's Program for International Student Assessment (PISA).

Objective: The purpose of this study is to understand strengths, weakness, opportunities and threats of the education system in South Korea, and identify policies which can be implemented in Indian Education system.

Methodology: In order to achieve the objective, descriptive method was used through reviewing the related literature to the research variables and also by analyzing the content of some studies which deal with these topics.

Findings: The study concludes that the whole nation stood up for the cause of Quality Education and the same can be implemented in Indian Education System.

Higher Education in Korea

Higher education is provided primarily by universities (industrial universities, teacher-training universities, broadcast and correspondence universities, cyber universities) and colleges (junior colleges, cyber colleges, technical colleges, colleges in company, graduate school colleges) as well as various other research and other institutions. A distinction is drawn between national institutions (funded and managed by the MOE), public institutions (funded and managed by local management boards) and private institutions (funded and managed by individuals or organizations). The three most prestigious universities are the Seoul National University Korea University and Yonsei, jointly abbreviated to SKY. The national universities also have a good reputation.

Adult and Distance Education

The sector for adult and distance education is very large, and is served by many different institutions and in a variety of ways, including secondary education. The Korea National Open University (formerly called Korea Air & Correspondence University) provides distance education to adults via television, radio (Educational Broadcasting System), CD-ROMs, Internet and video/cassette tapes. In 1990 the Educational Broadcasting System (EBS) was founded in order to expand opportunities for life-long learning. EBS broadcasts its cultural and social programmes daily via TV, radio and satellite.

Cyber universities and digital colleges provide distance education via the Internet. Since 2009 their number has increased and since then they no longer fall under the Lifelong Education Act as distance learning universities, but are now considered to be regular higher education institutions falling under the Higher Education Act. They offer 2- and 3-year junior college programmes (associate degree) and bachelor's programmes.

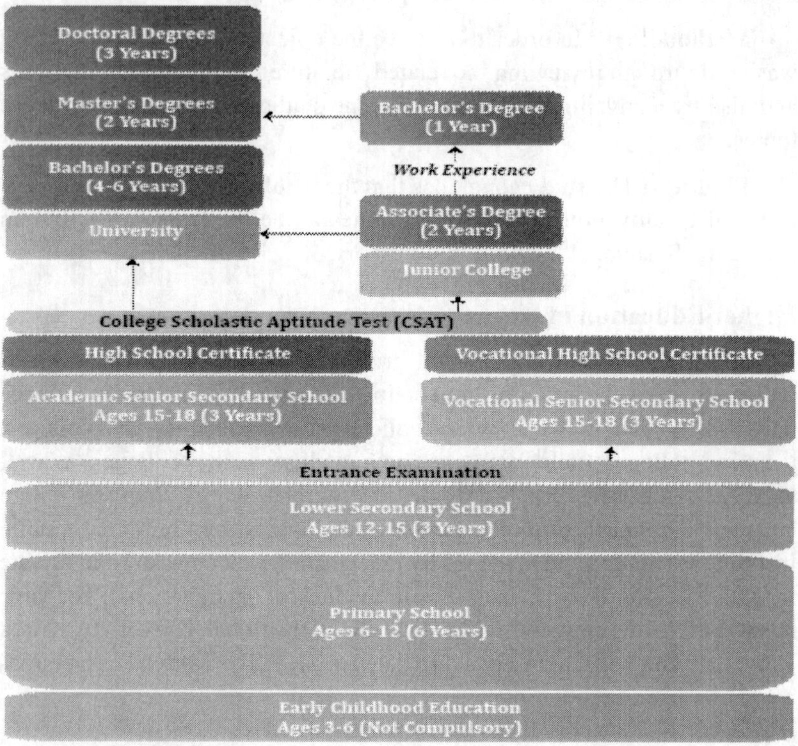

The Structure of South Korea's Education System

Importance of Education in South Korea

South Korea has experienced rapid and unprecedented economic and social achievements since the 1960s. From being one of the world's poorest nations, it has grown to become the ninth largest economy in the world with a GDP of US$1.75 trillion and per capita income of US$34,569 (OECD, current PPP, 2015). Once labelled as one of the four emerging Asian "Dragons," South Korea has repeatedly demonstrated that it has an identity of its own, as it strategically transformed itself into one of the world's high-technology and education superpowers. Much of this rapid development has been attributed to far-sighted, deliberate and government-regulated long-term education plans and policies, which have helped reshape the country and transform its occupational structures and prestige.

The nation has produced one of the most highly educated labour forces in the world by investing heavily in education. The proportion of those aged between 25 and 34 years old who had attained tertiary education in 2015 was 69 percent, the highest score among 36 OECD countries (OECD, 2017b) Population with tertiary education (indicator). South Korea's educational system is also producing 15-year olds that rank highly in world PISA scores: 7th in reading, 7th in math, and 11th in science (2015) (OECD, 2016d) PISA 2015 results. In 2011, South Korea led the OECD nations in the number of engineering graduates per capita, with 3,555 per 100,000. Clearly South Korea, and its government, has been very successful in educating its population and workforce.

The Importance of the CSAT

In Korea, children begin to prepare for the CSAT from the time they are about 4-5 years old so that they can ultimately reach the SKY – the collective nickname of Korea's 'big three' universities: Seoul National University (SNU), Korea University and Yonsei University. Getting into one of these three is the hope of every Korean child and her/his parents because not only will graduates from one of the big three have the best academic pedigree in the country, they will also have a strong alumni network – people tend to mentor and hire graduates from their alma mater. SKY graduates are also the most attractive marriage partners, along with women with degrees from Ewha Woman's University – so SKYE is the ultimate goal.

To make it into the SKYE, a student has to achieve a near perfect score on the CSAT and top grades in school. To improve their child's 'chances', parents enrol their children into special pre-schools, have them attend private institutes (hagwons) for extra math, science and English studies before and after school as well as on weekends. Those who can afford it also arrange for private tutoring in addition to the time spent in the private institutes. It is not unusual for parents to 'beggar' themselves as they invest in their child/children's future.

Extra Ordinary Measures by Govt and public for CSAT

As many as 5,95,000 students appeared for the examination. It is on the basis of this examination that students are admitted to the top universities. And to ensure that the students had no problems, the country came together collectively to assist the students. Here are the extraordinary measures undertaken by the country.

- Opening time of public offices, major businesses and the stock market was pushed back by an hour to ease the traffic and ensures that the students reached their respective centres on time for the examination which started across the country at 8:40 am and lasted till 5.40 pm
- In case of traffic situations, students could dial for police cars and motorbikes that would help them rush through the traffic and reach the exam centres.
- To facilitate the listening test, the country took measures to lower the volume and decibels across the country. In effect, all takeoffs and landings at South Korean airports were suspended for 25 minutes which coincided with an English listening test. Further, all the airborne planes were ordered to maintain at the altitude higher than 3,000 metres (10,000 feet). In effect, about 134 flights had to be rescheduled because of the exam as per the Transport Ministry.
- Electronic devices were strictly forbidden and students could not leave the school premises until the end of the examination.

Weakness:

Private tutoring in South Korea is quite pervasive. In 2006, the household sector spent 2.57 percent of the nation's GDP on private tutoring for primary and secondary school students. Government spending on those students was about 3.5 percent of GDP, which is about the average level among OECD countries. Empirical analyses indicate that students with high academic ability and high family income whose parents are highly educated spend more on private tutoring. Also, students in regions without school choice spend more on private tutoring. The estimated income elasticity of private tutoring is about 0.5. Pervasive private tutoring may create an inefficient as well as inequitable educational system. Korean experience studied in this article suggests that private tutoring should be studied as an integral part of the whole educational system.

Threats

The nation has one of the world's highest youth suicide rates. Also, according to a recent survey of South Korean households, the country's teenagers are some of the world's most depressed. Out of the 30 countries involved in the poll, South Korea ranked at the very bottom.

Conclusions

1. South Korean parents spend more on education (15 percent of their gross national product) than any other nation. Some parents drop close to 25 percent of their income on education, tutoring and supplemental educational materials. And most parents send their kids to extra private school after their regular school day.
2. Teachers in South Korea are another major factor in the students' success. South Korean teachers go above and beyond. "Korean teachers don't just do what is expected of them," "They are extremely dedicated to their jobs. They work very hard and make a huge effort." And society rewards them for it. Teachers in South Korea enjoy high social status, are paid very well and have great job security. No wonder teaching is *the* top career choice for young Korean's these days
3. The Korean Ministry of Education works hard to make sure *all* of their country's schools are tops as well. In 2008, they made several changes in an attempt to close the gap between kids in high-achieving urban schools and lower-achieving rural schools. They offered financial support to all middle school students, subsidized computers, offered meals and opened more schools in rural areas to make them more accessible.
4. South Korea is very savvy when it comes to leveraging technology to improve their schools. They topped PISA's digital literacy test in 2009, proving that when it comes to computers, their kids are on the ball. Every school in South Korea has high-speed internet. They also have digital textbooks to make learning materials more accessible, especially to lower income students. By 2015, they plan to go 100 percent digital and have all textbooks in all of their schools accessible from a computer, tablet or phone. The Ministry of Education has also recently created a Cyber Home Learning System, an online program designed to help kids with their after-school learning.
5. As reviewed in this study, the educational fever of the South Korea people was a major factor by which to achieve the wondrous development of the national economy as well as the rapid expansion of higher education. In particular, it is not too much to say that the economic growth in the 1960s and 1970s was the result of the

expansion of higher education. The rapid growth of higher education, the improvement of higher productivity, and the increment of higher earnings in contemporary South Korea support a human capital theory at large.

Suggestions

(1) India could seek to improve its education system with initiatives to support a long-term education policy, which has to include a clear plan to improve the accreditation process of teacher education institutes, the current salaries of teachers, the training of teachers, and the use of technology in schools.

(2) Putting education at the center of a long-term development strategy,

(3) Getting the right people to become teachers,

(4) Developing these people into effective instructors, and

(5) Prioritizing information and communications technology in education.

References

1. Daniel Carr, Liang Choon Wang. (2018) The Effect of After-School Classes on Private Tuition, Mental Health and Academic Outcomes: Evidence from Korea. Sociology 52:5, 877-897.
2. Ellinger, Thomas R; Beckham, Garry M.Phi Delta Kappan; South Korea: Placing education on top of the family agenda Bloomington Vol. 78, Iss. 8, (Apr 1997)624-625.
3. Choi, B. Y. (1994). Human capitalization through education in Confucian cultural Regions, The Universal and particular natures of Confucianism. Seongnam, Korea: The Academy of Korean Studies.
4. Lee, J. K. (2001). Korean experience and achievement in higher education. The SNU Journal of Education Research, 11, 1-23.
5. Ministry of Education & Human Resources Development and Korean Educational Development Institute (2002). Statistical yearbook of education. Seoul: Ministry of Education.
6. Bermeo, Elizabeth. (2014). South Korea's successful education system: lessons and policy implications for Peru. Korean Social Science Journal. 41. 135-151.
7. http://www.cee.org/what-we-do/center-on-international-education-benchmarking/top-performing-countries/south-korea-overview/south-korea-system-and-school-organization
8. https://www.clssbase.com/countries/South-Korea/Education-System
9. http://ncee.org/what-we-do/center-on-international-education-benchmarking/top-performing-countries/south-korea-overview/south-korea-education-for-all

10. http://ncee.org/what-we-do/center-on-international-education-benchmarking/top-performing-countries/south-korea-overview/south-korea-instructional-systems
11. Hyo-sik, L. (2008). Education spending hits record high. *The Korea Times,* 28 February. http://www.koreatimes.co.kr/www/common/printpreview. asp?category Code=123&newsIdx=19782.
12. Kim-Renaud, Y.-K. (2005). Korean education (introduction). *The Sigur Center Asia Papers,* 4 (1), 5–7.
13. Halyna Mykhailyshyn, Oksana Kondur, Lesia Serman, "Innovation of Education and Educational Innovations in Conditions of Modern Higher Education Institution", Journal of Vasyl Stefanyk Precarpathian National University, Vol. 5, No. 1, 2018, 9-16.
14. OECD, "Innovating Education and Educating for Innovation: The Power of Digital Technologies and Skills", OECD Publishing, Paris, 2016.

Chapter-43

Mentoring system in Higher Education: A Case Study of ICFAI Law School, Hyderabad

S. Kannan

Abstract

Education system in contemporary society possess many challenges in enhancing the skills of the students in both curricular, co-curricular and extra-curricular activities. In order to make the student more viable and productive in their respective field, mentoring system was introduced in higher educational institutions around the world and also in India. Further, many scholars have also agreed that mentoring system positively impact their abilities to succeed in college (Hurtado & Carter, 1997; Amaury Nora and Gloria Crisp, 2008). The studies on mentoring system remained more focused on medical, engineering and management stream students when compare to the other streams. Against this background, present study focus on effectiveness of mentoring system in legal education. The study was conducted in ICFAI Law School, ICFAI Foundation for Higher Education (Deemed University), Hyderabad, Telangana. The study used both primary and secondary information's to understand the effectiveness of mentoring system. The attendance details of the students were collected for the previous academic session at the beginning of the session and also at the end of the session. Finding suggest that mentoring programs aimed at providing experiences designed to assist students in adjusting to college life and becoming fully engaged in classroom and out-of-class activities. Unstructured interviews among the mentor's reveals that most of the time mentees were reluctant to meet them and the mentees opined that mentor system helps us in understanding the system, follow-up and circulation of the information regarding co-curricular and extra-curricular activities were helpful for them. At the end, the study suggest that for effective mentoring system, the regular interaction between devoted mentors and mentees will solve the purpose.

Keywords: *Mentor, Mentee, attendance, Law, interaction, skills*

Introduction

Higher education in the diverse and heterogeneous contemporary society, posses with many challenges in enhancing the skills and well-being of the students. Due to the advancement in technology and access to online resources in-hand exaggerated the student's life to a larger extent. Their behavior in the class room and out-side of the classroom was monitored through camera. Deteriorating formal teacher and student interaction and relationship is another emerging concern for the higher educational institutions. Further, students pursing the higher education are reported from the different cultural backgrounds, irregularity in attending the classes, higher level of usage of smart phones, more hunting towards entertainments in the name of celebrations, etc. These realities exemplifying the daunting challenge to higher education in India (Komarraju, Musulkin and Bhattacharya, 2010). In order to make the student more viable and productive in their respective field, mentoring system was introduced in higher educational institutions around the world, including India. Further, many scholars have also agreed that mentoring system positively impact their abilities to succeed in higher education (Hurtado & Carter, 1997; Amaury Nora and Gloria Crisp, 2008). It also has long been considered as a developmental and retention strategy for undergraduate education (Jacobi, 1991) and research suggests mentoring relationships are positively related to a variety of academic outcomes such as persistence and grades (Collings, Swanson, & Watkins, 2014; Khazanov, 2011). Mentoring programs and associated efforts can be effective means of supporting student development and academic success (Crisp and young, 2018). In sum, most notable outcomes of mentoring college students include increased academic performance and progress, skill development, program-related activities and overall quality of educational experience. In this context, the study explores the effectiveness of mentoring system in legal educational institution in support with empirical evidence.

Mentoring system: Origin and purpose

Mentoring is not a new concept as it may date back as far as the Stone Age (Dickey 1996). The origins of the word "mentor" stem from Greek methodology. In the Odyssey, the main character, Odysseus, entrusts his friend, Mentor, to help him prepare to fight in the Trojan War. Mentor serves as a wise, responsible and trusted advisor who guides Odysseus's development (Miller 2002). In the 1980s, Kram (1988) established mentoring as a workplace model and it has since proliferated in such forms as social psychology, learning theory, adult theory, organizational development, leadership theory and systems thinking. Mentorship historically involves training youth or adults in skills building and knowledge acquisition (Merriam, 1983), provoking the metaphor of mentoring as training. Technical mentoring involves the transfer of skills within authoritative and apprenticeship contexts whereas alternative mentoring questions hierarchical learning and favors new forms of socialization (Darwin, 2000; Hansman, 2003). The most recent comprehensive review of the mentoring literature was conducted by Crisp and Cruz (2009), who provided a critical synthesis of empirical research conducted between 1990 and 2007. Although findings pointed to the overall effectiveness of mentoring as a means to develop undergraduate students and support their academic success, the review also identified persistent conceptual, methodological, and theoretical weaknesses that impede the usefulness of findings in guiding the development of mentoring practice.

Within the context of higher education, the absence of a consistent definition of mentoring has been repeatedly recognized. Existing definitions of mentoring offered have often been extremely broad or even lacking entirely. For instance, Brown et al. (1999) and Murray (2001) broadly defined mentoring as a one-on-one relationship between an experienced and less experienced person for the purpose of learning or developing specific competencies. Blackwell (1989) has defined mentoring in more specific terms stating that mentoring "is a process by which persons of a superior rank, special achievements, and prestige instruct, counsel, guide and facilitate the intellectual and/or career development of persons identified as Protégés"

Mentoring models offer different ranges of interaction, involvement, and investment by the faculty. Some faculty foster mentoring relationships that are restricted to academic and research progress, dismissing issues of adjustment, family, emotion, or personal well-being. Mentorship that encompasses interpersonal competence and relational abilities (e.g., communicating empathy and respect), however, is most effective for academic transition and integration, and scholarship development. Further, many studies also opined that mentoring has the potential to support national and institutional goals to increase the number of persons completing college degrees by providing access to social capital—opportunities and resources provided through relationships and interpersonal networks (Palmer & Gasman, 2008)—and cultural capital, or social assets that promote mobility (Cole & Espinoza, 2008). Through mentoring programs, students participate in activities aimed at development in areas such as study skills, time management, and written and oral communication skills (Michael, et.al.,

2010; Salinitri, 2005), providing opportunities to identify ways of successfully navigating the college environment. The benefits of the mentoring system in higher education is summarized as follows:

- Enhances the students' confidence and challenges them by setting higher goals, taking risks and ultimately guiding them to achieve higher levels.
- Individual recognition and encouragement.
- Psychosocial support at the time of need.
- Routine advice on balancing of academic and professional responsibilities.
- Mentors act as role models and facilitate leadership by developing the interpersonal skills and helping students thrive in competitive environments.
- Students get access to a support system (Mentors) during the crucial stages of their academic, professional and intellectual development.
- Students get an insider's perspective on navigating your career in the right channel.
- Students get an exposure to diverse academic and professional perspectives, and experiences in various fields.
- The mentees get a direct access to powerful resources within your major or profession.
- The mentors lay the foundation for the students to reach greater heights in their professional lives- Thereby contributing to lasting personal and professional relationship.

The analysis of available literature on mentoring system clearly emphasis the need and importance of mentoring system in higher educational institutions and its major outcomes in the different parts of the world. The study on mentoring system in India is majorly focus among the students pursuing medical (Kukreja, 2017; Chhaya Saraf et. al, 2017; Singh et.al. 2014), engineering and business education.

Methodology

The present study focus on effectiveness of mentoring system in legal education. The study conducted in one of the potential legal educational institution in India, which is ICFAI Law School (ILS), ICFAI Foundation for Higher Education (Deemed University), Hyderabad, Telangana. The major objective of the study is to understand the need and importance of mentoring system and its effectiveness in the higher educational institution. In order to understand the effectiveness of the mentoring system in ILS, the attendance details of the students and interviews with mentors and mentees are taken into the analysis. The study used both primary and secondary information's to understand the effectiveness of mentoring system. The attendance details of the previous academic session of 2018-19, odd semester of the students were collected at the beginning of the session (after completion of one month of the session) and also at the end of the session. To gather primary data, interviews were conducted among the mentors and mentees in ILS. In previous academic session (2018-19) there are totally 23 mentor groups were existed, which was divided on the basis of section and semester-wise among BBALLB and BALLB courses.

About Study Area

The ICFAI Foundation for Higher Education (IFHE), Hyderabad, a Deemed to be University established under section 3 of the UGC Act, 1956 and accredited by the UGC NAAC with A+ Grade. The university offers management, Engineering and Law Program and provides world class, innovative, career oriented professional programs through inclusive technology-aided pedagogies to equip students with the requisite professional and life skills as well as social sensitivity and high sense of ethics. The University strives to create an intellectually stimulating environment approach for research, more particularly into areas bearing on the socio-economic and cultural development of the state and nation.

The ICFAI Law School is a significant segment of the IFHE and recognized by Bar Council of India. The institution is a promising destination for the students desirous of making law as their Dream Career. It offers five year full-time campus based integrated BBALLB (Hons.) and BALLB (Hons.) programs. In previous academic session (2018-19) there are 665 students pursuing the BBALLB and BALLB course (see table1). The student's strength is gender neutral. The students hailed from all over India to pursue the law course in ILS.

Table 1. Course and Semester-wise student's detail of ICFAI Law School

Course	Gender	Semester					Total
		I	III	V	VII	IX	
BBALLB (Hons.)	Male	87	69	40	48	33	277
	Female	98	65	47	37	25	272
	Total	185	134	87	85	58	549

(*Contd...*)

BALLB* (Hons.)	Male	24	14	12	-	-	50
	Female	35	19	12	-	-	66
	Total	59	33	24	-	-	116
Semester-wise total of BBALLB and BALLB		244	167	111	85	58	665

* BALLB course started from 2016-17 session onwards.

The institution also ranked 7th among the private law schools across the country by Career 360 for last 3 consecutive years. It is ranked 5th among the Top Law Schools of Eminence by Competition Success Review – Global Human Resources Development Centre (CSR-GHRDC). It ranked 1st in Telangana State by CSR GHRDC. It also ranked 15th among top law schools of India 2018 by India Today magazine. It is ranked one among the top 10 promising law colleges in India in 2018. It also offers one year LLM in Corporate and Commercial Laws and Tax Laws, Ph.D. fulltime and part time and Eight Certificate Courses in Law relating to cyber Law, Infrastructure, Financial Services, Immigration, Solid Waste Management, GST, International Trade and Forensic Science. The institution organized many international and national conference, seminar and events to bring out excellence in academic and co-curricular activities.

Mentoring system in ICFAI Law School

ICFAI Law School (ILS) implements mentoring process to help the students to strengthen their varied capabilities and to build an interpersonal relationship between the teachers (Mentors) and students (Mentees). Each mentors in the ILS is assigned with the task of mentoring 20 to 25 students. The students are divided into two groups on the basis of gender in each and every section consist of 50 to 60 students. ICFAI Law School is fostering 'peer mentoring'[14]. The process is conducted at two levels: group and personal. All the mentors conduct at least three group level interview of his group every semester. All mentors keep a confidential information in the register provided for that purpose. These reports are periodically evaluated by an academic coordinators or by the Head of ILS. Apart from the regular meetings, mentors meet their mentees and guide them with their studies and extra-curricular activities. They also provide advice relating to selection of electives, career guidance and personal problems. The mentors act as guides to the students during their summer and final projects.

The major functions of mentoring system at ILS:

(a) Mentors are assigned to monitor and guide students all through the five years.

(b) Mentors coordinate with the parents regarding the progress of the students.

(c) Mentors also keep track of the mentees' performance during the Legal Internship Program (LIP) offered during summer vacation for all the students. During LIP, the mentor's continuous interaction with the project guide designated to the student by the Law firms/ advocate/NGO.

(d) Mentors communicate with fellow faculty and promote mentees at the time of difficulty/opportunity to help them develop further in their areas of interest.

Apart from the above specified functions, the head of the institution also monitor the progress of the mentoring system and the students' progress in academic and non-academic activities by conducting review meetings. On the basis of the review meeting, administrative assistance, suggestions and advices has been provided to the concerned mentors from time to time to make the system more effective and beneficial to the students.

Effectiveness of mentoring system in ILS

The present study undertaken the empirical exercise on analyzing the effectiveness of formal mentoring system in ICFAI Law School in order to understand the benefits derived by the students from the mentoring process and also to identify the challenges faced by the mentors and mentees to strengthen the process. The attendance data were gathered from the system administrator and unstructured interviews were conducted among the mentors and mentees. Totally there were 23 peer mentor groups were existed in the ILS. The student's irregular to the classes is one of the major concern of the legal educational institutions in India. So the present study taken attendance as one of the major parameter to analyze the effectiveness of mentoring system in ILS. The Institution is maintaining 75 percentage minimum requirements (as in accordance with University Grants Commission rule and the regulation of Bar Council of India) for the students to appear in the final semester examinations. However, the institution allows the student's got 65 percentage, provided that they have genuine medical reasons. The institution also awarding marks for students maintaining above the minimum requirements (if the students maintains 76 percent to 80 percent one mark is awarded; 81 percent to 85 percent two marks; 86 percent to 90 percent three marks; 91 percent to 95 percent four marks and above 96 percent five marks were awarded). It motivates the students to attend the class room and to maintain the regularity. In spite of this initiative, students were unable to maintain regularity to the classes due to various reasons. In this context, the major responsibility assigned to the mentor to check the assigned mentees attendance progress on regular interval. In ILS, every fortnight, the attendance details of the mentees provided through email to the concerned mentors. The mentors will go through the attendance data and who ever fall shortage of attendance will be asked to meet the mentor and need to provide explanation for shortage of attendance. To verify the explanation provided by the mentee, the mentor will cross-check the information with the parents. This process consumes time for mentors, but student's regularity in attending class will be monitored and the student can able to achieve success at the time of completion of the course.

This is the process followed in the ILS to monitor the student's regularity in attending the classes under the mentorship program. To understand the effectiveness of mentorship system in ILS, the attendance information were gathered after one month completion of the session and at the end of the session. The purpose of analyzing this data is to analyze the effectiveness of mentors role in improving the ateendance. The semester-wise student's attendance at the beginning of the session (see table 2) were collected after completion of the one month.

Table 2. Semester-Wise student's attendance at the beginning of the session

Semester	*Attendance*					*Total*
	Less than 50 %	*51% to 65%*	*66% to 74%*	*&5 % to 90%*	*91% and above*	
I	7 (2.9%)	18 (7.4%)	34 (13.9%)	102 (41.8%)	83 (34%)	244 (100%)
III	4 (2.4%)	15 (9%)	27 (16.2%)	85 (50.9%)	36 (21.6%)	167 (100%)
V	1 (0.9%)	7 (6.3%)	26 (23.4%)	64 (57.7%)	13 (11.7%)	111 (100%)
VII	5 (5.9%)	15 (17.6%)	26 (30.6%)	35 (41.2%)	4 (4.7%)	85 (100%)
IX	3 (5.2%)	11 (19%)	14 (24.1%)	24 (41.4%)	6 (10.3%)	58 (100%)
Total	20 (3%)	66 (9.9%)	127 (19.1%)	310 (46.6%)	142 (21.4%)	665 (100%)

The data shows that at the beginning of the session 32 percentage of the students were below 75 percentage of attendance. The major reason gathered during personal interviews with mentors and mentees reveals that, late registration, family circumstances, late completion of internship programs and health issues. Further, the analysis shows that more than one-fifth of them (21.5 percent) attending classes very sincerely and nearly 50 percentage of them have normal attendance (75 percent to 90 percent).

The focus of the study is on the students gathered less than 75 percentage. It was analyzed in three categories, the student's attendance less than 50 percentage, between 51 percent and 65 percent, and between 66 percent and 74 percent. The chances for improvement of attendance by regular follow-up is feasible for the student's attendance in the range of 51 percentage to 74 percentage. The chances for less than 50 percentage is comparatively less, needs more intensive follow-up with the mentees and parents is required. The students in semester I, III and V their attendance were better (above 90 percent) when compare to the students in semester VII and IX. From this data (table 2), the mentors major task in the mentoring process has to improve the attendance of the 32 percentage of the students got less than 74 percentage attendance. In the process, the mentors should collect the list of students gathered less than 75 percentage, their phone numbers and their parent numbers. They have to ask explanation from the students at first stage (only for the student in the category of 66 percent to 74 percent of attendance), because they have bright chance to improve by mere warning. The next category (51 percent to 65 percent) needs rigorous follow-up of the students and also the parents because chances are there to improve his/her attendance. The last category needs counselling along with the parents with the Head of the Institution to know the reason for poor attendance. Sometimes genuine reasons will be there it needs to be recognized and given opportunity to partake in summer programme. The students to make-up his attendance, will partake in summer classes and exams will be conducted separately for this purpose. Hence, the students eventually acquire competence in their specific disciplinary area of research over the course of graduate program.

Table 3. Semester-Wise student's attendance at the end of the session

Semester	*Attendance*					*Total*
	Less than 50 %	*51% to 65%*	*66% to 74%*	*&5 % to 90%*	*91% and above*	
I	11 (4.5%)	6 (2.5%)	36 (14.8%)	134 (54.9%)	57 (23.4%)	244 (100%)
III	3 (1.8%)	6 (3.6%)	39 (23.4%)	96 (57.5%)	23 (13.8%)	167 (100%)
V	0 (0%)	7 (6.3%)	28 (25.2%)	72 (64.9%)	4 (3.6%)	111 (100%)
VII	0 (0%)	10 (11.8%)	24 (28.2%)	47 (55.3%)	4 (4.7%)	85 (100%)

(*Contd...*)

IX	1 (1.7%)	3 (5.2%)	10 (17.2%)	40 (69%)	4 (6.9%)	58 (100%)
Total	15 (2.3%)	32 (4.8%)	137 (20.6%)	389 (58.5%)	92 (13.8%)	665 (100%)

The data on the attendance of the students at the end of the session portrays that more than one fourth of them (27 percent) got less than 75 percentage of the attendance. However, the proportion of the students from 51 percent to 65 percent become half when compare with the attendance at the beginning of the session. The personal interview with mentees reveals that, mentors do continuous follow-up to improve our attendance and also they motivates us to participate in co-curricular and extra-curricular activities. In ILS, many co-curricular activities like, ICFAI Conference of Nations, intra and inter Moot court competitions, Lex-knot, etc., will conducted on annual basis and students will also be encouraged to participate in events conducted by other education institutions. Extra-curricular activities like sports meets, intra-cultural competitions, ethnic day, essay competition, etc., will be conducted semester-wise. The analysis also shows that the proportion of the students got above 75 percentage attendance (72.3 percent) was improved by the constant effort of the mentors. The attendance of the senior students (Semester VII and IX) was also improved better when compare to their attendance at the beginning of the session. The hard and sincere effort always gives it fruit in spite of lot of hurdles. Sometimes, parents also appreciate that mentorship program helps us to understand about their son/daughters performance in the institution.

Teacher and student relationship

The next major strength of the mentorship programme is to strengthen the teacher and student relationship. Most of the time the mentor will be the teacher who is not teaching any subject to them. The mentees, whenever they get free hours, they use to visit them and share their class room experience and personal problems. In the process, the students building good rapport with the teachers. On the other side, mentors also inform the important announcements/information's regarding academics/co-curricular/extracurricular activities to the students through their WhatsApp group and also through the registered email-Id. On the basis of the information shared by the mentor, students visit the mentor for further enquiry and clarification. This is the way the teacher and student interaction improves under the mentorship programme. Nevertheless, sometimes the mentees are not reporting to the mentors to provide explanation for their low attendance or for any other clarifications. In this case the mentors find it difficult to help the mentees and sometimes, the mentees are also not comfortable with mentors because they are not teaching them. Some other challenges also posed by mentors that sometimes they are unable to maintain the record in writing the call logs of their mentees and parents.

Summary and Conclusion

The empirical evidence clearly provides that, mentoring system benefits both the mentors and mentees in many ways, most particularly helps to maintain better teacher and student relationship. Further, analysis reveals that mentoring by college faculty has a positive impact on students' persistence and academic achievement in college (Crisp and Cruz 2009; Terenzini, Psacarella, and Blimling 1996) and helps prepare them to be successful in professional career (Schlosser, Knox, Moskovitz, and Hill 2003). Mentoring relationships frequently develop between mentors and mentees assigned to each other who discover the benefits of having a closer and ongoing relationship. (Schlosser and Gelso 2001). Mentees reported that mentoring helped them develop skills and behaviors necessary to succeed professionally. Most of the time students find it reluctant to meet the mentors to provide explanations for their low attendance. Because of it, the mentors find it difficult to improve the condition of the mentees.

To conclude, this paper discussed on formal mentoring programme for students pursuing legal education. The effort needed is small, as it is not difficult for committed faculty and student to find time for the interaction. Importantly, there are benefits for both mentors and mentees; also bonding and trust between teachers and students grow. Students with effective mentors as role models will imbibe their attributes and, in turn, be good mentors, and thus perpetuate the cycle. Depending on needs and cultural sensitivities, each institution should be encouraged to evolve its own mentoring programme. The problems faced by the mentors and mentees need to be sorted out at initial stage itself by conducting review meetings. In this was the teacher and student relationship will be strengthened in higher education.

References

1. Amaury Nora and Gloria Crisp, (2008), Mentoring Students: Conceptualizing and Validating the Multi-Dimensions of a Support System, *Journal of College Student Retention*, 9(3) 337-356.
2. Blackwell, J. E. (1989). Mentoring: An action strategy for increasing minority faculty. *Academe*, 75(5), 8-14.

3. Brown, M. C, Davis, G. L., & McClendon, S. A. (1999). Mentoring graduate students of color: Myths, models, and modes. *Peabody Journal of Education*, 74(2), 105-118.

4. Chhaya Saraf , Afreen Begum H Itagi, Shubhada Gade , Dimple Arora , Nitin Gosewade and Baishali Deb, (2017), Role of mentoring in improving academic performance among low achievers in a medical college of Chhattisgarh, India. Journal of Education Technology in Health Sciences, September-December, 4(3):107-111.

5. Cole, D., & Espinoza, A. (2008). Examining the academic success of Latino students in science technology engineering and mathematics (STEM) majors. *Journal of College Student Development*, 49(4), 285–300.

6. Collings, R., Swanson, V., & Watkins, R. (2014). The impact of peer mentoring on levels of student wellbeing, integration and retention: A controlled comparative evaluation of residential students in UK higher education. *Higher Education*, 68: 927–942.

7. Crisp, G and Young, Kelly Alvarado. (2018) The Role of Mentoring in Leadership Development, *New Directions for Student Leadership*, 158: 37-47.

8. Crisp, G., and Cruz, I. (2009). Mentoring college students: A critical review of the literature between 1990 and 2007. *Research in Higher Education*, **50**(6), 525–545.

9. Darwin, A. (2000). Critical reflections on mentoring in work settings. *Adult Education Quarterly*, 50(3), 197-211.

10. Dickey, C. (1996). Mentoring women of color at the University of Minnesota: Challenges for organizational transformation. Minneapolis: University of Minnesota. (ERIC Document Reproduction Service No. ED399838).

11. Hansman, C. A. (2003). Power and learning in mentoring relationships. In R. Cervero, B. Courtenay, & M. Hixson (Eds.), Global perspectives: Volume III (pp. 102-122). Athens, GA: University of Georgia.

12. Hurtado, S., and Carter, D. F. (1997), Effects of college transition and perceptions of the campus racial climate on Latino college student's sense of belonging. *Sociology of Education*, 70, 324-435.

13. Jacobi, M. (1991). Mentoring and undergraduate academic success: A literature review. *Review of Educational Research*, **61**(4), 505–532.

14. Johnson, W. B. (2007). Student-faculty mentorship outcomes. In T. D. Allen & L. T. Eby (Eds.), The Blackwell handbook of mentoring: A multiple perspectives approach (pp. 189-210). Malden, : Blackwell Publishing.

15. Khazanov, L. (2011). Mentoring atrisk students in a remedial mathematics course. *Mathematics and Computer Education*, 106–118.

16. Komarraju M., Musulkin S., and Bhattacharya G. (2010), Role of student-faculty interactions in developing college students' academic self-concept, motivation, and achievement, *Journal of College Student Development* ,332–342.

17. Kram, K. E. (1988). Mentoring at work: Developmental relationships in organizational life. Lanham, MD, England: University Press of America.

18. Kukreja S, Chhabra N, Kaur A, Arora R, and Singh T. (2017), Introducing mentoring to 1st-year medical students of a private medical college in North

India: A pilot study. *International journal of Applied and Basic Medical Research*, 7(5), pages. 67-71.

19. Meinel FG, Dimitriadis K, von der Borch P, Stormann S, Niedermaier S, and Fischer MR, (2011), More mentoring needed? A cross-sectional study of mentoring programs for medical students in Germany. *BMC Medical Education*, 24(11):68.
20. Merriam, S. (1983). Mentors and proteges: A critical review of the literature. *Adult Education Quarterly*, 33(3), 161-173.
21. Michael, A. E., Dickson, J., Ryan, B., & Koefer, A. (2010). College prep blueprint for bridging and scaffolding incoming freshmen: Practices that work. *College Student Journal*, 44(4), 969–978.
22. Miller, A. (2002). Mentoring students & young people: A handbook of effective practice. London: Kogan Page.
23. Murray, M. (2001). Beyond the myths and magic of mentoring. San Francisco: Jossey Bass.
24. Palmer, R., & Gasman, M. (2008). "It takes a village to raise a child": The role of social capital in promoting academic success for African American men at a Black college. *Journal of College Student Development*, 49(1), 52–70.

Chapter-44

Finances in Higher Education in India-An Introspection

Bibhudendu Das,

Abstract

The Recent Trend in Higher Education with the objectives to bring changes and reformation have attracted the policy markers, higher education regulatory authorities, Universities, Educationist, Colleges, Researchers, students and even parents as well. This trend has reflected the objectives and employability of the present system of higher education, when we are endeavouring to move from the existing higher education system to next generation and global education system. In fact, we have to create advanced educational institutions for skill, oriented, student centric and employability education to speed up the nation building process. Beside many issues and challenges relating to syllabus modification, infrastructure development, training of teachers community, objective research in the higher education, a balanced study skill with values, we are facing the financial issues in the Higher Education system. In this paper we are finding the alternatives and feasibility of funding the higher education for the management of the institution and the sponsoring the students expenses for the pursuing the degree.

Introduction

The statistics of India's higher education system shows that India is World's the third largest in terms of students, next to China and the United States. India provides approximately 11 per cent of its youth in higher education as compared to 20 per cent in China. The higher education institutions are categorized into three categories such as

1. Technical such as Polytechnics.
2. Post Graduate Diploma in Management recognized by AICTE.
3. Teacher Training such as District Institute of Education and Training recognized by National Council for Teacher Education.

4. Nursing Institutes recognized by Indian Nursing Council/State Nursing Council and

5. Institutes directly under the control of various Central Ministries.

Comprehensively it is Universities, College and Stand-Alone Institutions. All India survey on higher education for the year 2017-18 by the Government of India , Human Resources Development Ministry shows that there are 903 Universities, 39050 Colleges and 10011 Stand Alone Institutionslisted on AISHE web portaland out of them 882 Universities, 38061 Colleges and 9090 Stand Alone Institutions have responded during the survey. 285 Universities are affiliating i.e. having Colleges. 343 Universities are privately managed. 357 Universities are located in rural area. 15 Universities are exclusively for women, 4 in Rajasthan, 2 in Tamil Nadu & 1 each in Andhra Pradesh, Assam, Delhi, Haryana, Karnataka, Maharashtra, Odisha, Uttarakhand and West Bengal. In addition to 1 Central Open University, 14 State Open Universities and 1State Private Open University, there are 110 Dual mode Universities, which offer education through distance mode also and the maximum (16) of them are located in Tamil Nadu. There are 500 General, 126 Technical, 70 Agriculture & Allied, 58 Medical, 22 Law, 13Sanskrit and 10 Language Universities and rest 83 Universities are of other Categories. The top 8 States in terms of highest number of colleges in India are Uttar Pradesh, Maharashtra, Karnataka, Rajasthan, Andhra Pradesh, Tamil Nadu, Gujarat and Madhya Pradesh. Bangalore Urban district tops in terms of number of colleges with 893 colleges followed by Jaipur with 558 colleges. Top 50 districts have about 32.6 percent of colleges. College density, i.e. the number of colleges per lakh eligible population (population in the age-group 18-23 years) varies from 7 in Bihar to 51 in Karnataka and Telangana as compared to All India average of 28. 60.48 percent Colleges are located in Rural Area. 11.04 percent Colleges are exclusively for Women. Only 3.6 percent Colleges run Ph.D. programme and 36.7 percent Colleges run Post Graduate Level programmes. There are 33.75 percent Colleges, which run only single programme, out of which 83 percent are privately managed. Among these privately managed colleges, 55.1 percent colleges run B.Ed. Courses only. 78 percent Colleges are privately managed; 64.7 percent Private-unaided and 13.3 percent Private-aided.Andhra Pradesh & Telangana have about 82 percent Private-unaided colleges and Tamil Nadu has 76.2 percent Privateunaided colleges, whereas, Assam has 12.0 percent and Chandigarh has only 8.0 percent Private-unaided colleges.

Highest share of foreign students come from the neigh bouring countries of which Nepal is 24.9 percent of the total, followed by, Afghanistan (9.5

percent), Sudan (4.8 percent), Bhutan constitutes (4.3 percent) and Nigeria (4.0 percent). There are more than 78.0 percent colleges running in Private sector; aided and unaided taken together, but it caters to only 67.3 percent of the total enrolment. The total number of teachers are12,84,755, out of which about 58.0 percent are male teachers and 42.0 percent are female teachers. At all-India level there are merely 72 female teachers per 100 male teachers. Pupil Teacher Ratio (PTR) in Universities and Colleges is 30 if regular mode enrolment is considered whereas PTR for Universities and its Constituent Units is 20 for regular mode. Among non-teaching staff, the share of Group-C is the highest with 40 percent, followed by Group-D with 28 percent. Group-A and Group-B comprise of 15 percent and 17 percent non-teaching posts, respectively. The average number of females per 100 male non-teaching staff is 47. 34,400 students were awarded Ph.D. level degree during 2017 with 20,179 males and 14,221 females. B.A. (23.89 Lakh)degree has been awarded to maximum number of students. B.Sc. (11.52 Lakh)is the second highest followed by B.Com. (9.39 Lakh). At Post Graduate level M.A. pass number of students is maximum followed by M.Sc. and M.B.A The highest number of students (23.89 lakh)have graduated in Arts courses. At Ph.D. level, maximum numbers of students out-turn is in Science stream followed by Engineering and Technology. On the other hand at PG level maximum students out-turn is observed in Social Science and Management stream comes at number two. The share of Ph.D. student is highest in State Public University (31.6 percent) followed by Institute of National Importance (20.4 percent), Central University (15.8 percent) and Deemed University-Private (13.4 percent). Share of female students is lowest in Institutions of National Importance followed by State Private Open Universities, Deemed University-Government.

Policy Issues in Financing of Higher Education

The 1968 Education Policy and thereafter emphasis on

a. Radical restructuring of educational system.
b. Expansion of education facilities all over India.
c. Common structure of Education
d. Restructuring the existing courses by modifying the syllabus
e. Promotion of Post-graduation degree and research.
f. Reduction in disparities between rural and urban education facilities.

Expenditure in Higher Education-Sources

Expenditure for the financial year 2016-17 indicates that the education departments of the States/UTs and the Centre for various sub-sectors of Education. Departments other than the Department of Education also incur some expenditure on education and an effort has been made to include the budget estimates of their expenditure on education in order to get the complete picture of public expenditure on education in the country. The expenditure of other departments also includes the expenditure on training and research and development activities. The total amount of budget provisions on the revenue account made for education for the year 2016-17 by education departments for the States/UTs and the Centre works out to ₹ 462398.26 crore (₹ 390004.26 crore in State Sector and ₹ 72394.00 crore in the Central sector) which is 14.79 percent more than the revised estimates of ₹ 402811.71 crore for 2015-16. This amount constitutes 11.50 percent of the total budget provisions made on the revenue account in the States and at the Centre. Apart from the revenue account, the Education Departments of States/UTs also make some provisions for capital works. The total budget estimates on the capital accounts (including loans) accounted for ₹ 14376.64 crore. Taking into account both the revenue as well as the capital account, the total budget estimates for education for 2016-17 of the State Education Departments and the Education Departments of the Centre works out to ₹ 476774.90 crore, (which is 10.01 percent of the total budget estimates. The total budget provisions (Revenue Account) for 2016-17 made by the departments other than Education works out to ₹ 205996.87 crore.

Economic Reforms in Higher Education

Government is considering a proposal for the setting up of National Commission/Council for Higher Education and Research for prescribing standards of academic quality and defining policies for advancement of knowledge in higher educational institutions based on the principle of enhancing autonomy of universities and institutions of higher learning and research. The National Accreditation Regulatory Authority for Higher Educational Institutions Bill, 2010 recently introduced in the Parliament, proposes to make accreditation mandatory for all higher educational institutes. Prohibition of unfair practices in Technical Educational Institutions, Medical Educational Institutions and University Bill 2010 recently introduced in the Parliament, aims to curb malpractices in higher education. The Educational Tribunals Bill, 2010 recently introduced in the Parliament, provides for a two tier system of tribunals to deal with disputes between students, teachers and institutions. The Foreign Educational Institutions (Regulation of Entry and Operations) Bill, 2010 recently introduced in the Parliament, provides a time bound and transparent system for the approval process as also for regulation of Foreign Educational Institutions.

1. Transition to Higher Education
2. Establishment of New Central Higher Education
3. Improvement of Access to Higher Education institutions.
4. New Central Universities and Colleges.
5. Indian Institute of Managements.
6. Indian Institute of Technology,
7. Other Higher Educational Institutions.

Regulatory Needs to Ensure Proper Finances

The National Policy on Education (NPE, 1986) and the Programme of Action (PoA, 1992) that spelt out strategic plans for the policies, advocated the establishment of an independent National accreditation agency. Consequently, the NATIONAL ASSESSMENT AND ACCREDITATION COUNCIL (NAAC) was established in 1994 as an autonomous institution of the University Grants Commission (UGC). The mandate of NAAC as reflected in its vision statement is in making quality assurance an integral part of the functioning of Higher Education Institutions (HEIs). The NAAC functions through its General Council (GC) and Executive Committee (EC) where educational administrators, policy makers and senior academicians from a cross-section of Indian higher education system are represented. The Chairperson of the UGC is the President of the GC of the NAAC, the Chairperson of the EC is an eminent academician nominated by the President of GC (NAAC). The Director is the academic and administrative head of NAAC, and is the member-secretary of both the GC and the EC. In addition to the statutory bodies that steer its policies and core staff to support its activities, NAAC is advised by the advisory and consultative committees constituted from time to time.

Suggestion for Finances Higher Education

1. Promotion Public-Private Partnership Higher Educational Institutions.
2. Increase budgetary provision for higher Education.
3. Flexibility in providing students education loans for higher education.
4. Establishment of more number of National Institutions.
5. Collaboration of Corporate and Higher Education Institutions.

References

1. Azad, J.L. (1976) "Financing Institutions of Higher Education In India ; the need for realistic Policy. 1-7.
2. Azad, J. L. (1988). Higher Education in India: The Deepening Financial Crisis. New Delhi: Radiant. Bhagwati, J. (1973). 'Education, class structure and income equality', World Development 1 (5), 21-36.
3. Birdsall, W. (1988). 'Public spending on higher education in developing countries: too much or too little?', Washington D.C.: World Bank New York: Rockfeller Foundation (Draft), August 23.
4. Blaug, M. (1982). 'The distributional effects of higher education subsidies', Economics of Education Review 2 (3) 209-231.
5. Blaug, M., Layard, P. R. G. and Woodhall, M. (1969).
6. The Causes of Graduate Unemployment in India. London: Allen Lane the Penguin. Debi, Sailabala (1988).
7. Economics of Higher Education. Meerut: Anu Books. Education Commission (1966). Education and Development: Report of the Education Commission 1964-66. New Delhi: Government of India [reprint 1971].
8. www.mhrd.gov.in

Chapter-45

Role of Higher Education and Employability in India - Challenges and Solutions

Cyril T,

Abstract

Indian education is the third largest in the world, having 700 universities-national, state, deemed universities, autonomous colleges also 35,000 affiliated colleges. It serves 20 million students of the country. In spite of so much focus into the education of India, the nation is still striving to provide skilled employees. Higher education fails to prepare youngsters to become industry ready professionals. There has always been industry-academia gap with problems like outdated academic syllabus, language skills, insufficient practical sessions and absence of career counseling facilities are stopping the students to embrace the professional skills. A student to be employable must possess academic knowledge along with various soft skills. Since Indian education has not transformed from traditional to modern approach, students remain unskilled. There are few questions which need to be answered. Why are we lacking to blend academic-skills-industry in higher education syllabus? What employability skills include? What does an employer look for in new joiners'? This research will try to answer the above questions along with the objectives of higher education, problems in curriculum, skill sets lacking in our students, professional expectations of employers and at the end of this paper; suggestions would be given as how curriculum in higher education can be improved.

Keywords: *Higher education & employment, curriculum & employment, curriculum in India, higher education challenges.*

Introduction

Developing a nation depends on quality human resource and this can be created only with a good education. Right education contributes to making a good citizen; education means gaining knowledge, values & life skills.

The early Gurukul system diminished due to assaults & invasions this country experienced. The entry of Britishers also brought formal education system, post-independence India focused on giving education to all & maximising higher education as it understood the importance of providing professions like doctors, lawyers, engineers, scientists & good labour force. India is a developing country trying to match the developed, adapting to the growth of technology and advancement. Education becomes of vital importance to enhance this phase of the nation. Indian higher education is complex due to its dense population and diversity. It has had different requirements and crossed various phases - from the expansion of higher education to other phases such as improving curriculum, content, evaluation, governance & privatization of higher education. There has been a lot of initiatives taken by the government in forming teams & committees to regulate & recommend suggestions for improving higher education. Full employment is the goal of any nation for its economic & social development. Independent decision making & standard of living increases. Thus employment makes not just the individual happy but helps the nation to be happy and prosperous.

Today's higher education focuses on providing smart labour force and trying to give more importance to research and development. Even though India is seeing corporate investment, technology growth, IT requirements, there is a demand-supply gap. According to a study by NASSCOM (National Association of Software and Services Companies), only a few hundreds of millions coming out of universities/colleges/institutions are capable of becoming employees and this is due to lack of various skill sets.

"Presently, the challenge rests with the demand-supply gap. Despite numerous corporate initiatives, the availability of readymade talent is still an issue in the IT sector. To make students deliver, a lot of time and investment is done" (Saurabhgovil, 2013).

National Skill Development Corporation (NSDC) has observed that the Indian population is capable of the provided labour force for the world by 2020. But the industry claims that the graduates from Indian higher education have low-quality professional skills. The graduates passed out every year are not industry ready. As the industry does not get quality students to work, they take a lot of efforts in training the freshers with various skills to make him or her ready for work (Krishna, 2017).

National Skill Development Corporation (NSDC), first of its kind out in the open private association. It propels broad TVET programs (Technical and Vocational Education and Training for Youth). It attempts first-rate designs of activity for Technical and Vocational Education and Training for youth. At this moment, put ₹87.00 crore in 32 private for skilling 40 million youth (Krishna, 2017).

1.1 Research Problem

"Today, the youth invest time & money to get educated and hold qualification but lack skills in their job".

"Surveys have shown that 30 percent of our graduates are unemployable and the issue has to be addressed in far footing" (Narendra jadav, 2014). On an average, an Indian spend 18 years into education to complete his or her graduation and then get a job realising they need to now begin to learn work, develop their professional skills along with soft skills. This leads the educators to seriously think of the flaws in the education system and work towards improving them.

1.2 Research Questions

- Why are placements for graduating students a challenge?
- What are the factors contributing to this negative situation?

1.3 Research Objectives

- To explore the objectives of higher education in India
- To identify reasons for unemployability after graduation
- To explore the expectations of the industry

1.4 Limitations of the Study

- The existing reviews on higher education curricula & syllabi are considered and no primary data was collected.
- This research was carried out with time constraint.

1.5 Operational Definitions

1.5.1 According to Aristotle, "Education is the process of training man to fulfil his aim by exercising all the faculties to the fullest extent as a member of society".

1.5.2 Higher education comprises all post-secondary education, training and research guidance at educational institutions such as universities that are authorized as institutions of higher education by state authorities.

1.5.3 Employability refers to a person's capability of gaining initial employment maintaining employment, and obtaining new employment if required (Hillage and Pollard, 1998).

Methodology

This research uses content analyses of secondary data under qualitative research. It analyses available data through search and desk analysis of work already done on the related areas of this study. The researcher uses the literature available on the reports given by the government, non-government bodies, existing research in this field.

1.6 Content Analysis

Higher Education and Employability Skills - By Kalpathy Ramaiyer Subramanian, January 2017

This research journal article discusses the expectations of the employers and skills required to sustain employment after higher education. The paper holds strong on the importance of various soft skills required to get employed and sustain employment. The various skill sets are - Positive attitude and behaviour which includes being positive, motivated, flexible, confident about yourself, team player with honesty, integrity and personal ethics. Being innovative and resourceful by suggesting alternative ways of doing things to achieve goals. One's attitude to continuously learn, grow, give constructive feedbacks and open to take up new challenges. It is important to be well-organised meaning to be punctual, follow guidelines and norms of the company and be dependable. The employer must see difficulty without your presence to analyse facts, assumptions and giving practical solutions. Having initiative and enterprise skills, gaining knowledge and being a visionary, developing strategies, goals, ideas and effectively executing them. Learning skills becomes important where one learn to manage his or her own learning, sharing knowledge and experience at workplace with colleagues and juniors, also gaining self-management skills where one has personal vision and goals, evaluating and monitoring own performance, knowledge and confidence in own ideas and vision, taking responsibility and executing them with dedication, working ethically and working under pressure.

The paper discusses all these soft skills which are needed in an employee and this shows that every stage of life and education becomes crucial for an individual to become a responsible human being, citizen and employee.

1.7 Higher Education and Employability: Review - By Sarang Bhola and Sunil S. Dhanawade

Today it is not about the degree subjects a student studies in his higher education but his ability to understand and handle complex pieces of information, situations, think of creative solutions and to communicate effectively. Colleges see these skills as something after graduation but it becomes very difficult for students to develop these skills later as it takes time and practice.

Employers look for self-starters who can be motivated and initiate new things at work & leaders who can motivate co-workers. No longer academic qualification is sufficient to secure employment and this needs to be looked into with sincere efforts.

The National Association of College and Employers (NACE) has compiled a list of the top 20 skills requested by employers (2007). These skills in rank order are as follows

Rank	Skills	Rank	Skills
1	Analytical Skills	11	Leadership and Management Skills
2	Communication Skills	12	Motivation/ Initiative
3	Computer Skills	13	Organizational and Time Management
4	Creativity	14	Real Life Experiences
5	Detail-Oriented	15	Self-Confidence
6	Risk-Taker	16	Strong Work Ethics
7	Flexibility/ Adaptability	17	Tactfulness
8	Friendly	18	Teamwork Skills
9	Honesty/ Integrity	19	Technical Skills
10	Interpersonal Skills	20	Well-Mannered/ Polite

Source NACE 2007)

"Many feel that there is a skill gap between the manner in which students are prepared for the real world in a university setting and what they will need to be successful in the workplace and for life in general" (Shivpuri and Kim 2004). The faculty-student ratio should be close to 1:10, frequent revision of syllabus in consultation with the industry and institutions should create the students to become professionals with a global mindset so that they can adjust in different cultural & social settings as today at workplace people meet talents from around the nation and globe (Hannan 2003).

India post-independence has given a lot more importance to structure the higher education system. It has had different requirements and crossed various phases - from the expansion of higher education to other phases such as improving curriculum, content, evaluation, governance & privatization of higher education.

There has been a lot of initiatives taken by the government in forming teams & committees to regulate & recommend suggestions for improving higher education. Full employment is the goal of any nation for its economic

& social development. Decision making become independent & standard of living increases.

Conclusion

Indian education is heavily examination oriented, system sincerely follows a syllabus which emphasize more on subject knowledge and lacks to include and continuously practice skills in its subjects where skills play prominent role in getting employed and sustaining employment. When practicing skills fail to blend in higher education, graduates being unfit for employment. Skills cannot be learnt in a short span and hence it requires to be brought into undergraduate or postgraduate programs strategically from the beginning and it should continue until the completion of the program. This can be achieved only if policymakers, universities, employers and students come together to plan the future.

References

1. Subramanian, Kalpathy. (2017). Higher Education And Employability Skills. International Journal Of Combined Research & Development. Eissn:2321-225x;Pissn:2321-2241. Issue 1.
2. Bhola, Sarang & Dhanawade, Sunil. (2013). Higher Education And Employability - A Review. Ssrn Electronic Journal. 10.2139/Ssrn.2290103.
3. Higher Education In India: Issues, Concerns And New Directions(Publication). (2003). New Delhi, Delhi: University Grants Commission.
4. Krishna, H. G. (2018). A Study Of Employability Determinants In Pre And Post Employment Scenario With Reference To Kancheepuram District Tamilnadu State(Unpublished Master's Thesis). Chennai/Amet University. Retrieved January 16, 2019, Fromhttp://Hdl.Handle.Net/10603/198119.

Web References

5. Https://Www.Theguardian.Com/Higher-Education-Network/Blog/2013/Jan/22/Student-Development-University-Curriculum-Design.
6. Https://Www.Ijireeice.Com/Upload/2015/December-15/Ijireeice percent2031.Pdf.
7. Http://Www.Ppcrc.In/Blog/History-Of-Higher-Education-System-In-India-And-Present-State/.

Chapter-46

Role of Private Sector in Higher Education

Dr. N. Gopal,

Abstract

There are three levels of education; elementary, secondary and higher. The first two are imparted at the school level, whereas higher education is imparted at the college and university level. There may be two types of providers of education: public and private. Private institutions may be partly funded by the government (aided) or entirely self-funded (unaided). Public institutions are established, funded and managed by the government. Private providers of education often step in when the government has limited resources to provide universal access to education. In most markets, the private sector is characterised by a profit-motive. However, when it comes to education, the private sector is required to operate on a not for profit basis. Some experts are of the view that certain private providers of education dilute the quality of education due to a lack of regulatory oversight and restrict access due to charging high fees from students. On the other hand, some consider private involvement to be necessary to enhance investment and quality, as a result of increased competition, in higher education. The Standing Committee on Human Resource Development is currently examining the subject ,,Role of Private Sector in Higher Education. In this context, we present an analysis of the role of the private sector in providing higher education in India. This note maps out the regulatory framework and highlights key issues with regard to private higher education. Regulatory framework Constitutional provisions Education falls under the Concurrent List of the Constitution. This means that both the centre and states can enact laws related to education. In addition, the mandate of determining standards of higher education and research lies with the centre, as this falls under the Union List. Further, states have powers to incorporate, regulate and wind up universities as a subject under the State List. At the centre, the Ministry of Human Resource Development (MHRD) formulates policies, and implements laws and schemes related to education in the country. Under the Ministry, the Department of Higher Education is responsible for the higher education sector. At the state government level,

Departments of Education carry out similar functions. Institutions offering specialized professional disciplines in sectors such as health, agriculture, etc., are regulated by their respective ministries.

Introduction

India has four distinct types of higher education institutions: public universities, which are established by the central government through acts of the parliament; state universities, which are established by state legislation; private or "self-financed" universities, which are called "deemed-to-be-universities" and are governed by section three of the University Grants Commission (UGC) Act; and private universities in states, established through the Private University Act. The commonly called private universities do not receive any funding for development from the Indian Government. They subsist on the revenues that they gather from tuition fees. In India, the students, who are the most important stake holders and beneficiaries of the higher education system, clearly prefer private universities to public. This is mainly because the private universities offer more with respect to enhancement of the employability aspect of the student's repertoire. Moreover, private universities generally offer choices in programs that are career oriented such as engineering, management, and architecture, compared with public universities, which mainly focus on "general education" programs in humanities and social sciences.

The advancement of private higher education in India has been driven by a very compelling demand in the higher education demographic, and not public policy. The last decade has witnessed phenomenal growth of the private sector: In the year 2002, India had nearly 4400 professional colleges of which about 3150—upwards of 70 per cent—were in the private sector (Powar & Bhalla, 2005, as cited in Powar, 2012). This growth has continued unabated: In the year 2012, the total number of diploma granting institutions stood at 12,748, of which 9,541 were in the private sector. More importantly, the private sector has recorded growth at the broadest level: in the year 2012, as many as 64 percent of higher education institutions were in the private sector. This growth was reflected in other parameters as well—59 percent of student enrolment in higher education was in the private sector.

Notwithstanding the above, the Indian Government reserves its most stringent regulatory measures for the private institutions. Even more bizarre is the case that public universities, which receive government funding to the tune of millions of rupees, are allowed to operate with only minimal regulations. In an ironic twist, public intuitions, which do not enrol students to full capacity, are left off the hook, whereas private universities, which are highly selective in their student intake in spite of higher tuition, are burdened with inordinately heavy regulatory mechanisms. The recent nation-wide debates and protests over the University Grants Commission's stand on four-year undergraduate courses is a case in point. The fact of the Commission's attack on some such programs, without a modicum of investigation into the structure and components of the programs and the manner in which it was carried out, with shocking disregard for the students and institutions can only be considered worrying. Also curious is the case that the regulatory agencies come down the hardest on institutions that enjoy solid reputations for quality and integrity: the IITs, IISc, Symbiosis International University, and the Shiv Nadar University. Indeed, it is because these institutions have enjoyed greater autonomy that they tower over the legion of low-achieving state universities, which are the way they are partly because they enjoy far less institutional self-governance. One wonders what conceivable purpose is served by the government agencies' harmful interference, other than, of course, providing the bureaucrats an opportunity to make a show of being engaged with the higher education system.

Carl Lewis' thought comes to mind: "The task of the modern educator is not to cut down jungles, but to irrigate deserts." 2. Increasing role of private participants in the wake of "massification" Much like the rest of the world, the emergence of private contributors to higher education in India is an all-tooprominent phenomenon. Private institutions make the largest and the fastest growing segment (EY-FICCI, 2012). The chief lever of this trend is "massification"—the shift in access to higher education from "elite" to "masses," denoting a shift in both the extent and nature of demand for higher education. The other accounting factors also run common across India and other countries. First, state expenditure in higher education has borne the axe; meager public investments in higher education invariably presage undesirable outcomes. India's public expenditure on higher education as percentage of gross domestic product (GDP) is a low 0.6 percent. For this reason alone, it is important to open the system to competition from non-governmental sector and allow enough transparency that the "best man wins".

This will also facilitate surplus capital to be invested back into the sector, and draw in enterprise and talent. Second, the co-relation between higher education and employment has consolidated—a development to which private institutions has responded in a more timely fashion. Indeed, it is the dynamism of the Indian private sector that has allowed it to spawn and capture forte segments in higher education, even in the face of "over-regulatory" government fiats and missing policy direction. This is in stark contrast to the scenario in neighbouring countries to the south east, especially

Singapore, Malaysia, and Thailand. Third, the private sector, all across the world, has risen to the challenge of quality assurance. Of the top ten US universities in the QS World University Rankings® 2013-14, all are private institutions. In India, deemed universities, the vast majority of which are in the private sector, received higher grades by NAAC, an assessment and accrediting agency, than public universities (Powar, 2012). Fourth, internationalization, the new sine qua non of higher education, is also propelled forward by private universities in India.

Cross border higher education, the most prominent expression of internationalization, has made its biggest impression on the private sector. In fact, the increase in inbound mobility of international students is to be credited, at least partially, to the emergence of private participants. The specific expression of internationalization in India, as in much of South Asia and the Gulf region has been in the form of privately owned and managed international branch campuses. In a research study of Indian branch campuses in popular source countries, the OBHE (2006) noted that the vast majority of them were private institutions (Agarwal, n.d.a). 3. The "licence raj" of the regulatory structure The Indian Government's position on private participants is out of step with reality. An apt description is the proverbial "licence raj"—a system encumbered with excessively centralized regulations. The federal structure of the system, especially in the wake of the Forty-second Amendment to the Constitution" (1976) renders the system susceptible to political vagaries, even mishandling.

The UGC regulations, often punitive in nature, work to clamp down on private institutions' autonomy and self-determination. It is not enough that "checks and balances" are in place to hold existing institutions answerable; a responsible system must also provide resources to institutions so that they may be encouraged to continually enhance the deliverable. In the case of private institutions, this argument holds even better as these institutions do not receive any funding from the government, but are subject to more regulatory directives. The Ministry of Human Resource and Development's approach to higher education policy is largely governed by a rubric that derives from NPE (1986) and PoA (1992). Both documents have social-democratic reinforcement to them. As comprehensive as the two reports are, one might well ask how effectively they take in hand mounting gaps in higher education that result from India's growing participation in globalization.

This presents a significant obstacle to ushering in global advances in pedagogy and education, such as vocalization, specialization, advances in instructional technology, and research and development. None of these reforms would be possible until the policy makers decide to remodel a rulebook that was drafted over twenty-five years ago (in fact, the original version of NPE was drafted in 1968). Further, the UGC and the AICTE wield enormous power to "coordinate and determine standards" in higher education. This power is customarily translated to imply methodization, as in forging homogeny and symmetry by drawing up a centralized schema. Thus, the government assumes a paternalistic and directorial stance, leading to the locus classicus "over-regulation and under-governance". The "over regulation" is, in point of fact, fault-ridden at many levels: the enacted edicts are drafted with the intent to schematize not just the bigger pieces of the puzzle, but the "nuts and bolts" as well.

Consequently, the regulatory plan that oversees higher education goes into the brass tacks of curriculum, examination, evaluation, teacher – student ratio and such. Add to this cases that the regulators are sundry, the bureaucracy heavy-going, and academia divorced from policy makers. It is no surprise then that this positioning renders policy makers distrustful of initiatives that are dynamic and self-motivated, such as those undertaken by the private sector. The system indeed necessitates approaches that are diverse enough to target the large variety of demands and needs in the higher education demographic.

Conclusion

Whilst the structure of checks and balances is rigorous enough, the concern about how effective it is in achieving the end goal of enhancing the overall quality of education persists. The emergence of newer providers of higher education has rendered the quality control aspect of higher education more ineffectual than before. The present higher education scenario is marked by an upsurge in information and knowledge. This casts a welcome quandary to educators: While it is difficult to stay abreast with the ever growing expansion of specializations, inter-disciplinary and multi-disciplinary streams, delivery modes etc., herein lie latent opportunities for all stakeholders. In view of the consideration that private sector is no longer an outlying phenomenon but one that is securely grounded in the mainstream, it falls to the policy makers to sketch out policy that will shepherd the private higher education such that as it moves forward, it also addresses the systemic challenges of access, equity, and quality.

References

1. Adams, J., Pendlebury, D., & Stembridge, B. (2013). Building bricks exploring the global research and innovation impact ofnBrazil, Russia, India, China and South Korea. Thomson Reuters.

2. Agarwal, P. (2009). Indian higher education: envisioning the future. Thousand Oaks, US: Sage Publications.
3. Agarwal, P. (n.d.a). International India a turning point in educational exchange with the US. Retrieved January 13, 2013 from ttp://www.usief.org.in/USIHEC/Chapter percent204/Internationalization percent20of percent20Indian percent20Higher percent20Education.pdf
4. Agarwal, P. (n.d.b). Privatization and internationalization of higher education in the countries of South Asia: An empirical analysis. New Delhi, India: Indian Council for Research on International Economic Relations (ICRIER)
5. Altbach, P. (1999). Private Prometheus: Private higher education and development in the 21st century. Westport, US: Greenwood Press.
6. Altbach, P. (2009). One-third of the globe: The future of higher education in China and India. Prospects, 39
7. EY-FICCI (2009). Making Indian higher education ready. Retrieved January 17, 2012 from http://education.usibc.com/wpcontent/uploads/2010/09/EY-FICCI-report09-Making-Indian-Higher-Education-Future-Ready.pdf
8. EY-FICCI (2012). Higher education in India: Twelfth Five Year Plan (2012-2017) and beyond. Kolkata, India: Ernst & Young Pvt. Ltd.
9. Gupta, D. & Gupta, N. (2012). Higher education in India: Structure, statistics and challenges. Journal of Education and Practice. 3(2)
10. Powar, K.B. (2002). Indian higher education: A conglomerate of concepts, facts and practices. New Delhi, India: Concept Publishing Company
11. Powar, K.B. (2003). Internationalisation of higher education focus on India. New Delhi: Amity University Press
12. Powar, K. B. (2012). Expanding domains in Indian higher education. New Delhi, India: Association of Indian Universities Publications. pwc. (n.d.). India - Higher Education Sector Opportunities for Private Participation. Retrieved from
13. https://www.pwc.in/en_IN/in/assets/pdfs/industries/education-services.pdf UGC. (n.d.). Total no. of universities in the country as on 14.08.2014. Retrieved from http://www.ugc.ac.in/oldpdf/alluniversity.pdf
14. UNESCO. (n.d.). International student flow. Retrieved from http://www. uis. unesco.org/Education/Pages/international-studentflow-viz.aspx.

Chpater-47

A Study on Reformsin Education System in India

Ch.V. S Varma,
Y. Srinivasa Rao,

Abstract

It is unambiguous that Policy of the Government of India currently supports growth of assets for covering a bigger bit of expense of advanced education. Late strategy changes in India regularly support to redirect assets from higher to essential dimension of instruction and favors for full cost recuperation from understudies even out in the open advanced education establishments. Cost recuperation measures including increment in expenses, understudy advances at present worked by business banks and privatization will compound disparity in the general public. To be sure, there is by all accounts a nexus between the present understudy advance plan and full cost recuperation. Expanding dependence on understudy charges, understudy credits and privatization without considering the low-salary gatherings may deliver backward impacts in the general public. Under the profound floods of globalization and rivalry, imperative financial justification for government subsidizing particularly for advanced education is dismissed. Open help for advanced education stays fundamental to guarantee a fair accomplish-ment of instructive and social missions, aside from getting by in the learning based society. It is fundamental that subsidizing sources must be expanded hwever cost-offering to understudies has social and political points of confinement, and unnecessary commercialization of advanced education ought to be prohibited.

Keywords: *Reforms in Education, Current trends in Education.*

Introduction

Education is the foremost sector that shoulders the biggest responsibility of shaping the future of nation. India, though renowned since ancient time for higher educational institutions like Nalanda, is presently facing multiple challenges in education. Education is monetarily and socially speculation.

The idea of instruction start an element of state has late cause, both in the occident and the orient. In many creating nations, training is financed and gave transcendently by the state. The extension of instruction along these lines relies upon financial assets.

In the mid 90s a noteworthy financial emergency surfaced in many creating nations. Thus the administrations of different creating economies have pursued an approach of macroeconomic adjustment and have presented certain basic changes. The approach of an economical financial position about by containing open consumption is by all accounts the main way-out. Commonly, financing courses of action additionally result in the misallocation of open spending on training.

There is proof, gotten from different examinations that profits to essential training are higher than comes back to optional instruction, which thus are higher than to advanced education. Accordingly an extensive number of alumni are delivered in the fields like humanities; trade and so on while there is short age in different fields. With the monetary regulation, particularly unmistakable I advanced education, it is achievable to give more noteworthy job to private segment in financing with the presentation of broadly accessible understudy credits and a predetermined number of specific grant. The accessible credits would empower the understudies to fund the present training against future pay.

Along these lines, the issue for lower pay understudies would likewise be unraveled and training would not be constrained to candidates with important assets at the season of enrolment. Alongside this, the administration could give grants to low pay understudies to back educational cost and additionally everyday costs. A more prominent degree of decentralization is required.

A few academicians contradict decentralization on the ground that decentralization obliterates the limit of the focal government to guide neighborhood specialists to meet long range national requirements for preparing individual.

It keeps dynamic organization from forcing exclusive requirements of open ethical quality and effectiveness on in reverse neighborhood specialists. In any case, this can't be thought of to a great extent with unfavorable, macroeconomic conditions. Furthermore, more prominent decentralization including more space for private and network schools is empowering more noteworthy rivalry among them. On the off chance that opposition expands, better instructive administrations are accessible, the expense for, prompting more extensive selections of schools for guardians and understudies. This thus builds the proficiency of the school.

India is one of the biggest creating nations on the planet. The advanced education framework in India is exceptionally mind boggling. It is typically discovered that the higher education system got more flourished after the country got its independence. As the financial quality is one of most essential variables for the appropriate development of advanced education, India like other created countries has been rehearsing diverse techniques for financing advanced education all through the different eras.

Reforms in Current Education System:

This century has seen a restoration of advanced education changes around the world. India is no exemption. A few change measures as of late acquainted have contributed with the extension of the framework, quality enhancement and upgraded importance.

Extend the System :

India's advanced education area has moved from a time of moderate development and low gross enrolment proportions (GERs) to a time of remarkable extension. In the course of recent years, understudy enrolment has quadrupled to reach 34 million with a GER of 24 percent in 2015-2016

The extent of India's instruction framework has now outperformed the United States, turning into the world's second biggest after China.

Massification of the training framework has intensely depended on non-state subsidizing. Market benevolent changes presented by the state incorporate cost recuperation measures openly organizations and the advancement of the private division to claim and work colleges. While privatization began moderate, private colleges are multiplying, and now represent more than 60 percent of the enrolment share both as far as establishments and enrolment. Massification in India is likewise joined by persevering social imbalances and enlarging local disparities in enrolment in advanced education.

India set up outer quality confirmation offices and inward quality affirmation systems to improve advanced education quality. Despite the fact that accreditation is obligatory to get open financing, a lion's share of private advanced education organizations still remain non-licensed.

Positioning has been another push to upgrade quality. Indian establishments don't toll well on the planet positioning of colleges.

Accordingly, India started a national positioning procedure with the National Institutional Ranking Framework (NIRF) in 2015. The main outcomes distributed in April 2016 and 2017 plainly shown that the best positioning foundations are for the most part open financed focal colleges.

It is right now trusted that making world class colleges will support India's situation in the worldwide rankings. This incited India to plan to help the making of 20 world class colleges in the quick future. It creates the impression that India, in the same way as other creating nations, is on a most optimized plan of attack towards the reorientation of existing establishments into world class colleges.

Improve importance

Notwithstanding the part's development, numerous businesses in India have lost trust in the nature of the capabilities granted by the nation's colleges.

It is addressed whether these colleges offer the abilities and skills to its alumni obviously in the work showcase. So as to recapture the believability and improve the significance of college capabilities, India is presently during the time spent building up a National Higher Education Qualification Framework (NHEQF).

Conclusion

The massification of advanced education is joined by an extending of local inconsistencies, persevering social disparities and commercialization of the area. The test currently is to address the issues of value and assorted variety to give moderate, quality advanced education in a time of market-drove changes. It is normal that the national approach on training at present being developed will ideally address a portion of these worries.

References

1. http://www.iiep.unesco.org/en/reforms-revive-higher-education-india\.
2. http://www.insightsonindia.com/2018/05/09/insights-into-editorial-reform-higher-education-in-india-by-forming-a-common-higher-education-authority/.

Chapter-48

Higher Education in India: An empirical study of Jammu and Kashmir

Tariq Ahmad Malik, Haamid Amin Mir
Ajaz Ahmad Dass,

Abstract

The growth and development of a nation is essentially depending on its education system. Education is the fundamental need for everyone to grow up. In present World, surviving without education is difficult for an individual. It is the main constituent of innovation, contributor of prosperity and an asset in the long run of a nation. Higher education in modern times is considered as the backbone of a society. The government of India since independence execute numerous initiatives to improve the level of higher education in the country. Indian higher education system has showed outstanding progress over the last decade and is one of the largest in the World. In developing nations, the higher education system is facing various hardships. There is limited accessibility in rural areas, lack of quality, low enrolment, lack of standard infrastructure and high drop out. The institutions of higher education in India too lacks the modern facilities and equipment's and there is dearth of adequate number of quality institutes. The Jammu and Kashmir state suffers the most due its geographical and political situation. There are only few higher education institutes in the state and that too are lacking behind the modern facilities and the manpower is insufficient as compared to other states of the country. The purpose of this paper is to know the status of higher education in Jammu and Kashmir state in context of India and to provide some measures and suggestions to modernize the system.

Keywords*: Higher education, Development, India, Jammu and Kashmir.*

Introduction

Higher education has played an important role in the development of present advanced nations. It is a discretionary ultimate phase of formal education after secondary schooling. The right of access to higher learning is listed in various global human rights mechanisms. The 1966 UN International Covenant on Economic, \ in Article 13 avowed that "higher education shall be made equally accessible to all, on the basis of capacity, by every appropriate means and in particular by the progressive introduction of free education". Higher education is noteworthy for domestic economies, both as an industry and a basis of skilled and cultivated individuals for the economy.

The Indian higher education system has started from 1857 when the British's established universities at Bombay, Calcutta and Madras. According to statistics in India only one child among seven is a college student, and continues to decrease at university level. The system also suffers due to inefficient management of equity, access and relevance. It needs substantial improvement as compared to other developed /developing nations. India's higher education system at global level is the third largest in terms of students, next to China and United States, but regrettably lacking in terms of quality and modern infrastructure. The number of universities has increased from 30 in 1950 to 864 at present. There are also 40,026 colleges and 11,699 standalone institutions in the country. The Gross Enrolment Ratio(GER) of higher education has increased from 19.4 percent in 2010 to 25.2 percent in 2016, which is a noteworthy progress. Despite the growth India lacks behind in GER of higher education at global level. The comparison of India with some other countries is shown in the table below:

Table 48.1 Name of the Country
Gross Enrolment Ratio (GER) of Higher Education

Name of the Country	*Gross Enrolment Ratio (GER) of Higher Education*
Australia	90.3%
Brazil	50.6%
Chile	88.6%
China	43.4%
India	26.95
Russia	80.4%
Sri Lanka	19.8%
Thailand	48.9%
United Kingdom	56.5%
United States of America	85.8%

Source: UNESCO

The Gross Enrolment Ratio of higher education in India varies from state to state and across socio-economic groups in society. Chandigarh has the top GER of 56.1 percent, followed by Tamil Nadu at 46.9 percent while as Bihar has the lowest of 14.9 percent of its youth. The GER of Jammu and Kashmir stands at 25.6 percent which is very close to all India level of 25.2 percent and is lowest among the northern states of the country.

Review of Literature

Altbach (2005). in the study admitted that in the competition of knowledge India has a substantial gain in the present time. India has third largest in the world after China and USA in terms of students at higher education. English is used as primary language for higher education and research and has an old customary history of academics. However, the weakness are more than its strengths. The ratio of students at higher educations is 10 percent which is very low as compared to other nations of the globe. The author further points out that there is lack of sufficient number of quality institutions in the country.

Bhushan (2006). in his work analyzed that the higher education system from government level was not able to provide the adequate number of seats for the students and the private sector has grown instantly. "A substantial quantity of presumed private institutes is given status as 'deemed universities' and authorized to issue degrees, and the private sector played an important role in spreading the higher education and training in the country".

OECD (2007). in an economic survey recommended immediate improvement in the Indian education system. According to the study there is a lot of difference across social and gender backgrounds in execution of education system. Though, the first stage towards healthier result is to increase the enrolment of students. A lot of requirements are needed to improve the quality education with increasing the inducements of faculty members and enable proper appearance of students and training of teachers. The reforms of education sector in OECD countries and at state level advocated the devolution which will raise the competence and should be fortified.

Objectives of our study

(i) To analyze the scenario of higher education in India.

(ii) To know the status and development of Higher Education in Jammu and Kashmir.

(iii) To know the problems and make suggestions for improvement of higher education in J & K.

Methodology

The study is descriptive in nature and is mainly based on secondary data. The data is collected from various official and non-official reports, journals, books and newspapers. It includes reports of Planning commissions, Higher Education Department, University Grants Commission, Ministry of Human Resource Development, Economic Surveys of Central and State governments and other books and journals. The different sources of internet are also used for this study.

Scenario of Higher Education in Jammu and Kashmir

A society is known by the eminence of education of its people. Education is considered as the pillar of development of a nation or region. The social, economic and political development of a nation is impossible without the education of its citizens. Article 14 of the Indian Constitution confers that free and compulsory education be made available to all children in the age group of 06-14 years. Youth of Jammu & Kashmir were badly affected by the militancy and violence in the valley. The youth witnessed a setback in education; they couldn't compete with their elite counterparts as they had not the means to get better education. Educational Institutions in both Public and Private Sector increased as 24265, 5292 respectively in the state. The state has total enrollment increased to 27.98 lakh. The Gross Enrollment ratio for the state has increased from 10.36 percentin 2007-08 to 18.2 percent in 2011-12 which is higher than the National Gross Enrollment Ratio of 15 percent. The literacy rate increased from 55.50 percent to 68.74 percent during 2001-2011 decade. Moreover, the dropout rate has declined to 11 percent in 2012-13.

Education is one of the most important factors which disown the gender disparity and women empowerment. Increasing number of educational institutions has gradually increased the rural literacy and also increased the female literacy. Gender gap has drastically decreased from 25.06 percent in 1961 to 21.59 percent in 2001 and further to 16.68 percent in 2011. In J & K the establishing of number of educational institutions have lessen the distance per school and increased the rural and female literacy. Furthermore, the welfare programmes like *Sarva Shisksha Abhiyan, Beti Bachao Beti Padao* have uplifted the education system in the State. Sarva Shisksha Abhiyan gave 891.44 crore funds in 2013-14 against 508.6 crore. Rashtriya Madyamik Shiksha Abhiyan gave 135.78crore in 2013-14 against 109.36 crore in 2012-13 for the development of education in the state.

Development of Higher Education in Jammu and Kashmir

Higher education reflects the quantum of knowledge- general or specific and its impact on overall social cultural, aesthetic life of the students. It also shows how a student is able to express his achievements orally or in written. However, every desired student has not easy access to it in spite of number of measures taken by the government for its expansion. Gross Enrolment ratio is the tool through which access to higher education can be measured. Over the years, J&K has achieved many milestones in higher education. In 1950-51 there were only seven colleges out of which only one college was for female students. 1999-2000 witnessed the increase in number of colleges to 33 among which 07 colleges were for women. During 2013-14, the number of colleges increased to 95 having only 12 colleges for women. The state has two central universities one each at Jammu and Srinagar capitals of the J & K state. Moreover, the state has six other universities functioning in the state among them, two are state universities and four are govt. aided universities with intake capacity of 11,400 students. Besides 15 offsite campuses of Universities of Kashmir & Jammu have been approved among them 9 campuses have been established in far off places. The number of universities in Jammu and Kashmir is shown in the table below as:

Table 48.2

S. No.	***Name of the University***	***Year of Establishment***
1.	University of Kashmir	1949
2.	University Of Jammu	1969
3.	Sher-E- Kashmir University of Agricultural Science and Technology (SUAST) Kashmir	1982
4.	Sher-E- Kashmir University of Agricultural Science and Technology (SKUAST) Jammu	1999
5.	Shiri Mata Vaishno Devi University (SMVD)Jammu	2004
6.	Baba Ghulam Shah Badshah University	2005
7.	Islamic University of Science And Technology	2005
8.	Central University of Kashmir	2009
9.	Central University of Jammu	2011
10.	Cluster University Srinagar	2016
11.	Cluster University Jammu	2016

Source: J&K higher education reports.

In the state of Jammu and Kashmir there are total 364 colleges out of which 123 are government colleges and 241 are private colleges. There are total 214 colleges in Jammu region out of these 73 are government colleges and 141 are private colleges. In Kashmir region there are total 150 colleges, 50 are government colleges and 100 are private colleges.

Gross Enrollment Ratio in Higher Education

The GER in Higher Education in India for the year 2017-18 is 25.8 percent which is calculated 18-23 years of age group. GER for male population at all India level is 26.3 percent whereas the GER for Female population at all India level is 25.4 percent for Scheduled Castes it is 21.8 percent while as for Scheduled tribes it is 15.9 percent as compared to National GER of 25.8 percent. The GER of some states including J&K are shown in the table below:

S.No.	*State*	*All Categories*			*Schedule Castes*			*Schedule Tribes*		
		Male	*Female*	*Total*	*Male*	*Female*	*Total*	*Male*	*Female*	*Total*
1.	Jammu & Kashmir	26.4	29.0	27.7	15.3	19.0	17.1	15.4	14.9	15.1
2.	Himachal Pradesh	34.0	42.2	37.9	25.1	30.4	27.7	36.5	40.6	38.5
3.	Punjab	27.6	33.6	30.3	19.4	23.8	21.4	-	-	-
4.	Uttarakhand	36.3	36.3	36.3	26.4	26.7	26.6	42.1	42.5	42.3
5.	Haryana	27.0	30.7	28.7	18.0	19.4	18.6	-	-	-
6.	Delhi	44.9	48.0	46.3	31.7	32.0	31.8	-	-	-
7.	Rajasthan	22.7	20.6	21.7	18.2	16.2	17.2	19.8	17.2	18.5
8.	Uttar Pradesh	25.2	26.7	25.9	21.1	22.4	21.7	38.2	33.0	35.6

Source: Annual report on All India survey of higher education.

Snags in Higher Education System of India

The Indian higher education system agonizes numerous insufficiencies. The outcome of which is incipient scarcity of trained manpower and increasing number of unemployable alumni. The academic research status is diminishing and lowering. Higher education in India suffers from problems like rigid academic system, clumsy associating structure, restriction on sovereignty of institutions, irregular capability among different subjects, lack of modern labs and scarcity of financing are some well-known examples. The growth of higher education during the last two decades is mainly due to priv=ate sector creativities. The unpretentious disquiets are insufficient and manipulated system. Owing to inaptness of government, the growth of private sector is hectic and inadvertent. The monitoring authorities are unable to sustain the standard and instead make daunting access that create uninvited pavements. The Indian higher education system in spite of notable growth lacks behind in quality of top institutes. The reservation system for institutes is also the hindrance for quality outcome. The growing competition in institutes and decline of public funding further deteriorates the educational ideals of higher education in India. The tuition fee of higher institutes made it beyond the reach of poor students which compel them to not to opt for higher studies. These problems compelled the students to go abroad for higher studies which is distress.

Difficulties confronting higher education

They are generally divided into four major kinds: the truncated standard of training and learning process; the variance of supply and demand; the prospect to progress and access is rutted; and the aptitude of research and novelty is restricted.

The truncated standard of training and learning process

In higher education most possibly the shortage of quality faculty is considered as biggest challenge. It is estimated that thirty to forty percent of teaching faculty is vacant in the institutions. There is lack of training for teachers. The other concerns in teaching and learning process comprise as:

(i) Obsolete, inelastic syllabi and the lack of manpower and opportunity for the evolution of content and talents in learning.

(ii) The focus is on participation and memorizing the valuation and education. There is lack of innovation of transversal talents like developing analytical thought, critical perceptive, resolving of difficult glitches and concerted operations.

(iii) Absence of faculty members and high density of students in the class room.

(iv) Deficiency of investigation experience in initial period and the dividend of training and research.

(v) There is deficiency of coordination and futile eminence assurance among central and state administrations, scholars and other sponsors. These have ensued low employability among graduates throughout South Asia and cause for restricted enrollment in higher education and are considered as endemic problems in higher institutes of India.

The variance of Supply and Demand

The average growth rate during the last decade is increasing but still it lacks behind the various developing and developed nations. The GER ratio in J&K is below all India average of 26.95 percent which shows the grim situation in higher education in the state. The estimates show that hundred million qualified students are still unable to get admission in universities even if target of 30 percent GER by 2020 is fulfilled. There is significant need in India to raise the number of enrolment in universities. The multiplicity of courses at colleges and universities has contracted during the last decade has resulted in soaked bazaars for technical students, business experts and engineers.

The prospect to progress and access is rutted

There is wide gap in higher education across the country in rural and urban areas despite the efforts from authorities to locate the institutes. The gap is more in J&K as compared to other states of the country. The state government recently has announced more colleges in the state but the location is politically motivated and the deserved areas neglected by the authorities. The higher education institutes are located mostly in urban areas, there are multi-dimensional disparities in enrolment rates like rural and urban, poor and rich, men and women, majority and minority and persons with frailty. The need of the hour is inclusive growth in education system of India.

The aptitude of research and novelty is restricted

In the recent World University Rankings only a few were selecting in the top 500 institutes in India, which shows the grim situation of higher education. In top hundred universities no engineering and technology figures in India which is a shocking for the country which shows an increasing number of graduate pass outs every year. The quality of Ph.D. research is contracted due to over emphasis on degrees in order to get promotion. India needs to create some universities which compete at global level in order to get global level research and is productive for the scientific India as well as for World.

Some steps for the development of human resource by the Government of India

- The project of National digital library of eBooks for various topics and subjects. The online free of cost courses by highly qualified teachers from reputed institutes of IITs, IIMs and central universities.
- The central government has launched a distinct program 'Udaan' for meritorious girl students so that they will be able to get technical education and promote training and learning of science and mathematics at 10+2 level freely.

- The motive of the scheme is to increase the roll of girl students in prominent technical institutes so that they can access the incentives easily and became the role model in future leadership.
- A mission on the name of 'Pandit Madan Mohan Malviya' an educationist and freedom fighter was launched form a strong professional cadre of teachers. The project will address the issues of teachers, training techniques, preparation, experiment and curriculum development, designing and assessment of evaluation.
- The central government in order to address the issues of rural infrastructure, water management, renewable energy, organic farming and livelihood launched a project 'Unnat Bharat Abhiyan'. The scheme aims the technologies from the laboratory to the field. The organizing institute for the project is IIT Delhi and about 130 villages are adopted by different IITs and NITs in the country.
- A project 'Rastriya Avishkar Abhiyan' for reviving the interest in youth towards the technology for innovation based on observations and experiments has been started. This facilitates the direct interaction in and around the environment in educational institutions.
- A project "create a channel for US professors in science, technology, mathematics and engineering to teach in Indian academic and research institutions on short-term exchanges" as per the US Department of State website and Ministry of human resource development and department of science and technology India, under the Global Initiative of Academic Networks (GIAN) programme.

Suggestions

- To make India globally competitive and relevant in education there is need to adopt the innovative and transformational technique starting from primary to higher level.
- The development for organizing expert lectures, syllabus, projects, internships, counseling for career and placements should be in industrial cooperation for higher studies. there is need to advanced superiority, status and ensure credibility among student interaction, exchange programme for faculty and partnerships in high quality techniques at national and global level higher study institutes.
- There should be coordination among International reputed institutes with Indian higher education institutes for laboratory, research and idea sharing purposes to ensure better quality.

- The number of institutes should be increased in J&K. There should be more conferences, workshops and faculty development programmes in the state.
- The students at graduate level should be given the subjects of their preference and efficiency. This will reduce the unwanted rush at higher level of education.

Conclusion

Education is considered as an important aspect for the development of a nation. The investment in education sector is the only which remunerates high and rich dividends. The Indian Higher education system from last decade shows an improvement in the enrollment ratio. The number of institutes gradually increased in all the states of the country since independence. The GER ratio at higher education level in Jammu and Kashmir should be increased. The higher education in India is witnessing a substantial reforms and transformation. The institutes like IITs established few decades ago proved highly successful in providing specific and quality education. The development of science and technology and globalization of economic thought accelerated the emergence of modern higher education institutes. Higher education is of astonishing significance and reforms are often seen as substantial menace to particular, social measures that provide profits to influential people. The system needs change, development and importantly need an effectively plan for reforms.

Reference

1. Altbach (2005). "India: a World-Class Country without World-Class Higher Education". International Educator Nov-Dec.
2. Annual report of All India Survey on Higher Education (AISHE) Department of Higher Education, Ministry of Human Resource Development 2017-18.
3. Agarwal, P (2006). "Higher education in India: The need for change". New Delhi, Indian Council for Research on International Economic Relations. URL: www.icrier.org/publication/working papers 180.html.
4. Bhushan, S. (2005). "Foreign Universities in India: Market-Driven New Directions". International Higher Education.
5. Henard, F. (2008). Learning our Lesson: Review of Quality teaching in Higher Education.
6. Mukherjee, A. (2007). "Public Expenditure on Education: A Review of Selected Issues and Evidence", Working paper from financing Human Development paper 1, National Institute of Public Finance and Policy.
7. OECD (2007). www.oecd.org/dataoecd (viewed as on 16-01-2019).
8. www.google.com.

Chapter-49

Significance of Institutional Infrastructure in Development of Higher Education

M. V. Rama Mohan Rao,

Abstract

Although there have been challenges to higher education in the past, the most recent call for reform may provoke a fundamental change in higher education. This change may not occur as a direct response to call for greater transparency and accountability, but rather because of the opportunity to reflect on the purpose of higher education, the role of colleges and universities in the new millennium, and emerging scientific research on how people learn. These disparate literatures have not been tied together in a way that would examine the impact of fundamental change from the policy level to the institutional level and to the everyday lives of college and university administrators, faculty and students. Now the time has come to create a second wave of institution building and of excellence in the fields of education, research and capability building. We need higher educated people who are skilled and who can drive our economy forward. When India can provide skilled people to the outside world then we can transfer our country from a developing nation to a developed nation very easily and quickly and India become as an Education hub or to become a prosperous partner in Global Economy. India has already entered into the era of knowledge explosion. The role of higher education in the emerging scenario of knowledge economy is very crucial and multifaceted for any country in general and India in particular. Through the Cross Culture Programs one can understand about people, culture, arts, literature, religions, technological developments and progress of human society in the world. Environmental beautification and sanitation give the aesthetic impression conducive climate for teaching, learning, and research activities, healthy and secures lives in the school and its communities .The Governance of Higher education institutions namely universities encompasses many aspects such as, human resources management, funding, quality assurance, internationalization, academic and scientific planning etc. Higher Education (HE) plays a major role in building a nation's intellectual capital required for poverty reduction, sustainable development and positive engagement in the global knowledge economy the primary function of HE is the production, distribution, and consumption of knowledge, through teaching, research, and community engagement. The purpose of HE is traditionally viewed as an investment to build the necessary human capital for economic development.

Keywords: *transparency, capability building, resource management, sustainable development*

Introduction

Higher Education (HE) plays a major role in building a nation's intellectual capital required for poverty reduction, sustainable development and positive engagement in the global knowledge economy. The primary function of HE is the production, distribution, and consumption of knowledge, through teaching, research, and community engagement. India's higher education system is the world's third largest in terms of students, next to China and the United States. Unlike China, however, India has the advantage of English being the primary language of higher education and research. India educates approximately 11 per cent of its youth in higher education as compared to 20 per cent in China. The purpose of HE is traditionally viewed as an investment to build the necessary human capital for economic development. Society in the world. Environmental beautification and sanitation give the aesthetic impression conducive climate for teaching, learning, and research activities, healthy and secures lives in the school and its communities.

Need of the Study

This paper is an attempt to find out the gap in knowledge and awareness by analyzing the significance of the institutional infrastructure facilities for the development of Higher Education in India and its effects on living standard of people studying through the parameters like, physical resources ,staff capacity building ,learning resources, Access of e governance etc.

Need of the Hour

It is the need of the hour to free the higher education system from unnecessary constraints and political interference.

Methodology

The data has been based on secondary information, collected from various journals, reports, e-journals, books etc.

New Vision

A new vision for the future is required and we need to create an alternative society based on ecological sustainability and urbanization and promote competitive spirit among educated persons through the development of Higher Education in India.

The Main Emerging Issues

The role of higher education in the emerging scenario of knowledge economy is very crucial and multifaceted for any country in general and India in particular. There are many basic problems faced by higher education system in India. These include Lower level of teaching quality, Financing of higher education, More concentrated on theories and rather than practical knowledge, Traditional methods of teaching, Privatization, Inadequate facilities and infrastructure Quota system. Out dated and rigid curricula and pedagogy, lack of accountability and quality assurance and separation of research and teaching are raise questions on Indian education system. The system of Indian Higher education is the second largest in the world which fulfills the educational requirements of millions of students who come from different sections of the society since it is the student community that can help to generate healthy academic atmosphere in institutions of higher learning.

Financing of higher education

Expenditure on education in common and on higher education in particular by the government, is one of the parameters to judge the quality in Higher Education.

Traditional methods of teaching

Professors still stick to those older methods of teaching like board, marker. Also they are not up to date with the information available and what global industry demands.

Privatization

In the present scenario, privatization of higher education is apparently a fledgling but welcome trend and is essential to maintain creativity, adaptability and quality. In India both public and private institutions operate simultaneously. Private providers, in the interest of maximizing profit, have every incentive to 'minimize costs' by compromising on the quality of education provided in their institutions. Quality of teaching staff is one of the considerable issues for higher education sector to sustain in the future.

Inadequate facilities and infrastructure

In India, many of the universities don't have adequate infrastructure or facilities to teach students. Even many private universities are running courses without classrooms. Internet and Wi-Fi facility is still out of reach of many students

Quota system

Bringing the reservation and quota system for different categories in education lost its quality even deserving candidates of general categories also.

Physical Resources

Physical resources comprise land, building and furniture and it include physical facilities for teaching spaces and for ancillary rooms. The development of physical resources in higher education is complex and cost intensive and to ensure their quality and maintain world standards is very challenging. Maintenance, renewal and innovation are other determinants of the quality of the physical asset and facilities development effort of the institutions that will attract the students, staff and foreigners to the institutions. Environmental beautification and sanitation give the aesthetic impression that guarantees the serenity and conducive climate for teaching, learning and research activities, healthy and secured lives in the school and its communities. Quality assurance of these facilities right from their planning, to development and utilization will ensure effective realization of set goals and objectives in higher education institutions. The infrastructural development must be of international standard to attract foreign students, staff and recognition; and must be environmentally safe and of high sanitary standard. Physical resources include: availability, adequacy, student friendliness, maintenance culture, global accessibility and environmental safety and sanitation of the institutions. Performance also related to the quality, where quality term is use to reflect the degree of excellent product or service that fulfils or exceeds people expectations. Situations today make quality as a major weapon or tool for the organization to use in the drive to improve their performance. The development of institutional environment that is safe, clean and conducive to give students a sense of belonging, pride and beauty is urgently needed and developing a high level of maintenance culture.

Capacity Building in the field of higher education

The profile of staff involved in capacity-building projects is grouped in 4 categories:

Managers (staff category 1) carry out top managerial activities related to the administration and coordination of project activities.

Researchers, teachers and trainers (RTT) (staff category 2) typically carry out academic activities related to curriculum/training program development, development and adaptation of teaching/training materials, preparation and teaching of courses or trainings.

Technical staff (staff category 3) carries out technical tasks such as book-keeping, accountancy and translation activities.

Administrative staff (staff category 4) carries out administrative tasks such as secretarial duties.

Types of Activities Categories of Priorities

Curriculum Development: Subject Areas

Governance and Management: Improving quality of education and training and Improving Management and operation of HEI

Higher Education and Society: Developing the HE sector within society at large .Capacity-Building Projects are transnational cooperation projects based on multilateral primarily between higher education institutions (HEIs) from Program and eligible Partner Countries.

Access & Governance

A good higher education system is required for overall development of a nation. Electronic Governance (e - Governance) is the use of Information and Communication Technologies (ICT) for the planning, implementation, and monitoring of government programs, projects, and activities. E-Governance is expected to help deliver cost - effective and easy-to-access citizen services, and improve processing of transactions both within the government, and between the government and other agencies. E-Governance is understood as a set of activities involving the effective contribution of information and communication technology (ICT) for strengthening administration and management. Educational institutions may have various requirements that include computerization and management of processes such as registration, admission, student information, classes, time table, transport, attendance, library, salary and expenses, examinations, performance, grades, hostels, security and reports.

Management and Leadership

Aspiring academic leaders need to understand the organizational complexity of colleges and universities and the wisdom in shared decision-making. "Good management is essential: budgets must be balanced; facilities must be erected and maintained; essential services in food, transportation and housing must exhibit both functionality and quality. Creativity, entrepreneurship, innovation, educated citizens—all of the things we need from our great colleges and universities. Leaders must first know yourself—your strengths, weaknesses, aspirations, and predominant lens. Some leaders may be a bit more "born" to the job; but the skills required of a leader can be identified, learned, and practiced. James Downey (2001), former president of the University of Waterloo, confirmed the importance of the human relations and symbolic lenses in a quote about university leadership: "Visions in universities are not manufactured: they are harvested.

Competency

Competency concept may seem simple or merely a new label for a long-standing practice, \ offer new opportunities to rethink how Education is designed and delivered, student learning is demonstrated and degrees are granted.

1. Define learning out comes (or competencies) for college programs in clear, consistent terms that are transparent to students and aligned with employer expectations and continued education.
2. Measure student learning consistently, continuously and transparently with a multi-faceted approach that includes ongoing assessment and portfolios of student work.
3. Encourage innovative competency-based approaches that free colleges and students from the restrictions of credit hours and traditional academic calendars.

Purdue University professors have found a way to prepare students for ever- changing workforce demands. Faculty mentors meet with students to develop individualized plans of Study and then track student progress in each competency—rating them either developing, emerging or proficient. Students must show mastery of each competency to advance, either through experiences gained in the classroom or in extracurricular activities .Learning has always been the foundation of higher education.

Computers can be used extensively for educational administration.

- Pay Roll and Financial Accounting
- Administration of Student Data
- Personnel Records Maintenance
- Library System

E-Governance in Higher Education

India has one of the largest higher education systems in the world .Despite having the largest higher education system, the quality of education, in general, cannot be claimed to be the best. Technical and vocational Education in India has seen enormous growth in recent years with a large increase in total number of institutes imparting higher education. On one hand, this growth promises to produce more skilled youth to fulfill needs of ever growing Indian industry and on the other hand it poses a huge challenge for the governing bodies like UGC, AICTE, NCVT, NCTE, PCI, MCI, INC, DCI etc. and state technical education boards to maintain & improve the quality of education being imparted through these new & existing technical and Vocational institutes. But as has been reported by NASSCOM(National Association of Software and Service Companies) in its 2004 report, out of 3 million graduates and post-graduates added to the workforce in India every year only 25 percent of technical and 10- 15 percent of non-technical graduates are employable by growing IT, and other sector.

Benefits of e-Governance in Higher Education

The benefits of e-governance in an educational sector are improved efficiency, increase in transparency and accountability of educational administrative activities convenient and faster access to services, and lower costs for administrative services. The multi-faceted benefits of e-governance can be described as under these points.

Benefit to university

(i) Centralized information access from anywhere
(ii) Increase in student enrollment ratio.
(iii) Provide quality e-services, e-participation
(v) Inventive teaching tools
(vii) Less paper work

Benefits to students

(i) Increase participation in education affairs
(ii) Personalized login for each students
(iii) Information & transaction services
(iv) Job opportunities
(v) Students can access virtual lectures &Seminars.
(vi) Students can solve their problems like- examination queries, result verification etc.

Benefits to colleges

(i) Data can access easily
(ii) Electronic data exchange with university
(iii) Instant statistical report generation
(iv) Helpful for NAAC accreditation

Management and leadership

The art and science of formulating, implementing and evaluating cross functional decisions that enable an organization to full its objectives'. Strategic management is a holistic process with many components that must eectively interact and function together. These components include institutional culture; strategic planning; leadership; institutional research, resource allocation and financial management; personnel and human resources management; research and scholarly activity; student and campus support services; academic support services; internationalization; and external relations.

In the last few decades a countrywide problems/challenges have emerged in Higher Education system in India they are discussed as under.

Challenges

Our heterogeneous education system, based on geographical, rural-urban, rich-poor set up have posed in great challenge for the educational institutions. Varieties of colleges, universities, technical institutions have produced and different types and quality of students.

Economic Difficulties

Students hold part time jobs in order to pay for their educational expenses and should divide their attention between a job and College/ University education. Earn while learn scheme cannot adequately support student to face economic challenges.

Suggestions for improving quality of higher education

There are some suggestions and Expectations from Government, Industry, Educational Institutions, Parents and Students for improving quality of higher education.

Student-Centered Education and Dynamic Methods- Methods of higher education also have to be appropriate to the needs of learning to learn, learning to do, learning to be and learning to become. Student-centered education and employment of dynamic methods of education will require from teachers new attitudes and new skills.

Methods of teaching through lectures will have to subordinate to the methods that will lay stress on self-study, personal consultation between teachers and pupils, and dynamic sessions of seminars and workshops.

Examination Reforms- Examination reforms, gradually shifting from the terminal, annual and semester examinations to regular and continuous assessment of student's performance in learning must be implemented.

International Cooperation- Universities in India have been a primary conduit for the advancement and transmission of knowledge through traditional functions such as research, innovation, teaching, human resource development, and continuing education. With the increased development of transport and communication, the global village is witnessing a growing emphasis on international cooperation and action to find satisfactory solutions to problems that have global dimensions and higher education is one of them.

On 13th June, 2005 Government of India constituted a high level advisory body known as National Knowledge Commission (NKC) to advise the PM about the state of education in India and measures needed to reform this sector. It was headed by Sam Pitroda and submitted its report in November 2007. NKC has recommended setting up of 1500 universities by 2015 so that gross enrolment ratio increases to 15 percent. It has also called for establishing an Independent Regulatory Authority for Higher Education (IRAHE) to monitor the quality of overall higher education in India.

Cross Culture Programmes- After education, tour to every the places in India and world as far as possible with the cooperation of government is necessary so that one can understand about people, culture, arts, literature, religions, technological developments and progress of human society in the world.

Action Plan for Improving Quality

Academic and administrative audit must be conducted once in three years in colleges by external experts for ensuring quality in all aspects of academic activities. The self-finance colleges must come forward for accreditation and fulfil the requirements of accreditation. World Class Education - India must aspire for the international standard in education. Many national universities like in the USA, UK, Australia, etc. allow studies in higher education for foreign students in their countries and through correspondence courses as well.

Personality Development

Finally, education must be for the flowering of personality but not for the suppression of creativity or natural skill. In the globalized world opportunity for the educated people are naturally ample in scope. The world can be developed for peace, prosperity and progress by able and skilful men. A library must be online and conducive for serious study. Indian universities should concentrate more on providing quality education which is comparable to that of international standards.

Latest News

Sri Narendra Modi, Prime Minister of India on Monday announced 10 per cent reservation in government jobs and higher education for economically weaker sections in the general category.

References

1. Bolman, L., & Deal, T. (2013). Reframing organizations: Artistry, choice and leadership (5th ed.). San Francisco, CA: Jossey-Bass.Google Scholar.
2. Downey, J. (2001). Guest editor's introduction: Academic leadership and organizational change. Innovative Higher Education, 25, 235–238.Cross Ref Google Scholar.
3. Ashok Kumar (GIAN JYOTI E-JOURNAL, Volume 1, Issue 2, Jan – Mar 2012) E-Governance in Education Sector.
4. Dr.R.Krishnaveni and J. Meenakumari (International Journal of Environmental Science and Development, Vol. 1, No. 3, August. 2010) Usage of ICT for Information Administration in Higher education Institutions – A study.
5. Harshita Bhatnagar. (International Journal of Scientific & Engineering Research, Volume 4, Issue 5, May-2013) e-Governance in Higher Education: A Case Study of IGNOU, New Delhi.

Chapter-50

Impact of Globalisation on Higher Education in India – Challenges and Opportunities – An Insight

T. Y. Nirmala Devi,

Abstract

"Education is the most powerful weapon which you can use to change the world" ***Nelson Mandela***

Education is an important aspect of our lives, while some of us take it for granted, there are others who crave and struggle to get it. From Aristotle to APJ Abdul Kalam, every famous personality has time and again stressed on the importance of education in our lives. The world has advanced considerably throughout the decades and the need for higher education has been on the rise. Higher education has evolved to become one of the principal means in educating individuals in specific areas of study such as engineering, management, or the sciences etc. Education is a crucial determinant of human capital accumulation in the country and therefore, a source of economic growth. Universities and colleges are the places where people go seeking for higher education. Almost all the inventions that make our life easier today are the outcome of education. The higher education is treated as the educational pyramid at present times. The impact of globalization and the development of knowledge-based economy have caused much dramatic change to the character and functions of higher education. The major trend is the reforming and restructuring of private higher education in India to make it more competitive globally. Globalization clearly presents new opportunities, challenges and risks for higher education. This article examines both positive and negative impact of globalisation on higher education and challenges that the globalization brought to higher education in India. It is necessary to identify opportunities and threats to higher education sector and analyze them in a deep manner. The major objective is to make the segment of higher education in India more competitive globally.

Keywords *: Globalisation, Higher Education, Opportunities*

Introduction

The phenomenon of globalization, which transformed world trade, communications and economic relations in the latter part of the 20th Century, is having a similarly profound effect on education at the start of the 21st. Student options for higher education, in particular, are no longer constrained by national boundaries. For the first time in history, large segments of the world's student population truly have access to a "global marketplace" of higher education.

Globalization is a procedure, which has influenced numerous zones of human life, one of those being training. In the twentieth century, many creating nations have encountered development in the instructive offices accessible to them because of the section of organizations from the west. Some trust that this procedure is a priceless open door for the general population of the creating nations to raise their abilities and gauges of instruction. Others expect that it is just an advanced form of social dominion that will prompt the making of a general, at last western culture. No human movement has stayed unaffected by globalization and training is no special case. It conveys training to the forefronts. In the common talk, instruction is required to be the significant device for fuse into the 'learning society' and the mechanical economy.

In educational terms, there is a developing understanding that the neoliberal adaptation of globalization, especially as actualized (and ideologically guarded) by respective, multilateral, and worldwide associations, is reflected in an instructive motivation that benefits, if not straightforwardly forces, specific approaches for assessment, financing, evaluation, norms, instructor preparing, educational programs, guidance, and testing. Despite such weights, more investigation is required about neighborhood reactions to safeguard government funded instruction against the acquaintance of unadulterated market components with direct instructive trades and different approaches that try to diminish state sponsorship and financing and to force the board and productivity models obtained from the business division as a structure for instructive basic leadership.

The present globalization of advanced education makes the two difficulties and openings. The connection between colleges training and globalization gives unique consideration. Instruction will be the response to numerous issues raised by globalization. Instructive objectives are believed to be a territory of incredible worry in the time of globalization. It is here that colleges assume a significantly critical job, to make better society. It is difficult to overlook the worldwide; colleges need to consider the effect of globalization. They should draw in with the issues of globalization, both hypothetically as experts and specialists, and for all intents and purposes as scholarly labourers engaged with an undeniably globalized endeavor.

The probability of passage of outside colleges into India is an unavoidable outcome of globalization. Top class outside colleges are foreseen to add glory to India's advanced education. The desire is that remote colleges will bring truly necessary limit and new thoughts on advanced education the executives, educational programs, showing strategies and research, together with speculation. In spite of the fact that fear has been communicated that just business foundations will come to India and that Oxford and Cambridge will timid away, my speculation is that top class colleges will come to India, not to make benefit, but rather to benefit from the huge scholarly assets of the nation. The outside colleges bill has satisfactory shields against tossing open our advanced education to fortune searchers and corrupt business interests.

International Influences on Indian Higher Education

On the off chance that one outputs the skyline of Indian advanced education organizations today, the inheritance of earlier floods of worldwide, if not worldwide, impact can be seen in for all intents and purposes each field. India has a wide assortment of pre-Independence evangelist organizations – schools established in the late nineteenth and mid twentieth century by outside teachers of various religions. St. Joseph's College Trichy, St. Xavier's Chennai, Christian Medical College Vellore, St. John College Agra, Isabella Thoburn College Lucknow, and so on.

In the post-Independence period, the Indian Institutes of Technology, deliberately designed after the Massachusetts Institute of Technology in the U.S., got generous abroad help appropriate from the start. With help from four giver countries, the five IITs profited from visitor personnel from outside of India, the capacity to send Indian staff for preparing abroad, and commitments of current lab gear and offices. Comparative worldwide connections were built up by the Indian Institutes of Management: IIM-Ahmadabad, for instance, still keeps up solid associations with the Harvard Business School. Maybe the latest development in Indian advanced education, the Indira Gandhi National Open University (together with comparable, state sponsored Open Universities), drew vigorously on the UK involvement with separation training and the Open University idea.

Impact of Globalization on Higher Education in India

Globalization multi-dimensionally affects the arrangement of advanced education in India. It has underlined the requirement for changes in the instructive framework with specific reference to the more extensive use of data innovation, giving profitability measurement to training and accentuation on its innovative work exercises since training is a vital interest in building human capital. The advanced education framework in India experiences intense scarcity of assets, absence of self-sufficiency, weight of alliance. Then again the impact of globalization on instruction acquires fast improvements innovation, correspondence and learning economy.

1. Globalization and economic reforms in India have yielded significant changes in the role of state and restructuring of social welfares education, employment, agriculture and health system. In higher education it was always the monopoly of middle class and elite groups of the society.
2. Privatization of higher education-There has been an increasing trend towards privatization of higher education in India. The quality and content of the education are industry oriented due to privatization. In this day age of globalization and privatization with competition and to meet the new challenges of the 21st century higher education should be radically transformed. India is required to set up a chain of educational institutions which are accredited, globally acceptable. We should also keep in mind that quality can come only from quality teachers and quality infrastructure, under quality leadership.
3. Women education- Women literacy rate has grown over the three decades. Women education plays a very important role in the overall development of the country and improving the quality of life at home and outside.
4. Commercialization-Impact of globalization is commercialization of higher education due to which self financing courses have been introduced which has deprived many from getting higher education especially in countries like India where illiteracy still prevails and education is a dream to many. The existing policy of globalization of higher education is motivated by profits rather than social justice or the policy of the government. Its goals therefore are to meet the demands of the market.
5. Teacher education- In the global society today the aspects of rapid change, lifelong learning, flexible routes of learning and the use of technology have a major impact on all the areas of teacher education. Major steps to be taken qualitative expansion, value based, competency based and ICT based teaching learning.

6. Knowledge- The impact of globalization on higher education is the transition to a knowledge society towards universities as knowledge-centers.
7. Skill- Higher education is seeking ways to meet the demands and challenges put forth by globalization. Higher education today is expected to produce skilled and trained workforce who can compete in this global market.
8. Education policies- Globalization also impact the education policies on higher education in India. In the last two decades Indian government has formed various committees, commission and also different kinds of economic bodies came to existence like NAAC.
9. Entry of Foreign Universities- Foreign Direct Investment (FDI) is important tool of globalization. As government lack of funds FDI is allowed into higher education. The foreign universities is expected to bring the quality infrastructure in teaching, research as well as physical infrastructure This will attract large scale foreign investments into India and also to an extent reverse brain drain. However, the government will have to create a level playing field for all institutions and also ensure that other factors are considered. Their entry should also increase the qualities in research areas and so on, rather than focus on undergraduate programs.
10. Communication- The effects of globalization on education bring rapid developments in technology and communications. It changes the role of students and teachers and producing a shift in society from industrialization towards an information-based society.
11. E-learning-People with disability get benefit from globalization only if they endowed with knowledge, skills, capabilities and rights needed to pursue their basic livelihoods. The introduction of technology into the classroom is changing the nature of delivering education to students is gradually giving way to a new form of electronic literacy, more programs and education materials are made available in electronic form, teachers are preparing materials in electronic form; and students are generating papers, assignments and projects in electronic form. Video projection screens, books with storage device servers and CD rooms as well as the emergence of on-line digital libraries are now replacing blackboards. Even exams and grades are gradually becoming available through electronic means and notebooks are starting to give way to laptops. Also, students can be examined through

computer managed learning systems and do tutorial exercises on a computer rather than in a classroom.

One effect of globalization on training is the direness to build up a talented work constrain at all dimensions to meet the requests of expanding business condition. Rather than its conventional job of giving training as a welfare measure, the state is required to encourage privatization and deregulation in instruction, especially as the nature of instruction given by the state organizations has been somewhat poor. This is in no way, shape or form unfortunate, as privatization of training has expanded amount just as quality. Profiteering is a negative factor, yet its shrewdness is regularly balanced by the convenient and proficient use of human ability to create intensity around the world. Indians looking for work and contending effectively is no ongoing marvel. Globalization has only hurried the pace of relocation and made better positions around the world.

As the private segment's commitment in advanced education in India is picking up in quality, India can't take plan of action to article 1.3 of the GATS that permits exclusion for administrations given by the legislature. So as to adapt to the western nations, the measures required incorporate the selection of an acknowledge based semester framework for constant inner assessment. A cafeteria type choice to the understudies for the course to be offered and encourages of credit exchange. A greater part of customary colleges in India are a long ways behind, in any event in non-proficient courses. As the UGC, AICTE (All India Council of Technical Education) and other controlling offices are not in a situation to mediates viably and control the remote instructive establishments, the administration of India has set up a board of trustees under the NAAC, under its director Ram Takwale, to screen the applying outside colleges. At present 150 remote colleges (50 from UK, 45 from Australia. 30 from USA and the rest from Canada and other European nations that have been working in India. The UGC has chosen to welcome recommendations from organizations that are enthused about "sending out Indian instruction" to remote students under a "Study India Program". An ongoing report demonstrates that one in each 10 understudies examining in the US was an Indian, while under 0.6 percent of American Students were getting instructive kudos for concentrate in India.

The administration of India has perceived these unsafe wonders and belatedly began the way toward establishing a Committee for the Promotion of Indian Education Abroad under the Ministry of Human Resources Development, branch of training. Amid 2001, there were 54,664 Indian understudies in the United States alone, with the all out number abroad surpassing 10 lakhs. Interestingly, there were just 7,791 outsider understudies in India, for the most part from the creating nations like Bangladesh and nations of South and East Asia. Globalization and commercialization of instruction has subsequently turned into a reality and, India being a signatory to the WTO as additionally to the WATS, we must be particularly mindful about the working of the remote instructive organizations.

Pathways to A Global Future

Indeed, even an extraordinary hopeful person can't resist the opportunity to be unsettled by the numerous issues defying the Indian advanced education framework – a huge and clumsy framework included about 300 colleges and regarded colleges, in excess of 10,000 universities and some 6.5 million understudies. The circumstance is additionally entangled by the rigidities of India's unified advanced education administration, the political weights on advanced education organizations and the developing issue of debasement in different parts of college life (e.g., affirmations, examinations, advancements). In such an ambushed framework, in what manner can internationalization endeavors conceivably be successful? In the event that India needs to rise as favored area for advanced education in the globalizing scene it should build up a national approach to address the difficulties of sub-standard quality, insufficient frameworks of checking and control, red-tapism in development and improvement and political impedance.

Three pathways offer some expectation and guarantee for what's to come. The main way is named strategy change. It incorporates opening up space for private colleges, facilitating or dispensing with research confinements on remote researchers and graduate understudies, and empowering "outside coordinated effort" in the college area similarly such joint endeavors currently exist in private industry. More grounded associations should be produced between Indian colleges and colleges in different nations.

A second pathway for Indian internationalists has to do with associations. In fields, for example, designing, the executives and PC sciences, for instance, industry-college coordinated efforts can yield noteworthy advantages for the two sides. A progressively deliberate spotlight on institutional associations could likewise turn out to be a piece of India's way to deal with bi-horizontal academic trade programs. The last pathway centers around development and administration, two characteristics in most noteworthy need inside Indian advanced education today. Advancement can take an assortment of structures, running from the utilization of web innovation to create joint on-line courses among Indian and remote colleges to institutional developments like the activity by SNDT Women's University to set up an abroad branch grounds for ladies understudies in the Gulf locale. Effective development does not happen without initiative. For India to widen and grow its place in the worldwide commercial center of advanced education will require striking and creative initiative by college Vice-chancellors, political pioneers, managers and arrangement producers at the focal and state levels.

Conclusion

There is presently expanding worldwide challenge generally advantageous and most splendid understudies, as an ever increasing number of nations perceive the financial capability of advanced education as an administration send out segment and India isn't an exemption. The real worry of globalization has been "the means by which to satisfy the national goal of equity?" Interaction is required to enhance the nature of training and execution assessment at all dimensions of instruction which is giving more roads to the private schooling and thusly influencing the value thought. Changes in Indian instruction framework that unavoidable the center seems to continue as before just the thought of progress and the rate at which it happens shifts for all intents and purposes and spatially and in field tasks. Globalization of advanced education may assist India with taking favourable position of chances in the new worldwide condition.

With prescience, ability and assurance, the present chiefs of Indian colleges include it inside their capacity to make an alternate sort of globalization, one which asserts and values social distinction and supports more noteworthy versatility for all understudies. The universe of advanced education in the 21st century can genuinely be an outskirt less universe of information and thoughts which will yield corresponding advantages for all countries. There is no single, straightforward way to achieve this new worldwide future, yet rather, different pathways that lead toward "a world in one home".

References

1. Assocham–Icrier, Joint Conference on Globalization and Higher Education in India, November 1-2, 2006, New Delhi.
2. Draft Report of Working Group on Higher Education for the XI Plan, Planning Commission, Government of India (2007).
3. Gaynor, N. (2010). Globalizing higher education: Challenges and contradictions in policy & practice; A development Education Review, Vol.II
4. Higher Education and Globalization, 23rd Convocation Address by Dr. Panjab Singh, Oct. 14 2008, Rani Durgawati Vishwavidyalaya, Jabalpur.

5. Mishra, J. K., Abidi, N. and Sharma, R. (2008). Indian Higher Education: Global Challenges and Local Issues. JBS Working Paper Series.
6. Safaya, R. (2002). Current problems in Indian Education, Dhanpat Rai Publishing Co: New Delhi.
7. Scott, P. (1998). Classification, Internationalization and Globalization, in P. Scott (ed.), The Globalization of Higher Education, The Society for Research into Higher Education/Open University Press, Buckingham, pp. 108- 129.
8. Sharma, V. (2007). Indian Higher Education: Commodification and foreign direct investment. The Marxist, Vol.XXIII, No. 02.
9. Takwale, R. (2002). Presidential Address on 'Convergence of Educational Modes – An Opportunity for Evolving New Paradigm of Education' at the IDEA 2002 Conference held at University of Jammu, Jammu, during 1-3 March 2002.
10. Teichler, U. (2004), .The Changing Debate on Internationalization of Higher Education. Higher Education, Vol. 48, pp. 5-26.
11. Tilak, J.B.G. (2002). Education and Globalization: The changing concerns in Economics of Indian Education. Perspectives in Education, Vol. 17, Special Issue pp. 05-08.
12. Valimaa, J. (2004). Nationalization, Localization and Globalization in Higher Education. Higher Education, Vol. 48, pp. 27-54.

Chapter-51

The Commercialisation of Higher Education: A Paradigm Shift from Educating All to the Facilitating Few

Maruthi. O,

Dr. J. Rani Ratna Prabha

Abstract

Education in any form plays a vital role in human development and it helps in transforming society into a knowledge society. The role of higher education is even more essential as it directly contributes to the growth and sustenance of a knowledge society and internationally it is regarded as 'Tertiary Education'. The Indian education system in its present structure (English Education System) is the result of various reforms during the colonial period especially after the Charter Act (1813) for educational development in India. During the time of Independence, there were about 20 universities and 500 affiliated colleges. It was almost like Starting from Scratch and there were many other challenges in the newly independent country to establish stable and sustainable economic development. Despite serious handicaps of resources both in terms of human and capital, during the last seven decades a remarkable the change has been taken place. The large body of the education system has created a gigantic change in the utilisation of human resources and equipped them with a high order of scientific and technological capabilities, robust humanist and philosophical thought and creativity. Then after the higher education system started its move with remarkable changes.

The major outstanding achievements in the fields of education and employment were recorded only through public funding in the pre-globalisation period. But the Post- globalisation period experienced the laxity in support of public higher education and the decrease of public funding to meet the global challenges of education and employment. In a flipside, Private higher education sector has emerged and occupied the major portion of the education system. Though the evolution of the privatisation is a recent phenomenon, the private players have rapidly hegemonised their participation in the field of higher education. Within a decade period, they have occupied nearly 80 percent of the total higher educational institutions and accommodating more than 70 percent of the enrolments. Speedy commercialisation of higher education institutions and its services is the trending development in contemporary India as they offer only the profitable professional courses like Engineering, Medical, Management, and Computer application and others. On the other hand, the Indian society is highly stratified with the evils of caste, class, gender, and race, where the deprived sections like Scheduled Castes (SCs), Scheduled Tribes (STs) and Other Backward Classes (OBCs) are deprived of education and its amenities for centuries. The privatisation of higher education is one which badly affected the poor majority by undermining the equity and equal opportunity. In this regard, the present paper is an attempt to explore the structural changes happened in the higher educational system, and thus how it is affecting the public education system in the post globalisation period.

Keywords: *Higher Education, Privatisation, Hegemony, Globalisation, and Deprived Classes.*

Introduction

Education is one of the key instrument of development for a human being in both social and economic aspects. It is the master key which unlocks all the doors of development. The role of higher education is even more significant as the former crafts the society into a knowledge society and the later helps in the sustainability of the knowledge society. Higher education is greatly connected with the generating the new ideas, knowledge and in the enhancement of the skills for the individual and community development which ultimately leads to the sustainable development of a country. Education has become the major reason for the development of a conscious society in many countries many countries of the world. Access to education, especially at the higher levels can improve the economic outcomes of citizens and determine the prospects of future generations, especially in developing countries like India.

India is following the English education system, introduced by the European powers especially, the British during the early eighteenth century. "*Till the eighteenth century, India had three distinct traditions of advanced scholarship in the Hindu Gurukulas, the Buddhist viharas, and the Quranic madarasas, before the British set up a network of schools to impart western education in English medium" (Perkin, 2006)*[1] The genesis of modern English education and its adaptability was witnessed through many administrative proceedings.

The Post independent government at various period has adopted and continued the education system paved by the colonial powers during their two decades of their regime with the indigenous needs. According to Agarwal

(2006), *The higher education system in India grew rapidly after independence. By 1980, there were 132 universities and 4738 colleges in the country enrolling around five percent of the eligible age group in higher education.*[2] Today India had crossed more than seven decades where the education in general and higher education, in particular, have reached several milestones and a vast system of higher education has been developed. Indeed, the access and participation is still a nightmare for many marginalised communities like Scheduled Castes, Scheduled Tribes, Women, Physically Challenged and many other Religious Minorities. According to Thorat (2006), SC, ST, OBC, and other religious minorities such as Christian, Muslims, Sikhs, and Buddhist are also suffered from lower access to higher education as compared with their higher caste counterpart from these religions.[3]

History of Education System in India

In the infancy of humanity, education was quite unconscious (Das, S K 1930)[4]. The first phase of education to a human is through the observation, in order to try to get Food, shelter, and safety, man learns to observe nature. Later he has experienced and understood his physical and mental power in process of saving himself from the destructive forces with other animals. Later the assistance by the by the elders to their younger generation have created the mode of training as a mode of education. But the invention of domestication of animals, fire and the language became the major steps in the advancement of his prosperity through words, which helped him to be settled at one place and to form a societal relationship. Gradual man learns to control the things around him firstly from their family by imparting the patriarchal values, later he assumed the powers to a small community of living in the form of villages head and later formed and bounded by a certain customs and laws. This was considered as the genesis of conscious education during the ancient time.

The genesis and development of education as a system in India has a rich and interesting history and the bird-view on ancient India itself reveals that India does not belong to one race but different people at various stages have lived in the Indian soil and left their marks in the society. An anthropological inquiry, on the study of these races, has stated that the four major races had lived and proved their existence viz., Dravidians, Aryans, Scythians, and Mongolians. Certainly, the entire the ancient Indian education system was controlled by the Aryan race for many decades and the society is divided its people according to the dissection which was directed by the Varna System. Historical inspection on the education system states that access to education was restricted to the particular classes and people are divided into four Varnas as Brahmin the preaching class, Kshatriya the warrior class, Vaishya the trader class, and Shudra and Ati- Shudras as a service class. Inter-dining and intermarriages are strictly prohibited among these groups and pursuing education (learning of Vedas and other spiritual texts of Hindu religion) is the right of only Brahmins and to some extent only kings have those right to study or learn and undeniably, the other Varnas doesn't have any saying or right on the pursuing the education.

The advent of Buddhist and Jainist education system has been the first ever jolt on the rigid Hindu education system. unless the Hindu education system, the Buddhist monastic colleges began to impart education to the layman. Buddhism which has emerged out of the rebellion character against the Hindu caste system taught almost all the subjects which are taught by the gurukuls, but it also added the Pali language in their curriculum which was the layman's language with intention of even a corner man in the society should understand the essence of the education and its values. It was open to all without any discrimination though it was closed to Sudras in case of Hindu education.

Later during the medieval period education system was mainly dominated by the Muslim rulers, they followed the policy of laissez-faire for education which was considered the responsibility of society rather than the state. there was no particular department was formed by the Muslim rulers for imparting the education. the educational institutions were attached to the mosque or temple and the major aim of the education system in this period is the illumination and extension of knowledge and also the propagation of Islam religion. In many instances the Muslim rulers have shown the keen interest to develop the non-muslim languages especially the Sanskrit, they encouraged the translation of many Sanskrit literature works into Arabic and Persian languages. But the majority of Hindus regarded Muslims as impure and tried to avoid the contact with them. As a result, the Muslim education remained unconnected with the majority of Hindu communities.

India is following the current education system which is prevailed in India today was influenced by the European powers at the beginning of the nineteenth century. For the first time after Several centuries of Buddhist education system during the ancient period, the British have accommodated the downtrodden classes or the Dalits in the education system.

The saga continues even after the post-independence period government at various stages have implemented the several acts and regulations, especially affirmative action has to help the downtrodden classes to improve their qualities, as a result, Indian literacy rates has been increased from 16.67 percent in 1951 to the 74.04 percent in 2011 census report. In contrast with that still One-third of the Scheduled Castes, 42.72 percent of Muslims, 32.49 percent from Sikhs and 28.17 percent among Buddhists and 25.66 percent among Christians still remain as illiterates. Still, these are the most vulnerable group which often prone to many forms of discriminations and one can remember the caution given by Dr. B. R Ambedkar, during the constituent assembly debates *"On 26th January 1950, we are going to enter into a life of contradictions. In politics, we will have equality and in social and economic life, we will have inequality. In politics, we will be recognising the principle of one man one vote and one vote and one value. In our socio-economic life, we shall, by reason of our social and economic structures continue to deny the principle of one man one value. How long shall we continue to live this life of contradictions? How long shall we continue to deny equality in our social and economic life? If we continue to deny it for a long time we will do so only by putting our political democracy in peril. We must remove this contradiction at the earliest possible moment or else those who suffer from inequality will blow up the structure of political democracy which this Assembly has so laboriously built up"*[5]

At this juncture, it will clarify that though the existence of the best constitution in the world, implementation of its essence is not properly undertaken. Although, the constitution assembly suggested education to be listed in the Central list after 1947 education was listed in the concurrent list with promise of promoting the education as an instrument of social development and meanwhile central and state governments are encouraged the establishment of universities and colleges but, the post-independence governments especially, during the late 1990s have announced the decision of making the secondary and higher education as a non-merit good since then the government gradually and drastically reduced the subsidies on public education particularly on higher education. The major losers of this process are the marginalised classes such as Scheduled Castes, Scheduled Tribes, Muslims many other religious minorities.

Development of Higher Education in India

There has been the unprecedented growth of higher education in the country since independence. The growth of Higher education in India can be discussed in three phases, the first phase from 1947 to 1980s which evident the growth of grant-in-aid institutions or private aided institutions. The second phase of 1980 to 2000 covers the various developments in the national education policy and the wake of economic reforms in the early 1990s. It is generally recognised that 1991 was the landmark year for privatisation policy prescriptions in India (Naib 2004; Sengupta 2008).[6] The New Economic Policy of 1991 has invited the role of private players in the field of education by reducing public expenditure in the social sectors. Later in 1997, the government has identified the large scale of social and economic services and it also divided them into three categories as public goods, merit goods, and non-merit goods and proposed to reduce the subsidies for the non- merit goods and education up to the elementary level considered as a merit good and the later stage of education including higher education considered as the non-merit good. The third phase, from the year of 2000 onwards had to experience the demand of deemed-to-be universities and growth of pure private institutions across the state. The higher educational institutions are also considered as social institutions which play a major role in creating and disseminating the knowledge and also in constructing a knowledgeable society. After independence, the government of India was busy with the issues and problems of post-partition. the government was also concerned regarding the development of human resources. However, since the early 1950s, higher education has been diversified and extended its reach and coverage quite significantly. According to Tilak (2008) *"Conventionally higher education producing a huge set of externalities benefitting not only the individual but also the whole society. is regarded as the public good"*.[7] But during the late 1970s and early 1980s education across the world was facing in the crisis in terms of the high inflation rate, increase in pupil strength, cut- down in the public expenditure especially on the education and increasing the private ownership of the educational institutions. This phase is also experienced the Neo-liberal thinking led to the replacement of the welfare state to the free market philosophy. Traditional values and policies are gradually replaced with the new values and policies which led to the marketisation. By mid- 1990s this philosophy has also occupied the education sector and education nowhere remained as the public good and increasingly treated as the private good. The process of globalisation and internationalisation has gained its momentum and helped in spreading the new values across the country. So the development of higher education in the country until the 1980s is in the public nature and the later developments are characterised to the marketisation or private nature. Jomtien conference on education in 1990 under the umbrella of major international organisations like World Bank, UNESCO, UNICEF and UNFPA gave a serious call for the attention of the national and international communities to focus on the literacy and primary education thus improving the access to the higher education. Gradually the attempt was made to bypass the government control over higher education and all the policies and plan documents including economic survey mostly ignored the higher education and its public funding and focused entirely on the literacy and primary education.

During the late 1990s the policies which are supporting the liberalisation, privatisation, and globalisation, made the drastic reforms in the higher education sector. Since then there was a steady increase in private ownership in the higher educational institutions and decrease in the public institutions. Currently, there are 864 Universities, 40.026 colleges, and 11,669 stand-alone institutions in India. among the 824 universities, 1 Central Open University, 44 Central Universities, 33 Deemed Universities (Government), 5 Institutions under Legislature Act, 100 institutions on National Importance, 79 Deemed Universities (Private), 233 State Private Universities, 13 State Open Universities, 345 State Public Universities, Deemed Universities-Government Aided. In addition to this, there are various bodies regulating the higher educational institutions at various levels like NAAC for quality assessment of higher educational institutes in India. NBA, AICTE, AB, ICAR and more. World Trade Organisation (WTO) is the only international organisation dealing with global rules of trade between the nations.[8]

Till the year 1996 public services such as education, healthcare, and many other important services are classed as domestic activities, not included in the International trade agreement and it was difficult to trade across the boundaries The General Agreement on Trade in Services was a part of the trinity of Agreements upon in the Uruguay round included the 161 activities including education in the international trade agreement. According to this agreement educational systems are not exclusively provided by the public sectors and education particularly the higher education is no more becomes the free good and the agreement led to the financialisation of higher education.

Commercialisation of Higher Education v/s Issues of Access Quality and Equity.

Today the pure privatisation process is on the way to capture the entire educational system. Though private institutions are funded and subsidized by the state, it doesn't have any say at the administration level. The state is trying to abdicating from its responsibility of providing the equal opportunity to the each and every person without any discrimination. On the other hand, private educational institutions are working with the profit moto and primarily deprived of Social Ideas, Social Objectives, they look people at their economic status. These private institutes are depriving the marginalised classes like Scheduled Caste and Scheduled Tribes, OBC and RMs are still facing many problems related to equity, access, and quality.

The social structure of the Indian society is diversified comparatively to the other nations of the world. the demography of India reveals that more than 80 percent of the marginalised classes are still deprived of quality education. Out of 85 percent of marginalised classes, only 8 percent of Dalits, 6 percent of Tribes and less than 9 percent of Muslim children are able to graduate from class 12. It can be evident that more than 70 percent of children from the marginalised are still studying at the publicly funded institutions, the recent developments in the educational system have made them become dropouts due to various reasons associated with accessibility and quality.

During the early 1990s, The Government of India appointed two committees on both central universities and technical educational institutions. (1993 and 1994) The reports of the committees pressed the importance of state government financing and they have also suggested the possible measures to mobilise the non-governmental resources, funding for higher education such as rising the fees levels, the introduction of self-financing courses at the institutions, introducing the revitalisation of student loans. The government also found comfortable with these recommendations and adopted in its policy framework. Today a large number of institutions have launched many self-financing courses and many universities are subsequently increased the fee levels. Thus even today in a country like India, poor people go to public Institutions and most of the private Institutions are remained opened for the elites and other affordable sections especially at the Higher levels.

Though it is evident that most of the children from the Dalit and other marginalised communities are out of school and dropping out on the reason of economic inability no private institutions are ready to provide or reserve half of their seats for the socially and economically disadvantaged sections and no private institutions are ready to educate the rural mass with low-cost fees, they only concentrated in the urban world where it can exploit the readily available resources. Indeed today rural society is also experiencing the heat of privatisation in a quick way. These private institutions are charging higher fees and only those who can affordable are reaching to those institutions. It is unfair to a country like India to educate only 10 percent of the affordable classes to learn and keeping aside bright future of the 90 percent of the population. It will also affect the quality of education in overall because more than 60 percent of the population in the country lives in poor economic conditions, added to this there is an increased participation of private players in the education sector particularly in the higher education and the allocation of budget for education is reduced to less than three percent in the year 2015. In the higher education space, the total budgetary allocation has been reduced for IITs—from Rs 8,244.8 crore to Rs 6,326 crore in 2018-19. There is a cut in the budget allocations to IIMs as well as the University Grants Commission.[9]

Teachers are the major medium of communication in which student can learn directly by observing their virtue of knowledge. Teaching is also put under great risk through the privatisation. Today teaching has become one of the most unattractive profession. It is because the teachers are gradually replacing by the Online courses and lakhs of teachers across the nation are still appointing in the yearly contract basis with a salary of nuts. The privatisation of higher education is not only creating a gap between the students and teachers but also reducing the level of a teacher merely to a commodity. Thus the higher education in India through the process of privatisation seizing the future of the many students from the marginalised classes by depriving of the equality in access, participation and quality education.

Conclusion

The introduction of neo-liberal policies in the early 1990s has resulted in a momentous paradigm shift in the public approach to education: education nowhere remained as the public good character and meanwhile private sector is also gained its strength with a motive of profit-seeking and gradually Commercialisation of education, especially the higher education is on the step towards conquering entire education system.

Private education is not a new phenomenon in India, as there is a vast private sector, which is state-supported. However, the growth of '*pure private*' sector in education has been a recent one. The growth of such private sector, solely relying on student fees, has been very rapid in the last couple of decades, crowding out the public sector.

The decline in public investment in higher education, though essentially viewed as a factor contributing to the growth of the private sector, is also viewed as an outcome: as the private sector is growing, there is no need for growth in the public sector. All this poses serious problems relating to access, quality, and equity in education, resulting in dangerous cracks in the edifice of higher education and the erosion of public good nature of higher education.

AISHE report says, today the 34.2 million students were enrolled in the institutions of higher education out of that 22 million students (65 percent) are enrolled in private institutions and about 53 percent of college students are enrolled in private institutions because of there are not enough public higher educational institutions. In this hour of need, the state should intervene and should take the responsibility of educating all and It is the responsibility of a state to look at the welfare of the poor and marginalised classes through public funding. The state should take over the monopoly over the education system and it should have its say in all the decision process especially in the education sector.

References

1. Agarwal, P. (2006). *Higher education in India: The need for change* (No. 180). Working paper.
2. Agarwal, P. (2009). *Indian higher education: Envisioning the future*. Sage Publications India.
3. Chitnis, S., & Altbach, P. G. (1993). *Higher Education Reform in India: Experience and Perspectives*. Sage Publications Inc., 2455 Teller Road, Newbury Park, CA 91320, tele.
4. Deshpande, S. (2006). Exclusive inequalities: Merit, caste, and discrimination in Indian higher education today. *Economic and Political Weekly*, 2438-2444.
5. Kapur, D. (2012). Indian higher education. In *The Globalization of Higher Education* (pp. 177-208). Palgrave Macmillan, London.
6. Srivastava, P. (2010). Public-private partnerships or privatisation? Questioning the state's role in education in India. *Development in Practice*, *20*(4-5), 540-553.
7. Tijerina, K. H., & Biemer, P. P. (1988). The Dance of Indian Higher Education: One Step forward, Two Steps back. *Educational Record*, *68*(4), 86-91.
8. Tilak, J. B. (1991). The privatization of higher education. *Prospects*, *21*(2), 227-239.
9. Tilak, J. B. (2008). Higher education: a public good or a commodity for trade?. *Prospects*, *38*(4), 449-466.
10. Tilak, J. B. (2008). Transition from higher education as a public good to higher education as a private good: The saga of Indian experience. *Journal of Asian Public Policy*, *1*(2), 220-234.
11. Tilak, J. B. (2018). Private higher education in India. In *Education and Development in India* (pp. 535-551). Palgrave Macmillan, Singapore.

Notes

1. Agarwal, P. (2006). *Higher education in India: The need for change* (No. 180). Working paper. pp5
2. ibid

3. Thorat, S. (2006). Higher education in India: Emerging issues related to access, inclusiveness and quality. *Nehru Memorial Lecture. University of Mumbai, Mumbai.*

4. Hopkins, E. W., & Das, S. K. (1931). The Educational System of the Ancient Hindus.

5. Chand, S. (2007, December 11). Dr Ambedkar on Democracy. Retrieved December 12, 2018, from https://www.mainstreamweekly.net/article467.html

6. Srivastava, P. (2010). Public–private partnerships or privatisation? Questioning the state's role in education in India. *Development in Practice*, *20*(4-5), 540-553.

7. Tilak, J. B. (2008). Transition from higher education as a public good to higher education as a private good: The saga of Indian experience. *Journal of Asian Public Policy*, *1*(2), 220-234.

8. MHRD (2017). *All India Survey on Higher Education report of 2016- 17.* New Delhi, India.

9. Livemint. (2018, February 01). Education outlay in Budget 2018 set at Rs85,010 crore.

Chapter-52

Women in Higher Education: Issues and Challenges

Manjula A,

Abstract

"Unity is meaningless without the accompaniment of women, Education is fruitless without educated women and Agitation is incomplete without the strength of women"

D.R. Ambedkar

Education is one of the fundamental factors of economic development. Through the education a person can improve the efficiency of the labour force, by fostering democracy and thus creating better conditions for good governance, by improving health and so on. Education also raises people's productivity and creativity and promotes entrepreneurship and technological advancements. In recent scenario women's education is considered as a greater importance than that of men's education. Female education has powerful effects on the total fertility rate and hence on public population growth. Girl's education and the promotion of gender equality in education are critical to development, and policies and actions that do not address gender disparities miss critical development opportunities.

Dr.B.R.Ambedkar, Savitribai Phule and Mahatma Jotibha Phule who fought for the women's education and the Indian feminist movement is incomplete without these people contribution. They fought for women education and equality. Educate a woman, Agitate for the social issues and problems, Organise women to protect themselves through education. In the society women rights are equal to human rights. Women are the roots for preserving the caste, culture, religion, and property. In the twenty first century also women safety is questionable. While they are travelling from place to place for education so many sexual attacks are happening on girl students and women. Women safety is very important; as long as there is no safety for women it is difficult to achieve the development of the nation. A woman has to face discrimination from society as well as family also. Especially the girl child is given less importance and they are forced to stay back at home to assist in cooking cleaning and look after the young ones and grandparents. In rural

areas most of the women and Dalit women are backward economically, as well as socially in nature. One of the reasons behind this includes "Education". The Fourth Education commission (1964-66) remarks "for the full development of human resources, for the improvement of our homes and for moulding the character of children during the most impressionable years of infancy, the education of women is of even greater importance than that of men". The proper development of children largely depends upon the education of women. Mother is the foundation on which child's socialization process depends to a considerable period of time. Educated women can very easily share in decision making about everything in the family. (Goswamy, 1991).
The development of the women is possible through education only so the government should implement proper policies for the girl/women education. The present paper explores how difficult for women to get education and what are the difficulties women are facing while pursuing education and after pursuing the education.
Keywords: *Education, Women, Gender, Rights, Society.*

Introduction

Education can be viewed as a process of expanding human capacities to contribute to the making of a just and compassionate society. Education is the first step towards empowerment and the most crucial factor in the overall development of the individual and an effective instrument for social and economic development and national integration; it also helps one free from ignorance, exploitation, and poverty.

"Research worldwide shows that, in general, the economic benefits from the women's education-calculated as the economic rate of return to education- are comparable to those from men's education whereas the social benefits from investing in female's education are far greater than those from investing in males education."[1]

"Education is considered as a key of social change on one hand and on hand, it is considered as an instrument in creating social distension and perpetuating oppression. From ancient times education had been to subordinate certain groups such as Dalits and women"[2]

Education will help to develop one's personality and qualifies one in improving status an all respects. Education is the direct association to the socio-economic and political status of Dalit women (P.G.Jogdand).

The women's disadvantage in education is economically inefficient it prevails in most part of the world at varying degree. Female deprivation of education is particularly acute in the developing countries like India with high levels of poverty. The reality of gender inequality of higher education in India is very complex and diversified because it exists in every field like education, employment opportunities, income, health, cultural issues, social issues, economic issues etc.

In the ninth five year plan it is given assurance for the education, it says ensuring easy and equal access to education for women and girls and Elimination of gender bias in all educational programmes. It also stresses upon the Free education for girls up to college level including professional courses and Promoting skill development amongst women in modern upcoming trades etc.

G.P. Misra (1985) has remarked that the existence and persistence of spatial variations in the level of development is one of the basic structural characteristics of a developing country like India. If the adequate measures are not taken for the spread of education, the education chasm of economic disabilities, regional imbalance and social injustice will widen further, resulting in building up of disintegrative tendencies.

In India, women empowerment has taken a great change in the activities from the past few millenniums. Women enjoyed equal status with men in the Vedic period. The women situation was in pathetic condition from Mughal invaders and European invaders. The reformers B.R.Ambedkar, Raja Ram Mohan Roy, Pandita Rama Bai, and Eshawarchand Vidyasagar and some more others gave relief to women by educating them and making them know about their Rights. The British government has made some improvement in the status of women by "Abolition of the practice of Sati, Widow Remarriage Act in 1856. The Indian government made them get some more opportunities by constitutional laws, by the laws, there is no discrimination by the state on any grounds. And another law is Equality of opportunity (Article 16). Feminists have taken initiation in the 1970s and later that Many NGO's worked for the empowerment of the women. In 2001 the National Policy for the Empowerment was started by the Indian government for positive economic development and women got equal opportunity in health, education, anddecision-making process.

There is much importance for the empowerment women in this 21st century also. Women were degraded everywhere, they are brutally killed by people and commoditised, and they are sexually exploited by male and they are materialised. The reservation is granted for the women in Panchayat elections. As per the Indian constitution 73rd and 74th amendments, reservation is given to participating in Panchayat Raj elections but they are not functioning properly because of the male chauvinism in politics and society.

There must be empowerment in the women in social, educational ways also in the social empowerment the women status to be improved and have to reduce the maternal mortality rate. Women should take care of malnutrition. In India, the weaker sections face so much discrimination from society. They are exploited a lot in society. The authorities and social activist should look into the atrocities committed on the weaker section and they should try for the justice to be done to them. And for the victims some schemes to be introduced to help them. For empowerment of the women, awareness programs should arrange to know the rights. Education is very important for every woman, so the government should take an intervention to increase the literacy rate among women. Education is a tool to improve self-status in society.[3]

Disparities in women's education

Even though education has been considered important for women by various scholars, women even today are encountering various hurdles and discrimination. They are not equal opportunities to reap the benefits of education and literacy. Educational structures were inadequate and insensitive to women's needs and irrelevant to their daily lives. (UNESCO, 2001).

In India, the patriarchal society freedom and liberty were enjoyed by men only. In every family girl and boy were treated unequally. Girls were not allowed to pursue education. The reasons behind this are many; putting all together women's education is one of the limited opportunities. Most of the families don't send their daughters to school because it is a waste of expenditure on them. She will be with family till her marriage, after the marriage she will be a member of the other family so most the parents don't give importance to the girl child education. This type of feeling still exists in some families. As a result, Indian women are lacking in basic literacy.

In India "caste" is a deep-rooted phenomenon. Caste is the major determinant in deciding the social status of an individual and it can lead to a strong determinant to suppress an individual permanently. Scheduled caste's and scheduled tribe people are most backward in the Indian society. They were not treated equally in socially, politically and culturally. Discriminated in all possible ways for decades. The reservation had provided an opportunity to get equal education and employment. The enrolment of Sc's and St's is less in schools as well as in higher education.

Higher Education and Gender

From the period of civilization and after its existence also women were deprived of their right to equality in almost every field, including education, as it is the most important element of human overall development. In the patriarchal society, the subordination of women and discrimination on the basis of gender prevails irrespective of country, culture, society, and civilization.

The National policy of Education provides that "the education of girls should receive emphasis not only on the ground of social justice but also because it accelerates social transformation". In 1976, through the 42nd constitutional amendment, education was incorporated in the current list and it became a joint responsibility of both center and the state".

Education in General and Higher education in particular, was considered to be a privileged only meant for the higher castes, but Savitribhai Phule emphasised on secular education. She preached the importance of getting an education for both boys and girls. She was the reason thousands of women liberated and started living to fulfill their dreams. Savitribhai Phule was the crusader of women empowerment. Her contribution to the education field for girls and women is a remarkable history. At a time in India was plagued with women's outraged modesty, she played a key role for all those who were living a life of servitude. She was the first person who took the initiation to open the schools for the girls. Most of the upper caste people opposed the idea of opening schools but she faced all odds and she set up India's first women's school. She built 18 schools in the region. She had given a stipend to encourage them not stop schooling and the University of Pune was renamed as Savitribhai Phule University as an honor of her contribution in the field of education.

Right to education is a fundamental right of every citizen of India. The constitution provides equal rights to all gender. With 65.46 percent female literacy rate as per the 2011 census, women's education in India is still a point in question. It is still below the world average of 79.7 percent. The gender-based inequality in India can be measured by examining two important statistics: One is women constitute 46.2 percent of the total enrolment in higher education but the female labor force participation rate is a mere 27 percent.The second one is women form only 24 percent of entry-level professionals, out of which about 19 percent reach senior-level management roles and yet, paid 20 percent fewer salaries than men.

The problem arises in the family, parents negligence in girl child education. There are social and political reasons for girl child education. There is a lack of funding for the schools moreover the government schools are shutting down as there is no minimum number of students is not turning up for the education. No proper facilities and poor infrastructure of the school buildings. Parents are afraid of sending girls to long distant schools.

In the private schools the fee structure is very high; have to pay all basic fee, donation fee, sports fee, etc. Parents feel it as a burden and a middle-class family cannot spend that much expenditure. All these reasons put together the girl child education is neglected.

Conclusion

Education is the basic right of a human being but nowadays the private sector has occupied the public sector. Higher education contributes even more critical. Indeed, the burden has been increased in paying fees for the children and in this process parents are giving importance to the male child education than the girl child education. There are some factors responsible for low female literacy rate, gender-based inequality, social discrimination and economic exploitation, the occupation of the girl child in domestic chores and low enrolment of girls in schools. Most of the time parents fear about sexual harassment. Parents often complain about insecurity for girls attending schools. Instances of abduction, rape, and molestation of girls dampen the enthusiasm of parents and girl students in pursuing education beyond certain age; thereafter they remain bound to their homes. Education is an important facto and it enhances the self-respect of women. It also encourages a woman to participate in the changing process. It builds collective and alternative visions of their environment. Education helps them in questioning injustice and inequality. Helps women to assert themselves and modernizes the policies.

References

1. Bisht, D., & Rishi, S. (n.d.). Women Empowerment: A Challenge of the 21st Century. Shikshan Anveshika Shik. Anvesh., 68-68. Vol.7.
2. Chinarao, Y (2003). Dalit Struggle for Identity. New Delhi, Kanishka Publishers
3. Kingdon, G(2002), Education of Women and Socio-Economic Development" *Baha'I Studies Review,*
4. Jogdand, P. G. (1995). *Dalit women in India: issues and perspective*. Gyan Books.
5. Singh, S. C. (Ed.). (2009). *Gender Justice*. Serials Publications.

Notes

1. Kingdon, G (2002) , Education of Women and Socio-Economic Development" *Baha'I Studies Review,* Vol.7.
2. Chinarao, Y (2003). Dalit Struggle for Identity. New Delhi, kanishka Publishers.
3. Bisht, D., & Rishi, S. (n.d.). Women Empowerment: A Challenge of the 21st Century. Shikshan Anveshika Shik. Anvesh., 68-68. http://www.rmttc.com/images/new pdf/concept paper.pdf.

Chapter-53

Higher Education in India: Opportunities, Issues, Challenges and Suggestions

B. Venkateshwarlu,

Abstract

The world has realized that the economic success of the states is directly determined by their education systems. Education is a Nation's Strength. A developed nation is inevitably an educated nation. Indian higher education system is the third largest in the world, next to the United States and China. Since independence, India as a developing nation is contentiously progressing in the education field. Although there have been lot of challenges to higher education system of India but equally have lot of opportunities to overcome these challenges and to make higher education system much better. It needs greater transparency and accountability, the role of colleges and universities in the new millennium, and emerging scientific research on how people learn is of utmost important. India need well skilled and highly educated people who can drive our economy forward. India provides highly skilled people to other countries therefore; it is very easy for India to transfer our country from a developing nation to a developed nation. The current study aims to highlight the challenges and to point out the opportunities in higher education system in India.

Keywords: *Education, Opportunities, Challenges, Issues, Colleges, Universities*

Our university system is, in many parts, in a state of disrepair...In almost half the districts in the country, higher education enrollments are abysmally low, almost two-third of our universities and 90 per cent of our colleges are rated as below average on quality parameters... I am concerned that in many states university appointments, including that of vice-chancellors, have been politicized and have become subject to caste and communal considerations, there are complaints of favoritism and corruption.

Prime Minister of India

Introduction

India's higher education system is the world's third largest in terms of students, next to China and the United States. In future, India will be one of the largest education hubs. India's Higher Education sector has witnessed a tremendous increase in the number of Universities/University level Institutions & Colleges since independence. The 'Right to Education Act' which stipulates compulsory and free education to all children within the age groups of 6-14 years, has brought about a revolution in the education system of the country with statistics revealing a staggering enrolment in schools over the last four years. The involvement of private sector in higher education has seen drastic changes in the field. Today over 60 percent of higher education institutions in India are promoted by the private sector. This has accelerated establishment of institutes which have originated over the last decade making India home to the largest number of Higher Education institutions in the world, with student enrolments at the second highest. The number of Universities has increased 34 times from 20 in 1950 to 677 in 2014. Despite these numbers, international education rating agencies have not placed many of these institutions within the best of the world ranking. Also, India has failed to produce world class universities.

Today, Knowledge is power. The more knowledge one has, the more empowered one is. However, India continues to face stern challenges. Despite growing investment in education, 25 per cent of its population is still illiterate; only 15 per cent of Indian students reach high school, and just 7 per cent graduate. The quality of education in India whether at primary or higher education is significantly poor as compared to major developing nations of the world. As of 2008, India's post-secondary institutions offer only enough seats for 7 per cent of India's college-age population, 25 per cent of teaching positions nationwide are vacant, and 57 per cent of college professors lack either a master's or PhD degree. As of 2011, there are 1522 degree-granting engineering colleges in India with an annual student intake of 582,000 (Science and Technology Education, 2009) plus 1,244 polytechnics with an annual intake of 265,000. However, these institutions face shortage of faculty and concerns have been raised over the quality of education.

Despite these challenges higher education system of India equally have lot of opportunities to overcome these challenges and have the capability to make its identity at international level. However, it needs greater transparency and accountability, the role of universities and colleges in the new millennium, and emerging scientific research on how people learn is of utmost important. India provides highly skilled people to other countries therefore; it is very easy for India to transfer our country from a developing nation to a developed nation.

Opportunities in Higher Education

India is a large country, with an estimated population of young people aged between 18 to 23 years to be around 150 millions. The sheer size of the market offers huge opportunities for development of the higher education sector in India. India now boasts of having more than 33,000 colleges and 659 universities, which has been quite a remarkable growth during the last six decades. The year 2012 witnessed 21.4 million enrollments, which makes India the 3rd largest educational system in the world. Unfortunately, the educational infrastructure of India is inadequate to handle such huge volumes. In spite all the government spending in the educational sector, it is just too insufficient to meet the growing requirements. Therefore, higher Education sector has now been identified as one of the promising areas for private and foreign investments. It offers immense investment opportunities in both non-regulated and regulated segments. Indian higher education system is growing very fast irrespective of various challenges but there is no reason that these Challenges cannot be overcome. With the help of new-age learning tools, it is easy for country like India to overcome these problems and bring a paradigm shift in the country's higher education sector. With such a vibrant country with huge population properly educated, the possibilities are endless. If knowledge is imparted using advanced digital teaching and learning tools, and society is made aware of where we are currently lagging behind, our country can easily emerge as one of the most developed nations in the world. There are opportunities for strategic engagement and capacity building in higher education leadership and management at the state level. There are opportunities for India to collaboration at national and international level on areas of systemic reform, including quality assurance, international credit recognition, and unified national qualifications framework. Equality of educational opportunity in higher education is considered essential because higher education is a powerful tool for reducing or eliminating income and wealth disparities. The idea of equalizing educational opportunities also lies in the fact that "the ability to profit by higher education is spread among all classes of people. There are great reserves of untapped ability in the society; if offered the chance they can rise to the top. A great deal of talent of the highest level is, in fact, lost by an in egalitarian system of education". The need to enhance the employability of graduates is presenting entry points for collaboration in enterprise education and entrepreneurship, links with industry, research skills and the wide range of transferable skills, including English. The emerging interest in Indian higher education institutions in the vocational skills market provides areas for potential engagement with international partners. There is a need to build stronger relationships and increase mutual understanding in higher education by increasing support and participation in platforms which enable debate and dialogue with other countries of the world.

Critical issues in Indian higher education

As India strives to compete in a globalised economy in areas that require highly trained professionals, the quality of higher education becomes increasingly important. So far, India's large, educated population base and its reservoir of at least moderately well-trained university graduates have aided the country in moving ahead, but the competition isfierce; from China in particular. Other countries are also upgrading higher education with the aim of building world class universities. Even the small top tier of higher education facesserious problems. Many IIT graduates, well trained in technology, have chosen not to contribute their skills to the burgeoning technology sector in India; perhaps half leave the country immediately upon graduation to pursue advanced studies abroad, and most do notreturn. A stunning 86 percent of Indian students in the fields of science and technologywho obtain degrees in the United States do not return home immediately following their graduation. A body of dedicated and able teachers work at the IITs and IIMs, but the lure ofjobs abroad and in the private sector makes it increasingly difficult to lure the best and rightest to the academic profession.

The present system of higher education does not serve the purpose for which it hasbeen started. In general education itself has become so profitable a business that quality is lost in the increase of quantity of professional institutions with quota system andpoliticization adding fuel to the fire of spoil system, thereby increasing unemployment ofgraduates without quick relief to mitigate their sufferings in the job market of the country Critical issues in Indian higher education.

As India strives to compete in a globalised economy in areas that require highlytrained professionals, the quality of higher education becomes increasingly important. Sofar, India's large, educated population base and its reservoir of at least moderately well-trained university graduates have aided the country in moving ahead, but the competition is fierce; from China in particular. Other countries are also upgrading higher education with the aim of building world class universities. Even the small top tier of higher education faces serious problems. Many IIT graduates, well trained in technology, have chosen not to contribute their skills to the burgeoning technology sector in India; perhaps half leave the country immediately upon graduation to pursue advanced studies abroad, and most do notreturn. A stunning 86 per cent of Indian students in the fields of science and technology who obtain degrees in the United States do not return home immediately following their graduation. A body of dedicated and able teachers work at the IITs and IIMs, but the lure of jobs abroad and in the private sector makes it increasingly difficult to lure the best and brightest to the academic profession.

The present system of higher education does not serve the purpose for which it has been started. In general education itself has become so profitable a business that quality is lost in the increase of quantity of professional institutions with quota system and politicization adding fuel to the fire of spoil system, thereby increasing unemployment of graduates without quick relief to mitigate their sufferings in the job market of the country Critical issues in Indian higher education.

As India strives to compete in a globalised economy in areas that require highly trained professionals, the quality of higher education becomes increasingly important. So far, India's large, educated population base and its reservoir of at least moderately well-trained university graduates have aided the country in moving ahead, but the competition is fierce; from China in particular. Other countries are also upgrading higher education with the aim of building world class universities. Even the small top tier of higher education faces serious problems.

Many IIT graduates, well trained in technology, have chosen not to contribute their skills to the burgeoning technology sector in India; perhaps half leave the country immediately upon graduation to pursue advanced studies abroad, and most do not return. A stunning 86 per cent of Indian students in the fields of science and technology who obtain degrees in the United States do not return home immediately following their graduation. A body of dedicated and able teachers work at the IITs and IIMs, but the lure of jobs abroad and in the private sector makes it increasingly difficult to lure the best and brightest to the academic profession. The present system of higher education does not serve the purpose for which it has been started. In general education itself has become so profitable a business that quality is lost in the increase of quantity of professional institutions with quota system and politicization adding fuel to the fire of spoil system, thereby increasing unemployment of graduates without quick relief to mitigate their sufferings in the job market of the country.

Critical issues in Indian higher education

As India strives to compete in a globalised economy in areas that require highly trained professionals, the quality of higher education becomes increasingly important. So far, India's large, educated population base and its reservoir of at least moderately well trained university graduates have aided the country in moving ahead, but the competition is fierce; from China in particular. Other countries are also upgrading higher education with the aim of building world class universities. Even the small top tier of higher education faces serious problems. Many IIT graduates, well trained in technology, have chosen not to contribute their skills to the burgeoning technology sector in India; perhaps half leave the country immediately upon graduation to pursue advanced studies abroad, and most do not return. A stunning 86 per cent of Indian students in the fields of science and technology who obtain degrees in the United States do not return home immediately following their graduation. A body of dedicated and able teachers work at the IITs and IIMs, but the lure of jobs abroad and in the private sector makes it increasingly difficult to lure the best and brightest to the academic profession. The present system of higher education does not serve the purpose for which it has been started. In general education itself has become so profitable a business that quality is lost in the increase of quantity of professional institutions with quota system and politicization adding fuel to the fire of spoil system, thereby increasing unemployment of graduates without quick relief to mitigate their sufferings in the job market of the country.

So, the drawbacks of the higher education system underscore the need for reforms to make it worthwhile and beneficial to all concerned. Most observers agree that Indian higher education, the significant and impressive developments of the past few decades notwithstanding, faces major challenges in both quantitative and qualitative terms. Perhaps the clearest and boldest statement of this issue can be found in the "Report to the Nation 2006" of the National Knowledge Commission which concludes that there is 'a quiet crisis in higher education in India that runs deep', and that it has to do with both the quantity and the quality of higher education in India. Recognizing this dual challenge, the Indian Prime Minister, Manmohan Singh, severely criticized in a recent speech the serious qualitative deficiencies in Indian higher education while at the same time announcing plans for a major expansion of the system. Reflecting on the findings of a confidential report by the National Assessment and Accreditation Council, which is affiliated to the University Grants Commission (UGC), he expressed his concern over the fact that two thirds (68 percent) of the country's universities and 90 percent of its colleges are "of middling or poor quality" and that well over half of the faculty in India's colleges do not have the appropriate degree qualifications. Knowledge is the base for overall growth and if the nation has to be competitive and to be at par with the globalization pace, we will have to respond to the market forces.

Challenges in Higher Education in India

It is our 69th year of independence still our education system has not been developed fully. We are not able to list a single university in top 100 universities of the world. Various governments changed during these six decades. They tried to boost the education system and implemented various education policies but they were not sufficient to put an example for the universe. UGC is continuously working and focusing on quality education in higher education sector. Still we are facing lot of problems and challenges in our education system. Some of the basic challenges in higher education system in India are discussed below:

Enrolment: The Gross Enrolment Ratio (GER) of India in higher education is only 15 percent which is quite low as compared to the developed as well as, other developing countries. With the increase of enrolments at school level, the supply of higher education institutes is insufficient to meet the growing demand in the country.

Equity: There is no equity in GER among different sects of the society. According to previous studies the GER in higher education in India among male and female varies to a greater extent. There are regional variations too some states have high GER while as some is quite behind the national GER which reflect a significant imbalances within the higher education system.

Quality: Quality in higher education is a multi-dimensional, multilevel, and a dynamic concept. Ensuring quality in higher education is amongst the foremost challenges being faced in India today. However, Government is continuously focusing on the quality education. Still Large number of colleges and universities in India are unable to meet the minimum requirements laid down by the UGC and our universities are not in a position to mark its place among the top universities of the world.

Infrastructure: Poor infrastructure is another challenge to the higher education system of India particularly the institutes run by the public sector suffer from poor physical facilities and infrastructure. There are large number of colleges which are functioning on second or third floor of the building on ground or first floor there exists readymade hosieries or photocopy shops.

Political interference: Most of the educational Institutions are owned by the political leaders, who are playing key role in governing bodies of the Universities. They are using the innocent students for their selfish means. Students organize campaigns, forget their own objectives and begin to develop their careers in politics.

Faculty: Faculty shortages and the inability of the state educational system to attract and retain well qualified teachers have been posing challenges to quality education for many years. Large numbers of NET / PhD candidates are unemployed even there are lot of vacancies in higher education, these deserving candidates are then applying in other departments which is a biggest blow to the higher education system.

Accreditation: As per the data provided by the NAAC, as of June 2010, "not even 25 percent of the total higher education institutions in the country were accredited. And among those accredited, only 30 percent of the universities and 45 percent of the colleges were found to be of quality to be ranked at 'A' level".

Research and Innovation: there are very nominal scholars in our country whose writing is cited by famous western authors. There is inadequate focus on research in higher education institutes. There are insufficient resources and facilities, as well as, limited numbers of quality faculty to advice students. Most of the research scholars are without fellowships or not getting their fellowships on time which directly or indirectly affects their research. Moreover, Indian Higher education institutions are poorly connected to research centers. So, this is another area of challenge to the higher education in India.

Structure of higher education: Management of the Indian education faces challenges of over centralization, bureaucratic structures and lack of accountability, transparency, and professionalism. As a result of increase in number of affiliated colleges and students, the burden of administrative functions of universities has significantly increased and the core focus on academics and research is diluted.

Suggestions Improving the System of Higher Education:

(a) There is a need to implement innovative and transformational approach form primary to higher education level to make Indian educational system globally more relevant and competitive.

(b) Higher educational institutes need to improve quality and reputation.

(c) There should be a good infrastructure of colleges and universities which may attract the students.

(d) Government must promote collaboration between Indian higher education institutes and top International institutes and also generates linkage between national research laboratories and research centers of top institutions for better quality and collaborative research.

(e) There is a need to focus on the graduate students by providing them such courses in which they can achieve excellence, gain deeper knowledge of subject so that they will get jobs after recruitment in the companies which would reduce unnecessary rush to the higher education.

(f) Universities and colleges in both public private must be away from the political affiliations,

(g) Favoritism, money making process should be out of education system etc.

(h) There should be a multidisciplinary approach in higher education so that students knowledge may not be restricted only up to his own subjects.

Conclusion

Education is a process by which a person's body, mind and character are formed and strengthened. It is bringing of head, heart and mind together and thus enabling a person to develop an all round personality identifying the best in him or her. Higher education in India has expanded very rapidly in the last six decades after independence yet it is not equally accessible to all. India is today one of the fastest developing countries of the world with the annual growth rate going above 9 percent. Still a large section of the population remains illiterate and a large number of children's do not get even primary education. This is not only excluded a large section of the population from contributing to the development of the country fully but it has also prevented them from utilizing the benefits of whatever development have taken place for the benefit of the people. No doubt India is facing various challenges in higher education but to tackle these challenges and to boost higher education is utmost important. India is a country of huge human resource potential, to utilize this potential properly is the issue which needed to discuss. Opportunities are available but how to get benefits from these opportunities and how to make them accessible to others is the matter of concern. In order to sustain that rate of growth, there is need to increase the number of institutes and also the quality of higher education in India. To reach and achieve the future requirements there is an urgent need to relook at the Financial Resources, Access and Equity, Quality Standards, Relevance, infrastructure and at the end the Responsiveness.

References

1. Shaguri, Obadya Ray, Higher Education in India Access, Equity, Quality, EAN World Congress Scholar, Global Access to Postsecondary education, 2013.
2. Masani, Zareer, India still Asia's reluctant tiger, BBC Radio 4, 27 February 2008.
3. Newsweek, Special Report: The Education Race, August 18–25, 2011.
4. Science and Technology Education". Press Information Bureau, Retrieved 2009 08-08.
5. Mitra, Sramana, How To Save The World's Back Office of Forbes, 03.14.2008.
6. Henard, Fabrice, Report, Learning our Lesson: Review of Quality teaching in Higher Education, 2008.
7. Higher Education in India: Twelfth Five Year Plan (2012-17) and beyond FICCI Higher Education Summit 2012.

Chapter-54

Privatization of Higher Education in India

Md. Amzad,

Abstract

Education makes us more civilized and better educated. It helps us in making better position in the society and achieves dreamed position in the job. It makes us able to become a good doctor, engineer, officer, pilot, teacher, etc in the life whatever we want to become. Regular and proper study leads us towards success by making a goal of life. Earlier the education system was so tough and people from all castes were not able to get education according to their own wish. It was very tough to get admission in the proffered colleges because of high cost. But now it has become so simple and easy to go ahead in the education. Growing levels of private higher education "has resulted in a greater access but has made an alarming distress in the quality of the education. The UGC defines a private university as "an institution of higher learning established through a State or Central Act by a sponsoring body", such as a society registered under the Societies Registration Act, 1860, or any other corresponding law for the time being in force in a state or a public trust or a company registered under Section 25 of the Companies Act, 1956. As per law, for an institution to be given the status of a private university the State legislature conferring the status has to pass an Act by which the institution will acquire the status of a university. Private universities have to be recognised by the UGC so that the degrees awarded by them hold value. There are 262 Universities that can award degrees as specified by the UGC under Section 22 of the UGC Act with the approval of the statutory councils, wherever required through their main campus. In the wake of so much potential of setting up private universities, there is a strong need to explore challenges and opportunities of such private universities to impart higher education in terms of establishment, admission, formulating courses and curriculum. Also, innovations and about usage of ICT include that list. There is a need to investigate various aspects including advantages, disadvantages, and constraints of private universities for its stakeholders like students, faculty members, parents, industries and society. This article focuses on the privatization of Higher Education in India in the present day.

Keywords: *Higher Education, Private University, UGC.*

Introduction

Education has always been considered as the only key component of human development and greatest liberating force that contributes significantly to economic development. A well developed and equitable system of higher education that promotes quality learning as consequence of both teaching and research is pivot for success in the emerging knowledge economy. The developed world understood much earlier the fact that individuals with higher education have edge over their counterparts. They are the ones who always believed that any amount of investment in higher education was justifiable. So, it is important for developing countries like India to give due importance to both the quantitative and qualitative expansion of higher education, but the higher education system in India we inherited had been designed by a British government to suit their requirements since then no systematic efforts have been made to redesign and reorient the higher education system to meet the enormous task of economic regeneration, social transformation and political consolidation. It is not that nobody thought about modifying higher education; numerous committee reports, commission documents and national policies have made many valuable recommendations; but the higher education system remains unchanged, almost unaffected.

Higher Education Scenario in India

India's higher education system is the world's third largest interns of students, next to China and the United States. Unlike China, however, India has the advantage of English being the primary language of higher education and research. India educates approximately 11 per cent of its youth in higher education as compared to 20 per cent in China. The main governing body at the tertiary level is the University Grants Commission (India), which enforces its standards, advises the government, and helps coordinate between the centre and the State. Universities and its constituent colleges are the main institutes of higher education in India. As of 2011, India has 43 central universities, 130 deemed universities, 275 state universities, 90 private universities, 93 institutes of national importance and about 33,000 colleges. Most of these universities in India have affiliating colleges where undergraduate courses are being taught. Even after significant expansion in the post-independent period, access to higher education in India continues to be poor and more so for the disadvantaged groups. The mission of higher education is to achieve access, equality, justice, quality, employability, inclusiveness and create knowledge society and economy.

But the overall scenario of higher education in India does not match with the global Quality standards. Hence, there is enough justification for an increased assessment of the Quality of the country's educational institutions. Though India has a long heritage of quality higher education system it has failed to solve the problems of higher education until recent past. The deteriorating administration, unproductive practice, corruption and fund unavailability leads to break down of indigenous educational system. To tackle with the problem of unavailability of funds, instead of setting up new institutions, which require huge investments, priority of the government is to expand the capacity of existing institutions. This also infers that new education institutions in higher education would only be opened in private sector. None can deny the importance of private sector especially in tertiary education given the magnitude of challenge. But, government abdicating its responsibility for this crucial sector is fraught with grave implications. Public sector versus private sector accounts for about 62 percent of the total enrolment in higher education in India. The massive privatization of higher education would deprive a large section of Indians from Privatization Privatization means initiation of private ownership, management and control of organizations. The control is intermesh of decision making and responsibility of money and administration. In education privatization can be seen as expansion of private sector's control. Providing education to one and all has been one of the primary duties of the government. But there is a wave of privatization of education in our country. Actually government has diverted its focus from higher education to primary education and urged private sector to enter this sector which is term of higher education. .Privatization of higher education has emerged in several forms in the recent decade. Privatization within government higher education institutions takes place in the form of introducing self-financing courses within government institutions. Second form is converting government aided private institution in to private self financing institution. Third form of privatization is allowing self financing private institution with recognition and also without recognition. This may be termed as commercial private higher education institutions. Private Institutes are mainly allowed to set up state private universities, deemed university and academic institution with foreign collaboration, described the evolution of privatization in Indian higher education using a phrase, "from half-baked socialism to half bake capitalism." They argued that much of the massive privatization has not resulted from ideological commitments of key actors but is instead a result of collapse of the state system resulting in weak ideological and institutional foundations'.

Need of Privatization in Higher Education The need to privatize higher education is because of following reasons.

1. To increase competitive efficiency of public sector.
2. To meet the growing demand of higher education with rapid growth in population.
3. To reduce financial burden on government and for decentralization of educational institutions.
4. For imparting quality education and training and shaping of the curriculum according to global, national and local needs.
5. To fulfill the need for skilled manpower and to fulfill the need of the country in liberalization, privatization, and globalization.
6. To facilitate technological developments and information based economic development.

Impact of Privatization on Higher Education

Higher education in India has expanded rapidly over the past two decades. There are genuine concerns about many of them being sub standard and exploitative. Due to the government's ambivalence on the role of private sector in higher education, the growth has been chaotic and unplanned. The regulatory system has failed to maintain standards or check exploitation. The private institutions of present are motivated by profit. The large growths of these institutions (which make huge profits) represent commercialization of education. These institutions do not hesitate to admit students with poor academic credentials. The contributions of private sector to research and advanced level education are also found to be limited. (Tilak, 2005). It is rightly observed, "higher educationist far too expensive to be made privately profitable unless it is reserved for the rich or is of very poor quality.

Trends show that of the various forms of institutes of higher education that exists, the number supported by public funding have stagnated by growth (like the central and state universities, aided colleges, etc.) and rather the numbers with private funding have witnessed a speedily rising growth (like the private universities, deemed universities, unaided colleges, etc.). Within a small duration of five years from 2001–2006 the unaided private higher education accounted for 63 per cent (from 43 per cent in 2001) of the total higher education institutes and 52 per cent (from 33 percent in 2001) of the total higher education enrolments (FICCI, 2011). Since 2005–2011, the State Private Universities have witnessed fifteen-fold rise in the number of institutes from 6 to 94. Of the 130 Deemed Universities, 73 are in the private sector. About 1 per cent of colleges have been granted an autonomous status (FICCI, 2011). Quiet obviously most of this growth of private higher education has happened in the more marketable professional courses like engineering, medicine, management, computer applications, etc. ranging between 50 percent to 95 percent of the private institutions.

Suggestions

The massive privatization of higher education would deprive a large section of Indians from the ambit of higher education because they are too expensive. But, experience of deemed universities that turned to be teaching shops suggest that these caveats in policy do not stand during the implementation, so it is important to ensure that these institutes have adequate faculty, research facilities, relevant curriculum and adequate infrastructure among others as per Government norms. If we can impart high quality education to them we can reap the dividend. Otherwise, it would lead to demographic nightmare. So; we should follow the best practices in accreditation and assessment. Currently only handful of private institutions in India are accredited by NAAC and NBA.

Conclusion

The private initiative in education, especially higher education is not new to India. Some of the leading universities like Banaras Hindu University and Aligarh Muslim University came up with the efforts, dedication and financial support of community and since 1990's; trend towards privatization has-been on a large scale. Government cannot absolve its responsibility of regulating private institutes. So, some regulating agencies have to be formed which assure quality and transparency and prevent profiteering in private educational institutes. There is an emergence need to regulate quality but not growth of supply. Privatization of education has the potential to improve the quality of education as well as to reduce the cost. To ensure access to higher education by weaker section of society, government has to increase public expenditure on higher education. On the whole, an improvement in the standards of education could be achieved through a balanced relationship between public and private sector. Although there are many drawbacks of privatization of higher education but it has the positive point that education is accessible to all, even to the rural students now a days. In fact, privatization increases of number of degrees holders on one hand and unemployment on the other hand.

References

1. Agarwal, P. (2006). “Higher Education in India: The Need for Change.” ICRIER Working Paper, Indian Council for Research on International Economic Relations: No. 180.
2. FICCI. (2011). “Private sector participation in Indian higher education,” FICCI higher education summit 2011, Ernst & Young Pvt. Ltd., Kolkata.
3. Gautam,R.; Parihar, A.S.;Khare,S.(2015).”Analysis of Globalization/ Privatization of Higher Education in India, International Journal of Science, Technology and Management,Volume 4, Issue No. 1, pp 726-733.
4. Jonaki, B.; Prasenjit, P.(2016).” Higher Education in India: Recent Issues and Trends”, Research Journal of Educational Sciences, Volume 4 (1), 10-16.
5. Joshi, K. M.; Ahir, K.V.(2013). “Indian Higher Education: Some Reflections”, Intellectual Economics, Volume 7,No. 1(15), p 42-53.
6. Kapur, D.; Mehta, P.B. (2004). Indian Higher Education Reform: From Half-Baked socialism to Half-Baked Capitalism. Harvard University: CID Working Paper No. 108. September 2004.
7. Patel, I.G. (2003). Higher Education and Economic Development in JBG Tilak (ed),Education, Society and Development: National and International Perspectives, APH for NIEPA, New Delhi.
8. Tilak, Jandhyala BG (2005). Private Higher Education: Philanthropy to Profits’ in Higher Education in World 2006: The Financing of Universities, GUNI Series on the Social Commitment of Universities, Palgrave, New York and GUNI.
9. Times of India, 21st July, 2014, Article “Higher Education in India: An Introspection” Wikipedia-Higher Education in India.

Chapter-55

History of Higher Education in India

Dr. C. Kista Reddy,

Abstract

Development of any nation solely depends on the quality of human resources; and good human resource is produced through quality education. Education provides people with an opportunity to reflect on the social, cultural, moral, economic, and spiritual issues and contributes towards the development through propagation of specialized knowledge and skills. India, even after 70 years of its independence, is far away from the goal of universal literacy. The fact that India's higher education system is churning out millions of graduates who are unemployable speaks of the need to improve the quality of education in the country. However, on a positive note, India is engaged in the use of higher education as a powerful tool to build a knowledge-based information society of the 21st Century. Indian professionals are considered among the best in the world and are in great demand. This signifies the inherent strength of the Indian educational system.

Going Back to the Roots

Education in India dates back to its early civilization time where teaching and learning process revolved around the 'Gurukul System'. It was a residential concept wherein the students were educated under the guidance of a "Guru" in different areas of religion, philosophy and science. Historians speculate that these centers had a remarkable resemblance to the European medieval universities that came up much later. The initial education system in India gradually got obscured due to subsequent invasions and disorder in the country. In the early modern age, the Islamic influences enriched the traditional learning centers and brought in the disciplines of Geography, Administration, Law, and Arabic Mathematics to India.

A major change in the design of higher education was brought by the European rulers. The British established the formal system of higher education focused on languages, literature, history, and philosophy. These learning centers were focused on generating English-speaking working-class people for the British administrative services, army and trade. The British model of University system, inspired by the University of London, continued to expand across India, leading to a rising number of higher learning centers by 1947. The higher education system in India grew rapidly after independence. By 1980, there were 132 universities and 4738 colleges, enrolling around five per cent of the eligible age group in higher education. The number of institutions in India is four times more than the number of institutions both in the United States and the entire Europe.

Present-day Scenario

India is dashing headlong towards economic success and modernization. It is counting on high-tech industries, such as IT and Biotechnology, to propel the nation to prosperity. Currently, Indian higher education system has many favorable factors to its advantage. India has a large higher education sector, the third largest in the world. It uses English as a principal language of higher education and research and has an extensive academic tradition. Academic liberty is appreciated and there are a small number of high-quality institutions that can form the foundation of quality education. The fact that State Government, rather than Central Government, maneuvers vital responsibility for higher education, creates a rather cumbersome structure, but the system allows for a diversity of policies and approaches. Yet the weakness clearly outweighs the strengths. India educates approximately 10 percent of its youths in higher education. Even though, none of its universities occupy a solid position at the top. A few of the best universities have some excellent departments and centers, and there are a small number of outstanding undergraduate colleges. UGC recently released a report describing the current scenario of the Indian Higher Education System. It shows that despite the growing numbers of colleges and enrollments, it is not adequate enough to cater to the educational needs of the increasing young population.

Measures to Improve the Quality of Higher Education

One of the most efficient ways of tackling the problem of poor educational quality is by sharing the resources between private and public schools. It is vital to remember that the quality of education is directly linked to the resources available and it is important for the government to improve the resource allocation to bring about qualitative changes in the field of education. To enable the higher education sector to take on the emerging competition from the Asian countries, there is a need to loosen the hold of the government over the higher educational institutions.

The Government should undertake the following measures to improve the quality of higher education:

Encouraging Individuality

Albert Einstein once said, "*Everyone's a genius. But if you judge a fish on its ability to climb a tree, it will live its whole life believing that it is stupid.*" With the difference in ability, aptitude and interest of a student and the societal demands of expertise and specialization, the standardized testing and curriculum does not give much scope for the students to relate to the world of work and wages. Creativity that has nurtured our influences in almost all of life's passions and interests drops dead at standardized tests. The current educational system expects conformity and rewards predictable behaviors, both intellectually and emotionally.

Tech-Savvy Methods of Teaching

The new technologies offer vast opportunities for progress in all walks of life. The focus should not be on installing hardware but creating new, high-quality content such as intelligent teaching systems and tools that will help students to hone basic skills like reading and mathematics, and developing content in multiple Indian languages. Free high-speed internet connections can be provided to all schools through a simple scheme by which the government could reimburse internet service providers directly.

Making the Curriculum Dynamic

Currently, the curriculum in higher education is outdated in most cases. It is stale, dogmatic and teaches things that the world has moved on with. To infuse dynamism, the curriculum needs to be progressive in nature. Students need to be given the option of doing multiple courses. The spirit of curriculum should be projects-driven and not exams-driven.

High-Tech Libraries

The university libraries have a very good collection of books, but they are all in mess. A library must be online and helpful for serious study. Indian universities should concentrate more on providing quality education which is equivalent to that of the global standards. Instituting this notion in the education system will be of great help as anyone will be able to access the books and required study materials from anywhere with amazing effortlessness. Moreover, the E-libraries can be updated swiftly with new material and books.

The Power of Alumni

One of the most unappreciated potentials in Indian education system is the power of the Alumni. Excluding the IIT's and a few other top institutes, the concept of Alumni networking is non-existent. Once you launch a sincere network which is transparent, it would give the avenue as well as the confidence for the alumni to contribute in terms of money or academic expertise.

Keeping in perspective the rapid changes taking place in the society, higher education should possess various qualities like inculcation of confidence and ability to take responsibility and prepare students to be effective within the circumstances of their lives and work, and promote the pursuit of excellence in development and application of knowledge and skills. Government should take certain appropriate policy measures to improve the education system. India, today, is one of the fastest developing countries of the world. And hence, needs an educational system that is modern, liberal and can adapt to the changing needs of a changing society, a changing economy and a changing world.

Education in India

A well-established education system existed in India even in ancient times. There were old brahminical schools were theology, philosophy, arts, military education, public administration, etc.., was taught to the students. One major drawback about these schools was that education in India was a privilege and only children belonging to higher castes were allowed to receive the education. Ancient schools of India were mostly residential schools. The teacher and the pupils that used to receive the education stayed together till the education was completed. Education in India at that time was free; however students returned the favors by helping the teachers in daily chores. The teacher or Guru was the central figure and revered by all. In contemporary times, the great respect teachers and schools enjoy are somewhat related to the great honor bestowed in ancient times. Education in medieval India, new elements got fused in the education as foreign invaders brought with them their culture, their teachings and their life style. The growing influence of Islam also led to the establishment of schools for Muslims. Again the education primarily focused on theology. Thus two types of schools – the vedic schools and the Madrasas, were dominantly present in the pre-colonial India.

Education in India: Colonial Period

In the pre-colonial and early colonial period, India was not a strong nation in principle. The region comprised of separate small states that were often engaged in territorial disputes. Meanwhile, the renaissance period and great developments in the 14th, 15th and 16th century in Europe led them to explore new lands and further their movements. It was the time when missionaries started arriving in Asia and later in India. After the occupation of Indian states, the British, who had occupied a large part of India, felt the need to directly communicate with appointed officials. The interpreter or messenger system characteristic of the pre-existing monarchs came to an end, and British officials made English language necessary for Indian Officials; which was laid on English schools; oriental education, which were to include content as was made required in Western schools. The first English schools were seen as conspiracy measures to weaker the traditions and popular culture of Indian states. However, few reformers cashed on the opportunity and imbibed some essential traits, which later on changed the entire structure of Indian education system.

Modern Education – From Theology to Sciences

In the post-colonial period, the knowledge and great achievements by European states shifted the focus of education on sciences and popular studies that were being taught and learned in European countries. British left India in 1947, but the education system remained, though some reforms were incorporated in it. The popular school system, formal education, progressive learning, higher studies, and even the content were inherited. In the post-Independent period, the government, renowned educationists, social scientists and many leaders stressed on making the education India centric, with focus once again on the popular culture and traditions. But now there were slight difference, as both Western and our indigenous models got mixed up to shape into an altogether different entity. Thus, education in India got shape by influences and institutions in various periods, throughout the history.

"Changes does not necessarily assure progress, but progress implacably requires change. Education is essential to change, for education creates both new wants the ability to satisfy them" Henry S. Commager the educational instructions which provides the primary education to the maximum no of children is the world largest single enterprises. With the involvement of a bit of array of teachers the biggest no of pupil, a large no. of supervisors and administrators, this education of institutions is able to change the social value of human life with the help of education as such from the point of view of magnitude from the stand point of psychological preparedness, from the preponderance of the sociological influences, in view of the economic necessities, and the philosophical background and in view of scientific enlightenment and humanism, the role of primary education is extremely significant and crucial. Education works as a lever in raising financial and social status of the individuals. So, the expenditure on education is regarded as useful investment not only by the economists, but also by the educationists.

Education in India before Independence

The cultural and the traditional education were started from the beginning of the human civilization. Although the pattern of learning was different from today's curriculum yet, no one can deny that the human civilization was elaborated in a parallel manner in the presence of the cultural and the traditional education. (a) Education system in ancient period every aspect of life including education in ancient India was influenced by religion. However it is worth to mention that education aimed at many sided developments of the personality of the student of course with a religious orientation. The concept, aims and ideals of education were correlated with the ideals of life. Religion played an imperative part in life in ancient India. The whole social structure of those days was religious and the whole system of education surged with religious atmosphere. Teachers were usually priests, so they provided Liberal, Spiritual and Religious education. In ancient India the whole system of education ran on the specific systems of education called "GURUKUL SYSTEMS OF EDUCATION". 1. The main sources of teaching in the ancient education were Vedic literature with represent the most important and intrinsic part of life of the Indian people. In Vedic period, as the period is known, teacher or Guru used to give knowledge to their pupil on the basic of Vedic literature which consisted of eight different forms; the four Vedas, Six Vedanta's, Four Upavedas, Four Brahamans, One Hundred and eight Upanishads, Six systems of philosophy, Bhagwad Gita , and Three Smritis. 2. The Vedas deal with every branch of knowledge and provide basic material of all arts and science. In fact, they are the first source of wisdom. Ancient educators, considered knowledge as the third eye of man which gives him insight into all wordly and no wordly matters. 3. Teacher occupied a vital position in the Vedic system of education. The teacher was a parent surrogate, facilitator of learning, exemplar and inspirer, confident, detector friend and philosopher, evaluator, imparter of knowledge and wisdom and above all a guru, religious and spiritual guide. In vedic period forest was treated as a centre of education, which was far from the madding crowd's ignoble strife.

4. Demographic Characteristics of India's Population and Literacy Rates (1901-2011)

Year	*Population (Millions)*	*Literacy Rates (%)*		*Total*	*Decadal Growth (%)*	*Population Density (persqkm)*	*Sex Ratio (Female/1000males)*
		Male	**Female**				
1901	236	9.83	0.60	5.35	-	77	972
1911	249	10.56	1.05	5.92	0.57	82	964
1921	248	12.21	1.81	7.16	1.24	81	955
1931	276	15.59	2.93	9.50	2.34	90	950
1941	315	24.90	7.30	16.10	6.6	103	945
1951	360	24.95	7.93	16.67	0.57	117	946
1961	439	34.44	12.95	24.02	7.35	142	941
1971	548	39.45	18.69	29.45	5.43	177	930
1981	685	46.47	24.88	36.67	7.22	216	934
1991	844	64.20	39.19	52.19	15.52	267	927
2001	1028	75.3	53.7	64.8	12.61	325	933
2011	1210	82.14	65.46	74.04	9.24	382	940

Sources: Geography of population concepts, Determinants, and Patterns by R.C Chandha Kalyani Publishers New Delhi- 110002, and census of India Provisional Total 2011.

Globalization poses variety of complex trends in the economic, social and cultural fabrics of all societies. We live in an intensely interdependent world in which all immense differences of culture and historical experiences are compressed together in instant communication. The emerging digitization concept has altered this perception. The ascent of information and communication technology has given rise to e-commerce, e-banking, e-learning, medicine and e-governance. So, it is argued that government finds it increasingly difficult to cope up with technology driven activities. Because of that now a days education has turned out to be commodity of international trade. It is no more a public good on domestic scale but a private good on a global scale.

There are some trends that cut across all the issues relating to youth and education. Firstly, it is essential that governments and other sectors ensure that there is adequate funding to all schools to enable education capacity and quality and to make education accessible to all. Secondly, while they processes of globalization make education more accessible to the privileged, marginalized, disadvantaged and isolated groups are left behind. Generally, children who are fortunate in being born to educated parents or having caring, competent teachers do very well and are able to find jobs demanding high productivity. However, the average is appallingly low. The results are low productivity, poor skills and massive unemployment even after several years of schooling, or even college education. Varies studies have shown that children coming from a deprived background do not have supportive learning environment and feel alienated in schools. The government school teachers, even motivated ones, find it difficult to address their special needs.

Various literature studies state that ICT's facilitate the acquisition and absorption of knowledge, which provides developing countries unprecedented opportunities to enhance...revolutionize the way people work today and transforming education systems (Tinio 2002; Watson 2001).

But many studies (Mikre 2011; Noeth and Volkov 2004; Daggett 2010) also reveal that though ICTs Played equalization strategy for developing countries , but the reality of the digital divide i.e, the gap between those who have access to and control technology and those who do not, still exist. Thus integration of ICT's in different levels is extremely challenging.. failure to which will increase the knowledge gap and deepening of existing social and economic inequality among developed and developing countries.

Studies also reveal that improper usage of ICT in classrooms or at home by students increases their dilemma of making appropriate career choice for their future since the advantage of ICT overweighs the advantage in many ways than one like limiting students imagination; quandaries regarding which information is valid and reliable among the many widely available while making choice; limits students critical thinking and analytical skills; students neglect other learning resources due to computer an internet; students have less opportunity to use oral skills and handwriting; ICT usage is difficult for weak students because they may face problems working independently and so might need the support of the teacher; lack of proficiency in English resulting language barrier among students with English medium background and other regional language background; and one major negative physical side effect of computer based learning is vision.

Though technology advertises as speed, efficiency and comfort but it creates techno-illusion, ethical and pedagogical problems. It is changing the learners character, making them more technically conscious consumer of information and less critical, and reflexive, imaginative persons. The board-students interface becomes mechanical and superficial due to usage of smart classroom and as typing replaces handwriting, it creates harmful impact on the development of vital cognitive skills and tactile intelligence.

Conclusion

To sum up, we need to recognize that the knowledge, skills and productivity of our growing young and dynamic work force forms the backbone of our economy. To reap the benefits of such a young work force, we need to implement the reforms in the education system and also bring forth new factors of production, namely knowledge, skill and technology which have the ability to unleash the productive frontiers of the economy in the most efficient and dynamic way. Besides, taking a leaf from the western hemisphere, India should try to become "Knowledge economy" to promote inclusive growth. (i), therefore, would like underline three major areas to be focused to ensure that our education system is sustainable and meets global standards: Quality of education in terms of infrastructure, teachers, accreditation and etc. (ii) Affordability of education ensuring poor and deserving students are not denied education. (iii) Ethics in education voiding over-commercialization of education system.

Bibliography

1. Andrews, Ralph L.Post-Confederation Developments in Newfoundland Education 1949-1975.
2. Buffett, Rev. F.M The story of the church in Newfoundland. Toronto: General Board of Religious Education,1939.
3. Burke, Louis. "Some Irish Contributors and Contributions to Newfoundland Education in the last century ".M.Litt Thesis, University of Dublin,1975.
4. Canadian Press." Churches lose bid to overturn change to term 17. " The telegram (29 Feburary,2000)
5. Clement, Dominique." Searching for rights in the age of activism" The Newfoundland Labrador Human Rights Association, 1968-1982", Newfoundland Studies 19.2(2003): 347-372.

Chapter-56

Indian Higher Education System in India - Challenges and Suggestions

Dr. K. Peddi Raju,

India is at the crossroads of making a leap into a higher orbit and enter premier league of the world based on its strong human resources from a large population and seven decades of sustained efforts to (re) establish itself in various sectors of economic and intellectual activity. Indian universities are finding it difficult to grab a position among top 100 or top 200 Universities of the World. Some of the generic challenges observed are at level of operation or control of these universities or institutions and may serve as an input in prioritizing going ahead.

Higher education has been in the news with the government announcing some of the most far reaching changes in the sector in recent weeks. Proposing to rechristen the central higher education regulator, the University Grant Commission (UGC), as the Higher Education Commission of India (HECI), the Ministry of Human Resource Development (MHRD) has decided to go in for a complete overhaul by repealing the UGC Act of 1956. The HECI will be tasked with setting, maintaining and improving academic standards in Indian universities but the funding role of the UGC will be taken over by the HRD ministry. This was followed by the MHRD declaring six institutes as 'Institutes of Eminence' (IoE) under the highly ambitious scheme of the government for enhancing the quality of higher education in India. Though 10 public and 10 private institutes were to be granted exceptional autonomy under this plan so that they can work uninhibited towards moving into top 500 of the World University Rankings within 10 years, only six institutes could ultimately be finalized for this.

These are substantive changes in the higher education sector and will have a long term bearing on the health of higher education in India. Anyone with even a semblance of interest and experience of this sector can testify that status quo in higher education is not an option for India. In fact, many would even say that the time for debate is gone. India has to act now and act fast if it wants to salvage the future of its youth. The IoE debate has largely been overtaken by the Jio Institute's entry into the fray. What should really be a cause for concern is the fact that in a nation with more than 800 universities, the panel could not even name 20 institutions which met basic parameters of institutional excellence in higher education. Higher education institutions of all kinds have mushroomed around the country over the last three decades but they are mostly of substandard quality and established with dubious motives. Various reports have pointed out that almost 80 percent of our engineering graduates are unemployable and only 5 percent of our graduates in other disciples are employable.

The decline in India's higher education system can be traced to various factors. The blatant politicization of academia from 1970s onwards where academics of a certain ideological persuasion were privileged by powers that be. As a result, our universities, instead of becoming spaces where diverse ideas and genuine contestation can flourish, turned into monoliths of political correctness. Major central universities became parochial in their outlook as opposed to attracting talent from all over the country and outside. The marginalization of merit has had its own set of consequences where quest for excellence has given way to catering to the lowest common denominator. The idea that only my friends, my acquaintances, my students should get teaching and research positions irrespective of merit is now so pervasive that talented youngsters who are not connected dread their future in academia. As a consequence, we have witnessed a gradual withdrawal of Indian middle classes from the nation's higher education system. Those who can afford are now willing to send their kids abroad even for undergraduate studies.

The answers to this crisis so far have been rather inward looking. When challenged as to why Indian institutions do not appear in global rankings, we tend to cast aspersions on the rankings themselves, calling for an 'Indian' way to rank universities. When challenged as to why Indian academics are absent from global journals, our academics point to the incredibly tough time they face in their work environment. When challenged on the poor quality of our PhDs, we tend to talk of the huge number of PhDs in the system.

Initiatives taken by the government

- The Central Government has also launched a scheme called Unnat Bharat Abhiyan for the promotion of technologies from the laboratory to the ground. Under the scheme, higher educational institutes would connect with villages in their neighbourhood and address the various problems faced by them. The scheme would particularly looking for the solutions for water management, organic farming, renewable energy, infrastructure and livelihood. IIT, Delhi is the coordinating institute of this scheme. About 130 villages have so far been adopted by IITs, NITs across the country under the scheme.

- The focus of the project is to overcome the low enrolment ratio of girl students in prestigious technical institutions and enable them to receive special incentives and support so that they can join these institutions and go on to takes leadership roles in the future.
- A project has been taken up to made a national digital library of eBooks on various subjects and topics and another set up through which highly qualified faculty of centrally sponsored institutions like IITs, IIMs and central universities would offer online courses free of cost.
- Another special scheme called "Udaan" for girl students has launched by the Central government. Under this scheme mentoring and scholarship will be provided to enable meritorious girl students to transit from schools to technical education without any difficulty and also to promote teaching and learning of mathematics and science at senior secondary school level by providing free resources.
- Another interesting step is the launching of a mission named after freedom fighter and educationist Pandit Madan Mohan Malviya to build a strong professional cadre of teachers by addressing all the issues related to teachers, teaching, teacher preparation, professional development, curriculum design, design and development of more effective pedagogy and better assessment and evaluation methodologies.
- Ashtray Avishkar Abhiyan has launched to revive interest in the technology among youth through support for innovative learning based on observations and experimentation. The focus would be on learning outside the classroom through direct interaction with the environment around the educational institutions.
- Under the Global Initiative of Academic Networks (GIAN) programme, India's ministry of human resource development and department of science and technology will "create a channel for US professors in science, technology, engineering, and mathematics

to teach in Indian academic and research institutions on short-term exchanges", as per the website of the US Department of State.

Suggestions for Improving the System of Higher Education:

- In higher educational institutes Industrial co-operation must be there for the development of curriculum, organizing expert lectures, internships, live projects, career counseling and placements. 3 Sharma and Sharma: Indian Higher Education System: Challenges And Suggestions Published by CORE Scholar, 2015.
- There is a need to implement innovative and transformational approach form primary to higher education level to make Indian educational system globally more relevant and competitive.
- Government must promote collaboration between Indian higher education institutes and top International institutes and also generates linkage between national research laboratories and research centers of top institutions for better quality and collaborative research.
- Higher educational institutes need to improve quality, reputation and establish credibility through student exchange, faculty exchange programs, and other collaborations with high-quality national and international higher educational institutes.
- There is a need to focus on the graduate students by providing them such courses in which they can achieve excellence, gain deeper knowledge of subject so that they will get jobs after recruitment in the companies which would reduce unnecessary rush to the higher education. Conclusion In this paper we have presented the present situation of India in higher education.

Conclusion

The present study revealed the current scenario of higher education in India. The key challenges related to demand supply gap, enrolment, privatization, etc., indicate that the situation of higher education sector is not praiseworthy. However, the key initiatives from the government side provide comprehensive solution though not adequate. Accordingly the thrust of public policy for higher education in India has to be to maintain the high standards of education keeping pace with developments that take place in the fields of knowledge and technology.

References

1. Agrawal, M, (2008): "Education in Third World and India: A Development Perspective". New Delhi, Kanishka Pubublication, ISBN 81-8457-023-6.
2. Arunachalam, P. (2010): "Higher Education Sector in India: Issues and Imperatives" Journal of Global Economy, Volume 6 No 4, JULY AUGUST, 2010.
3. Deepti Gupta & Navneet Gupta, (2012): "Higher Education in India: Structure, Statistics and Challenges", Journal of Education and Practice, ISSN 2222-1735 (Paper) ISSN 2222-288X (Online) Vol 3, No 2.
4. Barnett, R. (1992). Improving Higher Education: Total Quality Core, Buckingham: SRHE & OU Agarwal, P. (2006).
5. "Higher Education in India: The Need for Change." ICRIER Working Paper, Indian Council for Research on International Economic Relations: No. 180.
6. PWC report on "India-Higher education system: Opportunities for Private Participation, 2012.
7. Sanat Kaul, "Higher Education in India: Seizing the Opportunity", Working paper no. 179, 2006.
8. British Council, Understanding India: The Future of higher education and opportunities for international cooperation, 2014.

References

Chapter-57

A Critical Analysis of Ranking System and Parameters and How They Result in Poor Ranking of Indian Universities and Institutions at Global Level

Dr. K. Raja Ram,

Abstract

The world ranking system of universities and the parameters they adopt to give ranking to the universities and institutions across the world are proving disadvantageous to the Indian universities and other premier institutions.

Though there are some truly world class premier institutes and universities in India, they are not able to make it to the top 100 ranking of the universities and institutes in the global level. Although there is plethora of reasons for the poor ranking of our institutions, the main reason stems from the very assessment method that the ranking agencies adopt which is proving disadvantageous.

Many premier institutions like Indian Institutes of Technology (IITs), Indian Institutes of Management (IIM), Indian Institute of Science (IISc) are competing at the global level in terms of hiring of their students by top companies, the other parameters like number of citations, number of patents, alumni contribution, number of foreign students, funding generated through consultancy and working of students in Fortune 500 companies etc., are turning out to be major impediments for better ranking.

Given the complex system of ranking assessment and the parameters they consider for ranking, it is unlikely that institutions or universities from India would make it to the top 100 anytime soon.

This is with reference to the QS Global Ranking, BRICS ranking and Times ranking systems and the parameters they use for the ranking of universities and institutions.

There must be concerted efforts and a bit of liberalized admission process for foreign students' admissions and specific measures at improving the research, publication and citations are the need of the hour to improve the ranking of our institutes and universities at the global level. There must be a greater public-private partnership for improved infrastructure and funding for research.

This paper takes a critical view of the assessment process and the reasons for poor ranking of our universities and institutions at the global level and would come out with suggestions for achieving better ranking to our institutions.

Introduction

The university ranking system at the global level is highly disadvantageous to universities in developing countries in general and universities in India in particular. The parameters, metrics or the indicators they consider are proving to be disadvantageous to the institutions in countries like India. The criteria like foreign students and faculty, citations, opinions of the academics on the reputation of the universities are all resulting in poor ranking to the universities in India.

There are two internationally prominent organizations i.e., QS World University Rankings and Times Higher Education World University Rankings that give rankings at the global level.

The QS World University Rankings organization takes the six main parameters which it calls as the metrics for assessing and ranking the institutions and universities across the globe. The metrics that are being followed by the QS World University Rankings are as follows.

1. Academic Reputation
2. Employer Reputation
3. Faculty/Student Ratio
4. Citations per Faculty
5. International Faculty
6. International Student Ratio

The Academic Reputation of the institution accounts for 40 per cent of the total assessment. This is the highest metric among all the parameters and it is arrived at through a massive survey of 80,000 individuals related to higher education across the globe. Their opinions will be based on the teaching and research quality in the universities.

With reference to the second metric i.e., Employer Reputation, the QS World Ranking claims that it takes the responses of over 40,000 employers asking them what are the institutions from which they hire their employees considering them as effective, competent and innovative. This is also called as the Employer Survey. It accounts for 10 per cent of the score in giving ranks to the universities.

The third parameter is Faculty/Student ratio this accounts for 20 per cent of the total assessment. The better the faculty/student ratio the institutions will get better score. This is viewed as the quality of teaching. If the number of teachers is less, the burden would be more and it is believed that the quality would suffer.

The fifth metric is citations per faculty, this account for 20 per cent of the assessment. This is in respect of the quality of research assessment in the institution. The total number of papers, published during the last five years is considered for the same and the total citations they received are divided by the total number of papers published to work out the citations per faculty. The citations are sourced from the Elsevier's Scopus database.

It is stated that more than 50 million citations were identified for more than 10 million papers published.

The sixth and final criterion is international faculty/international student ratio, as part of this the universities and institutions are assessed on their capability to attract international faculty and international students. This, in the assessment process, considers that the international outlook with the presence of international faculty and international students ensures the global outlook and multinational learning environment. The sixth metric accounts for five per cent each of the international faculty and international student ratios.

Going by the above metrics based assessment being followed by the QS World University Ranking in giving ranks to the universities at global level. The institutions and universities in countries like India obviously lag behind.

The criteria itself is working against the better ranking of the universities in developing countries. Especially the academic reputation which accounts for 40 per cent weighting in the assessment is faulty. The survey of 80,000 individuals related to the higher education may not include many from the developing countries. Obviously they may not give ranking to the institutions that are not much known in the west.

The employer reputation is another parameter that is also obviously going against the better ranking of Indian universities. The Fortune 500 companies, US-based or Europe-based employers give obvious preference to the western students as they do not, mostly, have the visa hassles.

The ever growing restrictions on the visas to foreign-based students certainly deter the employers to go for recruitment of prospective employees from developing countries; instead they prefer those who do not have visa hassles. Employers' preferences too vary depending upon the same.

In spite of the same, there are many reputed global organizations that prefer products of the Indian Institutes of Technology (IITs). But the same preference is not being given to the students of other universities in India.

The foreign faculty and foreign student ratios while assessing the rank of the universities are also working against the interests of the Indian universities. The expenses involved in attracting foreign faculty are too high for the fund-starved institutions in the country. Foreign students too prefer to go to those western countries that offer a remunerative employment in future where they dream of earning in dollars. And their preference for universities in India comes last. Incidentally India sends the second largest number of students for education abroad and it is next only to China.

Times Higher Education (THE) World University Rankings also use almost similar parameters to assess and give the global rankings. Their parameters are as follow:

1. Teaching: As the main assessment factor it accounts for 30 per cent of the score. This also includes the reputation survey, staff-student ratio, doctorates to bachelor's ratio and institutional income factor.
2. Research: This parameter also includes the reputation survey, volume of the research and productivity of the research and the income it has earned to the institution. On the whole, research accounts for equal 30 per cent score in assessment.
3. Citations: This also accounts for the 30 per cent score in the overall assessment of the universities as part of the Times Higher Education rankings.
4. International outlook of the institution: This accounts for 7.5 per cent of the score and this includes international-to-domestic students' ratio, international-to-domestic staff ratio and international collaborations by the university.
5. Finally the Income from Industry: This accounts for the remaining 2.5 per cent of the score. The income earned by the university through its works, services and consultancies from the industry are assessed as part of this.

The above criteria of the Times Higher Education World University Rankings also go against the interests of the Indian universities and the universities from other developing nations as they lag behind in staff-student ratios as a result of the understaffed universities, lack of funding, lack of research facilities due to the insufficient funding and lack of encouragement and absence of suitable research infrastructure. The international outlook is another factor that goes against the fund-starved Indian universities. Due to the negligible industry-academic collaboration, there is very little they earn from the industry thus lagging behind in the last parameter too.

Conclusion

It is evident that the methodology adopted by the global ranking institutions is not a level playing field for the Indian universities. There must have been some normalization process to make it a level playing assessment. The size and funding of the western universities is much higher than the Indian universities, it should have been assessed in terms of the funding and the results in different parameters in order to give a fair chance to the Indian universities to get deserving global rankings. If the same methodology using the same metrics and parameters is followed in future too, it is highly unlikely that any university from Indian would make to the top 10 for decades to come. The methodology adhered to is highly advantageous to western universities, while it continues to prove disadvantageous to Indian universities and no wonder our institutions and universities do not figure in the top 100 too and forget about the top 10 list.

References

1. https://www.timeshighereducation.com/world-university-rankings/methodology-world-university-rankings-2018#survey-answer.
2. https://www.topuniversities.com/forum/general-discussion/which-are-top-10-indian-universities.
3. https://www.topuniversities.com/university-rankings-articles/brics-rankings/indian-universities-2014-qs-university-rankings-brics
4. https://www.topuniversities.com/search/site/indian percent20universities percent20in percent20top percent20200#f
5. https://www.timeshighereducation.com/student/best-universities/best-universities-world

Chapter-58

Expansion in Indian Higher Education in Recent years: Impact of Technological Innovations for excellence

Dr. Santhosh Mathew

Introduction

The National Democratic Alliances (NDA) government, led by Narendra Modi, has been taking a series reforms initiatives in the Indian higher education to overhaul the entire system to meet the current and emerging domestic and global challenges. It is a fact that higher education in India is facing multiple challenges. Apex regulating agencies like University Grants Commission (UGC), All India Council for Technical Education (AICTE) and medical Council of India (MCI), etc. are obsolete bodies in the present circumstances. To a great extent, these agencies couldn't make striking progress to meet the expectations of the people which are well acknowledged by various commissions appointed by the government itself. In fact, they could not ensure a benchmark for institutions to compete with higher educational institutions abroad. Yes, there are progress and achievements in the sector during the past six-decades; however, the role of these apex watchdogs to make a great leap in this context is unimpressive. It is often viewed that the major policy decisions and important developments in the higher education sector have been happened as individual pursuit for excellence by some institutions themselves and expansion by governments without much involvement of these bodies. This situation is undesirable and damaging for a country like India in the era of rapid economic and social changes in all walks of citizens' life, particularly in the era of globalization. So, there is a pressing need to overhaul the higher education.

In this circumstance, the central government must take a leading and proactive role to bring reforms in the sector. In addition to that, the central government, along with state governments, has constitutional, political, and moral obligation to make vital reforms in this critical social sector of India. Unless and until the union government is not taking a leadership role in this field with special focus on radical reforms, India's future, and even the progress which we have achieved till today, will become meaningless. The great national vision of the makers of modern India will become grim. However, the recent initiatives of the central government is in the right direction to effect critical changes and this paper is going to discuss the reforms and related issues with the Indian higher education sector.

Higher Education Today

Today, higher education in India is meeting through more than 800 universities, 23 IITs and 21 IIMs, 31 NITs and 7 ISERs and 20 IIITs and a number of other recognized institutions[1]. As far students are concerned their overall strength is much higher and as per the government data it is estimated 2, 84, 84,746 which is very high.When the Modi governemt took over power in May 2014, they also decieded to contniue the education policy of "expansion; inclusion and excellence" of the previous Congress governemnt and continued to establsih new institions indifferent states. A major exapsion has been taken in the case of adding 7 IIMs and 6 IITs in states which do not represnted by these institions. Hovever, the new governemnt has very long term polciy with radical refoming agenda in the sector an this has been well articulated by the NDA government duirng the last three years. A major steps in this direction has been included in the union budget 2017-2018. Finance Minister Arun Jaitly has categorically stated that the "In higher education, we will undertake reforms in the UGC. Good quality institutions would be enabled to have greater administrative and academic autonomy"[2]. He stated that the government is committed to reform UGC and maximum permissible autonomy to institutions on the basis of ranking and their performance.

Nobody can say that Indian higher education is demonstration international quality though there are internationally reputed institutions in India. This is because; the sector is facing serious and systemic challenges for more long time. And the country could not be proud on the basis of these poor performance indicators of the sector. A major criticism is that in terms of research and innovation these institutions are far behind of global standards. Most of the premier national institutions itself is nowhere in the picture of international education ranking.

Arguably, this is a true fact also. Not a single remarkable or "earth shaking" innovation from these institutions during the last six-decades whereas the Massachusetts Institute of Technology has created in the last 50 years, path breaking invention like Global Positioning System, Bionic Prostheses and Microchip". In the words of Narayana Murthy, founding chairman of Indian Information technology major, Infosys, said these happened because students and faculty at MIT "walked the untrodden path, asked the unasked questions and used their intellectual prowess to take huge steps"[3] to address the real challenges of the people. Same concern is shared by President Pranab Mukherje, who the visitor of all central university. He strongly argued that research and excellence is the fundamental goal of these institutions but the present reality is raising number questions to us and we have to be improve our standard and quality in both spheres[4]. Globally, higher educational institutions are ranked and recognised on the basis of these two key parameters and the status of Indian educational institutions is abysmally very law. His cautious words are intended to have a serious introspection on the need to take serious reforms in the entire higher education sector without any delay.

Recent Initiatives

Soon after the NDA came to power, everybody was keenly waiting to see the higher education reform agenda and policy perspective of new government which is completely the previous governments. This higher education portfolio has great importance as it frames the education policy of the nation and implements the same with long term vision for a developed country with a vision of "Sabke Saath, Sbka Vikas" (collective efforts, inclusive growth). The Bharathiya Janatha Party (BJP), the party which leads the coalition at the centre has clearly outlined this policy in their manifesto. It says that "the basic objective of higher and professional education is not only rapid advancement of the affluent sector of the society but also to improve the lot of the last man in the line" in India[5]. This means that the government is committed rapid reform with inclusive agenda in the context of higher education and it also acknowledged that this field needs complete overhaul as the international scenario is rapidly changing and the country cannot, and should not be stand isolated in this era globalisation which India has huge stake. In a specific reference, BJP declared that UGC will be restructured with a new agency having a new mandate to ensure quality, standard and excellence in higher education with a "Higher Education Commission". An important aspects of this proposed body is its role is not to disburse grants to universities and individuals which has deeply reduced the role of UGC into a fund disbursing agency rather than being statuary body to push the higher education sector to compete with global standards and ensure skills and employability to students. In a careful reading of the principal document of the principal party of the NDA coalition, once can see that the reforms in education, particularly higher education has special focus. Since the last three years, the government is carrying out several reforms based on these broader frameworks.

In this above broader framework, government has started a serious of reform efforts to strengthen the regulatory system with transparency and openness. Initially, the government has been effecting changes in the administrative functions of higher educational institutions through various executive orders and delegated powers. The New Education Policy (NEP), which is yet to come up, is a welcome step as there is a wide disconnect between what the students learn from class room and what he/she does after education. Nobody can dispute that their employability and skill level is not in tandem with the demands of industry and academia. This leads a massive educated unemployment and frustration among youths who constitutes a significant number of Indian populations. The exercise conducted by the ministry to prepare a national policy has generated wide debate among all sections of society. But the follow up on this exercise and subsequent actions are yet to announce the government. Hover ever, in a twist and turn; the Finance Minister Arun Jailty has announced a drastic change in the functioning of UGC, in his 2017-2018 budget speech.

Restructuring Regulator

In a short, but a strong indication, the government has announced that UGC will be reformed and restructured. In addition to that, the government will free institutions with impeccable track record in excellence and standard, to ensure maximum autonomy to them[6] Press Information Bureau, This announcement is a significant step of the government to make drastic changes in the UGC in the long history of this statutory body. According to the human resources ministry which is the line department in charge of UGC, has maintained that there is no relevance to have an agency like this in the present context.

The action plan of the government is to give more freedom to good quality institutions rather than putting all of them into single umbrella organisation like UGC. For the first time in the existence of UGC, the government appointed a committee in 2014, headed by Hari Gautam, former UGC chairman, to review the function of the body. Though the committee submitted its report to the Ministry of Human Resources Development which is yet to come up in the public domain, recommended for fundamental changes in the body[7]. Since this report has submitted, it opened a serious debate among both policy makers and academic community about the urgent need for either reforms or disbanding the UGC with a new agency like other regulators, i.e. SEBI, TRAI, or IRDA.

The Hari Gautam Committee recommendation is an important one because the report made serious introspection about the functioning of this national body and its inability meet to its fundamental objectives whereas the overwhelming functions has been carried out during the last six-decades as fund disbursing agency. There is no need of a statutory agency to do the job of coordinating agency to release funds, conduct eligibility examinations, and make the higher education sector more centralising without considering the diversity of this nation and doing national ranking. It is an irony that all these are non-core functions of UGC but, the agency, unintentionally or may be lack of long-term vision, it miserable failed to do its basic functions. However, institutions which do not come under UGC have registered an impressive mark, even at very short pan of inception. For example, all the sixteen central universities established in 2009, is yet to make a mark in the National Institutions Ranking Framework (NIRF) of the government whereas institutions like ISER, IITs and IIMs, started in the recent years have achieved remarkable positions[8]. These institutions are not regulated like universities or they do not have compliance-commitment procedure for central or sate funds.

In fact, higher education regulatory bodies in India are functioning without any review or self-regulations. One can say that these are apex regulators without any external audit and self-evaluations, but very active to tighten regulations on non-mandate areas. It has to be functioned on the principle of self- accountability with greater role being an agency to frame guidelines and intervention where ever and whenever it necessitates. But the past record of the UGC is very critical in this context of pushing Indian higher education sector to ensure high quality, global competency and equity and access.

All these issues have got prime attention with the sustained initiates of NDA government to overhaul the UGC. And the government has assigned this duty to NITI Aayog to prepare roadmap for the revamping of UGC. The major task is of the NITI Aayog is to "improve the existing Higher Education regulatory framework in line with contemporary national and global requirements and to enhance the quality of Higher Education in India"[9]. In continuation to this objective, the government has directed committee comprising Higher education Secretary K. K.Sharma and NITI Aayog Chief Executive Officer Amitabh Kant to prepare a final policy document for revamping the UGC in line with the promises made, and policies announced by the Modi government. It is expected that this will be a game changer of the Indian higher education sector and this will also set new standards and greater objectives to transform the nation into a knowledge/economic power of the world.

Relying Technological Innovations

As discussed above regarding reforms and its great potential to transform India to be a knowledge/economic power in the world, innovative technologies have a pivotal role to accelerate this growth as real and sustainable. As far as technologies are concerned, like other advanced nations, it has penetrated into all walks of contemporary life of people in India, irrespective of their social, cultural, regional and economic divisions in society. In fact, it is unthinkable to imagine daily life without the influence of technology, and this situation has significantly reflected in higher education sector which is undergoing exceptional changes in recent years. Most impressive aspect's in this respect is adaptation and massive utilisation of technologies like Information Communication, Mobile Platform, Electronic Media, Satellite Technology, digitisation of contents. The All India Vice-Chancellors Conference, held in July 2018, had adopted a strategic plan for innovation, and reaffirmed the need for vigorous application of technology for higher education institutions across the country[10]. Because technology can make a lot of change in expansion and enrolment and quality of higher education. These three factors are very critical as far as higher education is concerned. Providing quality and affordable higher education to all, to a great extent, is achievable only through intense use of technology and innovation. One can see the central government's recent decision to establish "Innovation Cell and Atal Ranking of Institutions on Innovation Achievements (ARIIA)" is recognition of this fact[11] and right direction to achieve this goal. The National Mission on education through Information and Communication Technology is an important initiative in this direction[12] to tap the potential of technology in education and declaration of 2010-2020 as decade of Innovation in India shows the government's commitment to ensure a synergy between technology and innovation in higher education. Initiatives like MOOCs, SWAYAM, e-learning are some of the new initiatives in this way and attracting a lot of learners. The emerging scenario is redefining the role of teachers and classrooms and higher education is more becoming learner-centric and learner-friendly by the use of innovative technologies. It is a revolutionary change and unstoppable today.

Conclusion

Indian higher education, during the past six-decades, has miserably failed to address key issues dealing with the notion like standard, quality, excellence, equity, access, and research and innovation. Yes, it is a fact that there are some striking achievements, but these are isolated cases and mostly individual and institutional pursuits. So, one cannot attribute these as standard and level of achievements in higher education. A major reason for these under performance and under achievements in the sector is due to over regulation through multiple agencies and lack of technological advancements and innovations. The system has been functioning like a pyramid and most of the time regulators like UGC took the role of being at the top of the pyramid without any self-regulation and self-accountability. This exerted undue pressure to the bottom, and colleges and universities lost its creative role of being an active participant of the system. This has been a serious concern for the party in power and same had been recognized by various commissions in the past also. Because of that reason, the present government is showing a firm commitment to reform higher education in general and UGC, MCI and other regulators in particular.

The UGC and MCI and AICTE must be revamped. And in place of these bodies, government shall create an agency like other regulatory bodies to address the issues related with the sector rather than giving unreasonable faith and responsibly to maintain standard and to ensure quality. Because the country is passing through an age of rapid change with technological progress and economic growth, and people are expecting more transparent approach with greater flexibility and freedom which is missing today's context. While preparing a blue print for new agency in place of UGC, government may consider following as core objectives:

1. Autonomy with excellence
2. Social responsibly with effective participation of private players
3 Employability and skill acquisition
4. Creating separate good teaching and excellent research institutions at national and state level
5. Innovative curriculum
6. Aptitude and Exit exams at national level as a pilot mode at Post-graduate level.
7. Focus shall be on research and innovation.
8. Quality school education for enabling excellence and competency at higher education.

9. Mass application of technology for creating and environment for expansion and excellence in Higher education

If we are failing to make reforms and become unresponsive to the demand of people, particularly in higher education, the future of India will become dark and life of the people will become great misery and unpredictable. The country has achieved a remarkable progress and a global standard in the sphere of Informational Communication Technology and Digital Technology, if we apply this technology into Higher Education sector, India will become a global player and country can reinvent her legacy of being a knowledge hub in the ancient past.

Notes

1. See Budget Speech of Finance Minster Arun Jaitly, http://indiabudget.nic.in/ub2017-18/bs/bs. pdf.
2. Ibid.
3. Smita Gupta, Pranab Mukherjee: From din and clamour of politics to a pragmatic role http://www.thehindu.com/news/national/pranab-mukherjee-a-politicalpresident/article19332997.ece?homepage=true.
4. BJP Manifes to 2014, pp 23-24, http://www.bjp.org/images/pdf 2014/full manifesto english 07. 04. 2014. pdf.
5. Press Information Bureau, MHRD, http://mhrd.gov.in/sites/upload files/mhrd/files/Education%20in % 20Budget2017.pdf.
6. Akshay Mukul,Times of India,1 April 2015. http://timesofindia.indiatimes.com/home/education/news/UGC-a-failure-must-be-scrapped-HRD-panel/articleshow/46764087.cms.
7. Ibid.
8. MHRD Reply to Lok Sabha on 24 Novemebr 2016, http://mhrd.gov.in/sites/upload files/mhrd/files/ru996. pdf.
9. Press Information Bureau, "Three-Day VCs' Conference on Research & Innovation in Higher Education ends", New Delhi,28 July 2018.
10. Press Information Bureau, "Innovation Cell and Atal Ranking of Institutions onInnovation Achievements (ARIIA) launched by M/oHRD to foster culture of innovation in Higher Education Institutions" New Delhi:30August 2018.
11. Mukherjee, Pranab (2013), Convocation Address by President of India at IIT, Jodhpur, 10 July 2013.

Index

A

Aadhaar Act, 21
Aadhaar numbers, 21
Aadhaar Payment Bridge, 315
Absence of Entrepreneurship development scheme, 181
Absence of personality development program, 181
Academic and administrative, 239
Academic decision, 165
Academic development, 203
Academic environment, 80
Academic Performance Index, 61
Academic research status, 412
Academic staff college, 213
Access and Equity, 203
Accreditation Agency, 325
Action plan for improving quality, 57
Administration of Student Data, 422
Administration processes, 72, 84
Administrative reforms, 73
Administrative support, 223
Adult education, 239
Adult literacy programmes, 239
Adult theory, 372
Affiliated media centers, 214
Ahmadabad, 429
Ahmed Commission Report, 352
Ali Muslim, 27
All India Council of Technical Education, 432
All India Survey on Higher Education, 232
Ambani- Birla committee, 212
Ambani–Birla Report, 65
American companies, 187
Ancient gurukula, 198
Ancient Indian education, 77
Andhra Pradesh, 215, 232, 318, 386
Andhra Pradesh Reorganization Act, 231
Animal Care, 195
APJ Abdul Kalam, 427
Applied Sciences, 359
Approval Board, 332
Arabic and Persian languages, 440
Aristotle, 177, 427
Aryan race, 439
Aryans, 439, 440
Ashok Thakur, 35
Ashram Schools, 233
Assam, 215, 232
Assam, 386
Assertiveness training, 71
Audio-visual systems, 206
Aurobindo Ghosh, 77
Australia, 190, 425, 432
Autonomous body, 213

B

B. R Ambedkar, 441
B. Venkatesh Kumar, 35
Backbone of a society, 407
Bangalore Urban district, 386
Bangladesh, 433
Banking data, 19
Bar Council of India, 375, 377

Basic Education, 73
Benefits of Research in Eduction, 82
Bhutan, 387
Biological ecosystem, 226
Biotechnology sectors, 326
Birla Institute of Technology, 234
Bombay, 43, 408
Brain drain, 361
British Council, 40
British Indian, 74
British Raj, 212
Buddhist and Jainist education, 440
Buddhist viharas, 438
Build a great university, 221

C

Cabinet Committee, on Economic Affairs, 331
Cabinet Committee on Economic Affairs, 331
Calcutta, 43, 408
Canada, 190
Canada, 432
Capacity Building and Preparation, 338
Capacity utilization, 180
Capacity-Building Projects, 421
Central Advisory Board on Education, 331
Central and State Acts, 66
Central and state universities, 213
Central Board of Secondary Education, 311, 315
Central Government, 189
Central Ministries, 386
Central Open University, 232, 386
Central Plan Scheme Monitoring System, 315
Central Scheme, 309
Central Scheme to provide Interest Subsidy, 306, 309, 310, 319
Central Sector Scheme, 315, 319
Central Sector Scheme of Scholarship, 306, 309, 314, 319
Central universities, 178
Central universities and institutions, 329
Central University, 387
Centrally Sponsored Scheme, 328, 344
Centre for Cellular and Molecular Biology, 233
Certificate Courses, 376
Challenges in Indian Higher Education, 37
Challenges of higher education in India, 199
Chancellor's Office, 83
Chandigarh, 408
Changing Status of Indian Women, 359
Character of teachers, 182
Chennai, 188
China, 176, 198
China, 19, 33, 385, 418
Choice based credit system, 61
Christian Medical College Vellore, 429
Cinematograph films, 186
Co relational research, 81
Co-curricular activities, 380
College of Teacher Education,, 233
Colleges in company, 363
Commerce and Humanities, 314
Commercial Laws, 376
Commercial Laws and Tax Laws, 376
Common syllabus, 65
Commonwealth of Independent States, 324
Communication channels, 206
Communications technology, 368
Competition Success Review, 376
Competitive entrance examinations, 200
Computer centers, 213
Confidence-building, 71
Consent and Obligation to Notify, 195
Constituent Units, 387

Constitution of India, 327
Constitutional provisions, 399
Construction of women hostel, 213
Constructive tool, 207
Copyright, 186
Corporate image, 52
Correlation between Industries and Academic instit, 201
Council for Higher Education and Research, 388
Council for the Indian School Certificate Examinat, 315
Creative and motivated talent, 222
Creativity and security, 49
Crisis of Professional Ethics, 352
Critical analysis, 180
Cross border higher education, 400
Cross Cutting Applications, 207
Current Annual Plan, 335
Current Status of Indian Higher Education, 35
Curricular activities, 76
Cyber colleges, 363
Cyber Home Learning System, 367
Cyber Law, 376
Cyber universities, 363

D

Darjeeling, 164
Data Collection and Planning, 338
Data protection, 18
Data Protection Officers, 20
Data Storing, 206
Deception, 195
Deemed Universities, 234, 371, 374, 387
Defining University Research Ecosystem, 226
Delhi, 386
Delinking Between, 359
Delinking Between Education and Employment, 359
Delinking education with degrees, 171
Denmark, 341
Department of Higher Education, 331
Deprived Classes, 438
Deprived families, 28
Descriptive research, 81
Design registrations, 187
Designs, 186
Dharma, 359
Digital footprint, 18
Digital textbooks, 367
Direct Benefit Transfer, 315
Directive principles of State policy, 166
Disable children, 29
District Institute of Education, 385
District Primary Education Programme, 328
Dr. D.S. Kothari postdoctoral fellowship, 216
Dr. S. Radhakrishna post-doctoral fellowship, 216
Dr. Zakeer Hussein, 77
Dravidians, 439

E

East and South Asia, 324
East and South Asia region, 324
East and the West, 202
Eastern States of India, 344
Economic difficulties, 49, 55
Economic Surveys of Central and State governments, 410
Economical financial position, 404
Economically Weaker Sections, 309, 310, 426
Educated tribal youth, 239
Education for All, 201
Education Loan, 306, 309, 319
Education policies, 60, 358
Educational Backward Districts, 335
Educational Broadcasting System, 363, 364
Educational Commission, 76

Educational institutes, 28
Educational Institutions, 201
Educational Loan Scheme, 310
Educational policies, 29, 74
Educational Tribunals Bill, 388
Educationist, 385
Effective Collaboration, 208
Effective Networking, 208
Electronic Clearance Service, 315
Electronic data exchange with university, 424
Electronic Governance, 421
Eligible Partner Countries, 421
Employability Skills, 394
Empowerment in Learning, 208
English Education System, 437
Entry of Foreign Universities, 358, 431
Essential characters, 70
Establishment of Ashram School, 233
Establishment of New Central Higher Education, 389
Establishment of Public Private Partnership, 201
Ethical Conduct in Human Research, 194
Ethics among Researchers, 196
EU's Revolutionary Data Protection Rules, 19
European nations, 432
European powers, 440
European Union, 17, 19
Examination reforms, 56
Executive Committee, 389
Expectations from Government, 201
Expenditure Finance Committee, 331
Experimental research, 81
Extra-curricular activities, 201, 371, 376, 380

F

Faculty crunch, 79, 80
Faculty development program, 213, 215
Faculty Improvement, 338
Family environment, 237
Fault-ridden, 401
Financial Capital, 225
Financial problem, 237
Financial Resources, 27, 41, 203
Financial Services, 376
Financial Support System, 309
Financing, 179
Financing of Higher Education, 54
Fiscal policy, 165
Five year plan, 214
Five Year Plan, 314, 327
Five Year Plan period, 177
Five Year Plans, 327
Five-year plan, 214
Foreign companies, 187
Foreign Direct Investment, 358, 431
Foreign Educational Institutions, 388, 389
Forensic Science, 376
France, 216
French companies, 20
Functional quality, 52
Funeral system, 29

G

Gandhi:, 177
Gap in Supply and Demand, 179
General Council, 389
General Data Protection Regulations, 17
General universities, 212
Geographical barriers, 208
Germany, 189
Global Economy, 417
Global Human Resources Development Centre, 376
Global industry demands, 419
Global Initiative of Academic Networks, 415
Globalization of advanced education, 434
Good infrastructural facilities, 171

Governance Capital, 225
Government Degree Colleges, 178
Government educational institutions, 65
Government of France, 217
Governor General Lord William Bentinck, 74
Graded Autonomy, 219
Graduate program, 379
Graduate school colleges, 363
Great cultural achievements, 202
Gross cultural programmes, 56
Gross domestic product, 399
Gross enrollment rate, 179
Gross Enrollment Ratio, 24, 232, 329, 343, 408
Gross enrolment proportions, 405
Gross Enrolment Ratio
Gross Enrolment Ratio of India, 37
Gross National Product, 341
Gujarat, 386
Gulf region, 400
Gurkulas, 43
Gurukul system, 392

H

Harvard Business School, 429
Haryana, 232, 386
Health & Education, 312
Health issues, 378
Healthy practices, 77
Heavy dose of curriculum, 61
High drop-out rates, 23, 29
High tech libraries, 57
High technology libraries, 49
High-achieving urban schools, 367
Higher Education, 324, 354
Higher Education Commission of India, 36, 66
Higher Education Department, 410
Higher Education in India, 74
Higher Education in Jammu and Kashmir, 409
Higher Education in Korea, 363
Higher Education Institutions, 189, 232, 324, 389, 421
Higher Education sector, 176
Higher Educational Institutions Bill, 388
Higher National Diplomas, 177
Higher studies, 28
Himachal Pradesh, 331
Hindu Gurukulas, 438
Historical research, 81
Home Affairs, 312
Honors Degrees, 177
Huge human resource potential, 183
Human Capital, 24, 225
Human capital theory, 368
Human Development Report, 349
Human Dignities, 195
Human Research Ethics Committee, 194
Human Resource Development, 63, 386, 399
Hyderabad, 371, 374

I

IIT graduates, 198
Ill-equipped libraries, 79, 80
Impact of globalization, 430
Imperial economic policy, 74
Importance of Education, 26
Importance of Education in modern world, 26
Importance of Higher Education, 51, 177
Importance of technology, 18
Improve the education standards, 183
Improved communications, 72
Improvement of attendance, 379
Inadequate facilities and infrastructure, 54
Inadequate infrastructure, 80
Inadequate school infrastructure, 29
Inadequate teaching/learning material, 29
Inclusive Education for the Disabled, 328

Independent Regulatory Authority for Higher Education, 425
Indian academic institutions, 79
Indian Banks' Association, 310
Indian Certificate of School Education, 318
Indian companies, 21
Indian Education Abroad, 432
Indian Education Service, 63
Indian Institute, 35
Indian Institute of Chemical Technology, 233
Indian Institute of Managements, 389
Indian Institute of Science, 36
Indian Institute of Technology, 36, 234, 389, 429
Indian Institutes of Management, 36, 429
Indian market, 187
Indian Nursing Council, 386
Indian School of Business, 234
Indian Universities, 165
Indian universities and colleges, 214
Indira Gandhi National Open University, 429
Indira Gandhi scholarship, 216
Individual recognition, 374
Industrial growth, 63
Industrial Training Centres, 307
Industrial Training Institutes, 307
Industrial universities, 363
Inequity in Gender Difference, 76
Inferiority feeling, 237
Information and communication technologies, 25, 206, 421
Informative tool, 207
Infrastructure and learning and evolution, 77
Infrastructure development, 213, 385
Infrastructure facilities, 180
Innovation Achievements, 218
Innovative Practices, 201
Instant statistical report generation, 424
Institute of National Importance, 178, 387
Institutional imbalance, 215
Institutional Ranking Framework, 406
Institutional Restructuring, 338
Institutional Restructuring and Reforms, 338
Insufficient availability, 29
Insufficient availability of teachers, 28
Integrated Hostels, 233
Integration of telecommunications, 206
Intellectual property, 188
Intellectual property policy, 186
Intellectual property rights, 185
Inter -Disciplinary approach, 45
Interest Subsidy, 309
Interference of political factors, 55
Inter-Ministerial Committee, 312
International Cooperation, 56, 425
International Covenant on Economic, 407
International establishments, 40
International Labour Organisation, 326
International reputed institutes, 415
International Trade, 376
International treaties, 186
International universities, 359
Internet and Wi-Fi facility, 420
Internship programs, 378
Intra and inter Moot court competitions, 380
Intra-cultural competitions, 380
Isabella Thoburn College Lucknow, 429
Islam religion, 440
Issues and challenges, 44
Issues in the present university education, 60

J

Jammu, 163
Jammu & Kashmir, 215, 311, 312, 407, 410, 412

Jandhyala Tilak, 309
Japan, 187
Jharkhand, 215
Job-Oriented Courses, 202
Junior colleges, 363
Justice, 195

K

K. Kasturi Rangan Committee, 59
K. Kasturirangan, 64
Kakatiya University, 234
Kapoor & Mehta, 212
Karnataka, 232, 386
Kashmir Pandits, 313
Kashmir region, 412
Kashmir state, 407
Kasturba Gandhi BalikaVidyalaya Scheme, 328
Kasturi Rangan Committee, 59
Kerala, 36, 163
Knowledge Commission Report, 65
Knowledge-based society, 177
Kolkata, 188
Korea Air & Correspondence University, 363, 364
Korea National Open University, 363, 364
Korea University, 365
Korean Ministry of Education, 367
Korean War, 362
Kothari fellowship, 217
Kozhikode, 163
Kshatriya, 440

L

Lack of funds, 79, 80
Lack of library facilities, 170
Lack of modern labs, 412
Lack of moral values, 55
Lack of proper guidance, 237
Lack of proper monitoring, 237
Large scale changes, 207
Large vacancies, 199
Large-scale teacher vacancies, 29
Law Program, 375
Law School, 374
Leadership Development, 338
Leadership theory, 373
Learning approaches, 209
Learning theory, 372
Legal Internship Program, 377
Libraries with computers, 172
Library information system, 227
Library System, 422
Limited accessibility in rural areas, 407
Location of the Village, 237
Lord Curzon, 73
Lord Macaulay, 74
Low levels of learning achievement, 29
Low participation of girl students, 29
Lower level of teaching quality, 53
Lower-achieving rural schools, 367

M

Madhya Pradesh, 215, 386
Madras, 408
Maharashtra, 232, 318, 386
Mahatma Gandhi, 73, 77
Malaysia, 400
Management Information System, 338
Managerial style, 72
Massachusetts Institute of Technology, 429
Massive open online courses, 61
Masters Degrees, 177
Maulana Abul Kalam Azad National Urdu University, 233
Medical colleges, 234
Medical Educational Institutions, 388
Medieval period, 440
Meghalaya, 164
Mentors act as role models, 374
Mentorship programme, 380

Meritorious girl students, 414
Meritorious students, 216
Meta University, 61
Mid-day meal, 64, 239
Mid-Day Meal Scheme, 328
Ministries of Higher Education, 325
Ministry of HRD, 312
Ministry of Human Resource Development, 36, 66, 164, 325, 397, 410
Ministry of labor, 62
Ministry of Tribal Affairs, 232
Mission Authority, 332
Modern Indian society, 58
Modern World, 26
Mongolians, 439
Monitoring & Evaluation, 83
Moral Issues, 179
More Universities, 56
Most backward states in India, 311
Moving towards an innovative Society, 201
Multi-dollar business, 359
Mumbai, 188
Muslim rulers, 440

N

N. E. Hill University, 164
Nalanda, 43, 74
Narayana Murthy committee, 212
National Accreditation Regulatory Authority, 388
National Assessment and Accreditation Council, 76, 330
National Association of College and Employers, 395
National Association of Software, 423
National Association of Software and Services Comp, 392
National Commission, 388
National Commissions for Higher Education, 325
National Council for Teacher Education, 385
National Council for Vocational Training, 307
National Curriculum Framework, 327
National digital library, 414
National Education Policy, 59
National Electronic Clearing Service, 315
National Electronic Funds Transfer, 315
National Higher Education Mission, 331, 333, 339
National Higher Education Qualification Framework, 406
National Informatics Centre, 349
National Institute of Technology, 234
National Institution Ranking Framework, 60, 218, 406
National Institutions, 389
National Knowledge Commission, 425
National Loan Scholarship scheme programme, 309
National Merit Scholarship Scheme, 314
National Mission Authority, 332
National Overseas Scholarship, 233
National Policy on Education, 59, 60, 326, 389
National Programme of Nutritional Support, 328
National Quality Assurance Agencies, 325
National Remote Sensing Agency, 233
National Research Laboratories, 201
National Scheme of Incentive to Girls, 328
National scientific policies, 217
National Skill Development Corporation, 392
National student startup policy, 217
National System of Qualifications, 327
National universities, 203
National Vocational Education Qualification Framew, 327

Navratna universities, 214
Need of social Research Ethics, 194
Nelson Mandela, 427
New Central Universities and Colleges, 389
New Economic Policy, 442
New educational approaches, 208
New Educational vision, 202
New Model Degree Colleges, 335
New-age learning devices, 39
Nigeria, 387
Night school, 239
No Strategy, 181
Non-professional Colleges, 164
North Bengal University, 164
North-East State of India, 339
North-Eastern States, 331
Number of unemployable alumni, 412
Nursing Institutes, 386

O

Odisha, 386
On-demand board exams, 64
Open Universities, 198, 429
Organization for Economic Cooperation and Development, 362
Organizational management, 77
Original owner, 188
Osmania University, 233, 234
Other Backward Classes, 313, 438
Other Higher Educational Institutions, 389
Our heterogeneous education system, 55
Our school education system, 171
Outdated syllabus, 181
Overall development of the World, 326
Oxford and Cambridge, 429

P

Pali language, 440
Pandit Madan Mohan Malviya, 415
Parents want to work in early age, 237
Parents' organization., 165
Patents Act, 186
Pay Roll and Financial Accounting, 422
Pedagogical knowledge, 173
Personality development, 57
Personnel Records Maintenance, 422
Physical Capital, 225
Physically Challenged, 439
Plagiarism, 196
Plato, 177
Political Factor, 49, 179
Poor quality dissertations, 61
Poor quality of research, 168
Position of academic leader, 72
Post Graduate Diploma in Management, 385
Post Graduate Level programmes, 386
Post graduate levels, 70
Post- Graduation level, 314
Post secondary education, 50
Postgraduate programs, 177
Post-Graduation level, 314
Post-Independence period, 84, 429
Post-Matric Scholarship, 232
Post-Matric Scholarships, 232, 233
Post-secondary education, 393
Pre-independence period, 164
Prime Minister's Special Scholarship Scheme, 306, 319
Privacy, 195
Private and public sectors, 180
Private Degree Colleges, 178
Private engineering colleges, 234
Private higher education, 401
Private tutoring in South Korea, 366
Private universities, 178, 398
Private University Act, 398
Privatization, 54, 179
Privatization of higher education, 430
Privatization policy, 65
Problem of job relevance, 62

Problems of Tribal Education, 236
Professional Code of Conduct, 351
Professional Code of Ethics, 352
Professional colleges, 62
Professional relationship, 374
Programme of Action, 389
Programming of computer tasks, 206
Prohibition of unfair practices, 388
Project Approval Board, 332
Project Based Learning, 180
Prominence of Professional Ethics, 351
Proper guidance and counseling, 171
Psychosocial support, 374
Public and Private Sector, 410
Pupil Teacher Ratio, 387
Purdue University professors, 422

Q

Quality confirmation, 39
Quality education, 26, 46
Quality higher education, 84
Quality improvement and World Class Education, 203
Quality in Higher Education, 51
Quality Models, 41
Quality of education, 171
Quality of universities, 49
Quality Standards, 183, 203
Quick and reliable process of all kinds of data, 206
Quota System, 54, 179, 419

R

Rabindra Tagore, 77
Radhakrishnan Commission Report, 327
Rajasthan, 386
Rajiv Gandhi, 213
Rajiv Gandhi National Fellowship, 233
Rashtriya Madhyamik Shiksha Abhiyan, 328
Rashtriya Uchchatar Shiksha Abhiyan, 323, 331, 339
Rastriya Avishkar Abhiyan, 415
Recruitment of teachers, 23
Reforms in Current Education System, 405
Regional research culture, 227
Regulation of Entry and Operations, 388
Religious Minorities, 439
Reorganization of university education, 212
Reporting Results to Participants, 195
Republic of South Korea, 361
Research advisory committees, 172
Research and Development, 59, 189
Research Associates Funding Agencies, 227
Research consultancy and extension, 77
Research ecosystem, 226, 227
Research institutions, 212
Research Institutions and Professional, 164
Research resource management, 227
Research supervisors, 170
Residential Schools, 233
Respect for Intellectual Property, 195
Respect for Vulnerable Groups, 195
Responsibility for Avoiding Harm, 195
Responsible nature of Educational Institutions, 361
Revenue Account, 388
Revolutionary Data Protection Rules, 19
Right to Education Act, 34, 176
Role of a good academic leader, 72
Role of Central Government, 65
Role of higher education, 75
Routine advice on balancing, 374
Rural Area, 386
RUSA National Mission Authority, 332
Ruslina Ahmad, 26
Russian Federation, 189

S

Saakshar Bharat, 328
Sam Pitroda, 425
Sanskrit literature, 440
Sarva Shiksha Abhiyan, 328, 410
Satyapal Singh, 36
Scheduled Castes, 312, 313, 412, 438, 439, 441
Scheduled Tribes, 312, 313, 412, 438, 439
Scholarships and stipends, 171
School Board, 64
Science and Innovation Education, 34
Science and technology, 161
Scientific and technological capabilities, 437
Scientific methods, 167
Scientific research, 417
Scythians, 439
Selection of Faculty members, 44
Selection of research scholars, 172
Seoul National University, 364, 365
Shapoorji Pallonji Biotech Park, 234
Shillong, 164
Shiv Nadar University, 399
Shortage of attendance, 378
Shudra and Ati- Shudras, 440
Sikkim, 331
Singapore, 400
Situating tool, 207
Smart India Hackathon, 217
Smriti Irani, 64
SNDT Women's University, 434
Social inequalities and backwardness, 216
Social Sciences, 359
Socrates:, 177
Solid Waste Management, 376
Soner Yildirim, 25
South Africa, 20
South and East Asia, 433
South Asia, 400, 413
South Korea, 187, 189, 361, 365
South Korean airports, 366
South Korean households, 366
South Korean people, 362
Special assistance program, 213
Special Education Needs, 26
Special Groups of citizens, 30
Special Scholarship Scheme, 309, 311
Spiritualism, 359
St. John College Agra, 429
St. Xavier's Chennai, 429
Staff development programs, 71
Stand Alone Institutions, 342
Standing Committee, 397
State Board of Jammu & Kashmir, 311
State Education Departments, 388
State Governments, 189
State Higher Education Council, 331, 334
State Higher Education Sector, 331, 335
State Higher Education System, 325, 339, 344
State Nursing Council, 386
State Open Universities, 232, 386
State Private Open University, 386
State Public University, 387
State universities, 178
Statistical Cell, 83
Student support in progress, 77
Student's centric education and dynamic methods, 56
Student-Teacher ratio, 180
Swacch Campus Ranking, 218
Syllabus modification, 385
Symbiosis International University, 399
System of Higher Education, 182

T

T.S.R. Subramanian committee, 64
Takshashila, 43

Tamil Nadu, 32, 232, 386, 408
Task Force, 352
Tata Institute for Fundamental Research, 36, 234
Tata Institute of Social Science Research, 234
Tax Laws, 376
Teacher absenteeism rate high, 29
Teacher and student relationship, 380, 381
Teacher Education Scheme, 328
Teacher education Today, 358
Teacher Entrance Tests, 63
Teacher improvement programs, 70
Teachers Problem In tribal villages, 237
Teacher-training universities, 363
Teaching methods, 80
Teaching Quality, 178
Technical and Vocational Education and Training, 392
Technical and Vocational institutes, 423
Technical colleges, 363
Technical Educational Institutions, 388
Technical institutions, 212
Technical quality, 52
Technical Support Group, 333, 335
Technology and education, 65
Technology companies, 19
Technology growth, 392
Technology rich environments, 80
Telangana, 374, 386
Telangana State, 161, 233
Telangana Tribal literacy, 232
Telangana., 371
Telecom Regulatory Authority of India, 21
Telephone lines and wireless signals, 206
Thailand, 400
Thematic focus, 215
Top hundred universities, 414
Total budget estimates, 388
Total budget provisions, 388
Trademark registration, 186
Trademarks, 186
Tradition of Confucian education, 362
Traditional methods of teaching, 54, 419
Traditional target groups, 319
Training of teachers community, 385
Transformation education, 73
Transformational approach, 40
Transition to Higher Education, 389
Travel business, 206
Tribal Affairs, 312
Tribal literature, 238
Tribal regions, 238
Tribal residential colleges, 238
Tribal students enrollment, 235
Tribal Sub-Plan Areas, 233
Trojan War, 372
Twelfth Plan, 346
Types of Education Research, 81

U

Uganda, 162
Ujjaini, 43
Under graduate, 70
UNESCO Institute for Statistics, 324
Unfinished agenda, 77
United Kingdom, 216
United Nations, 186
United States, 33, 176, 198, 199, 385, 408, 418, 432
Universal Access, 327
Universal Achievement, 327
Universal adult literacy, 362
Universal Enrollment, 327
Universal Retention, 327
Universalization of Elementary Education, 327
Universities, 385
Universities of Kashmir & Jammu, 411
University autonomy, 165

University Bill, 388
University education, 74
University Education Commission, 74, 76, 212
University Grants Commission, 164, 198, 199, 201
University Grants Commission, 64, 83, 377, 389, 398, 399, 410
University level, 176
University of Calicut, 163
University of Hyderabad, 233
University of Jammu, 163
University of Waterloo, 422
University research ecosystem, 225, 227
University Students, 319
University system, 234
University teachers, 170
Unnat Bharat Abhiyan, 415
Unskilled manual workers, 319
US Department of State, 415
Uttar Pradesh, 386
Uttarakhand, 232, 331, 386

V

Vaishya the trader class, 440
Vallabi, 74
Value based Education, 46
Variance of Supply and Demand, 413
Varna System, 439
Varnas as Brahmin, 440
Video Conference, 71
Video projection screens, 431
Vikramashila, 74
Vocational Education, 24, 327

W

Warangal, 234
Warrior class, 440
Wealth of possessions, 163
Well-trained university graduates, 198
West Bengal, 164, 215, 232, 386
WhatsApp group, 380
Women education, 358, 430
Women literacy rate, 358, 430
Women's role in higher education, 75
World Bank, 50, 74, 88, 324
World Class Education, 57, 203, 425
World Intellectual Property Organisation, 186
World Trade Organization, 65
World University Rankings, 400, 414
World-class city, 221
Worldwide commercial center, 434

Y

Yashpal committee, 212, 218
Years of Schooling, 329
Yonsei University, 365
Young graduates, 180
Youth of Jammu & Kashmir, 410
Youth suicide rates, 366
Yuksel Goktas, 25

Z

Zahide Yildirim, 25